Contemporary Issues in Pharmaceutical Patent Law

This collection reflects on contemporary and contentious issues in international rulemaking in regards to pharmaceutical patent law. With chapters from both well-established and rising scholars, the collection contributes to the understanding of the regulatory framework governing pharmaceutical patents as an integrated discipline through the assessment of relevant laws, trends and policy options. Focusing on patent law and related pharmaceutical regulations, the collection addresses the pressing issues governments face in an attempt to resolve policy dilemmas involving competing interests, needs and objectives. The common theme running throughout the collection is the need for policy and law makers to think and act in a systemic manner and to be more reflective and responsive in finding new solutions within and outside the patent system to the long-standing problems as well as emerging challenges.

Bryan Mercurio is Professor and Vice Chancellor's Outstanding Fellow of the Faculty of Law at the Chinese University of Hong Kong.

Daria Kim is Doktorandin at the Max Planck Institute for Innovation and Competition.

Routledge Research in Intellectual Property

Available:

Intellectual Property and Traditional Knowledge in the Global Economy
Translating Geographical Indications for Development
Teshager W. Dagne

The Object of Copyright
A Conceptual History of Originals and Copies in Literature, Art and Design
Stina Teilmann-Lock

Well-Known Trade Marks
A Comparative Study of Japan and the EU
Hiroko Onishi

Forthcoming:

Intellectual Property and Conflict of Laws
Moral Rights and Alternatives to the Copyright Qualifications
Hanan Almawla

Intellectual Property Regimes in the Arabian Gulf States
Infidels at the Gates
David Price and Alhanoof AlDebasi

Pharmaceutical Patent Protection and World Trade Law
The Unresolved Problem of Access to Medicines
Jae Sundaram

Contemporary Issues in Pharmaceutical Patent Law

Setting the Framework and Exploring Policy Options

Edited by
Bryan Mercurio and Daria Kim

Routledge
Taylor & Francis Group
LONDON AND NEW YORK

First published 2017 by Routledge

2 Park Square, Milton Park, Abingdon, Oxfordshire OX14 4RN
52 Vanderbilt Avenue, New York, NY 10017

Routledge is an imprint of the Taylor & Francis Group, an informa business

First issued in paperback 2018

British Library Cataloguing in Publication Data
A catalogue record for this book is available from the British Library

Library of Congress Cataloging in Publication Data
Names: Mercurio, Bryan, editor. | Kim, Daria, editor.
Title: Contemporary issues in pharmaceutical patent law : setting the framework and exploring policy options / Edited by Bryan Mercurio and Daria Kim.
Description: New York : Routledge, 2016. | Series: Routledge research in intellectual property | Includes bibliographical references and index.
Identifiers: LCCN 2016046637 | ISBN 9781138934481 (hbk) | ISBN 9781315677972 (ebk)
Subjects: LCSH: Drugs. | Patent laws and legislation.
Classification: LCC K1519.D78 C66 2016 | DDC 346.04/86—dc23
LC record available at https://lccn.loc.gov/2016046637

ISBN: 978-1-138-93448-1 (hbk)
ISBN: 978-0-367-19338-6 (pbk)

Typeset in Galliard
by Keystroke, Neville Lodge, Tettenhall, Wolverhampton

Contents

Notes on Contributors

Carlos Correa is Professor and Director of the Centre for Interdisciplinary Studies on Industrial Property and Economics Law at the University of Buenos Aires.

Luis Mariano Genovesi is an Associate Professor at the University of Buenos Aires, School of Law.

Paul Grootendorst is Associate Professor in the Faculty of Pharmacy and the School of Public Policy and Governance at the University of Toronto.

Henning Grosse Ruse-Khan is University Lecturer and Fellow at King's College at the University of Cambridge and an Affiliated Senior Researcher at Max Planck Institute for Innovation and Competition.

Yaniv Heled is Associate Professor at Georgia State University College of Law.

Aidan Hollis is Professor of Economics at the University of Calgary.

Daria Kim is Doktorandin at the Max Planck Institute for Innovation and Competition.

Jakkrit Kuanpoth is Research Director, Thailand Development Research Institute (TDRI), and Visiting Professorial Fellow at the University of Wollongong.

Chang-fa Lo is a Justice on the Constitutional Court of Taiwan and Professor of Law at the National Taiwan University College of Law.

Bryan Mercurio is Professor and Vice Chancellor's Outstanding Fellow of the Faculty of Law at the Chinese University of Hong Kong.

Pedro Roffe is a Senior Associate at the International Centre for Trade and Sustainable Development, Geneva.

Roberto Romandini is a Senior Research Fellow at the Max Planck Institute for Innovation and Competition.

Xavier Seuba is a Senior Lecturer and Researcher, and Academic Coordinator and Judicial Training Manager at the Centre for International Intellectual

Property Studies (CEIPI), University of Strasbourg, and Senior Lecturer in Public International Law at the Universitat Pompeu Fabra, Barcelona.

Owais Hassan Shaikh is a recent PhD graduate from the Max Planck Institute for Innovation and Competition and currently provides consultancy in the area of trademarks prosecution and intellectual property management.

1 Introduction

A Holistic Approach to Pharmaceutical Patent Law and Policy

Bryan Mercurio and Daria Kim

Amongst the most important changes to the evolution of the world trading system was the formulation of the common minimum standards on the international protection of intellectual property (IP). This is not to downplay other significant results of the Uruguay Round of trade negotiations and the creation of the World Trade Organization (WTO), but to underscore the far-reaching impact of the incorporation of the Agreement on Trade-Related Aspects of Intellectual Property Rights (the TRIPS Agreement) into the trade regime on international trade and domestic legal order of the WTO Member States.

Negotiated with the aspiration to attain mutual economic benefits and further economic development, ostensibly, the key factor in the negotiation of the TRIPS Agreement was to connect trade and innovation.[1] The thinking at the time of industry and demandeur of the governments was that IP is inherent in most (if not all) trade in goods and that counterfeiting and piracy were costing inventors fortunes in lost revenue. With these goals in mind, negotiators crafted the most comprehensive international IP agreement, expanding on the earlier Paris and Berne Conventions in topical coverage and depth.

At the time, very few if any negotiating countries or non-governmental organizations (NGOs) attempted to evaluate to what extent and at what expense the final agreement contribute to the desired aspirations. More strikingly, even as more than 20 years have passed since the advent of the TRIPS Agreement, there still remains a dearth of solid, unbiased empirical research on the extent to which the initial objectives have been achieved and at what costs.[2] Despite what can be termed a lack of reflection among Members, and therefore with a limited understanding of the impact of the incorporation of IP upon the WTO on the domestic and global level, the international experiment of designing IP rules within the trade framework continues – predominantly, in the direction of the maximization

1 Preamble of the Agreement on Trade-Related Aspects of Intellectual Property Rights, Apr. 15, 1994, Marrakesh Agreement Establishing the World Trade Organization, Annex 1C, The Results of the Uruguay Round of Multilateral Trade Negotiations 320 (1999), 1869 U.N.T.S. 299, 33 I.L.M. 1197 (1994).

2 On the complexities of empirical assessment, see the Organisation for Economic Co-operation and Development, Enquiries into Intellectual Property's Economic Impact (2015).

of protection with the proliferation of bilateral and regional free trade agreements (FTAs).[3]

One of the areas where policy-makers, industry players and scholars have not spared resources and rhetoric is pharmaceutical patent law. Concerns over the increasing cost of healthcare, decreasing productivity of drug research and development and the need for an alternative system to promote medical innovation to replace or stand side-by-side to patents are subject to the ongoing debate. Meanwhile, the growing complexity of the global disease burden[4] and astronomical costs of developing and bringing a new successful drug to the market has led some commentators and governments to question the conventional system and search for new regulatory approaches. This suggests that the design of domestic and international IP rules is still very much a "work-in-progress", and Members of the WTO need not be constrained to what was agreed to in the Uruguay Round but instead should be more reflective and responsive in finding new solutions within and outside the patent system.

The present collection aims to contribute to the understanding of the regulatory framework governing pharmaceutical patents as an integrated discipline through the assessment of relevant laws, trends and policy options. Focusing on patent law and the related regulatory framework, this book deals with the most important and pressing issues governments are facing in an attempt to resolve the policy dilemma over competing interests, needs and objectives. In doing so, it undertakes a topical approach. Each chapter addresses a specific set of issues posed against the background of the pertinent international framework and discourse. The common theme throughout the collection is the need for governments to think and act in a systemic manner and break away from the "silo" method of dividing responsibilities between various government departments that rarely, if ever, communicate or act in concert.

The need for an integrated, systematic approach is of contemporary importance as critical aspects of pharmaceutical law are being determined through negotiations of FTAs. The latter have developed as the antithesis of a thorough and holistic government review and is troublesome for a number of reasons. Not least is the impact of pharmaceutical patent-related provisions upon the affordability of innovative medicines. Meanwhile, healthcare costs have been rising in most places at a far greater rate than gross domestic product (GDP). Given this it is surprising how few governments have ever taken steps to assess the impact of healthcare-sensitive provisions within the patent system since the adoption of the

3 For the analysis of the trend, see Michael Handler and Bryan Mercurio, "Intellectual Property" in Simon Lester and Bryan Mercurio (eds), *Bilateral and Regional Trade Agreements: Analysis and Commentary* (2nd edn, Cambridge University Press, 2016).

4 The World Health Organization, Global Burden of Disease: http://www.who.int/healthinfo/global_burden_disease/gbd/en/index.html; Institute for Health Metrics and Evaluation, University of Washington, *The Global Burden of Disease: Generating Evidence, Guiding Policy. Europe and Central Asia Regional Edition*, 2013; Warren Kaplan et al, *Priority Medicines for Europe and the World: 2013 Update* (2013).

TRIPS Agreement,[5] and how many have readily agreed to TRIPS-plus provisions in FTAs.

The premise of this collection is that international IP law provides a sufficient scope for countries to exercise flexibilities and align national laws and regulations with domestic needs and priorities.

The background

This book is a part of a larger government-funded project entitled "Intellectual Property Rights and the Pharmaceutical Industry: Evaluating Hong Kong's Regulatory Framework" (Hong Kong General Research Fund (GRF) No. CUHK450012). While this volume focuses on global issues and trends, its analytical framework and findings lay the groundwork for the subsequent monograph that explores law and policy options for Hong Kong.

In order to ensure a broad appeal, each chapter is structured in order to first provide the relevant context under international framework (i.e. the TRIPS standard) and recent trends (i.e. unilateral amendments or developments coming out of FTAs) before evaluating the situation in specific jurisdictions and potential policy options. In this way, readers can gain an appreciation of each issue from a broad, internationally relevant perspective and will be able to translate them into the local context.

The majority of the chapters are based on the conference hosted by the Faculty of Law of the Chinese University of Hong Kong on 23–24 June 2014. But unlike most conference collections, the conference was based upon the book project rather than the reverse. To ensure coherence and commonality among the various contributions, the editors carefully assigned each topic to the chosen contributors. A few chapters have been added later on in order to provide a more comprehensive topical coverage and to account for new developments.

Contributors and contributions

The remainder of the collection includes 10 chapters and is divided into three parts: Part I focuses on patent and related types of protection for pharmaceuticals; Part II explores flexibilities under the TRIPS Agreement; and Part III adopts a broader

5 Such exceptional pursuits include: the Center for Strategic Studies and Debates of the Brazilian Chamber of Deputies, *Brazil's Patent Reform. Innovation Towards National Competitiveness* (2013); Chan Park, Achal Prabhala and Jonathan Berger, *Using Law to Accelerate Treatment Access in South Africa: An Analysis of Patent, Competition and Medicines Law*, a study commissioned by the United Nations Development Programme Regional Service Centre for Eastern and Southern Africa (2013); Australian Government, *Pharmaceutical Patents Review: Draft Report* (2013); Canadian Intellectual Property Council, *Innovation for a Better Tomorrow: Closing Canada's Intellectual Property Gap in the Pharmaceutical Sector* (2011); Ministry of Economic Development of New Zealand, *Review of the Patents Act 1953: Boundaries to Patentability: A Discussion Paper* (2002).

view on incentives for pharmaceutical innovation and discusses approaches to impact assessment. The book concludes with a review of the recently completed Trans-Pacific Partnership (TPP) – perhaps the largest and most important FTA ever negotiated.

Following this introduction, Part I begins with a chapter by Roberto Romandini and Henning Grosse Ruse-Khan. The authors provide a detailed analysis of the scope of discretion that WTO Members have in defining standards of patentability for pharmaceutical inventions. Adopting an anecdotal approach, which looks deeply at issues raised before European, US and Asian courts, the authors scrutinize how Article 27 of the TRIPS Agreement applies to patentability of new medical uses and forms of known substances, and how it accommodates the specifics of biotechnological inventions. The authors also question the TRIPS-compatibility of the trend in FTAs to eliminate certain flexibilities which are themselves consistent with the WTO obligations.

In Chapter 3, Yaniv Heled focuses on the complex and emerging issues of biologics – a relatively novel and highly complex class of medicinal products promising unprecedented health benefits. The chapter reviews the approaches enacted in the European Union and the US to marketing approval and regulation of such medicines, discussing the latest developments in the context of the TPP. The author offers suggestions for countries seeking to institute their own regimes for approval of follow-on biologics that can balance the broad access to innovative medicines with the need to maintain incentives for innovation.

In Chapter 4, Owais Hassan Shaikh traces the evolution of test data exclusivity for pharmaceutical products in national laws implemented primarily through FTAs. Having developed a novel Index for Test Data Exclusivity and Access (IDEAS), Shaikh uses it as a tool for the comparative analysis of data exclusivity provisions under the FTAs and national laws by measuring their capacity to promote access to both originator and generics medicine. He argues that test data exclusivity lacks a plausible justification as an incentive for innovation in the presence of patent protection, and that it has a restrictive impact upon access to medicine. Using IDEAS, the author proposes recommendations for negotiating protection obligations regarding test data under FTAs, as well as their implementation in domestic laws.

In Chapter 5, Bryan Mercurio focuses on patent linkage – the practice of national pharmaceutical registration authorities of "linking" the grant of marketing approval for a generic drug with the patent status of an originator drug. The chapter begins with a review of current practices and highlights the differences in which patent linkage operates in various jurisdictions. Finding that potential negative effects of patent linkage are heavily dependent upon the construction of the patent linkage clause, Mercurio offers not only cautionary advice on the benefits and costs of this emerging practice, but also recommendations for a model patent linkage provision.

Part II begins with a chapter by Carlos Correa on the regulatory review exception (so-called the "Bolar exception"), which allows generic pharmaceutical companies to use the patented subject matter for the purpose of preparing an application for marketing approval prior to the expiration of the patents covering a branded drug. Following an introduction setting out the regulatory requirements for marketing approval of pharmaceutical products and examining the TRIPS-consistency of the exception given the important panel decision in *Canada vs Pharmaceutical Patents*, Correa reviews how certain countries have already instituted Bolar exceptions and offers a discussion on several issues that other jurisdictions need to consider in drafting Bolar-type provisions.

In Chapter 7, Justice Chang-fa Lo discusses the meaning and functions of compulsory licensing for patents, the requirements under the TRIPS Agreement, and trends of its application in relation to pharmaceutical products. Justice Lo recognizes the realities of its use, in particular, that affluent markets with an interest in maintaining a high level of IP protection are unlikely to make use of this flexibility absent national urgency. Focusing on the developing countries, the chapter outlines the factors that should be considered when adopting compulsory licensing in an attempt to maintain the balance between the accessibility of affordable drugs and protection of legitimate interests of patent holders.

In Chapter 8, Xavier Seuba, Luis Mariano Genovesi and Pedro Roffe make the case for the exception from patent protection for drug manufacturing for exportation. Novel and controversial, the authors argue that such exception is consistent with international norms of patent protection, when pharmaceutical products covered by patent(s) are manufactured and exported to countries where they are not protected. In doing so, the authors offer a detailed review of the existing TRIPS standards and flexibilities, with a particular focus on Article 30 of the TRIPS Agreement.

Part III begins with a chapter by Aidan Hollis and Paul Grootendorst. This contribution diverges from the usual normative analysis by offering empirical estimates of the financial impact of extending test data protection and patent term extension in a small upper-income jurisdiction with a high level of protection for intellectual property rights – Hong Kong SAR. The analysis finds that the costs to payers of such extensions are likely to be modest because generic entry is already relatively slow in Hong Kong. The authors also draw implications for other jurisdictions emphasizing that nominal exclusivity as defined by legal rules is not necessarily equivalent to the actual exclusivity.

In Chapter 10, Daria Kim from the Max Planck Institute for Innovation and Competition reflects on the concept of regulatory integrity in the pharmaceutical sector and addresses concerns related to the increasing role assigned to drug approval regulation in incentivizing pharmaceutical innovation. The analysis focuses on the interaction between the patent system and drug marketing approval regulation. After identifying complexities of welfare analysis of innovation incentives, and in view of the indeterminacy of their cumulative effect on innovation, Kim proposes an approach based on ecological and constructivist types of rationality in decision-making and concludes with policy recommendations. The chapter brings the entirety of the preceding contributions into perspective when discussing the facets of the integrated approach.

In the concluding chapter, Jakkrit Kuanpoth reviews the TRIPS-plus provisions under the comprehensive TPP and argues that they will have a significant impact upon access to essential medicines by limiting countries' ability to deal with public health problems and by restricting the measures the countries can take to pursue affordable drugs.

This collection offers deep analysis and useful insight into a dynamic area of policy and law-making. Of course, the covered issues and topics are by no means exhaustive. It is our hope and desire that this book can contribute to the field in a positive manner and act as a springboard for further and more targeted research.

Part I

Pharmaceutical Patents and Related Types of Protection

2 Patentability of Pharmaceutical Inventions under TRIPS

Domestic Court Practice Testing International Policy Space

*Henning Grosse Ruse-Khan and Roberto Romandini**

Introduction

During the last few years, an extensive body of literature has dealt with the latitude the World Trade Organization (WTO) Agreement on Trade-Related Aspects of Intellectual Property Rights (TRIPS) grants to WTO Members in the field of patent protection. The attention of scholars has centred on the possible limitations to the rights conferred by the patent and on the requirements for issuing compulsory licences. The leeway provided to the Members for defining their own standard of patentability was – at least until the proceedings before Indian courts[1] concerning the interpretation and the TRIPS-compliance[2] of Section 3(d) of the Indian Patent Act attracted public attention – less discussed.[3]

This chapter intends to address the latter aspect with specific reference to the pharmaceutical sector. This will not be done through an abstract analysis of the boundaries which TRIPS set for national courts and legislators. Instead, the

* Both authors have contributed to every part of this article and share the views expressed therein. However, while the Introduction and the Conclusions of the Article have been written jointly by the authors, the Section "*Evergreening*" *and the patentability of new forms and new uses of known compounds: Section 3(d) of the Indian Patent Act*" is attributable specifically to Henning Grosse Ruse-Khan, the Section "*Naturally occurring substances: The Myriad case before the US Supreme Court*" and the Section "*Absolute versus "purpose-bound" product protection: the Monsanto case before the European Court of Justice*" are attributable specifically to Roberto Romandini.

1 See Supreme Court of India, Judgment of 1 April 2013, Civil Appeal No. 2706–2716/2013.
2 See "Novartis AG v. Union of India" (2007) 4 Madras LJ 1153.
3 See, however, the contributions of Daniel Gervais, "Patentability Criteria as TRIPS Flexibilities: The Examples of China and India" and Ali Khader and Feroz Ali Ragavan, "Proof of Progress: The Role of the Inventive Step/Non-obviousness Standard in the Indian Patent Office" in Ruth L. Okediji and Margo A. Bagley (eds) *Patent Law in a Global Perspective* (Oxford University Press, 2014). On the flexibilities provided by the TRIPS Agreement as the substantive provisions on patents, see also Max Planck Inst. for Innovation & Competition, "Declaration on Patent Protection – Regulatory Sovereignty under TRIPS" (2014) 45 INT'L REV INTELL PROP & COMPETITION L 679 et seq. (with commentary by Matthias Lamping hereinafter: MPI Patent Declaration).

chapter adopts an anecdotal approach, taking up questions related to patentability raised before European, US or Asian courts, where the TRIPS-consistency of a domestic practice or interpretation has been an issue. In this context, we focus on scrutinizing whether TRIPS Article 27 allows:

1 denying composition claims for naturally occurring substances;
2 ruling out absolute product protection in all or specific technological fields;
3 excluding from patent protection new forms of known substances when they do not show an improvement in known efficacy; and
4 new uses of known substances.

The conclusions drawn on the above-mentioned issues are important for several reasons. *De lege lata*, they will outline the interpretative leeway national judges enjoy when applying their domestic patent laws. *De lege ferenda*, they will serve as examples of the flexibility WTO Members have in reforming internal legislation to pursue a specific national policy in the field of public health and pharmaceutical innovation. Finally, for the negotiation of new international intellectual property (IP) agreements, our findings may have a practical bearing firstly on the negotiation and secondly on the implementation of TRIPS-plus provisions.[4] If one takes the position that under TRIPS Article 1.1[5] a higher standard of protection may be *imposed* on Members only by multilateral agreements accepted by all Members (TRIPS Article 71.2),[6] then provisions going beyond TRIPS agreed in bilateral treaties would be allowed, but not binding. WTO Members may enter into such agreements *inter-se*, but compliance with TRIPS-plus provisions contained therein would, from a WTO/TRIPS perspective, remain at the discretion of Members.[7] A more conservative reading of Article 1.1 simply demands TRIPS-plus IP protection not to be *contrary* to TRIPS provisions – a standard that may be understood to give weight also to core flexibilities (such as those on patentability in TRIPS Article 27) which formed an important part of the overall WTO/TRIPS bargain agreed upon 20 years ago.[8] Such a perspective calls into question tendencies in treaty negotiations to explicitly prohibit approaches akin to Section 3(d) of the Indian Patent Act – to the extent that the latter are not more than an expression of agreed policy space under TRIPS.

4 The term "TRIPS-plus" refers to obligations included in other agreements – most notably free trade agreements – that are not included or go beyond that of the TRIPS Agreement. For more information and examples of TRIPS-plus provisions, see Michael Handler and Bryan Mercurio, "Intellectual Property" in Simon Lester et al (eds) *Bilateral and Regional Trade Agreements* (vol 1: Commentary and Analysis, 2nd edn, Cambridge University Press, 2015).

5 According to TRIPS Article 1.1 the Member States may implement in their domestic laws a higher standard of protection, if that is not contrary to TRIPS, but shall not be obliged to do so.

6 See Nuno Pires de Carvalho, *The TRIPS Regime of Patent Rights* (The Hague, 2010), 110.

7 Id.

8 See H. Grosse Ruse-Khan et al, "Principles for Intellectual Property Provisions in Bilateral and Regional Agreements" (2013) 44 INT'L REV INTELL PROP & COMPETITION L 878 et seq.

Naturally occurring substances: The *Myriad* case before the US Supreme Court

Premise

The issue of whether a substance that pre-exists in nature may be *per se* the subject of a patent is an old one. It was discussed in the German[9] and British[10] courts after World War II, and implicitly addressed, although not consistently answered, by even older US decisions.[11]

European countries originally adopted diverging attitudes based on their respective laws.[12] Before 1977, the German Patent Office excluded product claims to naturally occurring substances,[13] whereas the UK Patent Office accepted them if they were related to an isolated form of the compound.[14] The German Federal Patent Court took the same approach as the UK Patent Office in 1977,[15] as did the European Patent Office (EPO)[16] under the EPC 1978 from its inception. Later on, the EU Law-maker codified this "isolation doctrine" in the field of

9 See A. Hüni, "Absoluter oder zweckbeschränkter Stoffschutz und andere Harmonisierungsprobleme in der europäischen Rechtsprechung" (1970) Gewerblicher Rechtsschutz und Urheberrecht (GRUR) 9 et seq.; Holger Bunke, "Zur Patentfähigkeit von Naturstoffen" (1978) Gewerblicher Rechtsschutz und Urheberrecht (GRUR) 132 et seq.

10 See Ralph D. Satchell, "Chemical Product Patent Practice in the United Kingdom" (1970) INT'L REV INTELL PROP & COMPETITION L 179, 180.

11 See Bunke, see *supra* note 9, at 132; Christopher Beauchamp, "Patenting Nature: A Problem of History" (2013) 16 STAN TECH L REV 257, 271 et seq.; Tuo Ingram, "Association for Molecular Pathology v. Myriad Genetics, Inc.: The Product of Nature Doctrine Revisited" (2014) 29 BERKELEY TECH L J 384, 389 et seq.

12 Until the Convention on the Unification of Certain Points of Substantive Law on Patents for Invention (Strasbourg Convention) and the European Patent Convention (EPC), the substantive provisions on patentability of the European Member States were not uniform in Europe. The substantive provisions of the EPC (Articles 52–57 and 138) concern only European patents. In practice, however, all EPC states have harmonized the provisions concerning national patents to those provided under the EPC for European patents. See Karl Bruchhausen, "Interpretation and Application of European Patent Law and Harmonized National Patent Law" (1983) 14 INT'L REV INTELL PROP & COMPETITION L 732 et seq.

13 See the Guidelines of the German Patent Office of 14 September 1972; Blatt für Patent-Muster- und Zeichenwesen (1972) 298, 311 (quoted after Jasper Utermann, "Reflections on Patent Protection of Products of Nature" (1978) 9 INT'L REV INTELL PROP & COMPETITION L 409, 415 fn 11).

14 According to Section 4(7) of the UK Patents Act 1949, a claim to a new substance should be interpreted "as not extending to that substance when found in nature". According to R. S. Crespi, "Gene and Compound Claims: Another View" (2001/2002) 1 BIO-SCIENCE L REV 3, 5, this provision "was interpreted by the UK Patent Office to exclude patents for such products only as found in Nature but not exclude such products when isolated and purified for the first time".

15 See Federal Patent Court, "16 W(pat) 64/75, Decision of 28 July 1977" (1979) INT'L REV INTELL PROP & COMPETITION L 494 et seq.

16 See Joseph Straus, "Patenting Human Genes in Europe – Past Developments and Prospective for the Future" (1995) 26 INT'L REV INTELL PROP & COMPETITION L 920, 926.

biological material.[17] Pursuant to Article 3(2) of Directive 98/44/EC of the European Parliament and of the Council of 6 July 1998 on the legal protection of biotechnological inventions (hereinafter: Directive 98/44/EC),[18] "biological material which is isolated from its natural environment or produced by means of a technical process may be the subject of an invention even if it previously occurred in nature".[19] Other countries, such as China[20] and Japan,[21] have applied similar principles.

In the US, the Supreme Court did not rule expressly[22] on this issue until 2011 in *Association for Molecular Pathology versus Myriad Genetics* (*Myriad*), where the claims challenged by the plaintiff concerned biochemical substances. The product claims discussed were drafted to cover sequences of genomic deoxyribonucleic acid (DNA) and sequences of artificially created complementary DNA (cDNA). As in Europe, the controversy in the US did not concern method claims for obtaining and using the natural substance. Such method claims are possible in both jurisdictions if the claimed process or use is novel and inventive, and judicial or normative exceptions – such as those related to diagnostic methods under the European Patent Convention (EPC)[23] or to mental steps or abstract

17 See Tine Sommer, "The Scope of Gene Patent Protection and the TRIPS Agreement – An Exclusively Nondiscriminatory Approach" (2007) 38 INT'L REV INTELL PROP & COMPETITION L 30, 40.

18 See Directive 98/44/EC, of the European Parliament and of the Council of 6 July 1998 on the Legal Protection of Biotechnological Inventions, OJ L213, 13 et seq.

19 Id. The same principle provided for by Article 3(2) applies pursuant to Article 5(2) of Directive 98/44/EC to elements of human origin. Both provisions have been incorporated in implementing regulations of the EPC. See Rule 27 EPC 2000.

20 See SIPO, "Guidelines for the Examination of the SIPO" (Part II, Chapter 10, 2.1 "Natural Substances" 2006), www.english.sipo.gov.cn, 317, accessed 02/02/2016.

21 See JPO, "Examination Guidelines for Patent and Utility Model in Japan" (Part II, Chapter 1, at 1), www.jpo.go.jp, accessed 02/03/2016.

22 Two previous rulings of the Supreme Court did indeed deal with patents on natural products, but they decided the case based on lack of novelty and not on the basis of a product-of-nature exception. See *Am Wood Paper Co vs Fiber Disintegrating Co*, 90 US 566 (1874); *Cochrane vs Badische Anilinfabrik*, 111 US 293 (1883). See, however, *Funk Brothers Seed Co vs Kalo Inoculant*, 333 US 127 (1948) where the US Supreme Court decided on a mixture of known bacteria on the basis of the exclusion for law of nature. See also for a historical reconstruction of the product-of-nature doctrine, Beauchamp, "*supra* note 11, 257, 271 et seq.; Tup Ingram, "Association for Molecular Pathology vs Myriad Genetics, Inc.: The Product of Nature Doctrine Revisited" (2014) 29 BERKELEY TECH LJ 384, 389 et seq.

23 See Article 53(c) EPC; see also Rainer Moufang, "Methods of Medical Treatment under Patent Law" (1993) 24 INT'L REV INTELL PROP & COMPETITION L 118 et seq. The diagnostic use of gene sequences is eligible for protection in Europe. Article 53 EPC refers the exclusion only to methods practised on the human body. The concept of the human body pursuant to Article 53 EPC does not comprise samples, fluids, and substances isolated from the body of the patient. See EPO, "Guidelines for Examination" (G 4.2.1, 2013). For this reason, Article 53(c) EPC does not affect the patentability of DNA diagnostic tests since the latter are performed on a sample obtained from the body of the patient and not on the body itself. This conclusion is valid at least as long as the claim for performing the diagnostic test

ideas in the US case law[24] – do not apply. At dispute before the Supreme Court – because of the exclusion for products of nature – was only the validity of a *product* claim drawn to the isolated DNA and cDNA sequences.

One may wonder what the point is of excluding a product claim if claims for methods of using and methods of making the substance remain possible. The difference between the two categories of claims – product and process claims – is in the scope of protection, and in the possible effect on subsequent innovators. Product claims relating to the substance as such confer, as confirmed by TRIPS Article 28.1(a), a protection for the substance – however manufactured and for whatever purpose it may be used. This form of protection is defined as absolute by European scholars and case law.[25] By contrast, process claims cover only the method for obtaining or using the substance recited in the claim itself. If a third party identifies a new process for preparing the substance that is different from that claimed and a new use of the substance other than that claimed, it infringes neither the claim to the process for obtaining the substance nor the claim to the method for using it.[26]

The Myriad *case before the US Supreme Court*

In the *Myriad* case, the plaintiffs pleaded that claims relating to isolated DNA were not admissible under the "product of nature" exception. In fact, the biochemical structure of the claimed compounds was identical to that of native (genomic) DNA. The counter-argument of the patentee mirrored European case law: the claims concerned isolated DNA molecules (i.e. molecules removed from the chromosomal environment of the cells where they naturally occur). Once the covalent bonds of the chromosomal DNA are broken down, the molecule obtained is structurally different from native DNA. The challenged

in vitro does not comprise the taking of the bodily sample. See Decision T 964/99, 2004 OJ EPO 4 – Alternating polarity/CYGNUS Inc. An exclusion affecting even diagnostic methods performed on isolated tissues or samples of the human body would nevertheless be TRIPS-compliant. Under TRIPS Article 27(3), a patent may be denied protection for any diagnostic method, and not only for those which are practiced directly on the human body.

24 See *Alice Corp Pty Ltd vs CLS Bank Int'l*, 134 S Ct 2347 (2014). In the recent US case law, the exclusion for abstract ideas and law of nature seems to have become a significant obstacle for applicants seeking protection for diagnostic methods. See Dan L. Burk, "The Curious Incident of the Supreme Court in Myriad Genetics" (2014) 90(2) NOTRE DAME L REV 12, http://papers.ssrn.com/sol3/papers.cfm? abstract_id=2407094, accessed 02/03/2016.

25 See Alan W. White, "Gene and Compound per se Claims: An Appropriate Reward?" 6 BIO-SCIENCE L REV 239, 240 et seq.; Friction reductive additive/MOBIL OIL III, 1990 OJ EPO (G 2/88) 93, reasoning 5 of the decision. For an analysis of the case law see also Rudolf Kraßer, *Patentrecht* (6th edn, C. H. Beck Publishers, 2008) 139 et seq.; Rainer Moufang, "Stoffschutz im Patentrecht" in Gewerblicher Rechtsschutz und Urheberrecht (GRUR) (2010) 89 et seq.

26 For the US perspective, see Janice M. Mueller, *Patent Law* (4th edn, Wolters Kluwer Law & Business, 2013) 350.

patent claims comprised only the former and not the latter. The commercialization of cell lines, where endogenous genetic sequences corresponding to those patented are contained and active, would not interfere with the rights conferred by the patent on isolated DNA. Furthermore, isolated DNA can be used as probes for diagnostic purposes, which is not possible for native DNA.[27]

The United States District Court for the Southern District of New York endorsed the view of the plaintiff and declared void all claims of the patent, even those relating to cDNA.[28] The Court of Appeals for the Federal Circuit, however, adopted the European approach, upholding the validity of the claim for isolated DNA sequences based on the argument that the latter represent "naturally not occurring composition of matter" that allow uses which DNA sequences *in situ* do not.[29] The Supreme Court adopted an intermediate approach. On the one hand, it agreed with the Federal Circuit that cDNA segments are patentable because they are artificial biochemical compositions of matter. On the other hand, it followed the District Court's theory that isolated DNA sequences do not differ from genomic DNA, even if the covalent bonds are broken down. For this reason, merely isolated DNA sequences constitute a "product of nature" not eligible for protection under 35 USC § 101.[30]

Several *amicus curiae* briefs suggested that an exception to the patentability of native DNA sequences under the "product of nature" doctrine is at odds with TRIPS, since the latter mandates a protection *per se* for every product in all fields of technology.[31] Despite these pleadings, the US Supreme Court did not address the issue.[32] This is not surprising in light of Section 103 of the Uruguay Round

27 See the allegations of the defendant-appellant reported in the second decision of 16 August 2012, of the United States Court of Appeals for the Federal Circuit, *Ass'n for Molecular Pathology vs US Patent & Trademark Office*, 702 F Supp 2d 181 (SDNY 2010) aff'd in part, rev'd in part, 653 F 3d 1329 et seq. (Fed Cir 2011) cert. granted, judgment vacated sub nom.

28 See id.

29 Id.

30 See *Ass'n for Molecular Pathology vs Myriad Genetics, Inc.* 133 S Ct 2107, 2117–18, 186 L Ed 2d 124 (2013).

31 See Brief of Amicus Curiae "Federation Internationale des Conseils en propriete industrielle" in support of neither party; see also Brief of Amicus Curiae Alnylam Pharmaceuticals, INC. In Support of Defendants-Appellants, Supporting Reversal, 2010–1046, *Ass'n for Molecular Pathology vs Myriad Genetics, Inc.* 133 S Ct 2107, 2117–18, 186 L Ed 2d 124 (2013).

32 A possible violation of the TRIPS Agreement by invalidating the claim for native DNA was briefly considered in the first instance decision. Justice Sweet excluded a conflict with TRIPS by invoking Article 8 and Article 27.3 of the treaty. Both rules – according to his opinion – "permit governments to incorporate public health concerns into their intellectual property law and to exclude from patentability diagnostic, therapeutic, or surgical methods as well as particular inventions on the grounds of public interest". See *Ass'n for Molecular Pathology vs US Patent & Trademark Office*, 702 F Supp 2d 181 (SDNY 2010) aff'd in part, rev'd in part, 653 F 3d 1329 et seq. (Fed Cir 2011) cert. granted, judgment vacated sub nom. One might counter that a conservative reading of TRIPS Article 8.1 allows WTO Member States to adopt measures "necessary to protect public health and nutrition, and promote the public interest in sectors of vital importance to their socio-economic and technological

Agreements Act (URAA), which denies any direct effect of the WTO norms in the US legal system, and of Supreme Court jurisprudence that has reduced significantly their possible indirect effects.[33] Nevertheless, the question of TRIPS consistency remains relevant because it concerns the scope of patentable subject matter related to naturally occurring substances and may affect reforms of domestic rules in this field.

Assessment under TRIPS

There is a straightforward reasoning for the case that TRIPS allows patent protection to be denied for naturally occurring substances *per se*. TRIPS Article 27.1 mandates protection only for inventions, not for discoveries.[34] The agreement does not define the term "invention". Even if a WTO panel were to take it upon itself to define this legal concept, it would first, in applying the customary rules of treaty interpretation, resort to the ordinary meaning of the term.[35] The verb "invent" refers to the act of creating or designing "something that has not existed before", and the verb "discover" relates to the act of finding or observing "a place, substance, or scientific phenomena"[36] previously unknown.[37] It might be argued that if a product patent claim concerns a naturally occurring substance isolated from a biological or organic source, that subject matter – in its

development" only on the condition that "such measures are consistent with the provisions of the Agreement". In contrast to Article XX GATT, Article 8 hence appears not to entitle national lawmakers "to create exceptions to obligations otherwise imposed under the Agreement". See Justin Malbon, Charles Lawson and Mark Davison, *The WTO Agreement on Trade-Related Aspects of Intellectual Property Rights – A Commentary* (Cheltenham, 2014) 265. However, together with Article 7, Article 8 functions to ensure that interpreting open and ambiguous TRIPS provisions, for instance the concept "discrimination" under Article 27.1 or the exceptions under TRIPS Article 27.3 (b), can be conducted in a manner supportive of the right of WTO Members to protect public health and other interests mentioned in Article 8. See paras 4 and 5(a) of the Doha Declaration on the TRIPS Agreement and Public Health (WT/MIN(01)/DEC/2, 20 November 2001) where all WTO Member States emphasized the role of Articles 7 and 8 in achieving a public health consistent interpretation and implementation of TRIPS.

33 See John J. Barceló, "The Status of WTO Rules in U.S. Law" (2006) 36 CORNELL LAW FACULTY PUBLICATIONS 1, 3 et seq.

34 See C. M. Correa, *Trade Related Aspects of Intellectual Property Rights: A Commentary on the TRIPS Agreement* (Oxford, 2006) 272; see also "MPI Patent Declaration" (2014), *supra* note 3, at 5, 6–8, 11.

35 See Isabelle Van Damme, "Treaty Interpretation by the WTO Appellate Body" (2010) 21(3) EUR. J INT'L L 605, 619 et seq.

36 See *Oxford Dictionary of English* (3rd edn, 2010), sub voce "invent" and "invention". On the frequency with which the WTO Panels resort to the Shorter Oxford Dictionary *see* Van Damme, *supra* note 35, at 620.

37 See also, from the perspective of European Law, Ulrich Schatz, "Patentability of Genetic Engineering Inventions in European Patent Office Practices" (1998) 29 INT'L REV INTELL PROP & COMPETITION L 2, 4; Rainer Moufang, *Genetische Erfindungen im Patentrecht* (Köln et al., 1998) 164 et seq.

structural elements – was not "created" (but only extracted) through human intervention. Thus, the ordinary meaning of the treaty terms suggests that such substance may be excluded from patent protection as it is the subject of a discovery and not of an "invention" in the field of technology within the meaning of TRIPS Article 27.1. In addition, TRIPS' object and purpose would militate for an interpretation which offers WTO Members a sufficient degree of flexibility in interpreting broad and open treaty terms such as invention. Consequently, Member States may admit a product claim relating to a naturally occurring compound, but they are not required to do so under TRIPS Article 27.1.

Such arguments, however, have been subjected to the following contextual objections.[38] The agreement provides for an optional exception to patentability under TRIPS Article 27.3, according to which specific biological products and processes may be excluded from patent protection. With respect to products, the provision distinguishes between plants and animals whose patent eligibility may be limited, and microorganisms, whose patent eligibility must be recognized.[39] From a systematic perspective, TRIPS Article 27.3 concerns limited exclusions for subject matter that is, in principle, eligible for protection under TRIPS Article 27.1. Were this not so, then the optional exclusion provided for by TRIPS Article 27.3 would be superfluous. It would concern things which do not represent an invention and for which no patent has to be granted under TRIPS Article 27.1.

Since TRIPS Article 27.3 appears to mandate protection for microorganisms *per se*, it might be argued that this obligation applies regardless of whether or not the claimed microorganisms are different from organisms found in nature. If, however, a naturally occurring microorganism may constitute a patentable invention within the meaning of TRIPS Article 27.1, then the same should hold true for every other naturally occurring substance.[40]

This line of reasoning has its logical strengths, but it does not seem compelling to us for two reasons. Firstly, TRIPS Article 27.3 does not define the term "microorganisms".[41] It does not specify that the latter should be protected even in situations where its genomic structure coincides with that of a naturally occurring organism. Secondly, TRIPS Article 27.3 relates the optional exception to patentability of plants and animals, which implies – for the above mentioned reasons – that plants and animals represent subject matter in principle eligible for protection under TRIPS Article 27.1 as well. Assuming that TRIPS Article 27.3 requires the Members to consider a microorganism as a substance eligible for protection even if it occurs – with the same structure as that claimed – in nature, the same conclusion would follow for plants and animals. But the

38 See Joseph Straus, "Genomics and the Food Industry: Outlook from an Intellectual Property Perspective" in Vaver David and Lionel Bently (eds) *Intellectual Property in the New Millennium. Essays in Honour of William R. Cornish* (Cambridge, 2004) 124, 132 et seq.

39 See Carvalho, *supra* note 6, at 308.

40 See Straus, *supra* note 38, at 132 f.

41 See Sunil Mani and Richard R Nelson, "Conclusion" in Sunil Mani and others (eds) *TRIPS Compliance, National Patent Regimes and Innovation* (Cheltenham, 2013) 222, 230.

consensus among commentators is that a new insect or a new plant freely occurring in nature, as any other unaltered natural element, does not represent eligible subject matter. No Member needs to resort to the optional norm of TRIPS Article 27.3 for such limitation of patent eligibility. Instead, the latter is based on the concept of invention under TRIPS Article 27.1. This, by the way, is true under the EPC as well – where the mere discovery of a previously unrecognized plant or animal does not entitle the discoverer to a product claim for it, even if an industrial use has been disclosed.

For this reason, TRIPS Article 27.3 can only concern animals, plants, or microorganisms that incorporate a "product invention" within the meaning of TRIPS Article 27.1. However, TRIPS Article 27.3 does not specify when this is the case. As a consequence, the provision does not affect the discretion of Members to define in good faith what is understood by the word "invention" under their legal systems.[42] The practice of the Member States supports this reading of TRIPS Article 27.1. Several countries exclude product claims for isolated naturally occurring substances.[43] Now that the US has also adopted the stance that naturally occurring substances, even if claimed in isolated form, are not eligible for protection,[44] it seems even more unlikely that such legislation will be challenged before the WTO.

Practical implications for the pharmaceutical sector

If the conclusion drawn above is correct, Members allowing legal protection *per se* for substances found in nature are not required to do so by TRIPS and could revise their policies without repercussion. Nevertheless, the practical implications for the pharmaceutical sector would likely be minor. On the one hand, method claims for the production of the naturally occurring substance and for its uses would not be affected by the "product of nature exception". On the other hand, product claims relating to altered forms of the naturally occurring substance would remain possible, provided that their preparation implies an inventive activity.[45]

42 See Shamnad Basheer, "Limiting the Patentability of Pharmaceutical Inventions and Micro-organisms: A TRIPS Compatibility Review" (IP Institute, 2005) 56 et seq., http://ssrn.com/abstract=1391562, accessed 02/03/2016.

43 See for Brazil Article 18.3 of Law 9279/1996; for Argentina and India, see also Basheer, *supra* note 42, at 56 et seq. In Australia the High Supreme Court has denied the patent eligibility of genetic sequences, see *D'Arcy vs Myriad Genetics Inc.* (2015) HCA 35 7 October 2015 S28/2015; see on this judgment Jessica Lay, "D'Arcy v. Myriad Genetics: A Demand for the "Made" or "Non-Information" and Clear Subject Matter", (2016) 5 INT'L REV INTELL PROP & COMPETITION L 537 et seqq.

44 According to the "Interim Guidance on Patent Subject Matter Eligibility" released by the United States Patent and Trademark Office (USPTO) and published in Federal Register, vol. 79, no. 241/Tuesday, 16 December 2014, the judicial exception for natural products and the principles stated by the US Supreme Court in *Myriad* apply to all claims relating to nature-based products, that is, products which have a naturally occurring counterpart.

45 See again "Interim Eligibility Guidance", *supra* note 44, released by USPTO, Federal Register/vol. 79, no. 241, Tuesday, 16 December 2014, at 76422 et seq., according to which

Still, the purpose and the effect of such exclusion could be to keep naturally occurring elements in the public domain, thus creating an incentive for developing new methods for preparing or using them. This aspect seemed to be significant to some authors with regard to multifunctional compounds, such as genetic sequences or human proteins. A product protection in these situations – as was feared by European literature after Directive 98/44/EC was enacted – would create monopolies for all uses, even those not identified by the inventor, of natural substances for which no substitute exists.

It remains unclear whether such product patents have really had a deterrent effect on subsequent innovations in the biomedical field.[46] After the reference sequence of the human genome was made available to the public, granting product patents for unaltered human genes has become more the exception than the rule.[47] It is nevertheless still worth exploring, particularly because of its implications for the pharmaceutical and chemical sectors, whether TRIPS does mandate an absolute product protection – regardless of whether the substance concerned is naturally occurring or not.

"Absolute" versus "purpose-bound" product protection: the *Monsanto* case before the European Court of Justice

Premise

The question as to whether TRIPS mandates an absolute product protection for chemical or biological substances was intensively debated in Europe, particularly

a nature-based product may be eligible for protection only if it presents "markedly different characteristics from its naturally occurring counterpart".

46 There was a debate in the 1990s on the issue of whether patenting gene-related inventions – not specifically product patents on genes – could have caused a tragedy of anti-commons in the biomedical field. That is, a situation where because of the existence of too many overlapping IP rights owned by different entities over genetic sequences, the development of specific applications and products based on the subject matter of these overlapping rights could have been deterred. Whether these effects have really materialized – in the US and elsewhere – is unclear. Some empirical investigation came to the conclusions that these problems have not been significant in the US. See for a summary T. Caulfield et al, "Evidence and Anecdotes: An Analysis of Human Gene Patenting Controversies" (2006) 24 NATURE BIOTECHNOLOGY 1091, 1092, with further references. Other contributions question the methodology and the results of such studies. See, e.g., Paul A. David, "The Economic Logic of 'Open Science' and the Balance between Private Property Rights and the Public Domain in Scientific Data and Information: A Primer" (2003) STANFORD INST FOR ECON POL'Y RES 14 et seq. This debate did not concern specifically the issue of absolute product protection for genetic sequences. However, in *Myriad*, the plaintiff expressly invoked the tragedy of anti-commons when arguing its case for invalidity of the composition claims. See *Ass'n for Molecular Pathology vs US Patent & Trademark Office,* 702 F Supp 2d 181 (SDNY 2010) aff'd in part, rev'd in part, 653 F 3d 1329 et seq. (Fed Cir 2011) cert granted, judgment vacated sub nom.

47 I. Huys, G. Matthijs and G. Van Overwalle, "The Fate and Future of Patents on Human Genes and Genetic Diagnostic Methods" (2012) 13 NAT REV GENET 441, 446.

after the entry into force of Directive 98/44/EC. Some EU Member States did not accept, for several reasons, a product protection for polynucleotides, and enacted provisions requiring the applicant to indicate in the product claim drafted to such substances one possible use of the genetic sequence claimed.[48] Such statements of purpose, incorporated in the product claim, limit the protection conferred by the national patent to the function disclosed and claimed.

This development may surprise in light of the history of the EU legislative act. One of the purposes of Directive 98/44/EC was to ensure a legal protection for biotechnological inventions not only uniform in all Member States, but also consistent with WTO obligations.[49] The Committee on Legal Affairs of the EU Parliament assumed that TRIPS Articles 27 and 28 required the Member States to confer absolute product protection for chemical compounds.[50] For this reason, the committee suggested making such protection available for biological material, as well. Despite this premise, the European Court of Justice (ECJ) came to the opposite conclusion with respect to genetic sequences by interpreting the provisions of Directive 98/44/EC.

48 See for Germany § 1a(4) 3 Patent Act, as published on 16 December 1980 (Fed L Gazette 1981, 1), as last amended by Article 1 of the Act of 19 October 2013 (Fed L Gazette 3830). See also Christoph Ann, "Patents on Human Gene Sequences in Germany: On Bad Lawmaking and Ways to Deal with It" (2006) 7 GER LJ 279; Ralf Uhrich, *Stoffschutz* (Tübingen, 2010) 334 et seq.; for France, see Article L 611–18 of the Code la Propriété Intellectuelle. For a comment of this provision, see Sven J. R. Bostyn, "Protection of Biotechnological Inventions in France and Germany after Directive 98/4/EC" (2005) 1, 2 et seq., www.jetro.go.jp/world/europe/ip/archive/pdf/news_009_1.pdf, accessed 02/03/2016. In Italy, the legislature has excluded a protection for genetic sequences, as such. See Article 81 of the Code of Intellectual Property. All these domestic provisions limiting the patentability concerns only national patents and do not apply to European patents. See Articles 2(2) and 138 EPC; see also Ann, *supra* in this note, at 279 et seq.

49 See Article 1(1) and consideration no. 14 of Directive 98/44/EC.

50 See "Report on the Proposal for a European Parliament and Council Directive on the Legal Protection of Biotechnological Inventions" (COM (95)0661 – C4-0063/96 – 95/0350(COD)), in which the following comments are made: "The term 'product' as used in Article 27(1) of the TRIPS Agreement refers not to the end result of a process (e.g. a medicine) but to production material in the patent terminology sense of 'object' or 'substance'. The same is true of the terminology used in the rapporteur's amendments. When a medicine is patented, what is protected is the active ingredient which it contains: not, for example, the medicine called 'aspirin'. Protection of substances is compulsory under the TRIPS Agreement . . . Protection of substances is absolute. However, an inventor who discovers a new mode of operation of the substance and hence a new potential use may take out a patent on the application, provided that the other preconditions for granting of a patent are met. This gives rise to the following situation: the second inventor cannot exploit his patent on the new application because the first inventor has the rights to the substance (which are absolute). In virtually every case, these problems are solved by an agreement between the first and second inventors." As explained below, we do not agree with the opinion that the term product in TRIPS Article 27 has to be referred to the substance as such and not to the industrial product (pharmaceutical product, fertilizer, or insecticide) containing the compound; see *infra*, Section III, 3 of this contribution.

The* Monsanto *case

In *Monsanto versus Cefetra*,[51] the ECJ had to give its construction of Article 9 of Directive 98/44/EC.[52] This provision provides for a "horizontal" extension of the protection conferred by a patent for a genetic sequence, when the latter is incorporated as an exogenous element in biological or non-biological material and reads as follows:

> [T]he protection conferred by a patent on a product containing or consisting of genetic information shall extend to all material, save as provided in Article 5(1), in which the product is incorporated and in which the genetic information is contained and performs its function.

The case which triggered the referral was relatively straightforward.[53] The defendant in the national infringement proceeding, pending before the District Court of The Hague, had imported soy meal produced from genetically manipulated soy plants in Argentina. Monsanto argued that this soy meal was covered by the European patent that it asserted in the national proceeding against the importer. Monsanto's patent concerned the genetic sequence coding for enzymes able to make plants resistant to a herbicide, as well as the plants modified with the insertion of such genetic sequences. The production of soy meal from the genetically manipulated plants took place in Argentina, where no member of the patent family was in force. Monsanto could prove the presence in the imported soy meal of the patented fragments of DNA. It therefore requested an injunction on the basis of an alleged infringement of the product claim concerning said nucleotide sequences. The District Court of The Hague had to determine whether the import and commercialization of the soy meal infringed the product claim for the genetic sequence, even if the latter did not and could not perform any function in the material accused. Soy meal, as the court observed,[54] is "dead material", where the patented genetic sequences cannot express the enzymes to which the patent refers. The Dutch court held Article 9 Directive 98/44/EC to be determinative for the outcome of the case, and referred the following questions to the ECJ:

> 1. Must Article 9 of Directive 98/44. . .be interpreted as meaning that the protection provided under that provision can be invoked even in a

51 Case C-428/08, *Monsanto vs Cefetra et al*, 2010 ECR I-6765 at 77; see on this judgment Sven J. R. Bostyn, "A Decade After the Birth of the Biotech Directive: Was it Worth the Trouble?" in G. Ghidini and E. Arezzo (eds) *Biotechnology and Software Patent Law: A Comparative Review on New Developments* (Edward Elgar, 2011) 221, 230 et seq.

52 See Christopher Heath, "The Scope of DNA Patents in the Light of the Recent Monsanto Decisions" (2009) INT'L REV INTELL PROP & COMPETITION L 940 et seq.; Michael A. Kock, "Purpose-Bound Protection for DNA Sequences: In through the Back Door?" (2010) 7 J INTELL PROP L 495 et seq.

53 See *Monsanto*, 2010 ECR I-6765 at Reasonings 15 et seq.

54 See id. at Reasonings 26 et seq.

situation such as that in the present proceedings, in which the product (the DNA sequence) forms part of a material imported into the European Union (soy meal) and does not perform its function at the time of the alleged infringement, but has indeed performed its function (in the soy plant) or would possibly again be able to perform its function after it has been isolated from that material and inserted into the cell of an organism?

2. Proceeding on the basis that the DNA sequence described in claim 6 of patent No EP 0 546 090 is present in the soy meal imported into the Community by Cefetra and [Toepfer], and that the DNA is incorporated in the soy meal for the purposes of Article 9 of [the Directive] and that it does not perform its function therein: does the protection of a patent on biological material as provided for under [the Directive], in particular under Article 9 thereof, preclude the national patent legislation from offering (in parallel) absolute protection to the product (the DNA) as such, regardless of whether that DNA performs its function, and must the protection as provided under Article 9 of [the Directive] therefore be deemed to be exhaustive in the situation referred to in that provision, in which the product consists in genetic information or contains such information, and the product is incorporated in material which contains the genetic information?
3. Does it make any difference, for the purpose of answering the previous question, that patent No EP 0 546 090 was applied for and granted (on 19 June 1996) prior to the adoption of [the Directive] and that such absolute product protection was granted under national patent legislation prior to the adoption of that directive?
4. Is it possible, in answering the previous questions, to take into consideration the TRIPS Agreement, in particular Articles 27 and 30 thereof?

To deny infringement in the case at issue would not have required a general statement about the absolute product protection for genetic sequences.[55] Even in countries which allow absolute product protection, such as Germany, the mere existence of the patented compound in an incorporating material is not sufficient to find the patent infringed by selling or importing said material. It is necessary that the patented product performs a function in the incorporating material, even if not necessarily the function disclosed in the patent. Based on these premises, German case law excluded the infringement of a product claim to an intermediate, when the defendant imported end-products that were obtained abroad from the transformation of the patented intermediate and which contained a residual

55 See Anna Wolters, "EU & Germany: Denial of absolute product protection for DNA-patents (CJ decision in *Monsanto vs Cefetra*, C- 428/08) – a German perspective" (2011) 17 J OF COMMERCIAL BIOTECHNOLOGY 109 et seq.; see also Kock, *supra* note 52, at 499 (discussing Advocate General Paolo Mengozzi's Opinion that was then followed by ECJ).

amount of said intermediate – as long as the latter did not perform any function in the imported end-products.[56]

Despite that, the ECJ formulated general principles concerning whether Article 9 of Directive 98/44/EC allows an absolute product protection for DNA sequences, and came to the conclusion that it does not. According to the ECJ, Article 9 of Directive 98/44/EC limits the protection to the function for which the sequence was patented.[57] By the concept of function, the ECJ seems to understand the effect and use of which the genetic sequence is capable according to the specification of the patent. [58] As a result, no protection is possible under Article 9 of Directive 98/44/EC when the sequence does not perform any function in the material accused of infringing the patent, or when the sequence performs a function, but the latter is different from the function indicated in the patent. This principle seems to apply – in the reasoning of the ECJ – regardless of whether or not the function of the sequence has been indicated in the asserted product claim. Such understanding, however, could be in tension with the "primacy of the claims" in defining the scope of protection, as stated in Article 69 EPC and Article 8 of the Convention on the Unification of Certain Points of Substantive Law on Patents for Invention (Strasbourg Convention). As a consequence of this primacy, only functional and structural elements that are recited by the claim can limit the protection conferred by the patent. The direct implication of the *Monsanto* judgment for both the national patent offices and the EPO would be, therefore, to qualify the function of the polynucleotide claim as an integral part of the claimed technical teaching, and thus require the applicant to specify said function not only in the description, but also in the product claims of the application.[59]

The ECJ further considered the argument of the patentee according to which TRIPS would require an absolute protection for genetic sequences. The ECJ effectively denied any relevance of TRIPS Article 27.1. According to the ECJ, this provision deals with issues concerning the patentability and not the scope of protection. With respect to TRIPS Article 30, the court maintained that:

> [A]n interpretation of Article 9 of the Directive limiting the protection it confers to situations in which the patented product performs its function

56 See Joseph Straus, "The Scope of Protection Conferred by European Patents on Transgenic Plants and on Methods for Their Production" in A. Bakardjieva Engelbrekt et al (eds) *Festskrift til Marianne Levin* (Norstedts Juridik, 2008) 643, 651 et seq.

57 See *Monsanto*, 2010 ECR I-6765 at 77, Reasonings 49 and 50.

58 See id., Reasonings 43 and 44, that refer to Recitals 22 and 24 and Article 5(3) of the Directive 98/44/EC, that concerns the industrial application of the sequence that the applicant should disclose in the patent application as filed and seem to consider the terms "function" and "industrial application" within the meaning of Article 5(3) and Recitals 22–24 if not synonymous, at least interrelated.

59 See Jan B. Krauss and Toshiko Takenaka, "A Special Rule for Compound Protection for DNA-Sequences – Impact of the ECJ *Monsanto* Decision on Patent Practice" (2011) 93 J PAT & TRADEMARK SOC'Y 189, 202, 206.

> does not appear to conflict unreasonably with a normal exploitation of the patent and does not 'unreasonably prejudice the legitimate interests of the patent owner, taking account of the legitimate interests of third parties', within the meaning of Article 30.[60]

As a consequence, the ECJ held excluding an absolute patent protection for DNA molecules to be TRIPS-compliant. We agree with the conclusion of the ECJ, but not with the reasoning underlying it.

TRIPS-compliance

The question whether TRIPS requires an absolute product protection for chemical or biological substances is discussed controversially in the literature.[61] The debate, however, does not focus on the rights a patent grants under TRIPS. According to TRIPS Article 28.1(a), the patentee has the right to prohibit any use of the product claimed in the patent. If the product claimed by the patent is the "chemical entity" as such and the claim is valid, there is no doubt that the protection conferred under TRIPS Article 28.1(a) will be absolute. By contrast, if the allowable claim concerns not the chemical entity *per se*, but the industrial product containing it (a fertilizer, a colourant, a drug – i.e. the use of the chemical entity for a particular purpose, fulfilling a specific function),[62] it shall be equally undisputed that the protection will be limited to the right to prohibit the use and manufacture of the industrial product claimed (i.e. the fertilizer, the colourant, or the drug) and not of the chemical entity as such, because the former and not the latter is the "product" pursuant to TRIPS Article 28.1(a) the patent refers to.

Therefore, whether TRIPS mandates an absolute patent protection depends on what constitutes a product invention within the meaning of TRIPS Article 27.1. Hence, and contrary to the opinion of the ECJ, this issue of law is directly related to the question of what subject matter is eligible for protection[63] under TRIPS Article 27.1: the substance as such or the substance in relation to a specific industrial application? If one assumes that, under TRIPS Article 27.1, the technical problem solved by a product invention consists of the mere synthesis of the new

60 *Monsanto*, 2010 ECR I-6765 at 76.

61 See the analysis of Uhrich *supra* note 48, at 207 et seq., with further references; White, *supra* note 25 (2000/2001), 239, 241 et seq.; Crespi, *supra* note 14 (2001/2002), at 3 et seq.

62 These types of claims (e.g. pesticide containing the compound Y) were defined in the German practice as *Mittelansprüche*, and they granted according to the scholarship and case law a "purpose-bound" product protection. See Kraßer, *supra* note 25, at 486; German Supreme Court, Decision of February 24.02.1970 – Schädlingsbekämpfungsmittel, Gewerblicher Rechtsschutz und Urheberrecht (GRUR) 1970 361 et seq.; see also White, *supra* note 25, at 241 et seq.

63 See for a similar understanding of the issue with regard to the provisions of Directive 98/44/EC Meier Beck, "Aktuelle Fragen des Schutzbereichsbestimmung im deutschen und europäischen Patentrecht" (GRUR, 2003) 905, 911.

compound,[64] this would imply that TRIPS requires patents to be granted on the substance as such, and thus an absolute protection for it. If one assumes, by contrast, that a product invention exists only when the applicant has disclosed not only a method for the manufacture, but also an industrial use for the substance, and that the industrial use is an integral part of the technical teaching, then such use is to be indicated in the product claim. It will, therefore, limit the protection as well.

According to one opinion,[65] TRIPS allows only the first interpretation, and mandates a protection for the chemical compounds *per se*. In light of the following considerations, this view appears unconvincing. Admittedly, TRIPS Article 27.1 mandates a protection of all inventions, whether process or product. The provision, however, does not define what constitutes a product or an invention. It does not clarify whether, under the concept of "product" pursuant TRIPS Article 27.1 or TRIPS Article 28.1(a), the Members must encompass the chemical entity as such, or by contrast may subsume just the industrial product containing it. Therefore, it is up to the Members to decide whether the technical problem solved by a product invention in the chemical field consists in the synthesis of the new compound or whether the industrial use, of which the compound is capable, is an integral part of the invention itself. This interpretation of TRIPS Article 27 is supported by a systemic and contextual reading of the treaty provisions.

TRIPS Article 39.3 distinguishes between the "chemical entity" and "pharmaceutical or agricultural chemical products" which utilize or contain said "chemical entity".[66] In TRIPS Article 70.6, the obligation to grant patents for product inventions under TRIPS Article 27 refers to "pharmaceutical and agricultural products", and not to the "chemical entity". This implies that WTO Members can meet the obligations under TRIPS Article 27.1 when their domestic laws allow product claims for a pharmaceutical product or an agricultural product, as an "antivirus agent containing substance Z" or "fertilizer containing substance Y". The Members are not required to permit a claim for the chemical entity *per se*. Based on this view, TRIPS accommodates national laws that consider the use or function of the substance as an integral part of the product invention and an essential feature of the product claim.[67]

64 See for this thesis "the German Federal Supreme Court, Decision of 14.03.1972 – Case: X ZB 2/71" (1972) INT'L REV INTELL PROP & COMPETITION L 386 et seq.

65 See "Report on the Proposal for a European Parliament and Council Directive on the Legal Protection of Biotechnological Inventions" (COM (95) 0661 – C4-0063/96 – 95/0350(COD), at 36 et seq.

66 According to TRIPS Article 39.3 "Members, when requiring, as a condition of approving the marketing of pharmaceutical or of agricultural chemical products which utilize new chemical entities, the submission of undisclosed test or other data, the origination of which involves a considerable effort, shall protect such data against unfair commercial use." Admittedly, this provision does not deal with patents, but data protection. Despite that, it is relevant for the construction of TRIPS Articles 27.1 and 70.6, since it uses the same expression as in Article 70.6 (i.e. "pharmaceutical and agricultural chemical products").

67 See also "MPI Patent Declaration", *supra* note 3, at 679 et seq.

Against this conclusion two lines of arguments are possible, both actually older than the TRIPS Agreement itself.

First, patent law provides traditionally for two categories of patents (i.e. product and process patents). So does the TRIPS Agreement in Article 28.1(a).[68] The category of process patents includes patents for uses of a known substance.[69] If one excludes an absolute product claim for the chemical entity and admits only a "purpose-bound" product claim, then there would no longer be any distinction between a product and a process claim in this field.[70] More precisely, the argument is that there would be no difference between a "purpose-bound product claim" and a "use claim". This objection, however, was never really convincing.[71] A claim for a "fertilizer containing the substance Y" and a claim for the "use of Y as fertilizer" do not concern the same subject matter, and do not confer the same rights. The first claim remains a product claim within the meaning of TRIPS Article 28.1(a). Here, the preparation and sale of the fertilizer containing the chemical entity directly infringes the rights of the patentee. The use claim, on the other hand, is a method claim within the meaning of TRIPS Article 28.1(b). It protects only the activity recited in the claim, not the product as such. Thus, the preparation and sale of a fertilizer containing the compound thus do not directly infringe the patent. These acts can amount to a contributory infringement of the use claim in the Member States that provides the patentee with a right to prohibit indirect exploitation of the claimed invention, but this is an issue TRIPS does not address.

The second argument that could be raised against the conclusion of this chapter is that excluding absolute product protection for chemical or biological substances would discriminate this field against, for example, the mechanical sector. But this argument is not persuasive. Mechanical devices are characterized by a "unique and direct relation between structure and function".[72] This relation is, in most of the cases, expressed by the definition of the device itself. The product claim is not relating to an abstract geometrical form, but to, for example, "a rolling mill" or an "apparatus for straightening profiles" or a "straightening device" – that is,

68 Arguably, TRIPS Article 28 should have referred to process and product claims, and not process and product patents. Indeed the same patent according to the national legislation of almost all Member States may include claims belonging to both categories.

69 See *infra*, IV(c).

70 See in the recent literature Rochelle Cooper Dreyfuss and Esteban Donoso, "On Aiding Technological Development: The Max Planck Declaration on Patent Protection", 6 UC IRVINE LAW REVIEW (forthcoming); NYU School of Law, Public Law Research Paper No. 15-58; NYU Law and Economics Research Paper No. 15-27, http://ssrn.com/abstract=2698873, accessed 02/03/2016, at 5 et seq.

71 See discussion by Bernhard Geissler, *Der Umfang des Stoffschutzes für chemische Erfindungen* (1972) at 28 seq and 184 et seq.

72 See Vincenzo Di Cataldo, *I brevetti per invenzione e per modello* (3rd edn, Giuffrè, 2012) at 109 et seq.; Geissler, *supra* note 71 (1972) at 175 et seq.; Vincenzo Di Cataldo and Emanuela Arezzo, "Scope of the Patent and Uses of the Product in the European Biotechnology Directive" (2006), 1 ITALIAN INTELL PROP 11, 20.

a three-dimensional shape relating to a specific function.[73] Therefore, in this field, the protection conferred by the claim is implicitly always purpose-bound. By contrast in the chemical sector such strict relationship between the structure and the function does not exist.[74] On the one hand, from the mere description of the chemical structure of the claimed compound, no person skilled in the art can infer for which purpose – according to the invention – the compound should be used, as fertilizer, antiviral or whatsoever. On the other hand, the same chemical structure can be used for completely different purposes, for instance as ingredient of an antiviral drug and as component of a cosmetic product.

Against this background, a rule which admits the patentability of a substance only in relation to a specific use would be consistent with TRIPS Article 27 as well as with TRIPS Article 28 as long as it applies to all technical fields in a non-discriminatory fashion. It would, therefore, not be necessary to assess whether and under which conditions such provision may be admitted under TRIPS Article 30, as the latter disposition does not concern the issue of whether and in what form a product claim should be admitted, nor whether and to what extent a product, a substance, or information may be eligible as such for protection. TRIPS Article 30 concerns only the issue of whether domestic law may authorize third parties to perform specific acts related to the subject matter covered by a patent without the consent of the patentee. It stipulates a derogation from TRIPS Article 28, not from Article 27. It is thus not directly relevant for provisions, such as those enacted in Germany, France and Italy,[75] which exclude protection for a human genetic sequence *per se* and admit protection only when a specific use is indicated in the product claim. These provisions concern the issue of what is patentable, and not the issue of which uses of a patented subject matter infringe the patent and which are exempted.

If, however, the rule mandating only purpose-bound product protection were to apply only to a specific field, as is the case in German law, then its TRIPS-compliance would depend on whether this regulation implies only a differential, but objectively justified, treatment, instead of an unjustified discrimination. With specific reference to genetic sequences, the literature has provided several reasons why specific rules, departing from the general principles applicable to organic chemistry, may be appropriate in this field. Genetic sequences do have a double nature – they are indeed biochemical molecules, but at the same time they are

73 See Board of Appeal of the German Patent Office, Decision of 15 May 1952 at 38 767 IVd/12 o – 5 B 75/51, Gewerblicher Rechtsschutz und Urheberrecht (GRUR) 1952, 402. See also the comment by Hans Dersin, "Über einige Fragen aus der Praxis des Deutschen Patentamts (unter besonderer Berücksichtigung der Chemie)", 1952 Gewerblicher Rechtsschutz und Urheberrecht (GRUR) 360, 366.

74 See Cataldo, *supra* note 72 (2012) at 109 et seq.; Geissler, *supra* note 71(1972) at 175 et seq.

75 See *supra*, note 48 of this chapter.

essential carriers of information.[76] Furthermore, the same sequence may be able to perform several functions and – because of the alternative splicing mechanism[77] – may be involved in the coding of several functionally and structurally different polypeptides.[78] Other contributions have raised some doubts about the relevance of these differences. They have argued that traditional chemical compounds as well are multifunctional; in fact, they may be used for different purposes even more frequently than a genetic sequence. However, it is not necessary to reproduce this broad discussion[79] here, and it is not the purpose of this chapter to advance it.

Implication for the pharmaceutical sector

If one agrees with the position adopted above, then it is up to the Members to decide whether to allow absolute or "purpose-bound" product claims for chemical compounds and biological material.[80] If a Member decides to allow only a purpose-bound product protection, the practical implications of this solution for the pharmaceutical sector depend on how broad or narrow the statement of purpose must be. If the applicant may draft the purpose-bound product claim to cover *any* possible medical uses of the compound, as is the case in the practice of the EPO with respect to the first medical use of known compounds ("drug containing substance Y"),[81] the differences between a system permitting absolute product protection and a system rejecting it will be of little practical importance. By contrast, if domestic law requires the applicant to indicate in every independent product claim the specific use which was disclosed in the application, then the differences would become significant. In that case, if the application describes only the use of the compound as an agent able to reduce high blood pressure, the patent claims will have to be limited to an antihypertensive drug containing the substance concerned. If a third party identifies a method for using the

76 See Moufang, *supra* note 37, at 179 et seq., discussing the possible implication of the DNA's double nature under the perspective of the exclusion of abstract information provided under Article 52 EPC.

77 See for the concept of alternative splicing B. Roy, L. Haupt and L. Griffiths, "Review: Alternative Splicing (AS) of Genes as an Approach for Generating Protein Complexity" (2013), 14 CURRENT GENOMICS 182 et seq.

78 See Joseph Straus, "An Updating Concerning the Protection of Biotechnological Inventions including the Scope of Patents for Genes – An Academic Point of View", OJ EPO 2003, 166, 172.

79 See Wolrad Prinz zu Waldeck and Pyrmont Waldeck, "Special Legislation for Genetic Inventions – A Violation of Article 27(1) TRIPS?" in Prinz zu Waldeck and Pyrmont et al (eds) *Patents and Technological Progress in a Globalized World: Liber Amicorum Joseph Straus* (Springer, 2009).

80 This is also the opinion of Uhrich, *supra* note 48, at 211, and Niclas Kunczik, *Geistiges Eigentum an genetischen Informationen* (Baden-Baden, 2007) 90 et seq.

81 See Rainer Moufang, "Patentability of Pharmaceutical Innovations: the European Perspective" in Josef Drexl and Nari Lee (eds) *Pharmaceutical Innovation, Competition and Patent Law* (Edward Elgar, 2013) 54, 66 et seq.

compound and a method for making it different from that possibly claimed in the first patent, then the patentee will not be able to stop the entry into the market of the drug containing the same substance, but marketed for a different indication.

"Evergreening" and the patentability of new forms and new uses of known compounds: Section 3(d) of the Indian Patent Act

One of the core negotiated achievements of proponents for a strong, harmonized international IP system has been the introduction of an obligation to provide for patent protection "in all fields of technology" under TRIPS Article 27.1. However, based on the transition periods of the agreement, developing countries had until 2005 to introduce product patent protection in areas not protectable prior to TRIPS.[82] As a country that since the 1970 revision of its Patent Act had rejected product patents for pharmaceuticals in order to boost generic drug production and enhance access to affordable medicines, India's shift to full patent protection in accordance with TRIPS Article 27.1 has been watched around the world with great interest. This is not least due to the fact that India serves as the "pharmacy of the third world" by supplying generic medicines to poor countries around the globe which often do not have domestic manufacturing capacity in the pharmaceutical sector.

Section 3(d) and the Novartis *case*

When India adopted its Patent Amendments Act in 2005, allowing the grant of product patents for pharmaceutical substances for the first time since the 1970 Act, a revised version of Section 3(d) of the Patent Act aimed to tackle the practice of patent "evergreening" and to ensure continuous availability of affordable medicines in India.[83] Under the disputed term "evergreening" a part of the literature and the case law understands the practice of filing subsequent patents for minor modifications or improvements to an earlier patented invention in an attempt to

82 See TRIPS Article 65(4). Those countries nevertheless had to introduce a so-called "mailbox system" where patent applications from 1995 onwards could be filed in order to be examined once the country became fully bound by TRIPS. See TRIPS Article 70(8). In addition, those countries had to grant "exclusive marketing rights" to products subject to an application in the mailbox system under certain conditions. See TRIPS Article 70(9).

83 As F. Abbott summarizes, "Section 3(d) was proposed by the government with the stated purpose of addressing concerns raised by members of Parliament that the introduction of pharmaceutical product patent protection would substantially inhibit the availability of medicines for the population of India and developing countries more generally." See F. Abbott, "The Judgment in *Novartis v. India*: What the Supreme Court of India Said" (2013), 4 INTELL PROP WATCH, www.ip-watch.org/2013/04/04/the-judgment-in-novartis-v-india-what-the-supreme-court-of-india-said/. For a review of the drafting history of Section 3(d), see decision of the Indian Supreme Court in *Novartis AG vs Union of India & Others*, 1 April 2013, at pp31–48.

effectively extend the period of protection especially for pharmaceutical products.[84] In the strict legal sense, the so-called "secondary patents" that result from this practice can, of course, not limit access to the subject matter disclosed in previous publication and patent applications. However, they can be the basis for switching or hopping product strategies based on a combination of product, authorization withdrawal and patent filings that could as a result delay generic competition.

Under Chapter II, entitled "Inventions Not Patentable", Section 3(d) provides that the following are not inventions within the meaning of the Patent Act (PA):

> (d) *the mere discovery of a new form of a known substance which does not result in the enhancement of the known efficacy of that substance* or the mere discovery of any new property or new use for a known substance or of the mere use of a known process, machine or apparatus unless such known process results in a new product or employs at least one new reactant.
>
> *Explanation: For the purposes of this clause, salts, esters, ethers, polymorphs, metabolites, pure form, particle size, isomers, mixtures of isomers, complexes, combinations and other derivatives of known substance shall be considered to be the same substance, unless they differ significantly in properties with regard to efficacy.*[85]

This provision has been at the core of a highly debated decision of the Indian Supreme Court concerning the patentability of the Swiss pharmaceutical giant Novartis's cancer drug commonly sold under the brand name Glivec. After having received patents *inter alia* in the US,[86] Novartis filed an Indian "mailbox" application in July 1998 for a patent claiming the use of an active ingredient, Imatinib Mesylate (IM), in its beta crystalline form for the treatment of certain forms of cancer. Since it had been disclosed prior to 1995, Novartis could not hope to obtain a patent for the original IM form used in Glivec via the mailbox system in India.[87] Instead, it stated in the specification of the "mailbox" application

84 See A. Ramanujan and R. Sen, "Pruning the Evergreen Tree: Section 3(d) of the Indian Patents Act 1970" (2009) 10 EUR INTELL PROP REV 1, 4.

85 Section 3(d) of the Patents Act, 1970 – as amended by the Patents (Amendment) Act, 2005. Emphasis added to indicate the changes by the 2005 amendment.

86 After Novartis was granted a patent in the US covering the drug "Imatinib" in its free base form and pharmaceutically acceptable salts, it filed for the "beta crystalline" form of the salt, for which it later was granted US Patent No. 6894051 B1. Interestingly, the US patent examiner initially denied the patentability of the claimed subject matter, but its decision was reversed by the Board of Patent Appeals and Interferences. See Abbott, *supra* note 83; see also "Ex Parte Joerg Zimmermann, Bertrand Sutter and Hans Burger", Appeal No. 2003–0919, Application No. 09/463/097.

87 See S. Barazza, "Incremental Pharmaceutical Innovation in India: The Supreme Court's Judgment in the Novartis *Gleevec* Case" (2013), 8 J INTELL PROP L & PRAC 776, 777. On the mailbox system and exclusive marketing rights, see TRIPS Article 70(8)–(9) and the explanation, *supra* note 82.

that the subsequently developed beta crystalline form of IM had better flow properties, enhanced thermodynamic stability, and lower hygroscopicity than earlier forms of IM.[88] Novartis obtained exclusive marketing rights for Glivec in India under the Indian implementation of TRIPS Article 70(9) in 2003. Based on the grant of these rights, the price for treatment of leukaemia using Glivec in India increased by the factor of ten up to a price of US$26,000 per year. With an average annual income below US$1500, this placed Glivec out of reach of the vast majority of leukaemia patients in India.[89]

When Novartis's mailbox application was examined in late 2005 by the Assistant Controller of Patents, several NGOs and generic companies filed pre-grant oppositions. The application was rejected in March 2006 on the grounds that the beta crystalline form of IM had been anticipated by the earlier US patent (i.e. lacked novelty) and was obvious to a person skilled in the relevant art. In addition, the Assistant Controller of Patents held that Novartis's invention fell under the new version of Section 3(d) and hence was not patentable in India.[90] In response, Novartis challenged the Orders of the Assistant Controller to the Intellectual Property Appeals Board (IPAB) and the TRIPS consistency and constitutionality of Section 3(d) to the Madras High Court. While the court rejected the claim of a breach of the Indian Constitution and denied its jurisdiction for judging TRIPS - compliance in August 2007,[91] the IPAB upheld the denial of a patent based on Section 3(d) in June 2009.[92] Later that year, the Supreme Court of India agreed to hear the petition of Novartis against the IPAB order.

On 1 April 2013, the Indian Supreme Court issued its decision, essentially confirming that the beta crystalline form of IM was not patentable in India. It held that the earlier US patents on Glivec, especially the so called "Zimmermann" patent of 28 May 1996, already covered and disclosed not only the free base form of Imatinib, but also Imatinib Mesylate (IM) – the latter hence could not qualify as an "invention" that is new, inventive and industrially applicable within the

88 See Indian Patent Office, Application No. 1602/MAS/1998; see the analysis of the patent application in *Novartis vs Union of India* (2009 IPAB TA/1-5/2007/PT/CH, Order 100/2009 of 26 June 2009), www.ipab.tn.nic.in/Orders/100-2009.htm, accessed 02/03/2016.

89 See G. Murdur, "Indian Patients Go to Court Over Cancer Drug" (2004), 329 BRITISH MED J 419, 419; Janice M. Mueller, "Taking TRIPS to India – *Novartis*, Patent Law, and Access to Medicines" (2007), 356 NEW ENG J OF MED 541, 541.

90 See "*Novartis AG vs Natco Pharma*, Indian Patent Office" (Application No. 1602/NAS/1998), http://lists.essential.org/pipermail/ip-health/2006-March/009200.html, accessed 02/03/2016.

91 See "*Novartis AG vs Union of India*" (2007), http://judis.nic.in/judis_chennai/qrydispfree.aspx?filename=11121, accessed 02/03/2016. The Madras High Court found Section 3(d) as not arbitrary and vague and hence rejected a breach of Article 14 of the Constitution of India.

92 See *Novartis vs Union of India*, 2009 IPAB TA/1-5/2007/PT/CH, Order 100/2009 of 26 June 2009, *supra* note 88.

meaning of Section 2(1), (j) and (ja) of the Patents Act.[93] It is therefore the beta crystalline form of IM that – as "a new form of a known substance" (the latter being IM itself, rather than the free base form of Imatinib) – had to meet the requirements of Section 3(d).[94] The key issue under Section 3(d) then was whether the beta crystalline form "result[s] in the enhancement of the known efficacy" of IM, and how to interpret the notion of enhanced efficacy.[95]

According to the Indian Supreme Court, efficacy means "the ability to produce a desired or intended result" – whereas in the case of a medicine that claims to cure a disease, the test of efficacy can only be "therapeutic efficacy", which must be judged "strictly and narrowly".[96] In light of its emphasis that "not all advantageous or beneficial properties are relevant", the court held that while "more beneficial flow properties", "better thermodynamic stability" and "lower hygroscopicity" can improve "processability" and "storability" of a drug, they do not, in themselves, bring an enhancement in efficacy.[97] The court felt no need to decide whether only enhanced curative effect or also "safety or significantly reduced toxicity" fall under the notion of therapeutic efficacy, as neither had been shown by Novartis.[98] The Court did, however, make clear that increased bioavailability (i.e. the degree to which the medicine can be absorbed by the human body) alone does *not necessarily* lead to an enhancement of therapeutic efficacy – as the latter must be "established by research data".[99] In this regard, Novartis essentially lost its long battle for patentability of Glivec in India because it was unable to present sufficient data which satisfied the requirement of enhanced therapeutic efficacy. That, however, has *not* been due to a very narrow reading of Section 3(d), as Abbott aptly summarizes:

> It is important to note what the Supreme Court did not say. It did *not* say that a new form of known compound may never be patented. It did *not* say that improving the bioavailability characteristics of the drug may never result in enhanced efficacy. It left open the question whether enhanced efficacy refers narrowly to curative effect, or more broadly to improved safety profile and reduced toxicity.[100]

93 See *Novartis AG vs Union of India*, Indian Supreme Court Judgment of 1 April 2013, at pp131–136, 157.
94 Id. at p171.
95 The court assumed for the sake of argument that the beta crystalline form was new and left open the question whether it represented an inventive step. In light of its application of Section 3(d), it did not find it necessary to pass judgment on this point. Id. at p158.
96 Id. at p180.
97 Id. at pp172–173, 180.
98 Id. at pp185–187.
99 Id. at p189.
100 See Abbott, *supra* note 83.

Assessing compliance with TRIPS

Premise

Section 3(d) and the Supreme Court interpretation have initiated a debate about its consistency with the TRIPS Agreement, as well as the wider policy question on how to deal with minor modifications and incremental innovation in the pharmaceutical sector.[101] In the following subsection, this chapter focuses only on the former question. The matter is of interest beyond India, as several (developing) countries and emerging economies are considering Section 3(d)-style measures as part of national patent laws. In response, the US has suggested including a clause explicitly prohibiting its trading partners from introducing or maintaining Section 3(d)-type provisions in the text of the Trans-Pacific Partnership Agreement (TPP). Based on the text of Article 18.37(2), however, such a suggestion did not make it into the final version of the TPP – as under that rule TPP contracting parties only confirm the availability of new use patents in their national laws.

It is necessary to point out that Section 3(d) incorporates at least four different exclusions, including exclusions for: (i) a new form of a known substance which does not result in the enhancement of the known efficacy of that substance; (ii) the mere discovery of any new property; (iii) new uses of a known substance; and (iv) the mere use of a known process, machine, or apparatus unless such known process results in a new product or employs at least one new reactant. Two of these exclusions are more relevant to the pharmaceutical sector: new forms of known substances and new uses of known compounds.

The exclusion for new forms of a known substance

At the core of the consistency issue of the exclusion of a new form of a known substance which does not result in the enhancement of the known efficacy is TRIPS Article 27.1, which requires that "patents shall be available for any inventions, whether products or processes, in all fields of technology, provided that they are new, involve an inventive step and are capable of industrial application". In particular, "patents shall be available and patent rights enjoyable without discrimination as to the place of invention, the field of technology and

101 On the question of TRIPS consistency, see, for example, C. Correa, "Is Section 3(d) Consistent with TRIPS?" (2013), 48(32) ECON & POL WEEKLY 40; Shamnad Basheer, "India's Tryst with TRIPS: The Patents (Amendment) Act 2005" (2005), 1 INDIAN J OF L & TECH 15; Shamnad Basheer and P. Reddy, "Ducking TRIPS in India: A Saga Involving *Novartis* and the Legality of Section 3(d)" (2008), 20 NAT'L L SCH OF INDIA REV 131; L. Lee, "Trials and TRIPS-ulations: Indian Patent Law and *Novartis AG v. Union of India*" (2008), 23 BERKELEY TECH L J 281; Z. Turrill, "Finding the Patent Balance: The Novartis Glivec case and the TRIPS Compliance of India's Section 3(d) Efficacy Standard' (2013), 44 GEORGETOWN J INT'L L 1555; R. Bhattacharya, "Are Developing Countries Going Too Far on TRIPS? A Closer Look at the New Laws in India" (2008), 34 AM. J OF L AND MED 395.

whether products are imported or locally produced". In that regard, the most common argument against Section 3(d), as interpreted by the Indian Supreme Court, is that "the decision appears to confirm that *India's law creates a special, additional criterion for select technologies, like pharmaceuticals*, which could preclude issuance of a patent even if the applicant demonstrates that the invention is new, involves an inventive step, and is capable of industrial application".[102]

At first sight, this argument seems firmly based on some of the statements made by the Indian Supreme Court in the *Novartis* case: rejecting the proposition that Section 3(d) simply reiterates that mere discoveries do not amount to inventions under the PA,[103] the Supreme Court emphasized:

> The amended portion of Section 3(d) clearly sets up a *second tier of qualifying standards for chemical substances/pharmaceutical products* in order to leave the door open for true and genuine inventions but, at the same time, to check any attempt at repetitive patenting or extension of the patent term on spurious grounds.[104]

The court goes on to explain that, when reading the definitions of "invention" under Section 2:1(j)[105] and of "inventive step" in Section 2:1(ja)[106] with Section 3(d):

> it would appear that the Act sets *different standards for qualifying as "inventions" things belonging to different classes, and for medicines and drugs and other chemical substances, the Act sets the invention threshold further higher*, by virtue of the amendments made in Section 3(d) in the year 2005.[107]

Finally, at the end of its decision, the Supreme Court – while leaving somewhat open the nature of Section 3(d) either "as setting up the standards of 'patentability' or as an extension of the definition of 'invention'" – comes back to the main effect of Section 3(d):

> Section 2(1)(j) defines "invention" to mean, "a new product . . ." but the new product in chemicals and especially pharmaceuticals may not necessarily

102 United States Trade Representative (USTR), Special 301 Report, at 38 (2013) (emphasis added).

103 See *Novartis AG vs Union of India*, Indian Supreme Court Judgment of 1 April 2013, at p101.

104 Id. at p103 (emphasis added).

105 Under Section 2:1(j) PA, ("invention" means a new product or process involving an inventive step and capable of industrial application).

106 Under Section 2:1(ja) ("inventive step" means a feature of an invention that involves technical advance as compared to the existing knowledge or having economic significance or both and that makes the invention not obvious to a person skilled in the art).

107 *Novartis AG vs Union of India*, Indian Supreme Court Judgment of 1 April 2013, at p104 (emphasis added).

> mean something altogether new or completely unfamiliar or strange or not existing before. It may mean something "different from a recent previous" or "one regarded as better than what went before" or "in addition to another or others of the same kind." However, in case of chemicals and especially pharmaceuticals if the product for which patent protection is claimed is a new form of a known substance with known efficacy, then the subject product must pass, in addition to clauses (j) and (ja) of section 2(1), the test of enhanced efficacy as provided in section 3(d) read with its explanation.[108]

Section 3(d), as applied by the Supreme Court, indeed raises several potential questions when analysing its consistency with the international standards set out in TRIPS Article 27.1. In light of the common critique, exemplified in the quote from the United States Trade Representative (USTR) Special 301 Report, one could ask whether it establishes an additional condition for patent protection – one beyond the requirements of novelty, inventiveness, and utility and hence not mentioned and not allowed in Article 27.1. More worrisome still, in light of the statements by the Supreme Court about "setting different standards" and "higher thresholds" for the patentability of pharmaceuticals and chemicals, one may find it difficult not to consider Section 3(d) as discriminating between fields of technology. The purpose of this chapter, however, is not to search for and discuss potential justifications for individual, and to some extent diverging, statements in a single court decision. Our objective rather is to point to ways of construing and interpreting national provisions such as Section 3(d) in a manner so as to avoid conflicts with TRIPS.

A starting point from this perspective is to acknowledge that every WTO Member is free to design its domestic IP protection system to suit domestic needs – subject to the minimum standards of TRIPS. The agreement's objective is that IP protection and enforcement contributes to both technological innovation and dissemination of technology, serves the interests of users and producers of technology, and overall facilitates social and economic welfare.[109] In the specific context of public health, all WTO Members agreed in the Doha Declaration on TRIPS and Public Health that TRIPS "can and should be interpreted and implemented in a manner supportive of WTO Members' right to protect public health and, in particular, to promote access to medicines for all".[110] The declaration then lists an interpretation of all TRIPS provisions in light of the balancing

108 Id. at p192.

109 See TRIPS Article 7. Under the customary principles of treaty interpretation in international law, the object and purpose of a treaty form one of the core elements driving the treaty interpretation exercise; see Article 31(1) of the Vienna Convention on the Law of Treaties (VCLT) which serves as the main source of guidance for treaty interpretation in the WTO.

110 "Doha Declaration on TRIPS and Public Health", WT/MIN(01)/DEC/2 (14 November 2001), at p4.

objectives in Article 7 and public interest principles in Article 8 in order to ensure that TRIPS supports, rather than counters, public health policies.[111]

Against this background, it will not be easy to show that a national law is violating TRIPS because it decides, in balancing between promoting (future) pharmaceutical innovation and access to medicines, against protecting new forms of known substances unless they show enhanced efficacy. A WTO Member complaining about a Section 3(d)-type measure would have to establish (and bear the burden of proving) that there is a *prima facie* case for a breach of Article 27.1 (or any other TRIPS provision).[112] In light of the open-textured nature of the key terms used in TRIPS Article 27.1, which lend themselves to several possible interpretations, Members enjoy significant policy space in designing domestic patent policy.[113] The remaining discussion in this chapter will focus on the flexibilities relevant for Section 3(d)-type measures that follow from the notion of "invention" and "discrimination" under TRIPS.

One possible starting point is to perceive national provisions akin to Section 3(d) as subject matter limitations to what otherwise comprises an invention under patent law. Indeed, Section 3(d) is systemically positioned in Chapter II of the Indian Patent Act, entitled "Inventions Not Patentable". The provision defines – by virtue of its title – "What are not inventions" and thereby excludes from the definition of inventions under Section 2(j), *inter alia*, the mere discovery of a new form of a known substance unless this results in enhanced efficacy. Based on the broad definition of invention in the Indian Patent Act, this leaves room for various, more specific understandings of Section 3(d) – for example, as a clarification of the *inventive step* requirement, or as an inherent, not otherwise generally defined aspect of the concept of invention.[114]

The question, then, is whether any of these approaches are inconsistent with TRIPS. The agreement requires WTO Members to make patents available "for *any* inventions, whether products or processes, in *all* fields of technology" – but it does not otherwise define the notion of invention and inventive step. Some argue that neither the ordinary meaning of the qualitative term invention nor its treaty context prohibit an interpretation which excludes new forms of known substances (without enhanced efficacy) from the concept of invention.[115] On the other hand, contextual arguments based on the transitional provisions of the

111 Id. at 5(a).

112 On the general burden of proof of the party asserting the affirmative of a claim or defence, see "U.S. – Wool Shirts and Blouses" (Appellate Body Report 1997), at p14. Based on the established jurisprudence in WTO dispute settlement, only once sufficient evidence is produced "to raise a presumption that what is claimed is true, the burden shifts to the other party, who will fail unless it adduces sufficient evidence to rebut the presumption". See ibid; see also "EC – Hormones" (Appellate Body Report 1998), at pp98, 104.

113 See "MPI Patent Declaration", *supra* note 3, at pp5, 6–8, 11, and §§ 1.2, 1.3, 2, 3.1, 3.3.

114 In *Novartis*, the Indian Supreme Court seems critical about the favour of the former approach (see pp99–102), but essentially leaves the question open (see p190).

115 See Correa, *supra* note 34, at 271–272; Cynthia M. Ho, "Should All Drugs Be Patentable?: A Comparative Perspective" (2015), 17 VAND J ENT & TECH L 295, 341.

TRIPS Agreement support findings that pharmaceutical products under TRIPS do include new forms of a chemical substance.[116] According to TRIPS Article 70.8 pharmaceutical products represents a subject matter in principle eligible for protection within the meaning of TRIPS Article 27.1.[117] The concept of pharmaceutical product may be argued to include any drugs. Whether the ingredient of the drug is a new chemical entity or the derivative of a known class of compounds does not matter, since TRIPS Article 27 distinguishes the concept of subject matter that is in principle eligible for protection – an invention in the field of technology – and the requirements for its protection – novelty, inventive step and industrial applicability.[118] Therefore, as a technical solution remains an "invention" within the meaning of TRIPS Article 27 even if it is not novel or not inventive, so a drug remains a "pharmaceutical product" within the meaning of TRIPS Article 70.8 even if it is not novel or inventive and for this reason no patent can be granted.

While rationalizing Section 3(d) based on a wide notion of the concept of invention hence appears debatable, a justification based on a wide understanding of the inventive step requirement is a more promising alternative. Enhanced efficacy, then, is essentially a specific expression of the required advance over the state of the art in the field of pharmaceuticals. This approach is actually not much different from the position taken by the EPO and United States Patent and Trademark Office (USPTO) with regard to the inventiveness of new forms of known substances.[119] Those new forms will often be structurally obvious. As a consequence, a national law that allows their patenting under the condition that they show enhanced efficacy as a specific type of a surprising (and thereby inventive) effect is certainly within the boundaries of possible constructions of the inventiveness standard in TRIPS.

The remaining question, nevertheless, is whether this construction of an inventive step for pharmaceutical innovation is a form of discrimination under TRIPS Article 27.1. Since Section 3(d) on its face applies to all chemical inventions, and not only to the pharmaceutical ones, there is no case for a *de jure* discrimination.[120] If one, however, assumes – for the sake of analysis – that the provision in practice affects patent applications relating to pharmaceutical inventions more often than patent applications relating to chemical inventions, it may nevertheless be considered *de facto* discriminatory. This would fall within the scope of the non-discrimination test in TRIPS Article 27.1 that covers both

116 See Case no. C-414/11 (18 July 2013), *Daiichi Sankyo Co Ltd, et al vs DEMO Anonimos Viomikhaniki kai Emporiki Etairia Farmakon*, Reasonings 65 et seq.

117 See ibid, Reasonings 65 et seq.

118 See Roberto Romandini, "Flexibilities Under TRIPS: An Analysis of the Proposal for Reforming Brazilian Patent Law" (2016), 15 J MARSHALL REV INTELL PROP L 150, 171.

119 See id. at 25–26.

120 See Romandini, *supra* note 118, at 173; Gesine Berthold, *Evergreening von Arzneimittelpatenten* (Baden-Baden, 2011) 186.

de jure and *de facto* discrimination.[121] At the same time, not all forms of differential treatment amount to discrimination.

As a starting point, one should point out that the policy considerations underlying Section 3(d) find further support in more general TRIPS provisions. All WTO Members have agreed that the object and purpose of TRIPS, primarily embodied in its Articles 7 and 8, serve to achieve an interpretation and implementation of TRIPS which is supportive of public health. In TRIPS Article 27.1, this flexibility militates for a wide understanding of both invention and inventive step which encompass national laws that – in order to reduce the number of so called "secondary patents" and facilitate in this way access to medicines – adopt Section 3(d)-type restrictions on patent protection. More generally, the balancing objectives in Article 7, as well as the concept of sustainable development in the preamble to the WTO Agreement, suggest that finding the appropriate balance between competing economic, social, and environmental interests is – within the boundaries of ordinary meaning and treaty context – a matter for WTO Members to decide in the process of treaty implementation, and not for WTO adjudicators in the process of treaty interpretation.[122]

With these general considerations in mind, the allegation that Section 3(d)-type measures discriminate between fields of technology seems less persuasive. The core question is what is to be understood by the open term "discrimination" in Article 27.1 and how much flexibility exists for WTO Members to distinguish on the basis of domestic policies, in particular those accepted in TRIPS as valid grounds for regulating IP. In the only WTO dispute so far where this issue has been addressed, the (then) European Community (EC) complained *inter alia* about an exception in the Canadian Patent Act which allowed the use of a patented invention for the purpose of obtaining regulatory approval as discriminating against pharmaceutical patents.[123] Although the panel carefully avoided defining the term "discrimination" in general terms,[124] it clarified that "Article 27 does not prohibit bona fide exceptions to deal with problems that may exist only in certain product areas."[125] Instead, the notion of discrimination "extends beyond the concept of differential treatment. It is a normative term, pejorative in connotation, referring to results of the unjustified imposition of differentially disadvantageous treatment."[126]

121 See the discussion of Canada – Patents Panel Report (DS114, 2000), *infra*.

122 See, for a detailed discussion, H. Grosse Ruse-Khan, "The Principle of Integration in WTO/TRIPS Disputes" in M. Cordonier-Segger (ed) *Sustainable Development Principles in the Decisions of International Courts and Tribunals 1992–2012* (2015), http://ssrn.com/abstract=1939859, accessed 02/03/2016.

123 See Canada – Patents Panel Report (DS114, 2000).

124 See id. at 7.94, 7.98.

125 See id. at 7.92.

126 See id. at 7.94.

In other words, even if Section 3(d)-type measures primarily affect pharmaceutical patents, this does not necessarily imply discrimination. Instead, the panel in *Canada–Patents* demanded:

- a *de facto discriminatory effect* in the sense that the actual effect of the measure "is to impose differentially disadvantageous consequences"; and
- a *lack of justification for the disadvantageous effects*: "an inquiry into the objective characteristics of the measure from which one can infer the existence or non-existence of discriminatory objectives".[127]

On the first point of a *de facto* discriminatory effect, a closer reading of the Indian Supreme Court is instructive. While the court admits that Section 3(d) "clearly sets up a second tier of qualifying standards for chemical substances/pharmaceutical products", it does so only "*in order to leave the door open for true and genuine inventions but, at the same time, to check any attempt at repetitive patenting or extension of the patent term on spurious grounds*".[128] Section 3(d), hence, may be understood as simply dealing with a particular problem (evergreening) in a particular field of technology (pharmaceuticals, but also chemicals) by ensuring that a new form of a known substance shows enhanced efficacy (and thereby enforcing in particular the requirements of inventiveness). In that case, Section 3(d) simply treats different areas of technology differently for reasons inherent in the field of technology – something which does not amount to "differentially disadvantageous consequences" and hence is not discrimination.[129] Pointing to state practice, Correa has shown that it is not uncommon for WTO Members to treat different areas of technology differently.[130]

Of course, a WTO Member claiming a breach of the non-discrimination standard in TRIPS Article 27.1 might be able to show that evergreening or similar types of attempts for patenting slight improvements over earlier inventions exist also in other fields of technology. This in turn may suggest "differentially disadvantageous consequences" for those technological sectors affected by a Section 3(d)-type measure *vis-à-vis* those which are not. However, even in these circumstances, the second element of a discrimination claim, namely a lack of justification for the disadvantageous effects, still needs to be shown. In the context of pharmaceutical products, a WTO Member will usually attempt to rely on public

127 See id. at 7.101.

128 *Novartis AG vs Union of India*, Indian Supreme Court Judgment of 1 April 2013, at p103 (emphasis added).

129 The argument that Section 3(d) is understood by the Indian Supreme Court as primarily dealing with a particular problem in a particular field of technology is further supported by paragraph 192 of the judgment, emphasizing that a "new product in chemicals and especially pharmaceuticals may not necessarily mean something altogether new" or "not existing before", but rather something "different from a recent previous" or "in addition to another or others of the same kind".

130 See Correa, *supra* note 34, at 282–284.

health as an objective that justifies a *de facto* or *de jure* less advantageous treatment. As explained above, the TRIPS balancing objectives and public interest principles, as well as paragraph 4 of the Doha Declaration, militate strongly for the "right [of a WTO Member] to protect public health" [and] "to promote access to medicines for all".[131]

Against such public health justification, one could counter that Section 3(d)-type exclusions apply only when the claimed new form has no better (therapeutic) effect than the forms of the compound already known. If the claimed new form of the compound implies a therapeutic improvement over the compound already known, Section 3(d) does not exclude patentability. The requested patent, provided that the other requirements for protection are met, can be granted. It thus might be argued that since only new forms of the known compound which do *not* involve therapeutic improvements are excluded from protection, no health-related public interest may exist to ensure access to the subject matter excluded by Section 3(d). As a consequence, the justification for differential treatment of pharmaceutical inventions covered by Section 3(d) on health or humanitarian grounds may appear as a case of *venire contra factum proprium*. The argument would be that the rule does not, in effect, serve the purpose to improve access to life-improving or life-prolonging medicines (as those remain patentable if they are more therapeutically effective than the closest prior art).

By contrast, one might allege that the effect, if not the chief aim, of the provision is to promote the domestic generics industry. Indeed, new forms of existing substances arguably are often not (significantly) more effective than the closest prior art, but may rather be commercially more profitable or successful because of other properties than those related to their therapeutic effect. That is why giving the generics industry the freedom to market the new forms of the substance improves its competitiveness. On the other hand, one may counter that protecting only new forms with enhanced efficacy is not about what is excluded from patent protection and hence freely accessible. Instead, Section 3(d)-like measures can be understood primarily as a tool for directing pharmaceutical research towards those new forms which indeed show enhanced therapeutic efficacy. The public health rationale then lies in what is protected, not in what is excluded under Section 3(d).

Which of the arguments above prevail will usually depend on the specific domestic circumstances within which a Section 3(d)-type provision operates. A provision like Section 3(d) – as any exception to patentability or requirement for protection – may serve different purposes and can be the result of different political patterns. Even where it may be seen as promoting industrial policy rather than public health, these rationales are often interlinked. On the one hand, minor advancements in storage capacity, shelf life, and other non-therapeutic enhancements can be quite important from a public health perspective. This may lead to a normative argument for incentivizing them under the patent system, but it does not necessarily translate into a legal argument for having to protect all of

131 Doha Declaration, *supra* note 110, at p 4.

those advancements under TRIPS. As shown above, a WTO Member may well decide, in exercising its discretion in defining what amounts to an inventive step, that certain types of incremental advancements, while socially desirable, do not deserve a patent because they only amount to an obvious advancement over the state of the art. In the context of justifying differential treatment, such discretion equally extends to choosing the types of advances a country considers so desirable from a public health perspective that it wants to reward them with a patent.

On the other hand, public health and industrial policy objectives are intertwined when Section 3(d)-type provisions are relied upon to tackle "evergreening" strategies of originator companies to prevent, delay, or at least discourage generic competition in practice. It should be clarified that concerns about evergreening are much less of legal, but of practical nature. A fundamental principle of patent law is that no patentee may prevent third parties from practising the prior art and obvious modification thereof. Therefore, successive filings of patent applications on new forms or new uses of known compounds do not allow the owner of a patent on a chemical entity or on its first medical uses to prolong the legal exclusivity for that chemical entity or its uses disclosed in the original patent applications.[132] Once the original patent expires, that chemical entity and its disclosed uses are in the public domain. Exclusions such as those provided under Section 3(d) are, from a black-letter law perspective, not necessary to prevent evergreening. To the extent that new form or new use patent claims comprise the prior art and any obvious modification of the prior art, the patent is not valid for lack of novelty or inventive step.[133]

Despite that, a Member State may reasonably and in good faith assume that these so called "secondary", "ancillary" or "peripheral" patents – all definitions not accurate from a legal perspective – for incremental modifications of the basic substance can have a deterring effect on generic competition. Firstly, the threat of long and costly infringement litigation may serve as an effective means to deter generic companies from entering the market for ingredients which technically are no longer under patent protection, but for which such a further patent exists. Secondly, such secondary patents might favour collusive or unilateral efforts to delay generic competition. For instance, they might give rise to reverse payment settlements.[134] Thirdly, they may be instrumental to – *per se* legitimate – "product hopping" strategies of the originator.[135]

132 See Scott Parker and Kevin Mooney, "Is 'Evergreening' a Cause for Concern? A Legal Perspective" (2007), 13 J COM BIOTECHNOLOGY 235, 237 et seq.; Dorothy Du, "Novartis AG v Union of India: 'Evergreening', TRIPS, and 'Enhanced Efficacy' under Section 3(d)" (2015) 21 J INTELL PROP L 223, 238 et seq.

133 Novelty and obviousness are mandatory requirements for protection under TRIPS Article 27.

134 See Scott Hemphill, "Unjustified Delays in Generic Drug Competition", OECD, 18 June 2014, DAF/COMP/WD(2014)76 (6 June 2014).

135 See J. Cheng, "An Antitrust Analysis of Product Hopping in the Pharmaceutical Industry" (2008) 108 COLUMBIA L REV 1507 et seq.

Finally, the design of the domestic patent litigation and enforcement system may further enhance evergreening risks – for example, the option to bifurcate validity and infringement proceedings in a way that infringement is decided early on, while challenges to validity are addressed in separate proceedings which usually take much longer.[136] In such circumstances, an "injunction gap" of up to two years would allow originators to maintain exclusivity and prevent generic competition on the basis of an injunction even though a later decision holds the new form or new use patent to be invalid. Similarly, high standards of proof – higher, for example, than the balance of probability usually applied in civil litigation – for proving the facts establishing invalidity of the granted claims can affect the chances of generic competitors challenging such patents. While these problems are perhaps best addressed within the patent enforcement system where they arise, strategic use of litigation (threats) to extract high amounts of compensation or defer market entry in out of court settlements can certainly inform the decision of policy-makers to introduce Section 3(d)-type provisions in order to improve the bargaining position of generic competitors.

We do not want to pass judgement on whether, when, and where practical "evergreening" is so significant and entails such negative effects on consumer welfare as to suggest the enactment of a broad exclusion as that incorporated in Section 3(d) of the Indian Patent Act. Often, the evidence for drawing or rejecting such a conclusion is limited.[137] In the end, such considerations concern primarily

136 For an analysis of the German Bifurcation system and its implications for challenging patent validity, see Katrin Cremers and others, "Invalid but Infringed? An Analysis of Germany's Bifurcated Patent Litigation System" (Max Planck Inst. for Innovation & Competition Research Paper No. 14–14, 13 September 2014), http://ssrn.com/abstract=2504507, accessed 02/03/2016.

137 Admittedly, some empirical studies focused on the US market seem to suggest that so-called secondary patents are inefficient in delaying generic competition, and that in the last 30 years the average effective term of protection for new chemical entities has remained almost the same despite these evergreening attempts. See C. Scott Hemphill and Sampat N. Bhaven, "Weak Patents Are a Weak Deterrent: Patent Portfolios, the Orange Book Listing Standard, and Generic Entry in Pharmaceuticals" (2011), National Bureau of Economic Research Working Paper; C. Scott Hemphill and Sampat N. Bhaven, "Evergreening, Patent Challenges, and Effective Market Life in Pharmaceuticals" (2012), 31 J HEALTH ECON 327, 328, both quoted after Benjamin N. Roin (2014) 61 UCLA L REV 672. However, the authors of these empirical investigations observe that these results, even if they were confirmed by further evidence, could be due to the unique features of US law, and more precisely of the Hatch-Waxmann Act, and for this reason "a lack of similar institutions in other jurisdictions may explain why our findings diverge from those of the EU Sector Report, which suggests strong effects of evergreening on competition in European pharmaceutical markets". Further investigation is therefore required in Europe and elsewhere to draw a conclusion with regard to the issue of whether so-called secondary patents – in conjunction with the use of regulatory provisions and switching product strategies – are really able to slow the onset of generic competition with respect to the ingredient drug and indications thereof disclosed by the original, already expired patent. See C. Scott Hemphill, "Unjustified Delays in Generic Drug Competition" (OECD, 18 June 2014, DAF/COMP/WD (2014) 76, 6 June 2014).

the normative desirability, rather than the TRIPS consistency of a Section 3(d) type of provision. The evaluation of these aspects hence must take place within a domestic law context, focusing on the (positive and negative) practical implications of allowing patents over incremental improvements and deciding which of those advances "deserve" a patent as a matter of policy. A good faith attempt to design a national policy in view of these aspects should offer reasonable grounds to justify any alleged differential treatment adopted by Section 3(d) not (or not only) from an industrialist or protectionist perspective, which is foreign to TRIPS Article 8, but also on health-related grounds.

New uses of known substances

The exclusion of new uses of known substances under Section 3(d) of the Indian Patent Act was not discussed in the Glivec case. As far as compliance with TRIPS is concerned, a succinct analysis will suffice.

New uses of a known item may constitute a technical invention. They can also be novel and inventive, for instance when the prior art did not suggest using the known substance for the purpose disclosed by the applicant and/or such use presents unexpected advantages. Therefore, the exclusion under Section 3(d) for the new uses of a known substance does not clarify the concept of invention and is not based on the requirement for inventive activity. Indeed, Section 3(d) prohibits use claims regardless of whether or not the use claimed is novel and inventive. The provision therefore establishes an exception to patentability. Despite that, as far as it relates to medical uses, the provision is TRIPS-compliant. The use of a compound for treating a human or animal disease constitutes a medical method. For this reason, it may be excluded from protection under TRIPS Article 27.3(a) as a diagnostic, therapeutic, or surgical method for the treatment of humans or animals.

Even if the patent claims were related to a medicine comprising the known compound ("first medical indication") or to a medicine comprising the known compound for the treatment of a specific disease ("second or further medical indication"), the application may be rejected without violating TRIPS Article 27. In Europe, such patent claims would indeed be possible.[138] But this is the case only because of a legal fiction provided for by Articles 54(4) and 54(5) EPC.[139]

138 See Dieter R. Schneider, Patenting of Pharmaceuticals – Still a Challenge? (2008) INT'L REV INTELL PROP & COMPETITION L 511, 513 et seq.; Moufang, *supra* note 81, at 54, 66 et seq.

139 Articles 54(4) and (5) EPC read as follows: "(4) Paragraphs 2 and 3 shall not exclude the patentability of any substance or composition, comprised in the state of the art, for use in a method referred to in Article 53(c), provided that its use for any such method is not comprised in the state of the art; (5) Paragraphs 2 and 3 shall also not exclude the patentability of any substance or composition referred to in paragraph 4 for any specific use in a method referred to in Article 53(c), provided that such use is not comprised in the state of the art." The first paragraph regulates medical product claims for the first medical

Based on these provisions, even if the compound is known, European law permits (purpose-bound) product claims pertaining to it where the novel feature is only the medical use of the compound.[140] Such a fiction was introduced to allow protection for inventions that otherwise would not be eligible for protection since the medical use claim would fall under the exclusion for medical methods. But WTO Members are not required under TRIPS to adopt this legal fiction and to follow this practice. The compounds claimed by the pharmaceutical product claims mentioned are actually known and hence form part of the prior art. The inventive step is derived only from the medical effect which the compound or the drug containing the compound is capable of achieving. There is no legal necessity for the other WTO Members to adopt such a legal fiction to allow a product patent for a medical use of a known substance which would otherwise be included in the exclusion for medical methods provided by domestic law.[141] Member States are required under TRIPS Article 27 to allow a product claim – whether absolute or purpose-bound – only when the compound itself is novel and inventive. If the compound is already known according to the domestic concept of novelty and prior art, they are required to allow a process claim for new uses of it, but only when no exceptions – such as that under TRIPS Article 27.3(a) – apply. For this reason, they are entitled to reject purpose-bound product claims for the first or for the second or further medical indications of known compounds as they are permitted to prohibit use claims for such new medical indications.

By contrast, to the extent that no medical uses are concerned, the exclusion under Section 3(d) of the Indian Patent Act is more problematic. It excludes from patentability a certain category of inventions even if they are novel and inventive and no optional exception to patent eligibility under TRIPS Article 27.2 or Article 27.3 may be invoked. But this aspect of the provision is not relevant for the pharmaceutical sector, which is the focus of this chapter, and therefore does not need to be addressed further.

Conclusions

The principal conclusion of this chapter is that the obligations under TRIPS Article 27, at least for the pharmaceutical sector, are actually more limited than might be expected in view of the criticism surrounding the Agreement. It is true that under TRIPS Article 27, WTO Members are required to admit patent

indication of a known compound; the second paragraph allows purpose bound-product claims for the second and any further medical indication of a known compound.

140 See G 2/08 of 19 February 2010, OJ EPO 2010, 456, Reasoning 6.3 – Dosage regime/ Abbott Respiratory, where the Enlarged Board of Appeal observes: "By virtue of a legal fiction Article 54(4) and (5) EPC acknowledges the notional novelty of substances or compositions even when they are as such already comprised in the state of the art, provided they are claimed for a new use in a method which Article 53(c) EPC excludes as such from patent protection."

141 See Carvalho, *supra* note 6, at 308.

protection for pharmaceutical products and methods for obtaining the ingredients of such products.

However, as far as product patent protection is concerned, the Members are free to exclude from such patent grant: (i) naturally occurring substances and (ii) derivatives from known compounds, unless the latter present (surprising) superior properties – for example, in the form of enhanced efficacy. Further, they may limit product protection for new and inventive chemical entities to the industrial uses disclosed in the patent application. As far as process patents are concerned, the Members, under TRIPS Article 27.3(a), may deny patent protection for all inventions concerning new medical uses of a known compound. No patent protection is therefore due under TRIPS Article 27 for a significant part of pharmaceutical innovation, such as that concerning the development of new indications, new dosages and regimes of administration of previously known substances.

The fact that such exclusions from patent protection are legally possible under TRIPS does not imply that they would also be sound policy. This has been argued particularly for the exclusion concerning new medical indications of known compounds. Companies from emerging economies may be more active with respect to this type of innovation than in creating new chemical entities. Therefore, according to several authors, in emerging markets such exclusion would mainly hurt domestic innovators, depriving them of an incentive to invest in pharmaceutical research.[142]

Such an assumption, however, may prove to be speculative. Changes in national patent legislation do not necessarily affect the behaviour of domestic companies. This holds true even in fields such as the pharmaceutical sector, where a causal link between patents and innovation appears somewhat more likely than in other areas. Whether national legislations influence the economic behaviour of national companies, and their decisions on whether and how to invest in innovation, depends on the relative importance of the domestic market for those companies. For a company located in Hong Kong, for example, the legal protection available in the Chinese or US market is more significant than the protection available under its domestic legislation, because the market covered by the former is by far more important that the market covered by the latter.[143]

142 See Janice M. Mueller, "The Tiger Awakens: The Tumultuous Transformation of India's Patent System and the Rise of Indian Pharmaceutical Innovation" (2007), 68 UNIV OF PITTSBURGH L REV 491, 558; Du, *supra* note 132, at 223, 255.

143 See Edith Tilton Penrose, *The Economics of the International Patent System* (Baltimore, 1951) 110 et seq.; see also Nuno Pires Carvahlo, "The Rule of Patent Law (RPL) as Established by the TRIPS Agreement and Its Role of Promoting Trade Rather than Invention" in Ruth L. Okediji and Margo A. Bagley (eds) *Patent Law in Global Perspective* (OUP, 2014) 675; Romandini, *supra* note 118, at 33. Of course, if other countries, and more specifically those with significant markets such as the EU or China, were to adopt a patent exclusion like that incorporated in Section 3(d), this could prevent innovative companies – wherever they are located – from investing resources in the discovery of new applications or better formulations for existing drug ingredients. That said, some authors

More generally, whether or not enacting exclusions such as those provided under Section 3(d) of the Indian Patent Act is desirable from a policy perspective depends on the purposes pursued by law-makers in reforming domestic legislation. If the main objective of a reform is to keep down the prices of pharmaceutical products and to foster the domestic generics industry, Section 3(d)-like exclusions could be significant tools to this end. Such a provision may likely facilitate the refusal or the revocation of patents for incremental improvements of existing compounds, which, even if they do not imply a superior therapeutic effect, might nevertheless present some other advantages that are able to affect the choice of consumers between a generic equivalent to the subject matter covered by the older patent and the modified drug protected by the younger patent.

If the purpose of a prospective legislature intervention is by contrast to avoid legal "evergreening", provisions such as those incorporated in Section 3(d) are not necessary from a purely technical legal perspective. Even where such a provision does not exist, no company can prohibit third parties, on the basis of a subsequently filed patent application, from using, selling or importing the ingredient of a drug already fully disclosed in a previous patent application. The same holds true for patents granted on new applications of known compounds. Applications of the compound already known would remain patent-free. It is a general principle of patent law that no one may be prevented from practising the prior art and any obvious modification thereof. A broad prior art defence[144] – like the one enshrined in Chinese law[145] – is sufficient to avoid any legal ambiguity in this respect.

By contrast, if the purpose of the possible reform is to prevent not the evergreening of patents, but the extension of a factual privileged market position of an originator through a combined use of subsequent patent applications, authorization or marketing withdrawals and switching products strategies, then Section 3(d) is an effective tool in improving generic competition. The "secondary

view this as a positive development: i.e., it would foster originators to invest more in the development of the new chemical compounds than in the research of new uses or forms of known compounds: see Amy Kapczynski, "Engineered in India: Patent Law 2.0" (2013) NEW ENG J MED. Such an opinion, however, is based on the assumption that the development of new uses or formulations is less significant for advances in medicine or technology than the development of new molecules, an assumption that has been questioned for a long time; see with respect to new uses of known compounds Geissler, *supra* note 71, at 23 et seq. Medical use claims can also offer protection to important and significant innovations. Indeed, the medical relevance of an invention does not depend on whether or not the basic compound is novel within the meaning of patent law; see on the issue of use claims Romandini, *supra* note 118, at 168 et seq.; see Kraßer, *supra* note 25, at 249, observing that the first medical use found for a compound is often not the most valuable.

144 See Romandini, *supra* note 118, at 179.

145 See "Article 63 Patent Law of the People's Republic of China" (as amended up to the Decision of 27 December 2008, regarding the Revision of the Patent Law of the People's Republic of China), www.wipo.int/wipolex/en/text.jsp?file_id=178664, accessed 02/03/2016.

patents", whose granting a Section 3(d)-like provision might limit, are one necessary element for successfully implementing product hopping strategies. At the same time, the availability of patents for new uses or new forms of existing compounds, if they can reduce the competition among originators and generic companies, can also be seen as promoting competition between different originators. Empirical analysis suggests indeed that such "secondary patents" are obtained very often also by competitors of the originator.[146] Without the prospective of patent protection such competitors would likely not invest in developing new forms or new uses of a known class of compounds or they would not invest in getting a market authorization in countries that deny such a protection. A law-maker should be aware of the potential ambivalent effects from a competition perspective of such exceptions to patentability. Finally, if the aim of a possible reform is to render the country more attractive for innovative clinical or non-clinical research, exemption from the rights conferred by the patent, such as a broad "Bolar" and "experimental" exemption,[147] may often be equally if not more effective than the limitations to patentability considered in this chapter.

Overall, the policy choices are ones which countries should make by way of an informed decision in light of the specific domestic circumstances. Here, it is important that the international legal framework for the regulation of IP, in general, and pharmaceutical patents, in particular, be sufficiently flexible to accommodate means to give effect to the different policy choices. That, in turn, requires that states think carefully before they forego the important flexibilities TRIPS leaves for this purpose – in particular, through the acceptance of comprehensive and detailed IP provisions in bilateral or regional agreements. Regardless of the substance of these rules and whether they currently reflect sound policy choices in the pharmaceutical sector or elsewhere, it is hard to imagine that such a degree of specificity, if cast into the stones of international law, will leave sufficient leeway to adapt domestic IP rules to a continuously developing technological, economic and social environment. If we have learned one thing from the history of IP protection it is probably that laws representing a tailored IP policy at one point in time will not necessarily continue to reflect sound IP policy 10, 20 or 30 years down the line.

146 Mike Lloyd, "Evergreening by Whom? A Review of Secondary Patents for Omeprazole" (2013) 2(6) PHARM PAT ANAl 737 et seq.

147 See Katherine A. Helm, "Outsourcing the Fire of Genius: The Effects of Patent Infringement Jurisprudence on Pharmaceutical Drug Development" (2006), 7 FORDHAM INTELL PROP MEDIA & ENT LJ 153 et seq.

3 Biologics, Biosimilars and Other Idiosyncrasies

*Yaniv Heled**

Introduction

Biological pharmaceuticals, also known as biologics,[1] are a broad class of therapeutics whose uniqueness lies in the methods by which they are obtained. Rather than being chemically synthesized like most traditional pharmaceuticals,[2] biologics are produced by and isolated from living organisms. As such, biologics are, generally speaking, complex. They are large in size, sensitive to environmental

* I wish to thank Cynthia Ho, Pamela Brannon and Elizabeth-Ann Weeks for their comments and assistance in preparing this chapter.

1 The American Food and Drug Administration (FDA) defines biological pharmaceutical products as "any virus, therapeutic serum, toxin, antitoxin, or analogous product applicable to the prevention, treatment or cure of diseases or injuries of man". Biological Products, 21 C.F.R. § 600.3(h) (2014). According to the FDA Center for Biologics Evaluation and Research (CBER):

> . . . [b]iological products include a wide range of products such as vaccines, blood and blood components, allergenics, somatic cells, gene therapy, tissues, and recombinant therapeutic proteins. Biologics can be composed of sugars, proteins, or nucleic acids or complex combinations of these substances, or may be living entities such as cells and tissues. Biologics are isolated from a variety of natural sources—human, animal, or microorganism—and may be produced by biotechnology methods and other cutting-edge technologies . . . . Biological products often represent the cutting-edge of biomedical research and, in time, may offer the most effective means to treat a variety of medical illnesses and conditions that presently have no other treatments available.
>
> . . .
>
> In contrast to most drugs, which are chemically synthesized and have a known structure, most biologics are complex mixtures that are not easily identified or characterized. Biological products, including those manufactured by biotechnology, tend to be heat sensitive and susceptible to microbial contamination.

"What Are 'Biologics': Questions and Answers", U.S. Food & Drug Admin., www.fda.gov/AboutFDA/CentersOffices/OfficeofMedicalProductsandTobacco/CBER/ucm133077.htm, accessed 9 December 2014.

2 Medicines produced in such a manner are commonly referred to as "small-molecule drugs" or simply "drugs" for short.

changes (both during production and afterwards), and expensive to develop and manufacture. But in their complexity also lies their advantage: unparalleled effectiveness in the treatment of serious, and sometimes previously untreatable, ailments that renders biologics, in many cases, nothing short of wonder drugs.[3] As such, biologics have been growing in number and importance, playing an increasingly dominant role both as therapeutics and as a component of the healthcare economy.[4]

The complexity of biologics, however, comes at a cost that is well reflected in their typically high price tag.[5] As policymakers strive to make biologics more accessible to larger groups of patients, significant public policy challenges come to bear that go to the heart of intellectual property, innovation, and pharmaceutical regulatory policies as well as one's right to health and bodily integrity inasmuch as it depends on access to life saving technology. These issues are by no means unique to biologics or even to biomedicine. Indeed, the balancing of incentives for innovation against the public interest in making technology freely accessible has been with us for as long as technology itself. Yet, the unique context of biomedical technology in general, and cutting edge biologics, in particular, accentuates these policy issues and makes them stand out. Moreover, the complexity of biologics makes the production of follow-on biologics especially challenging, as the science and regulation of comparing follow-on biologics to original products is confounded with peculiarities and uncertainties that are often product-specific.[6] With the maturation of biologics technology, which is accompanied by an expiration of patents covering important biological products, these policy debates come to the surface, making them unavoidable to policymakers and stakeholders alike.

In particular, the pressure to make biologics more widely accessible has resulted in the emergence of laws in Europe, the United States, Japan, India, Canada, Australia, and a handful of other countries aimed at creating pathways for the approval of follow-on versions of existing biological products. This chapter will

3 Examples include such biologics as *Humira* (*adalimumab*), *Enbrel* (*etanercept*), *Rituxan* (*rituximab*), *Remicade* (*infliximab*), *Avastin* (*bevacizumab*), *Herceptin* (*trastuzumab*) and *Gleevec* (*imatinib*) for the treatment of such ailments as rheumatoid arthritis, Crohn's disease, psoriasis and various cancers, including colorectal cancer, non-small cell lung cancer, breast cancer, and gastric cancer. See Stacy Lawrence and Riku Lahteenmaki, "Public Biotech 2013 – The Numbers" (2014), 32 NATURE BIOTECH., 626, Table 8 (listing the top-ten-selling biologic drugs of 2013).

4 See IMS Institute for Healthcare Informatics, "The Global Use of Medicines: Outlook through 2017" (2013), 9 (projecting that whereas biologics were responsible for 11% of the global pharmaceutical sales in 2002, they are expected to have a 19–20% market share by 2017).

5 See, e.g., Andrew Pollack, "Costly Drugs Known as Biologics Prompt Exclusivity Debate" (2009), N.Y. TIMES, B1 (describing the relatively high prices of biologics); Robert Langreth and Cynthia Koons, "Investors Bet $100,000 Prices For Cancer Drugs Are Here to Stay" (2015), 9 LSLR 315.

6 See Ameet Sarpatwari, Jerry Avorn and Aaron S. Kesselheim, "Progress and Hurdles for Follow-on Biologics" (2015), 372 N. ENGL. J. MED., 2380, 2381 (describing challenges involved in receiving regulatory approval for follow-on versions of biologics, mostly due to known and unknown changes between the compared molecules).

survey these laws and the "track record" of the regulatory pathways that they have created, highlighting prominent features of these regimes. It will be followed by a short review of biologics- and biosimilars-specific sections in international trade agreements and proceed with some recommendations for countries seeking to create their own regulatory pathways for the approval of biologics and follow-on versions thereof.

National regulation of biologics and biosimilars

Biologics and biosimilars regulation in the European Union (EU)

The European Medicines Agency (EMA), located in London, is the European Union's (EU) centralized agency responsible for evaluating biological product candidates for all EU member countries.[7] Under EMA procedures, which are at least formally the same for biologics and small-molecule drugs, an applicant seeking EMA evaluation of its biological product must submit a marketing authorization application (MAA) to the EMA. Upon completion of the evaluation process, the EMA issues a scientific opinion regarding the product, which may then serve as the basis for a grant of the MAA by the European Commission, and which allows the applicant to market its product in all EU member states and European Economic Area states.[8] In 2003, the EMA began laying down the regulatory groundwork of what is now the oldest and most robust regulatory framework for evaluating biosimilar versions of previously approved biologics.[9] To date, this framework led to the approval of 19 biosimilar products for marketing in the EU.[10] In making biosimilarity determinations, the EMA relies

7 Regulation (EC) 726/2004 of the European Parliament and of the Council of 31 March 2004 laying down Community procedures for the authorization and supervision of medicinal products for human and veterinary use and establishing a European Medicines Agency [2004], OJ L 136 1. Notably, the EMA is only the *centralized* European hub for approval of medicines and is not exclusively responsible for approving medicines for marketing in the EU, as it is also possible to apply for approval of medicines with relevant national agencies in EU member states in accordance with their own national procedures. A review of such Member State agencies and their respective procedures as they pertain to biologics, however, exceeds the scope of this chapter.

8 See EMA/437313/2014, THE EUROPEAN REGULATORY SYSTEM FOR MEDICINES AND THE EUROPEAN MEDICINES AGENCY, 2 (2014), ("Once granted by the European Commission, the centralised marketing authorisation is valid in all EU Member States").

9 CHMP/437/04 COMMITTEE FOR MEDICINAL PRODUCTS FOR HUMAN USE (CHMP), GUIDELINE ON SIMILAR BIOLOGICAL MEDICINAL PRODUCTS, 4 (2005), [hereinafter EU GUIDELINE ON SIMILAR BIOLOGICAL MEDICINAL PRODUCTS]; additional general guidance documents are www.ema.europa.eu/ema/index.jsp?curl=pages/regulation/general/general_content_000408.jsp&mid=WC0b01ac058002958c, accessed 19 January 2015.

10 See www.ema.europa.eu/ema/index.jsp?curl=pages%2Fmedicines%2Flanding%2Fepar_search.jsp&mid=WC0b01ac058001d124&searchTab=searchByAuthType&alreadyLoaded=true&isNewQuery=true&status=Authorised&keyword=Enter+keywords&searchType=name&taxonomyPath=&treeNumber=&searchGenericType=biosimilars&genericsKeywordSearch=

on four criteria: the product's safety, efficacy, quality and biological activity.[11] The evaluation itself is done in accordance with procedures laid down in general guidance documents,[12] as well as numerous product- and product-class-specific guidance documents.[13] Interchangeability[14] determinations, however, are not within the purview of the EMA and are left for the discretion of the numerous national agencies operating within EU member states.[15] Significantly, as of mid-2013, there does not seem to be any local agency in any EU member country to have made an interchangeability determination with respect to any biosimilar product.[16] Similarly, the EMA is not involved in setting the price of approved biologics and biosimilars or in decisions regarding reimbursement for such products, which are reserved for the national healthcare system of each EU member country.[17]

Submit, accessed 15 January 2015. EPA has also adopted a negative opinion, recommending the refusal of a marketing authorization application for the biosimilar Alpheon meant for the treatment of hepatitis C due to differences between Alpheon and the reference product, lack of data on the stability of the active substance and the product, and concerns regarding the validation process used for making the finished medicine. See EMA, "Questions and Answers on Recommendation for Refusal of Marketing Application for Alpheon" (2006), 2, www.ema.europa.eu/docs/en_GB/document_library/Summary_of_opinion_-_Initial_authorisation/human/000585/WC500017451.pdf, accessed 15 January 2015.

11 See CHMP/437/04 Rev 1 COMMITTEE FOR MEDICINAL PRODUCTS FOR HUMAN USE (CHMP), GUIDELINE ON SIMILAR BIOLOGICAL MEDICINAL PRODUCTS, 4 (2014).

12 See EU GUIDELINE ON SIMILAR BIOLOGICAL MEDICINAL PRODUCTS, n. 9.

13 The EMA has product-specific biosimilarity evaluation guidelines for the following product classes: Recombinant follicle-stimulating hormone, interferon beta, monoclonal antibodies, recombinant erythropoietins, low molecular weight heparins, recombinant interferon alpha, recombinant granulocyte-colony stimulating factor, somatropin, and recombinant human insulin and insulin analogs. See EMA, scientific guidelines on biosimilar medicines webpage, www.ema.europa.eu/ema/index.jsp?curl=pages/regulation/general/general_content_00040.jsp, accessed 15 January 2015.

14 Interchangeability is a regulatory determination that the clinical safety and efficacy profiles of two pharmaceutical compounds are sufficiently similar to make it possible for physicians to prescribe one instead of the other and vice versa and for pharmacists to substitute such products with one another.

15 See CHMP/437/04 Rev 1 3; EMA, "Questions and Answers on Biosimilar Medicines (Similar Biological Medicinal Products)", EMA/837805/2011 (2012) ("EMA . . . evaluations do not include recommendations on whether a biosimilar should be used interchangeably with its reference medicine. For questions related to switching from one biological medicine to another, patients should speak to their doctor and pharmacist.").

16 Lynne Taylor, "Germany: 'EU's Most Favourable Market for Biosimilars' (2013), PHARMATIMES DIGITAL, http://www.pharmatimes.com/tagresults/13-05-30/Germany_EU_s_most_favourable_market_for_biosimilars.aspx (quoting Henry Grabowsky saying that "[n]o EU state currently allows substitution for biosimilars"), www.pharmatimes.com/article/13-05-30/Germany_EU_s_most_favourable_market_for_biosimilars.aspx, accessed 15 January 2015; notably, several EU countries, including the United Kingdom, Spain and France, explicitly prohibit substitution of one pharmaceutical with another, at least where there is no explicit approval to do so from the prescriber. See Joan Rovira et al, *The Impact of Biosimilars' Entry in the EU Market*, 19, 21 (2011).

17 See EMA/437313/2014 (n. 8) 3.

Importantly, the EMA does not play a role in creating and enforcing linkage between biological products and any intellectual property thereof. In other words, specifically, the agency does not provide information on patents as they pertain to biologics and does not employ procedures related to the evaluation and approval of biological products that are dependent on the status and scope of such patents.[18] Nevertheless, the EMA does enforce a market exclusivity[19] period of 10 to 11 years during which the EMA will not approve an MAA for follow-on products seeking to rely on a previously-approved marketing authorisation granted to an earlier product.[20] In addition, the EMA also enforces a concurrent data exclusivity[21] period of eight years during which follow-on applicants are unable to reference data submitted as part of an application for marketing approval of an original, previously-approved product.[22] It is important to note, however, that while the EMA generally does not consider clinical data commercially confidential and has been regularly publishing clinical data submitted to it as part of MAAs since 1 January 2015,[23] it also will not, as a general rule, publish data submitted as part of MAAs that is identified as commercially confidential information.[24]

In addition to its regulatory role, the EMA maintains professional ties with counterpart agencies within the EU and around the world as well as with international organizations such as the World Health Organization (WHO).[25] These relationships foster the development of harmonized regulatory standards and facilitate exchange of regulatory and scientific information, subject to mutual confidentiality agreements.[26] Further, as part of these relationships, the EMA, in

18 See EMA website, "Frequently Asked Questions", www.ema.europa.eu/ema/index.jsp?curl=pages/about_us/q_and_a/q_and_a_detail_000114.jsp&mid=WC0b01ac058035b2b0#section7, accessed 15 January 2015; see also Bryan Mercurio, in this collection.

19 See Yaniv Heled, "Regulatory Competitive Shelters" (2015) 76 OHIO ST. L. J. 299, 315 (defining market exclusivity).

20 See EU Directive 2001/83/EC, [2011] | OJ L 311 67. Articles 6, 10(1). The 10-year period is extended to 11 years if "during the first eight years of those ten years, the marketing authorisation holder obtains an authorisation for one or more new therapeutic indications which . . . are held to bring a significant clinical benefit in comparison with existing therapies." Ibid. Directive 2001/83/EC further requires that the additional period of one year shall only be granted once "provided that significant pre-clinical or clinical studies were carried out in relation to the new indication". Ibid Article 10(5). Notably, this period of data exclusivity is applicable for products for which a marketing authorization application has been submitted as of 20 November 2005. See EMA, *EMA Procedural Advice for Users of the Centralised Procedure for Generic/Hybrid Applications*, EMEA/CHMP/225411/2006, 6 (2013).

21 See Heled (n. 19) 316 (defining data exclusivity). See also Owais Hassan Shaikh, in this collection.

22 See EU Directive 2001/83/EC (2011) OJL 311, Articles 6, 10(1).

23 EMA, *European Medicines Agency Policy on Publication of Clinical Data for Medicinal Products for Human Use*, 4, EMA/240810/2013 (2014).

24 Ibid at 4, 7.

25 See EMA/437313/2014 (n. 8) 4 (describing the EMA's relationships with international fora as well as counterpart agencies within the EU and internationally).

26 Ibid.

cooperation with the WHO, performs evaluation of medicines that are intended for use outside of the EU.[27]

Biologics and biosimilars regulation in the United States

Following in Europe's footsteps, in March 2010, the US Congress passed the Biologics Price Competition and Innovation Act of 2009 (BPCIA).[28] BPCIA provided an infrastructure for the approval of follow-on biological products similar to the one implemented in the EU in its flexibility and recognition that establishing therapeutic equivalence in biologics is more complicated than in small-molecule drugs.[29] Like the EU framework, BPCIA provides for a period of 4 years of data exclusivity as well as a lengthy period of 12 years of market exclusivity,[30] but also for a period of up to 3.5 years of generic exclusivity[31] to the first follow-on applicant to have its biosimilar approved as interchangeable with a previously-approved product.[32]

Unlike the European framework, however, the approach to the approval of biosimilar products in the United States is more centralized and leaves it to the Food and Drug Administration (FDA) – the federal agency in charge of implementing the BPCIA – to approve biosimilar products for marketing (rather than just make recommendations, like the EMA) and make therapeutic interchangeability determinations (rather than leave such determinations to the states).[33] Similar to Europe, in making biosimilarity determinations, BPCIA instructs the FDA to consider the compared products' safety, purity and potency.[34]

Also in variance with the European framework, BPCIA establishes an elaborate if not convoluted patent dispute resolution process that includes several rounds of exchange of technical and legal information between an original product

27 Ibid.

28 Patient Protection and Affordable Care Act (2010) Pub. L. No. 111–148, §§ 7001–7002, 124 Stat. 119 (adding § 351(k)-(m) to the PHSA ch. 373, 58 Stat. 682 (1944); coded at 42 U.S.C. § 262(k)-(m)).

29 This is evident, for example, in the conceptual separation of biosimilarity and interchangeability as well as the broad discretion afforded to the Secretary of Health and Human Services (HHS) (and through her, by delegation, to the FDA) with respect to the kind of information necessary for biosimilarity and interchangeability determinations. See 42 U.S.C. § 262(k)(2)–(3).

30 42 U.S.C. § 262(k)(7). Both exclusivity periods are extendable by an additional period of six months for conducting additional studies of the relevant biologic in paediatric populations. See 42 U.S.C. 262(m)(2)(A), (3)(A).

31 See Heled (n. 19) 317 (defining generic exclusivity).

32 42 U.S.C. § 262(k)(6).

33 42 U.S.C. § 262(k)(2) (giving the Secretary of HHS the authority to approve biological products for marketing as biosimilar and interchangeable). Notably, it is still within the purview of the different states to determine whether and how substitution of a certain biologic for a biosimilar would take place.

34 42 U.S.C. § 262(h)(2)(B). In making these determinations, BPCIA makes clear that the FDA may consider a wide variety of data, as it deems necessary. See 42 U.S.C. § 262(k)(2)-(4).

manufacturer and a follow-on applicant.[35] The BPCIA patent dispute resolution framework does *not*, however, create linkage between the status of patents covering reference listed biological pharmaceutical products and evaluation and approval of follow-on versions of such products.[36]

To date, the FDA, has issued a total of six guidance documents on biosimilars,[37] and is currently soliciting public comments on a seventh.[38] Not much has happened, however, by way of approval of biosimilar products during the time since the passage of BPCIA; and although the FDA has been accepting

35 42 U.S.C. § 262(l). See Yaniv Heled, "Patents vs. Statutory Exclusivities in Biological Pharmacuticals – Do We Really Need Both?" (2012), 18 MICH. TELECOMM. TECH. L. REV. 419, 441–42. The Court of Appeals for the Federal Circuit has held, however, that following the BPCIA's patent dispute resolution framework (aka "patent dance") is not mandatory. See *Amgen Inc. vs Sandoz Inc.* [2015] Fed. Cir. 794 (2015) F.3d 1347, 1354–57 (affirming that Sandoz's refusal to engage in 42 U.S.C. § 262's disclosure and dispute resolution process was within its rights).

36 See 42 U.S.C. § 262(l)(6)(C) (requiring only that the Secretary of HHS be notified of a filing of a patent complaint against a biosimilar applicant and that the Secretary publish a notice of receipt of such complaint in the Federal Register); 42 U.S.C. § 262(l)(8) (requiring that biosimilar applicants provide 180-day notice to original product holders of intent to commercially market a biosimilar product and making it possible for original product holders to seek a preliminary injunctive order from a court prior to commencement of such commercial marketing). Notably, the FDA has voluntarily chosen to publish a registry of biologics and biosimilars as well as any exclusivities thereof, which is similar to the Orange Book listing instituted under the Hatch-Waxman Act, which plays a crucial role in facilitating linkage in small-molecule drugs. See FDA, *Purple Book: Lists of Licensed Biological Products with Reference Product Exclusivity and Biosimilarity or Interchangeability Evaluations*, www.fda.gov/Drugs/DevelopmentApprovalProcess/HowDrugsareDevelopedandApproved/ApprovalApplications/TherapeuticBiologicApplications/Biosimilars/ucm411418.htm.

37 Department of Health and Human Services, Food and Drug Administration, Draft Guidance for Industry on Scientific Considerations in Demonstrating Biosimilarity to a Reference Product, 77 Fed. Reg. 8,883 (15 February 2012); Department of Health and Human Services, Food and Drug Administration, Draft Guidance for Industry on Quality Considerations in Demonstrating Biosimilarity to a Reference Protein Product, 77 Fed. Reg. 8,884 (15 February 2012); Department of Health and Human Services, Food and Drug Administration, *Draft Guidance for Industry on Biosimilars: Questions and Answers Regarding Implementation of the Biologics Price Competition and Innovation Act of 2009*, 77 Fed. Reg. 8,885 (15 February 2012); Department of Health and Human Services, Food and Drug Administration, *Draft Guidance for Industry on Formal Meetings Between FDA and Biosimilar Biological Product Sponsors or Applicants*, 78 Fed. Reg. 19492 (29 March 2013); Department of Health and Human Services, Food and Drug Administration, *Draft Guidance for Industry on Clinical Pharmacology Data To Support a Demonstration of Biosimilarity to a Reference Product*, 79 Fed. Reg. 27622 (14 May 2014); Department of Health and Human Services, Food and Drug Administration, *Draft Guidance for Industry on Reference Product Exclusivity for Biological Products Filed Under Section 351(a) of the Public Health Service Act*, 79 Fed. Reg. 45448 (5 August 2014).

38 Department of Health and Human Services, Food and Drug Administration Agency Information Collection Activities; Proposed Collection; Comment Request; General Licensing Provisions; Section 351(k) Biosimilar Applications, 80 Fed. Reg. 5,761 (3 February 2015). Notably, none of the FDA's guidance documents provides direction on approval of biosimilar products as interchangeable under 42 U.S.C. § 262(k)(4).

applications for biosimilar products,[39] currently, there is only one biosimilar product approved for marketing in the United States.[40] Similarly, as of November 2015, no party has initiated any patent dispute resolution procedures under the scheme laid down in BPCIA.

Biologics and biosimilars in Japan

As one of the earliest countries to create a regulatory framework for the approval of biosimilars, in early 2009, Japan published its own comprehensive framework for the approval of biosimilars.[41] Shortly thereafter, in June 2009, the Japanese Pharmaceuticals and Medical Devices Agency (PMDA)[42] recommended the approval for marketing of the first biosimilar product in Japan.[43] From 2009 through May 2014, PMDA also recommended three other types of biosimilar products for marketing in Japan.[44]

The Japanese framework for the approval of biosimilar products highly resembles that of the EU, and PMDA has a mutual confidentiality and information exchange agreement with the EMA.[45] Similarly, like in Europe, none of the

39 As of September 2014, the FDA received 15 biosimilar investigational new drug applications (IND). See Number of Biosimilar Investigational New Drug Applications (INDs) Received in the Month, www.accessdata.fda.gov/scripts/fdatrack/view/track.cfm?program=cder&status=public&id=CDER-RRDS-Number-of-biosimilar-INDs&fy=2014.

40 See Media Release "FDA Approves First Biosimilar ZarxioTM (Filgrastim-sndz) from Sandoz" (6 March 2015), www.novartis.com/newsroom/media-releases/en/2015/1900097.shtml.

41 See Evaluation and Licensing Division, Pharmaceutical and Food Safety Bureau, Ministry of Health, Labour and Welfare, *Guideline for the Quality, Safety, and Efficacy Assurance of Follow-on Biologics*, PFSB/ELD Notification No. 0304007 (4 March 2009; translated 19 April 2013).

42 Like the EMA, the Japanese PMDA does not actually grant marketing approval to pharmaceutical products but rather submits its recommendations based on its evaluation of such products' safety, efficacy, and quality, to the Japanese Ministry of Health, Labour and Welfare (MHLW). See PMDA, *Drug and Medical Devices Review*, www.pmda.go.jp/english/service/outline_s.html.

43 See PMDA, Products Approved in FY 2009: New Drugs, www.pmda.go.jp/english/service/pdf/list/NewdrugsFY2009.pdf (listing the approval of a biosimilar somatropin product on 22 2009).

44 These products include: epoetin alfa (one manufacturer), filgrastim (five different manufacturers), and infliximab (two different manufacturers). See PMDA, Products Approved in FY 2009: New Drugs, www.pmda.go.jp/english/service/pdf/list/NewdrugsFY2009.pdf (listing the approval of a biosimilar epoetin alfa product); PMDA, New Drugs Approved in FY 2012, www.pmda.go.jp/english/service/pdf/list/NewdrugsFY2012.pdf (listing filgrastim biosimilar products); PMDA, New Drugs Approved in FY 2013, www.pmda.go.jp/english/service/pdf/list/NewdrugsFY2013.pdf (listing a filgrastim biosimilar product); and PMDA, New Drugs Approved in May 2014, www.pmda.go.jp/english/service/pdf/list/NewdrugsFY2014.pdf (listing infiximab manufacturers), accessed 15 February 2016.

45 The agreement was signed in 2007 and is currently valid through 2018. See Letter from Guido Rasi, Executive Director, EMA and Andrzej Rys, Director – Health Systems and Products in the European Commission to Yoshiyuki Kikura, Director General, Pharmaceutical

PMDA-approved biosimilar products was designated as interchangeable or substitutable with the reference product.

Notably, Japanese patent law provides up to five years of term extension for patents covering an approved pharmaceutical product to account for the time during which it was not possible to practise the patented invention while the biological product was being evaluated by PMDA.[46] Japanese law also provides an eight-year market exclusivity in newly approved pharmaceutical products, including biologics, which is extendable by an additional period of two years for completion of additional studies in paediatric populations.[47]

Biologics and biosimilars in India

With its own set of "similar biologics" guidelines coming into effect in September 2012, India is probably the country with the most permissive biosimilars regime instituted to date.[48] While the Indian Central Drugs Standard Control Organization (CDSCO) had been approving products similar to previously-approved biologics long before 2012 on a case-by-case basis,[49] the CDSCO guidelines have streamlined the approval process.

The regulatory flexibility afforded by the Indian Guidelines on Similar Biologics is currently unique as compared to the more stringent respective frameworks instituted in the EU, United States and Japan. Perhaps most illustrative of this

and Food Safety Bureau, Ministry of Health, Labour and Welfare and Tatsuya Kondo, Chief Executive, PMDA (2 February 2012), and letter from Kikura and Kondo to Rasi & Rys (2 February 2012), respectively www.ema.europa.eu/docs/en_GB/document_library/Other/2012/02/WC500122828.pdf and www.ema.europa.eu/docs/en_GB/document_library/Other/2012/02/WC500122828.pdf, accessed 15 February 2016.

46 John A. Tessensohn and Shusaku Yamamoto, "Patent Term Extensions for Biologic Innovators in Japan" (2011), 29 NATURE BIOTECH., 34, 36 (describing the Japanese patent term extension mechanism).

47 Japan Pharmaceutical Manufacturers Association English Regulatory Information Task Force, PHARMACEUTICAL ADMINISTRATION AND REGULATIONS IN JAPAN (2012), 159 www.jpma.or.jp/english/parj/pdf/2012.pdf, accessed 15 February 2016.

48 CDSCO, *Guidelines on Similar Biologics: Regulatory Requirements for Marketing Authorization in India* (2012), www.cdsco.nic.in/writereaddata/Bio%20Similar%20Guideline.pdf, accessed 15 February 2016. India has been approving follow-on versions of biologics based on an ad-hoc process long before CDSCO (or any other agency for that matter) issued its *Guidelines on Similar Biologics*. See Editorial, 'Similar Biologics' Approved and Marketed in India", 2 GENERICS AND BIOSIMILAR INITIATIVE (GABI) JOURNAL 50 (2012; updated 2015), www.gabionline.net/Biosimilars/General/Similar-biologics-approved-and-marketed-in-India, accessed 15 February 2016 [hereinafter GABI] ("India has, by far, demonstrated the greatest acceptance of 'similar biologics'. According to our research at GaBI Online, the first 'similar biologic' was approved and marketed in India for a hepatitis B vaccine in 2000. In recent years over 50 biopharmaceutical products have been approved for marketing in India, with more than half of them being 'similar biologics'").

49 See GABI; CDSCO, *Guidelines on Similar Biologics* 1 ("so far . . . similar biologics were approved . . . using an abbreviated version of the pathway applicable to new drugs on a case by case basis").

approach is the fact that the Indian Guidelines on Similar Biologics allow for the approval of follow-on, similar versions to reference products that were never originally approved for use in India so long as a reference product has been licensed and marketed for at least four years in a country with a well-established regulatory framework.[50] India's flexible approach has thus far resulted in the largest number of biosimilar products approved in any single market to date.[51]

Biologics and biosimilars in other countries

In Australia, new biologics are evaluated and approved by the Therapeutics Goods Administration (TGA) in the Department of Health based on their quality, safety, and efficacy.[52] In July 2013, the Australian TGA issued a set of specific guidelines for the evaluation of biosimilar products and has been accepting applications for such products ever since.[53] Notably, the Australian TGA's guidelines incorporate by reference several of the EMA's guidelines pertaining to biosimilars' evaluation as well as guidelines issued by the International Conference on Harmonization of Technical Requirements for Registration of Pharmaceuticals for Human Use (ICH).[54] Further, Australian law makes certain allowances for the evaluation of applications for biologics and biosimilars that were approved in at least two other "acceptable countries".[55] The Australian Therapeutic Goods Act creates a data exclusivity period of five years in information pertaining to registered pharmaceutical products.[56] To date, Australia has approved at least four biosimilar drug products.[57]

In Canada, pharmaceuticals in general, including biologics, are regulated by Health Canada under the Food and Drugs Act[58] and the Food and Drug Regulations.[59] In early 2010, Health Canada published final guidelines for submission of data in connection with applications for subsequent entry biologics

50 See *Guidelines on Similar Biologics* (n. 48) 4–5.

51 According to GABI, as of early 2015, India had over 50 "similar biologics" approved for marketing, of which at least 15 were approved subsequent to the entry into force of CDSCO's *Guidelines on Similar Biologics* in September 2015. See GABI (n. 4).

52 See Therapeutic Goods Act (1989) §§ 25, 32A.

53 TGA, Evaluation of Biosimilars (2013), www.tga.gov.au/file/6914/download.

54 See ibid n. 8, 11 and 14.

55 See Therapeutic Goods Regulations §§ 16C-16D (1990). "Acceptable countries" are determined by the Minster of Health.

56 Ibid § 25A.

57 See TGA, *Biosimilar Medicines – Information for Health Professionals*, archived at www://web.archive.org/web/20140211232239/http://www.tga.gov.au/hp/hp-information-biosimilars.htm#.VYWxY1xVikp, accessed 2 August 2014 (listing the products Tevagrastim, Nivestim, Zarzio, and Novicrit as biosimilars approved in Australia); Australian Public Assessment Report for prescription medicines (AusPAR), www.tga.gov.au/browse-auspars-product-name (listing Tevagrastim, Nivestim, and Zarzio as products belonging to Submission Type "biosimilar" or "similar biological medicinal product").

58 Food and Drugs Act (1985) §§ 8–15.

59 Food and Drug Regulations (2014) C.R.C., c. 870 §§ C.08.002, C.08.002.1.

(SEBs), as they are called in Canada.[60] Like other jurisdictions, Health Canada also accepts and allows the use of information generated in connection with foreign applications for reference biologics and biosimilars.[61] And as in virtually all other jurisdictions to date, Canada also has yet to recognize a follow-on biologic as interchangeable with an existing product.[62] In addition, the Canadian Food and Drug Regulations provide for a data exclusivity period of six years[63] and a market exclusivity period of eight years in original drug products, which is further extendable by another six months for additional testing in paediatric populations.[64] As of March 2015, Health Canada has approved three biosimilars.[65]

China and Hong Kong are among the more recent entrants into the field of biosimilars regulation. In late 2014, the Hong Kong Drug Office published Guidance Notes for Registration of Biosimilar Products,[66] which was met with industry support provided that certain conditions are met, including the enforcement of an eight-year data exclusivity period in original biologics.[67] Shortly afterwards, in early March 2015, China's Food and Drug Administration (CFDA) issued its own Technical Guideline for Development and Evaluation of Biosimilars

60 See Notice: Release of Guidance for Sponsors: Information and Submission Requirements for Subsequent Entry Biologics (SEBs), 10-10569-330 (5 March 2010), www.hc-sc.gc.ca/dhp-mps/brgtherap/applic-demande/guides/seb-pbu/notice-avis_seb-pbu_2010-eng.php, accessed 15 February 2016. Health Products and Food Branch, *Guidance for Sponsors: Information and Submission Requirements for Subsequent Entry Biologics (SEBs)* (2008) 2–3 (defining biologics and subsequent entry biologics) [hereinafter, "Canadian SEBs Guidance"].

61 See Canadian SEBs Guidance (n. 60) 5 (addressing the consideration for the use of non-Canadian reference biologics).

62 Although Health Canada does not have the authority to declare two biologics automatically substitutable as such substitution is solely within the discretion of pharmacists, and although Health Canada states that it would "review data that supports therapeutic interchangeability and make a recommendation as to whether this can be done safely and effectively by physicians", at this point in time, "Health Canada *does not support automatic substitution* of a Subsequent Entry Biologic for its reference biologic drug and recommends that physicians make only well-informed decisions regarding therapeutic interchange." See Questions & Answers To Accompany the Final Guidance for Sponsors: Information and Submission Requirements for Subsequent Entry Biologics (SEBs), www.hc-sc.gc.ca/dhp-mps/brgtherap/applic-demande/guides/seb-pbu/01-2010-seb-pbu-qa-qr-eng.php#q13 (emphasis added).

63 Food and Drug Regulations § C.08.004.1(2).

64 Ibid §§ C.08.004.1(3)-(4). Notably, these exclusivity periods are *not* specific to biologics but rather apply to all pharmaceutical products approved by Health Canada.

65 Letter from Office of Regulatory Affairs, Biologics and Genetic Therapies Directorate, Health Canada to Heled (12 March 2015), on file with author (the approved SEBs are Omnitrope, Remsima, and Inflectra).

66 While the Hong Kong guidance document itself is apparently not available to the public, the pharmaceutical industry's response to it is. See Hong Kong Association of the Pharmaceutical Industry (HKAPI), *Responses to the Draft Guidance Notes for Registration of Biosimilar Products* (2014), www.hkapi.hk/images/newsletter/HKAPI%20response%20to%20biosimilar%20guidelines%20(web)_14102014_161606.pdf, accessed 15 February 2016.

67 Ibid 1.

(Interim) instituting a regulatory process for applying for approval of biosimilar products.[68]

Other countries that have thus far established regulatory frameworks for the approval of biosimilar products include Brazil, Malaysia, New Zealand,[69] Russia,[70] Singapore and South Korea.[71]

Biologics and biosimilars in international trade agreements

The variety of biologics and biosimilars regulatory regimes discussed in the previous section are a testament to the flexibility that ultimately governs the regulation of biologics in international trade agreements. Of the several international trade agreements that have bearing on the regulation of biologics and biosimilars, the Agreement on Trade-Related Aspects of Intellectual Property Rights (TRIPS)[72] does not directly address the regulation of biologics and biosimilars, but is of importance, nonetheless. Indeed, TRIPS merely requires that all signatory countries provide for patent protection of biologics, as they would for any other technology.[73]

Yet, TRIPS includes several options to exclude certain patentable subject matter that are of particular importance in the context of biologics and biosimilars. First, TRIPS provides that "[m]embers may exclude from patentability inventions . . . to protect *ordre public* or morality, including to protect human, animal or plant life or health or to avoid serious prejudice to the environment, provided that such exclusion is not made merely because the exploitation is prohibited by their law".[74]

68 See China Food and Drug Administration, *CFDA Issues Technical Guideline for Development and Evaluation of Biosimilars* (5 March 2015), www.eng.cfda.gov.cn/WS03/CL0757/115203.html, accessed 15 February 2016. Katherine Wang, "China Announces Final Biosimilars Guideline" (2015), Ropes and Gray News & Insights, www.ropesgray.com/news-and-insights/Insights/2015/March/China-Announces-Final-Biosimilars-Guideline.aspx, accessed 15 February 2016.

69 Medsafe, New Zealand Medicines and Medical Devices Safety Authority, "Medsafe Position on Biosimilar Medicines", www.medsafe.govt.nz/profs/RIss/Medsafe%20position%20on%20biosimilars.pdf; Medsafe, www.medsafe.govt.nz/profs/RIss/Biosimilars.asp, accessed 15 February 2016.

70 Ministry of Healthcare Working on Several Documents Ensuring the Enforcement of Amendments to the Federal Law "On Circulation of Pharmaceuticals" (2 February 2015), KPMG Pharma bulletin (reporting that the Russian Ministry of Healthcare was in the process of implementing Federal Law No. 429-FZ "On Circulation of Pharmaceuticals", including in the context of pharmaceuticals).

71 Jun Wang and Shein-Chung Chow, "On the Regulatory Approval Pathway of Biosimilar Products" (2012), 5 PHARMACEUTICALS 353, 364 (discussing the regulatory frameworks of Brazil, Malaysia, Singapore and South Korea).

72 Agreement on Trade-Related Aspects of Intellectual Property Rights (1994) 1869 U.N.T.S. 299, 33 I.L.M. 1194 (1994) [hereinafter TRIPS Agreement].

73 See TRIPS Agreement, Article 27(1) ("patents shall be available for any inventions . . . in all fields of technology . . . [and] without discrimination as to . . . the field of technology").

74 Ibid Article 27(2).

This exclusion may be of particular relevance to biological technologies derived from or involving practices that certain cultures may consider immoral or repugnant. A notable example of such exclusion is the European denial of patentability to human embryonic stem cells (hESCs) and technologies that require the destruction of human embryos.[75] Second, under TRIPS, members may exclude from patentability "diagnostic, therapeutic and surgical methods for the treatment of humans or animals".[76] This exclusion, in effect, makes it possible for signatories to except from patent protection any methods of treatment involving biologics (or any other pharmaceutical for that matter).

Still, while TRIPS itself mandates that signatories institute patent regimes,[77] it leaves considerable flexibilities when it comes to the formulation of protection for data submitted as part of regulatory proceedings for approval of pharmaceutical products.[78] Hence, the data, market and generic exclusivity periods instituted under the EU, US and other countries' regulatory frameworks are not explicitly echoed in TRIPS itself. Rather, such exclusivities are provided for in several bilateral and regional trade agreements containing so-called "TRIPS-plus" provisions.

The vast majority of such TRIPS-plus agreements do not address biologics explicitly but rather only pharmaceuticals more broadly.[79] Notable examples of

75 European Patent Convention Rule 28(c) ("European patents shall not be granted in respect of biotechnological inventions which, in particular, concern . . . uses of human embryos for industrial or commercial purposes"); see also *Brüstle vs Greenpeace* [2011] E.C.J., No. C-34/10 (holding unpatentable any technology requiring the destruction of human embryos); EPO, Enlarged Board of Appeal, *WARF*, G02/06 (2008) (denying patentability of hESCs and holding that biotechnological products are to be denied patentability when they require the use of human embryos even where such use was not explicitly part of the claims); EPO, Boards of Appeal, Technion Research and Development Foundation Ltd., T2221/10. (2014) (holding that inventions which make use of hESCs obtained by de novo destruction of human embryos or of publicly available hESC lines which were initially derived by a process resulting in the destruction of the human embryos are excluded from patentability).

76 TRIPS Agreement, Article 27(3)(a).

77 See Mark Janis, 'Second Tier Patent Protection' (1999) 40 HARV. INT'L L. J. 151, 152 ("the TRIPs agreement dutifully establishes minimum substantive standards for each of the major intellectual property regimes but fails explicitly to mention second tier protection, leaving WTO member countries free to formulate or reject second tier protection regimes as they see fit").

78 See TRIPS Agreement, Article 39.3 (stipulating that such data whose origination "involves a considerable effort" should be protected from "unfair commercial use" and "disclosure, except where necessary to protect the public, or unless steps are taken to ensure that the data are protected against unfair commercial use").

79 See Brook Baker, "With One Exception Current Trade Agreements Do Not Appear to Include Biologic Medicines in their Data Protection/Data Exclusivity Provisions – Implications for TPP Negotiation" (2013), 2–3, www.infojustice.org/wp-content/uploads/2013/08/baker082013.pdf With only one possible exception, current US trade agreements do not provide data exclusivity for biologics, but rather only for pharmaceuticals containing "chemical entities" The only US trade agreement that is ambiguous in this regard

such agreements include the North American Free Trade Agreement (NAFTA)[80] and the Korea–US Free Trade Agreement (KORUS).[81] As a result, arguably, the vast majority of existing TRIPS-plus agreements providing for further exclusivities in pharmaceutical products do not apply to biologics.[82] A few notable exceptions to this inapplicability of TRIPS-plus agreements to biologics may be found in the Trade Agreement between the EU and Colombia and Peru,[83] which is special in that it explicitly addresses biologics as such rather than only pharmaceuticals more broadly[84] as well as the United States–Singapore Free Trade Agreement whose definition of "pharmaceutical products" is, apparently, inclusive of all types of pharmaceuticals, including biologics.[85] Another exception to the general rule that

is the United States–Singapore Free Trade Agreement . . . which covers all, not just new, pharmaceutical products.

80 See NAFTA, Article 1711.5–7, www.sice.oas.org/trade/nafta/chap-172.asp#A1711 (providing for a period of data exclusivity in "pharmaceutical or agricultural chemical products that utilize new chemical entities").

81 See KORUS, Article 18.9.1–2, www.ustr.gov/sites/default/files/uploads/agreements/fta/korus/asset_upload_file273_12717.pdf, accessed 15 February 2016 (providing for a minimum period of five years of market exclusivity in "a new pharmaceutical . . . product" and three years of market exclusivity in a new use of a pharmaceutical product containing a chemical entity that was already previously approved in the relevant territory). KORUS also provides for a notice requirement to the owner of an original pharmaceutical product of submission of follow-on applications to its product as well as an opportunity to sue follow-on applicants for patent infringement. Ibid Article 18.9.5.

82 See Baker (n. 79) 2–7 (arguing that any exclusivities afforded in international trade agreements to "new chemical entities" do not apply to biologics). Professor Baker makes a compelling argument, which is based on the historical dichotomy drawn in legislation and regulation between small-molecule drugs (that are chemically synthesized) and biologics (which are made by utilizing processes taking place within the cells of living organisms). Ibid 3–4. Baker's position is further bolstered by the fact that the recently agreed upon language of the Trans-Pacific Partnership also creates a dichotomy between "pharmaceutical products" and "biologics" as well as provides a definition of biologics. See Trans-Pacific Partnership §§ 18.50, 18.52.1, 18.52.2, www.medium.com/the-trans-pacific-partnership/intellectual-property-3479efdc7adf, accessed 15 February 2016.

83 See Trade Agreement between the European Union and its Member States, of the one part, and Colombia and Peru, of the other part, Article 231 (26 July 2012), www.trade.ec.europa.eu/doclib/html/147704.htm (setting a market exclusivity period of at least five years for pharmaceutical products containing "new chemical entities").

84 See ibid, Article 231.1, note 72 (clarifying that the EU's and Colombia's commitment to protect undisclosed data related to the safety and efficacy of pharmaceuticals includes the protection of such data as it pertains to biological and biotechnological products).

85 United States–Singapore Free Trade Agreements, Article 16.8.1, n. 16–14, www.ustr.gov/trade-agreements/free-trade-agreements/singapore-fta/final-text (the requirement to provide a minimum of five years of market exclusivity in pharmaceutical products "[w]here a Party [has] in place a system for protecting pharmaceutical . . . products not involving new chemical entities from unfair commercial use that conferred a different form or period of protection shorter than that specified in paragraph 1 of Article 16.8"). Notably, unlike the trade agreements between the United States and Korea and the United States and Australia, the trade agreement between the United States and Singapore does not include any reference – direct or indirect – to pharmaceuticals as containing a "chemical entity". See KORUS,

sections in free trade agreements (FTAs) addressing pharmaceutical new chemical entities do not apply to biologics may exist where local laws explicitly include biologics within the statutory definition of new chemical entities, as in the case of Chile.[86]

Yet, the FTA most significant for the regulation of biologics and biosimilars is the Trans-Pacific Partnership (TPP) Agreement, a long-anticipated and prominent TRIPS-plus agreement between Australia, Brunei, Canada, Chile, Japan, Malaysia, Mexico, New Zealand, Peru, Singapore, the United States and Vietnam.[87] The Intellectual Property Chapter of the TPP requires that the signatories provide for a data exclusivity period of eight years in new biologics.[88] Alternatively, signatories may provide for a data exclusivity period of only five years so long as they are able to guarantee a comparable market outcome to that of the eight-year data exclusivity that TPP otherwise requires.[89] TPP does not clarify what would be considered a "comparable market outcome" and how "market outcomes" may be quantified and measured, if at all. This flexibility in the TPP, while seemingly blurring the lines between *de jure* standards of protection of biologics and *de facto* outcomes of such protection, may reflect the realization of signatories that under current market and regulatory realities biologics might not be as vulnerable to competition from biosimilars as they are sometimes argued to be. In that same vein, apparently, TPP further "[recognizes] that international and domestic regulation of new pharmaceutical products that are or contain a biologic is in a formative stage and that market circumstances may evolve over time" and

n. 73, Article 18.9.1(c) (clarifying that a "new pharmaceutical product" under the agreement "is one that does not contain a chemical entity that has been previously approved", while not mentioning biologics); United States–Australia Free Trade Agreement, Article 17.10.1.(d), www.ustr.gov/trade-agreements/free-trade-agreements/australian-fta/final-text. ("For the purposes of this Article, a new product is one that does not contain a chemical entity that has been previously approved for marketing in the Party" [emphasis omitted].)

86 Chilean Ley no. 20.724, Modifica el Código Sanitario en Materia de Regulatión de Farmacias Y Medicamentos § 95 (2014) (defining pharmaceuticals as including biologics); see also Baker (n. 79) 7 ("some countries may have unilaterally adopted data exclusivity or interpreted existing data exclusivity legislation to apply to biologics").

87 Trans-Pacific Partnership, www.ustr.gov/trade-agreements/free-trade-agreements/trans-pacific-partnership/tpp-full-text [hereinafter TPP]. As of December 2015, TPP has not been signed yet and its currently available versions are still "[s]ubject to [l]egal [r]eview in English, Spanish and French for [a]ccuracy, [c]larity and [c]onsistency [S]ubject to [a]uthentication of English, Spanish and French [v]ersions". Ibid, Preamble, www.ustr.gov/sites/default/files/TPP-Final-Text-Preamble.pdf. According to some accounts, the members of TPP represent "nearly 40 percent of global [growth domestic product]". See U.S. Trade Representative, *Overview of the Trans Pacific Partnership*, www.ustr.gov/tpp/overview-of-the-TPP.

88 Ibid § 18.52.1.(a). Notably, the eight-year data exclusivity period applies cross-nationally such that it would be impossible to reference or rely on data submitted in *any* other territory (not just a signatory territory) to secure the approval of a biologic before the lapse of eight years from the date of marketing approval of the biologic in that other territory. Ibid § 18.50.1.(b).

89 Ibid § 18.52.1.(b).

stipulates that signatories "shall consult after 10 years" to review the periods of exclusivity provided under the agreement.[90]

In addition to several specific accommodations made to certain signatories,[91] TPP, however, recognizes several important general limitations to its own stipulations, including those pertaining to biologics and biosimilars. First, under Section 18.6 of the TPP, signatories may construe and implement their obligations under the Intellectual Property Chapter "in a manner supportive of each Party's right to protect public health and, in particular, to promote access to medicines for all".[92] Section 18.6 further acknowledges that "[e]ach Party has the right to determine what constitutes a national emergency or other circumstances of extreme urgency . . . including those relating to HIV/AIDS, tuberculosis, malaria and other epidemics".[93] In addition, similar to TRIPS, Section 18.37 of TPP also recognizes that signatories may exclude from patentability "inventions, the prevention within their territory of the commercial exploitation of which is necessary to protect *ordre public* or morality, including to protect human, animal or plant life or health . . . [including] diagnostic, therapeutic and surgical methods for the treatment of humans or animals".[94] Finally, specifically with respect to biologics, TPP holds that signatories may take measures to protect public health in accordance with the Doha Declaration on TRIPS and Public Health[95] and any subsequent waivers granted under the Declaration by the World Trade Organization.[96]

Given the anticipated prominence of TPP,[97] it is to be expected that once finalized its provisions may well set minimum standards for the regulation of biologics and biosimilars globally. Hence, for example, the TPP may dictate to a large extent the terms of the Transatlantic Trade and Investment Partnership (TTIP) agreement between the United States and the EU as they pertain to biologics and biosimilars.

90 Ibid § 18.52.3. Importantly, TPP stipulates that such review of exclusivity periods will be conducted "with a view to providing effective incentives for the development of new pharmaceutical products that are or contain a biologic, as well as with a view to facilitating the timely availability of follow-on biosimilars". See ibid.

91 Ibid §§ 18.83.4.(a)(vi), 18.83.4.(b)(viii), 18.83.4.(c)(v), 18.83.4.(e)(ii), 18.83.4.(f)(xxiv), Annex 18-B § 1, Annex 18-C § 1 and Annex 18-D, Part 2.

92 Ibid § 18.6.1.(a).

93 Ibid.

94 Ibid § 18.37.3.(a).

95 Declaration on the TRIPS Agreement and Public Health (2001) WT/MIN(01)/DEC/2, www.wto.org/english/thewto_e/minist_e/min01_e/mindecl_trips_e.htm.

96 TPP §§ 18.50.3, 18.52.1.

97 According to the United States Trade Representative (USTR), the signatories of the TPP Agreement represent 40 per cent of global gross domestic product (GDP). See USTR, "Overview of the Trans Pacific Partnership", www.ustr.gov/tpp/overview-of-the-TPP.

An IP roadmap to a regulatory framework for approval of biologics and biosimilars

While there are several sources of possible guidance on the clinical and scientific aspects of testing and approving biologics and biosimilars,[98] there appear to be no good sources of direction on the intellectual property aspects of doing so. The discussion thus far draws an intricate picture of conflicting interests and international commitments that countries seeking to institute a pathway for approval of biosimilar products must consider and balance. At the same time, most if not all of the surveyed regulatory arrangements share certain commonalities that offer lessons as well as guidance for new frameworks. The international trade agreements create the boundaries within which such frameworks may reside.

Thus, for example, it is important to point out that none of the frameworks discussed earlier offers a pathway for approval of biosimilar products as interchangeable or substitutable with previously approved biologics and that as of yet no biological product has been deemed interchangeable with another product. The only notable exception to this is the yet-to-be-implemented legislation in the United States, which explicitly grants the FDA the authority to deem certain biosimilar products interchangeable with existing products, provided a high standard of clinical substitutability is met.[99] This, in turn, indicates that while the clinical and scientific aspects of biologics development may not have reached a point in which it is possible to establish clinical substitutability, developers of regulatory frameworks for approval of biologics and biosimilars would do well to leave sufficient flexibility in such frameworks so as to allow for the approval of products as interchangeable once this becomes practicable. It is more advisable to follow the example of the United States framework in this respect than that of the EU, which is dictated by political considerations particular to the EU and which creates an unnecessary dichotomy—and, potentially, redundancy[100] – between the

98 See, e.g., World Health Organization Expert Committee on Biological Standardization, GUIDELINES ON EVALUATION OF SIMILAR BIOTHERAPEUTIC PRODUCTS (SBPS) (2009), www.who.int/biologicals/areas/biological_therapeutics/BIOTHERAPEUTICS_FOR_WEB_22APRIL2010.pdf.

99 See 42 U.S.C. § 262(k)(4); (n. 38).

100 Evaluators of clinical data for the purpose of biosimilarity determinations are presumably in the best position to also determine if two biological products, a reference and a follow-on product, are clinically interchangeable such that similar evaluation further down the regulatory road may well be repetitive, quite possibly wasteful, and potentially ethically unjustified. This, however, is not to say that interchangeability is necessarily synonymous with automatic substitution, which heavily depends upon the status and scope of intellectual property in the reference product as well as the permissibility of such substitution under the laws of relevant jurisdictions. See Rovira et al (n. 16) 15 ("Although substitutability and interchangeability are often used as synonyms . . . interchangeability essentially refers to the doctor's ability to prescribe a biosimilar in place of the reference product and substitutability is to allow pharmacists to dispense a biosimilar rather than the reference drug" [internal quotation marks omitted]).

initial approval of biologics as biosimilars by the EMA and, then, their subsequent approval as interchangeable by the multiple local agencies in EU member states.[101]

Another reoccurring theme in the regulatory pathways for approval of biologics and biosimilar products is regulatory agencies' ability to learn from each other's experience and defer to the findings – clinical and regulatory alike – of counterpart agencies with respect to biological products. In this respect, it appears that virtually all of the surveyed jurisdictions have instituted a means of saving time and conserving resources by opening up their regulatory processes to information obtained from trusted institutions in other jurisdictions.[102] Most flexible in this regard is the Indian regulatory framework, which allows not only for approval of biologics based on data produced for the purpose of regulatory proceedings elsewhere, but also where such data was produced with respect to reference products that have never been previously approved for use in India.[103] The only conditions set by the Indian regulatory authorities in this regard are that the reference product was approved and marketed for at least four years, and that the approval and marketing took place in a country that has what the regulatory authorities in India consider a sufficiently established regulatory system, such as those in the United States and the EU.[104] The Indian guidelines further make it possible to reduce or even waive altogether the required period of four years "[i]n case no medicine or only palliative therapy is available or in national healthcare emergency [*sic*]".[105] The flexibility of the Indian framework reflects an emphasis on access to biologics, which may be appropriate for other nations with similar socio-economic circumstances.

Finally, with the exception of India, all of the jurisdictions surveyed earlier in this chapter provide for periods of market, data, and generic exclusivities, or any combination thereof in biologic and biosimilar products.[106] While the nature and length of these exclusivity periods seem to vary according to each country's internal considerations and bilateral international obligations,[107] the provision of *some form* for extra-patent exclusivities in biologics technology is commonplace.[108] It is therefore necessary to bear in mind that the rationale behind the provision of such exclusivities (especially market exclusivities) has been, primarily, to

101 See n. 15 and accompanying text.

102 See nn. 25–27, 45, 50, 55, 61 and accompanying texts.

103 See CDSCO, *Guidelines on Similar Biologics: Regulatory Requirements for Marketing Authorization in India* (2012) §§ 5, 6.1, 13, www.cdsco.nic.in/writereaddata/Bio%20 Similar%20Guideline.pdf.

104 Ibid.

105 Ibid §§ 5, 6.1.

106 See nn. 20–22, 30–32, 47, 56, 63–64 and accompanying texts.

107 As mentioned earlier, the TRIPS Agreement does not require any particular extra-patent protections for any kind of technology. See *supra* Part III.

108 Notably, as emphasized by Professor Baker, under TRIPS, low- and middle-income countries remain free to conclude that extra-patent exclusivities for biologics are not required and are even counter to the interests of their citizens, healthcare systems, and their economies. See Baker (n. 79) 5.

compensate product developers for what has, controversially, been described as an insufficiency of the incentives provided by patents for technological innovation in the area of biologics.[109] Accordingly, in weighing whether to provide further exclusivities in biological products in addition to those afforded by patents, developers of regulatory frameworks for approval of biologics and biosimilars should strive to avoid potential risks of waste and exclusivity misuse (including patent misuse)[110] by taking the following precautions. First, they ought to tailor any extra-patent exclusivities in such a manner that does not provide excessive protection to the interests of biologics and biosimilar developers as it is well known that over-protection of intellectual property (IP) rights may be just as injurious to innovation as under-protection.[111] Admittedly, reaching a balanced policy in this regard is no simple matter, as it requires careful calculation of the costs of bringing biologics and biosimilars to market in the particular market in which the jurisdiction resides against the anticipated ability to leverage exclusivities towards super-competitive profits on biologics and biosimilars. Some of the factors that developers of regulatory frameworks for approval of biologics and biosimilars should look to when evaluating whether and how to protect proprietary interests in biologics and biosimilars include:

1 the cost of development of a biological pharmaceutical, including the ratio of success-to-failure in the relevant jurisdiction;
2 the cost of manufacturing and distributing biological products, including the cost of regulatory compliance;
3 what forms of intellectual property protection are already available or unavailable for biologics developers in the relevant jurisdiction; and
4 the need to make biologics widely accessible upon expiration of IP.

It is also important to keep in mind that rational actors in the market regularly do and will take advantage of regulatory loopholes, and so it is important to make sure that the regulatory regime does not provide incentives for brand and generic to collude in a manner harmful to consumers (e.g., by entering pay-for-delay arrangements).

Second, developers of regulatory frameworks for approval of biologics and biosimilars ought to make sure that extra-patent market exclusivities do not run concurrently with patent protection by making the onset of such exclusivities

109 See Heled (n. 31) 440, n. 92 and Part III.C.1 (describing these risks in the context of BPCIA).

110 For a fuller description of these risks and how to avoid them, see Heled (n. 31) Parts III.C.2-3.

111 See Nancy Gallini and Suzanne Scotchmer, "Intellectual Property: When is it the Best Incentive System?" in Adam Jaffe et al (eds) *Innovation Policy and the Economy, Volume 2* (MIT Press, 2002) 51, 67 www.nber.org/chapters/c10785, accessed 7 January 2017 ("A danger of intellectual property that has been debated from its inception to the present . . . is that intellectual property can stifle innovation and slow progress").

dependent upon a commitment not to enforce any concurrently running patents.[112] In other words, upon the potential triggering of a market exclusivity period in a biologic, the regulatory agency instituting and enforcing the exclusivity should have the potential beneficiary choose whether it would rather have the agency enforce the market exclusivity (by not approving applications for marketing approval of follow-on products) or the ability to enforce its patents against potential competitors seeking regulatory approval for their follow-on products. Should the potential beneficiary elect to have the agency enforce the exclusivity, it should be required to commit to the agency not to attempt to enforce patents covering the approved product that is the subject of the potential market exclusivity against such potential competitors. To clarify, this is not to say that such commitment would make such patents unenforceable under any circumstances against any possible defendant, but rather that such patents ought to be unenforceable only against potential third party defendants whose own products are or were blocked to some extent by the otherwise concurrent extra-patent exclusivity. If, on the other hand, the potential beneficiary were to elect to maintain its ability to enforce its patents against developers of follow-on products, the regulatory agency should refrain from enforcing the market exclusivity period in the originally approved product and grant follow-on products regardless of any patent enforcement proceedings involving such products that take place.

Conclusion

As the significance of biologics and their proportion among pharmaceuticals available to treat patients increases, it also becomes more important to create and streamline regulatory pathways for the approval of biologics and biosimilars. This is especially true for countries that have not yet taken full advantage of the healthcare benefits that biologics and biosimilar offer. The experience gained from the regulation of biologics and biosimilars thus far in the EU, the United States, India, Japan, Australia, Canada and other countries offers several valuable lessons to countries seeking to develop their own regulatory framework for evaluation and approval of biologics and biosimilars. First, developers of such regulatory frameworks should build into these frameworks pathways for evaluating and approving certain biosimilar products as interchangeable with one another, while avoiding unnecessary dichotomies between biosimilarity and interchangeability determinations.

Second, developers of new regulatory frameworks for approval of biologics and biosimilars would do well to ensure that their regulatory frameworks are sufficiently "porous" to allow for "diffusion" of clinical and regulatory findings from other jurisdictions – possibly ones with similar yet more established frameworks – into their own regulatory processes, which could save time, money, and – ultimately

112 See Heled (n. 31) Part III.C.4 (describing a proposed amendment to BPCIA that is meant to achieve this result).

– human lives. And, third, developers of regulatory frameworks for approval of biologics and biosimilars should only provide for extra-patent exclusivities to the extent necessary to incentivize further innovation in the area of biologics and, regardless, to avoid such extra-patent market exclusivities from running concurrent with patent protection in the same products.

This checklist of elements recommended for incorporation into newly crafted regulatory frameworks for approval of biologics and biosimilars is by no means exhaustive. Indeed, every country seeking to establish a regulatory framework for approval of biologics and biosimilars would need to carefully consider and balance its own socio-economic needs, cultural and ethical norms, intellectual property laws, and international obligations. Nor is the list of recommended elements a guarantee for the success of such newly crafted frameworks. But it is a good start.

4 Index of Data Exclusivity and Access (IDEAS)

An Analysis of Test Data Exclusivity Provisions in Free Trade Agreements and National Laws

Owais Hassan Shaikh

Introduction

Test data exclusivity is being increasingly accepted as a new form of intellectual property (IP). From being conceived as a mechanism for easing entry of generic pharmaceuticals in the US market, test data exclusivity is now promoted as a new must-have in the national mix of IP protection as an incentive for pharmaceutical research and development (R&D). The branded pharmaceutical industry as well as developed countries are promising that data exclusivity will bring benefits such as a healthier future, increased investment in local pharmaceutical R&D and manufacturing as well as early access to originator products. Nonetheless, the empirical evidence shows that these promises have not come to fruition so far. But what is more disturbing is that through the introduction of test data exclusivity in their national laws, an increasing number of developing countries are contributing to redefining the flexibility inherent in Article 39(3) of the TRIPS Agreement with regard to protecting test data against "unfair commercial use" to one that exclusively means test data exclusivity. Such an interpretation was considered and rejected during TRIPS negotiations. This development has primarily come about through the extensive use of bilateral and regional trade agreements (collectively called free trade agreements (FTAs)) in the last 20 years where countries have willingly traded TRIPS flexibilities in return of short-living trade benefits in non-IP areas. This chapter questions the arguments forwarded in favour of test data exclusivity, traces its development path from its birth until today, discusses the implications of the recent developments in this area and offers recommendations to countries in connection with FTAs and national laws.

The remainder of this section introduces the concept of test data exclusivity, differentiates it from patent and trade secret protection and presents empirical evidence of its impact on selected countries. The second section analyses the reason for the existence of test data exclusivity. The third section sketches the evolutionary picture of test data exclusivity from its birth up till now. The fourth presents the Index of Data Exclusivity and Access (IDEAS), which enables comparison of test data exclusivity provisions in FTAs and national laws. The last part discusses the implications of these developments and offers some recommendations to countries that have already concluded FTAs providing for test data exclusivity or for countries that are or will negotiate this exclusivity in the context of an international trade agreement.

Test data exclusivity, defined

Test data exclusivity may be defined both as a *positive* and a *negative* right. The International Federation of Pharmaceutical Manufacturers and Associations (IFPMA) considers test data exclusivity an intellectual property right (IPR) which "provides the holder with specific rights, namely that the data generated by the holder may not be referred to or used by another person or company for a specific period of time".[1] According to this definition test data exclusivity is a negative right. At the same time, IFPMA also defines this exclusivity as a positive right claiming that it "provides a limited duration of time during which only the owner or generator of . . . preclinical and clinical trial data can *use* it for purposes of marketing authorization " (emphasis added).[2] Test data exclusivity comes into play when a generic pharmaceutical's applicant makes reference to the originator product or when the drug regulatory authority relies on the originator's test data for approval of a generic pharmaceutical product, and therefore acts to restrict such reference or reliance for a specific period of time.

Difference from patents and trade secrets

In certain cases the protection conferred by test data exclusivity may overlap with other forms of protections such as trade secrets and patents. Trade secrets protect test data as such whereas patent protection extends to the pharmaceutical product. Although protection through test data exclusivity differs from these two, the effect of all of these protections is the same. They impose restrictions on the introduction of generic pharmaceutical products in the market and may result in higher prices.

Historically, test data has been considered a valuable business secret of the R&D pharmaceutical manufacturers (originators). Therefore, generic manufacturers could not use it to support their marketing applications. They were required to generate their own test data to support their applications. Alternatively, they had to acquire authorization to use the originator's data. The requirement was waived

1 International Federation of Pharmaceutical Manufacturers and Associations (IFPMA), *Data Exclusivity: Encouraging Development of New Medicines*, 2011, p1 [hereinafter "IFPMA (2011)"], www.ifpma.org/fileadmin/content/Publication/IFPMA_2011_Data_Exclusivity__En_Web.pdf, accessed 8 December 2015.

2 International Federation of Pharmaceutical Manufacturers and Associations (IFPMA), "Encouragement of New Clinical Drug Development: The Role of Data Exclusivity" (2000), 5 [hereinafter "IFPMA (2000)"], www.who.int/intellectualproperty/topics/ip/en/DataExclusivity_2000.pdf, accessed 8 December 2015.

where the drug regulatory authority (DRA) could make determination of the generic product's safety and efficacy based on publicly available information. However, the onset of test data exclusivity as the most important mode against generic competition has taken the shine off trade secrets protection for test data. This is because after the expiry of the test data exclusivity period, generics are allowed to enter the market based on the originator product's test data and the competitive advantage secured by the trade secret is neutralized.

Unlike trade secrets, patent protection is conferred upon the originator's pharmaceutical product and not directly upon the test data. Patent protection is available to pharmaceuticals that pass the criteria of novelty, inventive step and industrial application under the national patent law. As the two protections have different objects, it is possible that an originator product enjoys both test data exclusivity and patent protection. Moreover, as both protections are aimed at excluding generics competition, sometimes both are useful whereas in certain circumstances one becomes redundant.[3]

For example, the test data exclusivity period generally lasts between five to ten years, whereas the minimum term for patent protection is 20 years from the date of filing. Therefore, where an originator product is approved early in the patent life and the test data exclusivity term is short, the former subsumes the latter. Test data exclusivity is useful when it is longer and marketing approval is granted later in the patent term. It may be noted that even in these cases, the importance of test data exclusivity may be mitigated where the law also provides extension of the patent term because of delays in approval of the pharmaceutical product by the DRA.

Test data exclusivity is also beneficial in the case of successful validity challenges to related patents. In such cases, patent protection may be denied but test data exclusivity is still available. Moreover, despite being shorter in duration, test data exclusivity may override exceptions to patent protection, for example compulsory licences, which normally cover only patents and not test data. As a result, at least in theory, generics may still not be able to bring their product to the market during the exclusivity period. Similarly, test data exclusivity may also render ineffective the "regulatory review exemption" (also called the "Bolar

3 There are several differences between the two protections. For example, test data exclusivity is automatically granted with marketing approval of the originator product whereas an application has to be made for grant of patent protection. Similarly, the originator does not have to petition the DRA or the Court to prohibit acceptance or approval of a generic application, as the DRA cannot accept a marketing approval application or if accepted, cannot approve for launch in the market during the test data exclusivity period under the law. On the other hand, as patent right is a private right, the patentee has to enforce it through courts every time it is infringed. Under the patent law, once a patent right on an invention is granted, if another person later comes up with the same invention independently, practising it without authorization from the patentee will be an infringement, whereas test data exclusivity does not preclude another applicant from obtaining the marketing approval by generating its own set of test data, or relying on publicly available information where accepted by the DRA.

exemption") for a patented pharmaceutical. Under this exemption, a competitor, normally a generics manufacturer, is allowed to prepare application for its generic product during the originator's patent term. However, test data exclusivity renders this exemption useless as it applies only to patent protection.

Flexibility of international test data protection regimes

Unlike patent protection, countries have considerable leeway in constructing test data exclusivity protection in their laws. The only international reference point for test data protection is Article 39(3) of TRIPS. Article 39(3) requires that World Trade Organization (WTO) Members protect test data against "unfair commercial use" and "disclosure". The requirement of protection against disclosure is straightforward; however, there is considerable debate as to what is meant by "protection against unfair commercial use". The TRIPS Agreement does not define this term, there is no reference made to test data exclusivity and there has been no guidance provided by a WTO Panel so far. However, it has been argued, applying the customary rules of interpretation according to Articles 31 and 32 of the Vienna Convention on the Law of Treaties, that Article 39(3) TRIPS does not require test data exclusivity.[4] WTO Members would fulfil "protection against unfair commercial use" if they outline in their laws, protection against misappropriation of test data.[5] This assertion is based on Article 39(3)'s link with Article 39(1) of TRIPS and by that reference to Article 10*bis* of the Paris Convention. Article 10*bis*, relating to "unfair competition", aims to restore competition in the market in the absence of exclusive rights. Therefore, interpreting "protection against unfair commercial use" as requiring test data exclusivity would fail to give effect to Article 39(1). Moreover, as will be discussed in the section on 'Evolution' below, test data exclusivity was excluded from the TRIPS Agreement after being discussed, debated and actually being included in various earlier drafts. This shows that the *common intention* of the parties engaged in the negotiation of the TRIPS Agreement was not to consider test data exclusivity as the exclusive interpretation of "protection against unfair commercial use" in Article 39(3).[6] It must be noted, however, that Article 39(3) does not prohibit WTO Members from providing test data exclusivity protection, because the exclusivity approach encompasses protection against misappropriation.

4 Jakkrit Kuanpoth, "Intellectual Property Protection after TRIPS: An Asian experience" in Justin Malbon and Charles Lawson (eds), *Interpreting and Implementing the TRIPS Agreement: Is it Fair?* (Gloucestershire: Edward Elgar Publishing Limited, 2008) 88.

5 Carlos M. Correa, "Data Exclusivity for Pharmaceuticals: TRIPS Standards and Industry's Demands in Free Trade Agreements" in Carlos M. Correa (ed), *Research Handbook on the Protection of Intellectual Property under WTO Rules: Intellectual Property in the WTO Volume I* (Gloucestershire: Edward Elgar Publishing Limited, 2010) 713.

6 On the other hand, the developed countries as well as the R&D pharmaceutical industry claim that test data exclusivity is the only interpretation of Article 39(3) TRIPS. IFPMA (2000), 5.

Impact upon access to medicine

The negative impact of test data exclusivity upon access to affordable medicine is quite obvious. As mentioned above, its effect is the same as that of patent protection (i.e., delaying the market entry of generic pharmaceutical products and extending the originator product's exclusivity). Although there is still a dearth of empirical evidence of the impact of test data exclusivity on access to medicine, as it has been introduced in most countries only recently, its negative impact has already been confirmed in a few countries. For example, in 2007, Oxfam International studied the impact of the US–Jordan FTA on access to medicine in Jordan. The study revealed that 79 per cent of the drugs launched in Jordan between 2001 and 2006 did not face any generic competition due to test data exclusivity.[7] Jordanians, therefore, paid an additional sum between US$6 to $22.04 million for pharmaceuticals.[8] The report made comparison of drug prices in Jordan with those in Egypt, which did not grant test data exclusivity, and found that in the former, the prices for drugs for diabetes and heart diseases were up to eight times more expensive.[9] The promise of foreign direct investment (FDI), which is used as an incentive for introducing test data exclusivity, was also not fulfilled. Similarly many originator drugs available in the US were not launched in Jordan, despite the provision of this protection. Similar conclusions were drawn from studies conducted in Guatemala[10] and Colombia.[11]

Delaying originator entry in the national market

Another important implication of test data exclusivity has been overshadowed by the focus on access to affordable *generic* pharmaceuticals. Test data exclusivity may also affect the availability of originator product in a specific national market. Normally, generic manufacturers make reference to an originator drug that has been earlier approved in the same jurisdiction. Where there is no national approval, generic manufacturers would make reference to an approval from another jurisdiction acceptable by the national DRA. After approval, the generic product can be marketed in that country even in the absence of an originator product.

7 Oxfam International, "All costs, no benefits: How TRIPS-plus intellectual property rules in the US-Jordan FTA affect access to medicine" Oxfam Briefing Paper, March 2007, [hereinafter "Oxfam (2007)"], www.oxfam.org/sites/www.oxfam.org/files/all%20costs,%20no%20benefits.pdf, accessed 8 December 2015, p9.

8 Oxfam (2007) 14.

9 Oxfam (2007) 10.

10 Ellen R. Shaffer and Joseph E. Brenner, "A Trade Agreement's Impact On Access To Generic Drugs" (2009) 28(5) Health Affairs 957, www.content.healthaffairs.org/content/28/5/w957.full.pdf+html, accessed 8 December 2015.

11 M. E. C. Gamba, F. R. Buenaventura and M. D. V. Serrano, "Impacto de 10 años de protección de datos en medicamentos en Colombia" (2012) 2 Serie Buscando Remedio, www.web.ifarma.org/images/files/buscandoremedio/BuscandoRemedio_2.pdf, accessed 8 December 2015.

Certain FTAs and national laws restrict this possibility.[12] This may result in absolute absence of pharmaceuticals in a country's market. This is especially true if the national law also does not require the originator to file application for approval with, or within certain time from, the first approval or filing elsewhere. The originator company is thus enabled to reserve these markets for the future, when their exclusivities end in more profitable markets.

In summary, test data exclusivity can delay launch of both generic and originator products, can empower the originator to control the market and can restrict the ability of the state to override patent protection when the need arises. The following section discusses whether such a proprietary right is justified on the grounds of promoting innovation similar to other mainstream intellectual property protection mechanisms.

Justification

The case of the R&D pharmaceutical industry

The argument in support of test data exclusivity is based on protection of investment as an incentive for innovation in pharmaceuticals.[13] As explained in the first section, an originator pharmaceutical product application is accompanied by test data generated through clinical trials. Even though all pharmaceutical products need to prove that they are safe (they do not cause unnecessary risks for the patients) and effective (they do what they claim to do), generics products can be approved on the basis of comparative studies known as bioequivalence information, showing identity and interchangeability with the relevant originator pharmaceutical.[14] The DRA uses the originator product's test data as reference, relieving the generics applicant from generating their own test data. In the presence of the originator product's test data such a requirement would be deemed unnecessary and financially and ethically questionable.[15] The generic manufacturers, therefore, save the costs of conducting clinical trials and their financial outlay for proving safety and efficacy of their product is limited to the cost incurred in generating

12 See the third and fourth sections.

13 Bruce N. Kuhlik, "The Assault on Pharmaceutical Intellectual Property" (2004), 71 University of Chicago Law Review 96 [hereinafter "Kuhlik (2004)"]. Also see generally IFPMA (2000) and IFPMA (2011).

14 United States Food and Drug Administration, "Abbreviated New Drug Application (ANDA): Generics" (2014), www.fda.gov/Drugs/DevelopmentApprovalProcess/HowDrugsareDevelopedandApproved/ApprovalApplications/AbbreviatedNewDrugApplicationANDAGenerics/, accessed 8 December 2015; European Medicines Agency, *Guideline on the Investigation of Bioequivalence* (2010), 4, www.ema.europa.eu/docs/en_GB/document_library/Scientific_guideline/2010/01/WC500070039.pdf, accessed 8 December 2015. Generally, bioequivalence information acts as a signal that the generic is as safe and effective as the originator drug.

15 Repetition of clinical trials needlessly consumes finite financial and non-financial resources of the society and also exposes animals and human lives to unnecessary dangers of drug testing.

bioequivalence information. The R&D pharmaceutical industry argues that the savings to generics manufacturers only from this one head can run into hundreds of millions of dollars.[16] Generic manufacturers free ride on originators investments, putting them at a disadvantage, as generics are made available in the market at a fraction of the originator pharmaceutical's price.[17] The originator pharmaceutical industry argues that in order to level the playing field, the generics should be prevented by law from (mis)using the former's test data. Accordingly, it argues that test data exclusivity is the best or even the only mechanism through which this can be achieved and the originator is assured recoupment of its R&D expenses.[18]

Despite the apparent forcefulness of this argument, the contention of the R&D industry is by no means a settled issue. It is doubtful whether protection of investment in clinical trials through test data exclusivity, especially in the presence of patent protection (and new ways of extending this protection through patent term extensions), provides incentives for creation of new and innovative pharmaceutical products. In the light of the discussion in section 1, it appears that test data exclusivity acts more as a safety net than a real mechanism for promoting targeted innovation in the pharmaceutical industry. Thus what needs to be asked is whether test data exclusivity is imperative for innovation in pharmaceuticals and whether it is worth the pain of compromising access to affordable medicine through this arrangement. Put simply, does test data exclusivity protection increase *dynamic* competition at the cost of *static* competition?

Is test data exclusivity an incentive for pharmaceutical innovation?

Test data is information about the safety and efficacy of a pharmaceutical product. As public goods, information is *non-rival* and *non-exclusive*. It is non-rival as one person's consumption does not reduce the consumption possibilities of others and it is non-exclusive as it is almost impossible to exclude someone from consuming it once created.[19] According to the incentive theory, on which

16 According to recent industry estimates, the cost of developing a new drug has long crossed the high mark of $1 billion and is marching onwards to reach $2 billion. See "Pharmaceutical Research and Manufacturers of America, 2013 Profile: Biopharmaceutical Research Industry" (2013), 37–38, www.phrma.org/sites/default/files/pdf/PhRMA%20Profile%20 2013.pdf, accessed 8 December 2015. Roughly half of this amount is spent on research on the new drug and the other half on developing the drug through the different phases of clinical trials, in which test data is generated. See Joseph A. DiMasi and Henry G. Grabowski, "The Cost of Biopharmaceutical R&D: Is Biotech Different?" (2007), 28 Managerial and Decision Economics 469. Generics drug manufacturers save expenditures under both these heads.

17 Kuhlik (2004) 95.

18 IFPMA (2000) 1.

19 Joseph E. Stiglitz, "Knowledge As a Global Public Good" in Inge Kaul, Isabelle Grunberg, and Marc A. Stern (eds), *Global Public Goods: International Cooperation in the 21st Century* (United Nations Development Programme, New York: Oxford University Press, 1999) 308.

much of the justification for intellectual property rights is based,[20] there is an enormous upfront cost for generating commercially beneficial information. However, being a public good, excluding others from unauthorized use or copying of information is difficult. At the same time, using or consuming it can be achieved at very low cost. Hence, without some kind of statutory protection, the producer of information or knowledge is unable to recoup the upfront costs leading to under-production even when demanded by the society. Test data exclusivity too, like other intellectual property exclusivities, precludes the DRA and the generics manufacturer for a specific period of time from reliance on or reference to the originator's test data for approval of a subsequent generic pharmaceutical application. However, does this preclusion result in pharmaceutical innovation?

As mentioned earlier, the basic premise for test data exclusivity is protection of investment in clinical test data. The argument for test data exclusivity is that in its absence there will be no clinical trials and in turn there would be no new and innovative pharmaceutical products in the market. However, there is a catch in this logic. Test data is only an intermediate good, like other inputs, for another good i.e., the pharmaceutical product whose creation is already incentivized by the society through the patent system. The decision of generating test data is already part of the decision of developing an originator pharmaceutical product. From this perspective, clinical trials are simply an input cost for producing an originator product, which must be considered when taking the decision to invest in the R&D for an originator product.

Another counter-argument regarding the *dynamic* competition justification of test data exclusivity is that if at all, it fails to incentivize innovation in pharmaceutical products in a systematic manner. As discussed above, the relevant consideration for qualifying for test data exclusivity protection is that it must provide proof of safety and efficacy of the pharmaceutical product. Test data exclusivity is available regardless of whether the product has therapeutic advantage over the ones already existing. Thus, test data exclusivity may impose additional costs on the society such as higher prices for pharmaceuticals with low or no added value and by keeping cheaper generics out of the market. Moreover, when test data exclusivity outruns the patent protection period, the societal decision to limit the patent protection for a certain period of time to promote static competition is compromised. Hence, not only is there no assurance that test data exclusivity would lead to creation of better pharmaceutical products, it also creates frictions with the societal decision to put a limit on the duration of patent protection.

Even though the separate effect of test data exclusivity has not been studied on pharmaceutical R&D and innovation, it has been documented that the originator pharmaceutical industry has increasingly focused on marginal innovation and imitative research.[21] Hence, financial, human and technical resources that

20 Edwin C. Hettinger, "Justifying Intellectual Property" (1989), 18(1) Philosophy and Public Affairs, 47.

21 Bernard Munos, "Lessons from 60 Years of Pharmaceutical Innovation" (2009) 8 Nature Rev. Drug Discovery 959 and National Institute for Health Care Management (NIHCM),

should have been directed towards finding breakthrough medical solutions for the society are consumed by projects that apparently focus on providing increased returns on investment. Test data exclusivity is increasingly becoming an important mechanism, with its probable objective on securing the latter.

Evolution

The importance of test data exclusivity on an international level has evolved over time from a purely domestic legal subject. Today, test data exclusivity is part of the national legal system of more than 50 countries[22] and is an integral part of bilateral and regional trade agreements concluded by the United States (US), European Union (EU) and European Free Trade Association (EFTA).

Birth of test data exclusivity

Due to the requirement of proving safety and efficacy of pharmaceuticals under the United States Food, Drug and Cosmetic Act (FDCA)[23] and an opaque policy competition from generic pharmaceuticals had continually declined.[24] The FDCA requirement of test data submission resulted in increased prices of originator products as well.[25] To address this situation, the FDCA was amended through the Drug Price Competition and Patent Term Restoration Act (more commonly known as the Hatch-Waxman Act) of the US in 1984.[26] The goal was

"Changing Patterns of Pharmaceutical Innovation: A Research Report by the National Institute for Health Care Management Research and Educational Foundation" (2002), www.nihcm.org/pdf/innovations.pdf, accessed 8 December 2015.

22 IFPMA (2011).

23 The safety requirement was included in the Federal Food, Drug and Cosmetic Act (FDCA) of 1938 whereas the efficacy requirement was added in 1962. See §102 Drug Amendments of 1962, Public Law 87–781, 10 October 1962, www.//uscode.house.gov/statutes/pl/87/781.pdf, accessed 8 December 2015.

24 James J. Wheaton, "Generic Competition and Pharmaceutical Innovation: The Drug Price Competition and Patent Term Restoration Act of 1984" (1986) 35 Catholic University Law Review 439–440; Elizabeth S. Weiswasser and Scott D. Danzis, "The Hatch-Waxman Act: History, Structure, And Legacy" (2003) 71 Antitrust Law Journal 585. An abbreviated pathway – so-called the *paper-NDA* (NDA: new drug application) – was established for generics in 1962 to ensure supply of cheaper generic pharmaceuticals. However, the FDCA secrecy requirements regarding safety and efficacy data made filing *paper-NDAs* quite difficult. At the same time, generic pharmaceuticals were considered to be "new" drugs, requiring safety and efficacy data as well. *United States vs Generix Drug Corp.* (1983) 460 U.S. 453, 461. ANDA was only available for products approved before 1962 and filing a paper-NDA was not easy.

25 Jeremy A. Greene and Schott H. Podolsky, "Reform, Regulation, and Pharmaceuticals – The Kefauver – Harris Amendments at 50" (2012) 367(16) New England Journal of Medicine, 1482.

26 Drug Price Competition and Patent Term Restoration Act, (1984) Pub. L. No. 98–417, 98 Stat. 1585 (codified as amended at 21 U.S.C. § 355; 28 U.S.C. § 2201; 35 U.S.C. §§ 156, 271,282).

to promote both *static* and *dynamic* competition through granting exclusivities for five (new chemical entity exclusivity) and three years (new clinical study exclusivity) to originator pharmaceuticals containing a new chemical entity[27] and their modifications,[28] respectively. After these periods, generics applicants were allowed to rely on the formers' test data for approval. Thus the Hatch-Waxman Act was the first national law to introduce test data exclusivity.

In Europe, test data exclusivity became part of Directive 65/65/EEC[29] in 1986 through amendments made by Directive 87/21/EEC.[30] Article 4 of Directive 65/65/EEC was amended to provide that essentially similar[31] generic pharmaceutical products that relied on an originator product already on the market for either six or ten years (depending upon the Member State), were not required to provide results of physico-chemical, biological or microbiological tests, pharmacological and toxicological tests and clinical trials.[32] Alternatively, a generics application could be filed where the applicant obtained authorization from the originator to rely on its results (informed-consent application) or where it relied on detailed published scientific literature, in the case of pharmaceuticals with well-established medicinal use (bibliographic application).

Internationalization of test data exclusivity

On the international level, multilateral trade negotiations in the General Agreement on Tariffs and Trade (GATT) Uruguay Round, launched in 1986, had

27 A new chemical entity is defined as "a drug that contains no active moiety that has been approved by US FDA in any other application under section 505(b) of the [FDCA] Act". 21 CFR § 314.108.

28 The purpose of this exclusivity is to promote research in new uses/indications of the already approved chemical entities. Such new uses/indications may include modification in the dosage, route of administration, new indications, strength, patient population, etc.

29 Council Directive 65/65/EEC of 26 January 1965 on the approximation of provisions laid down by Law, Regulation or Administrative Action relating to proprietary medicinal products [1965] OJ 022/0369.

30 Council Directive 87/21/EEC of 22 December 1986 amending Directive 65/65/EEC on the approximation of provisions laid down by law, regulation or administrative action relating to proprietary medicinal products, [1986] OJ L 15/36.

31 The notion of essential similarity was not defined in the Directive. The European Court of Justice (ECJ) ruled on this concept in the Generics decision in 1998, holding that "a medicinal product is essentially similar to an original medicinal product where it satisfies the criteria of having the *same qualitative and quantitative composition* in terms of active principles, of having the *same pharmaceutical form* and of being *bioequivalent*, unless it is apparent in the light of scientific knowledge that it differs significantly from the original product as regards safety or efficacy". Case C-368/96, *The Queen and Licensing Authority of the Department of Health, ex parte Generics (UK) Limited* [1998] ECR I-8001, para 36.

32 High-technology products were protected for a period of ten years across the European Communities (EC). High-technology products were defined in the Annex to Directive 87/22/EEC.

an extended mandate including intellectual property. The US[33] and Switzerland[34] presented initial proposals on test data exclusivity as part of broader trade secrets protection, calling for ten-year and unlimited test data exclusivity respectively with limited exceptions. These proposals were fiercely opposed by developing countries[35] who were against the inclusion of trade secrets and test data exclusivity.[36]

The individual proposals were followed by draft proposals for the future TRIPS Agreement. The US, Switzerland and European Communities (EC) proposals contained test data exclusivity provisions. They all linked protection of test data against unauthorized disclosure and use to Article 10*bis* of the Paris Convention for the Protection of Industrial Property. The EC proposed a reasonable period of exclusivity to be determined according to the efforts and expenditures in generating test data, its nature and availability of other forms of protection.[37] The US proposed exclusivity to last for a reasonable period of time, in contrast to the initial proposal of ten years. A relaxed liability rule, requiring reasonable value of the use, was included as an alternative.[38] The Swiss draft was similar to its initial proposal and contained an unlimited restriction use of test data.[39] The draft from developing countries contained no such provision.[40]

The various draft proposals were consolidated into one text on the basis of which the negotiations continued.[41] Finally, a draft text was presented in the Brussels Ministerial Meeting on 3 December 1990 containing an admixture of

33 GATT, Suggestion by the United States for Achieving the Negotiating Objective: Revision (1988) MTN.GNG/NG11/W/14/Rev.1, par III.D.6.

34 GATT, Standards and Principles Concerning the Availability, Scope and Use of Trade-Related Intellectual Property Rights, Communication from Switzerland: Addendum On Proprietary Information (1989) MTN.GNG/NG11/W/ 38/Add.1, para2(v).

35 The European Communities also proposed trade secret protection in their submission, though there was no mention of protection of test data against third party/government use or disclosure. See GATT, Guidelines and Objectives Proposed by the European Community for the Negotiations on Trade-Related Aspects of Substantive Standards of Intellectual Property Rights (1988) MTN.GNG/NG11/W/26, para III.D.3(g). The Canadian delegation also submitted their initial proposal containing provisions related to trade secrets. See GATT, Standards for Trade-Related Intellectual Property Rights, Submission from Canada (1989) MTN.GNG/NG11/W/47, 1989, para 18.H.

36 GATT, Meeting of Negotiating Group of 12–14 July 1989: Note by the Secretariat, MTN. GNG/NG11/14, 1989, para 90.

37 GATT, Draft Agreement on Trade-Related Aspects of Intellectual Property Rights (1990) MTN.GNG/NG11/W/68, Article 28.

38 GATT, Status of Work in the Negotiating Group: Chairman's Report to the GNG, MTN. GNG/NG11/W/76, 1990, Article 33.

39 GATT, Draft Amendment to the General Agreement on Tariffs and Trade on the Protection of Trade-Related Intellectual Property Rights: Communication from Switzerland (1990) MTN.GNG/ NG11/W/73, Article 243(1).

40 GATT, Communication from Argentina, Brazil, Chile, China, Colombia Cuba, Egypt, India, Nigeria, Peru, Tanzania and Uruguay (1990) MTN.GNG/NG11/W/71.

41 GATT, Status of Work in the Negotiating Group: Chairman's Report to the GNG (1990) MTN.GNG/NG11/W/76.

the US, European Communities and Swiss draft test data exclusivity proposals.[42] Accordingly, GATT Parties would protect test data against disclosure and *unfair commercial use*, which was taken to mean test data exclusivity. The Parties could not rely on the submitted test data without permission, for at least five years. The only exception to protection against disclosure was to protect the public. The various qualifying conditions such as new pharmaceutical or agricultural chemical product, considerable effort, etc. were retained from the EC's draft proposal. Most of the operative text of Paragraph 3 was in square brackets meaning that there was no consensus on the text of the provision.

The GATT negotiations continued in the new decade and the final draft of TRIPS was produced on 20 December 1991. Article 39(3) of the draft provided for test data protection. Square brackets from the paragraph were removed. But so was the reference to test data exclusivity! This meant that the test data exclusivity was no longer the authoritative interpretation of "unfair commercial use". The relationship with the unfair competition rules of the Paris Convention (Article 10*bis*) was also retained through Article 39(1). The reference to protection against unauthorized disclosure was retained in Article 39(3) that would be waived when necessary to protect public or where the data is protected against unfair commercial use. Eventually, Article 39(3) of the final draft became Article 39(3) of the TRIPS Agreement.[43]

The failure to include an explicit reference to test data exclusivity in the TRIPS Agreement made its proposers active on other fronts. For example, the US pressured its trading partners through various means, to provide test data exclusivity in their domestic laws.[44] For instance, selected countries that did not provide test data exclusivity were put on one of the lists of the *301 Special Report*[45] and

42 GATT, Draft Final Act Embodying The Results Of The Uruguay Round Of Multilateral Trade Negotiations: Revision (1990) MTN.TNC/W/35/Rev.1, Annex III, Article 42(3).

43 Article 39(3) TRIPS read as follows:

> Members, when requiring, as a condition of approving the marketing of pharmaceutical or of agricultural chemical products which utilize new chemical entities, the submission of undisclosed test or other data, the origination of which involves a considerable effort, shall *protect such data against unfair commercial use.* In addition, Members shall *protect such data against disclosure*, except where necessary to protect the public, or unless steps are taken to ensure that the data are protected against unfair commercial use.

44 This happened despite the fact that unilateral pressure to provide TRIPS-plus in domestic law runs afoul of Article 1(1) TRIPS, which states that "Members may, but shall not be obliged to, implement in their law more extensive protection than is required by this Agreement, provided that such protection does not contravene the provisions of this Agreement."

45 §182 of the US Trade Act (1974) requires the US Trade Representative (USTR) to identify countries that "deny adequate and effective protection of [IPRs]" or "deny fair and equitable market access to United States persons that rely upon [IP] protection". For explanation of different categories in which trading partners are classified see United States International Trade Commission (USITC), The Year in Trade 2009, Operation of the Trade Agreements Program, 61st Report (2010) 2–9, www.usitc.gov/publications/332/pub4174.pdf, accessed 8 December 2015.

threatened with trade sanctions such as withdrawal of benefits under the Generalized System of Preferences (GSP). Hence, Australia featured on the "Watch List" solely for failing to provide adequate test data protection in 1996[46] followed by Denmark in 1997[47] and South Africa in 1998.[48] Among the developing countries, Argentina was put on the "Priority Watch List" in both 1997 and 1998 for not providing protection to test data exclusivity.[49] In 2000, the US requested for consultation with Argentina under the WTO rules. It was alleged that "Argentina fails to protect against unfair commercial use of undisclosed test or other data, submitted as a requirement for market approval of pharmaceutical or agricultural chemical products" in accordance with the requirements of Article 39(3) TRIPS.[50] However, a "Mutually Agreed Solution" was notified to the WTO by the two countries where the two parties "reached an agreement on all of the matters raised by the US".[51] Hence, to this date there has been no authoritative interpretation from a WTO Dispute Settlement body as to what is meant by "protection against unfair commercial use".

Free trade and intellectual property agreements

US FTAs

Because of the failure to include test data exclusivity in the TRIPS Agreement, its proposers pushed it through bilateral and regional trade agreements. The trend started as early as 1994 with the conclusion of the North American Free Trade Agreement (NAFTA) between the US, Canada and Mexico. Article 1711(5) of NAFTA is similar to Article 39(3) TRIPS to the extent of protection against disclosure. The innovation over TRIPS is Article 1711(6), which provides for test data exclusivity for a period of normally not less than five years from the date of approval of the originator pharmaceutical. As per Article 1711(7) where reliance

46 United States Trade Representative (USTR), *USTR Announces Two Decisions: Title VII and Special 301*, (1996) 11, http://keionline.org/sites/default/files/ustr_special301_1996.pdf, accessed 8 December 2015.

47 United States Trade Representative (USTR), *USTR Report on Special 301 Annual Review*, (30 April 1997) [hereinafter "USTR (1997)"] , www.keionline.org/ustr/1997special301, accessed 8 December 2015.

48 United States Trade Representative (USTR), *USTR Announces Results of Special 301 Annual Review*, (1998) 21 [hereinafter "USTR (1998)"], www.keionline.org/sites/default/files/ustr_special301_1998.pdf, accessed 8 December 2015.

49 USTR (1997); USTR (1998), 10.

50 WTO, "Argentina – Certain Measures on the Protection of Patents and Test Data: Request for Consultations by the United States" (2000), WT/DS/196/1 and IP/D/22.

51 WTO, "Argentina – Patent Protection for Pharmaceuticals and Test Data Protection for Agricultural Chemicals" (WT/DS171); "Argentina – Certain Measures on the Protection of Patents and Test Data" (WT/DS196); "Notification of Mutually Agreed Solution According to the Conditions set forth in the Agreement" (2002) WT/DS171/3 and WT/DS196/4.

is made on an originator product's foreign approval, exclusivity would start from the date of that approval. Similar provisions were included in Intellectual Property Agreements with Sri Lanka, Ecuador, Latvia and Cambodia.[52]

In October 2000, the US signed an FTA with Jordan that contained test data exclusivity provisions. Its wording is identical to Article 39(3) TRIPS and further provides for exclusivity at least for the same period as in the US (Article 4.22 read with footnote 11). Moreover, it provided for three years' exclusivity for new uses/indications of already approved chemical entities (footnote 10). Australia, Singapore and select others introduced test data exclusivity protection in their domestic laws in the 1990s as well.

Since 2000, the US has concluded 11 FTAs that include provisions on test data exclusivity. FTA partners include Singapore and Chile in 2003, Australia, Morocco, CAFTA-DR and Bahrain in 2004, Oman Colombia and Peru in 2006, and Korea and Panama in 2007. For each agreement the US relied on a template provision, tweaked for regional and economic differences. For example, Colombia, Peru and Panama have provisions that are identical to NAFTA test data exclusivity provisions (NAFTA Model). On the other hand, Bahrain and Oman have almost identical provisions (Middle East Model). However, FTAs with countries like Singapore, Korea and Australia differ from others in details.

The standard period of test data exclusivity in the US FTAs is five years, although, in FTAs with Australia, Singapore, Korea and those based on the Middle East Model, this is a minimum period. In NAFTA Model FTAs, there is a possibility of curtailing the period based on a case-by-case analysis. On the other hand, NAFTA Model FTAs require *data* exclusivity[53] whereas the others require *market* exclusivity.[54] Reliance on foreign marketing approvals is prohibited in Australia, Singapore, Korea, and Middle East Model FTAs and CAFTA-DR. Middle East Model FTAs and those with Australia and Korea provide for additional three-year test data exclusivity for new uses/indications.

US FTAs also relax various Article 39(3) TRIPS conditions. For example, Singapore, Korea and Middle East Model FTAs do not require that test data be undisclosed.[55] The Singapore FTA, arguably, also covers biologics. The chemical entities do not have to be universally new, a flexibility present in Article 39(3) TRIPS as well as in NAFTA and the Jordan FTA.[56] Similarly, the requirement of

52 See www.tcc.export.gov/Trade_Agreements/Intellectual_Property_Rights/index.asp, accessed 8 December 2015.

53 Under *data* exclusivity, the DRA cannot accept generics application relying on the test data until the exclusivity period ends. This provides a *de facto* exclusivity to the originator product equal to the time taken by the DRA to approve the generics product.

54 Under *market* exclusivity, the DRA can accept the generics application within the test data exclusivity period. However, generics can only be launched after this period ends.

55 Ironically, the *undisclosed* nature of the test data was the main argument for its protection.

56 These FTAs provide that "a *new product* is one that does not contain a chemical entity that has been previously approved for marketing in the Party". See, for example, Article 17.10.1(d) US–Australia FTA.

considerable effort is absent from Australia, Singapore, Chile and Middle East Model FTAs as well as the CAFTA-DR.

US FTAs do not contain many exceptions to test data exclusivity protection. Provisions on public interest measures are absent from most FTAs. In Bahrain, Oman and Morocco FTAs, *side letters* for protection of public health have been issued with ambiguous practicality and usefulness.[57] Therefore in the later FTAs with Peru, Colombia, Panama and Korea the text of side letters was included in the main text of the FTA "to eliminate any ambiguity in future".[58]

EFTA FTAs

The European Free Trade Association has concluded 14 FTAs containing provisions on test data exclusivity. They include FTAs with Chile in 2003, with Lebanon and Tunisia in 2004, with Korea in 2005, with Egypt in 2007, with Colombia in 2008, with Serbia and Albania in 2009, with Peru and Ukraine in 2010, with Hong Kong and Montenegro in 2011, and with Central American States (Costa Rica and Panama) and Bosnia and Herzegovina in 2013.

Most EFTA FTAs provide that undisclosed information should be protected in accordance with Article 39 TRIPS. This means that all the limitations of Article 39(3) are automatically incorporated in these FTAs unless they are specifically contracted out. The latter is true for more recent EFTA FTAs. For example, EFTA FTAs with Hong Kong, Central America, Montenegro, and Bosnia and Herzegovina extend test data protection to biological products, unlike Article 39(3) TRIPS which limits exclusivity to pharmaceutical products containing a chemical entity. In the case of the Central America FTA, Article 39(3)'s requirement of considerable effort is also removed.

In addition, most EFTA FTAs require stringent *data* exclusivity[59] with exceptions only in Chile, Colombia, Peru and Egypt FTAs. Test data exclusivity for new uses or indications is provided in recent Ukraine, Bosnia and Herzegovina, and Montenegro FTAs. However, reliance on foreign approval of the originator product is allowed. The downside of EFTA FTAs is the duration of the exclusivity. Half of the EFTA FTAs, including the recent ones, require protection for more than five years. For example, duration in Serbia, Albania, Hong Kong, Bosnia and Herzegovina and Montenegro FTAs is eight years.

57 For instance, these side letters only allow FTA partners to take *necessary* measures for protection of public health in contrast to the Doha Declaration that did not use this qualifier. See Bryan Mercurio, "TRIPS-Plus Provisions in FTAs: Recent Trends" in Lorand Bartels and Federico Ortino (eds), *Regional Trade Agreements and the WTO Legal System* (Oxford: Oxford University Press, 2006) 234.

58 Committee on Ways and Means – US Congress H. Rept. 108–627, Report from the Committee on Ways and Means to Accompany H.R. 4842, United States–Morocco Free Trade Agreement Implementation Act, together with additional views (2004), 23–4, www.gpo.gov/fdsys/pkg/CRPT-108hrpt627/pdf/CRPT-108hrpt627.pdf, accessed 8 December 2015.

59 See n. 53.

The EFTA FTAs are more problematic than the US FTAs when it comes to exceptions to test data exclusivity. Only the Colombia and Peru FTAs contain reference to the Doha Declaration. Reliance on test data against compensation is provided only in the Lebanese, Tunisian and Korean FTAs. When recent EFTA FTAs are compared with earlier ones, it becomes clear that the EFTA is gradually raising the test data exclusivity bar.

EU FTAs

The EU only began including data exclusivity provisions in 2010 and has concluded lesser FTAs containing provisions on test data exclusivity. The exclusivity appears in EU FTAs concluded with Peru (Colombia was later added) and Korea in 2010, Central America (Panama, Guatemala, Costa Rica, El Salvador, Honduras and Nicaragua) in 2012 and with Moldova, Georgia and Singapore in 2013.

All EU FTAs, except that with Georgia, require protection for a period of five years. In the FTA with Peru and Colombia it is *normally* for a period of five years whereas in the Korean, Central American and Singaporean FTAs it is the minimum period of protection. Peru and Colombia, Central America and Singapore FTAs require *market* exclusivity,[60] whereas the Korean FTA requires *data* exclusivity.[61] Exclusivity for new uses/indications is absent in these FTAs.

The approach in Moldovan and Georgian FTAs is slightly different. The Georgian FTA requires six years of *data* exclusivity as well as one year of exclusivity for a new use/indication if the application for this indication is filed within the *data* exclusivity period. The Moldovan FTA is a combination of five years of *data* exclusivity, an overlapping seven years of *market* exclusivity and a one-year exclusivity for new uses/indications.[62] Both Georgia (Article 187(5)) and Moldova (Article 315(5)) are required to ultimately align their domestic laws with the EU standards to become an EU member state.

As compared to Article 39(3), the EU FTAs have a broader scope. For example, all EU FTAs, except that with Peru and Colombia, can be interpreted as requiring protection of biologics' test data. Similarly, no EU FTA, except Peru and Colombia and Korea, include considerable effort requirement. In most cases, it is also hard to argue for public interest exception to test data exclusivity in these FTAs, even though reference to the Doha Declaration is explicitly provided with regard to patents in some cases (Article 10.34 Korea-EU FTA, Article 313 Moldova-EU FTA and Article 185 Georgia-EU FTA). Reference to the Doha Declaration with respect to test data exclusivity is limited to Peru and Colombia and Central America FTAs. A special feature of EU FTAs is that all of them allow parties to

60 Ibid (n. 59).
61 Ibid (n. 58)
62 Article 315(2). This structure is similar to the EU law, which also provides for all three types of exclusivities.

take measures against anti-competitive use of test data exclusivity. The EU FTAs also do not restrain generic applicants from relying on foreign approvals.

Trans-Pacific Partnership (TPP) Agreement

The Trans-Pacific Partnership Agreement (TPP) is one of the most recent regional trade agreements that includes provisions on test data exclusivity. The TPP represents 40 per cent of the global gross domestic product (GDP), which demonstrates its importance in world trade.[63] The negotiating parties to the TPP include both developed and developing countries.[64] The draft TPP Agreement provides five-year test data exclusivity protection for both chemical[65] and biological pharmaceutical products (which can be increased up to eight years for the latter).[66] The generics applicants cannot rely on foreign marketing approvals as well. An additional three-year exclusivity is provided when new clinical information is submitted with the application for new indication of a previously approved pharmaceutical. A provision on protection of public health is also included that is structured on similar provisions in other US FTAs.[67]

National laws in the new millennium

There has been a flurry of national laws adopted in the first decade of the new millennium. These laws were primarily driven by the FTA commitments. The EU and the US modified their national laws as well.

The EU's test data exclusivity system was overhauled by Directive 2004/27/EC.[68] The Directive harmonized the exclusivity regime across the EU by providing eight year's *data* exclusivity, overlapping ten years' *market* exclusivity and an additional year of new use/indication exclusivity if the application for approval is filed within the *data* exclusivity period. The new use/indication must also show significant clinical benefits over existing therapies.

The US implemented law for approval of follow-on biological pharmaceuticals or biosimilars through the Biologics Price Competition and Innovation Act of 2009 (BPCIA), in 2010.[69] Unlike the Hatch-Waxman Act, the BPCIA combines

63 "After Trans-Pacific Partnership Deal Reached in Atlanta, Focus Shifts to Ratification" (*Bridges*, 8 October 2015), www.ictsd.org/bridges-news/bridges/news/after-trans-pacific-partnership-deal-reached-in-atlanta-focus-shifts-to, accessed 8 December 2015.

64 The negotiating countries, apart from the US, include Canada, Mexico, Chile, Peru, Australia, New Zealand, Brunei Darussalam, Japan, Malaysia, Singapore and Vietnam.

65 Article 18.50.

66 Article 18.52.

67 Article 18.50.3.

68 The EU repealed Directive 65/65/EC of 26 January 1965 through Directive 2001/83/EC of 6 November 2001but the substance of the test data exclusivity regime remained unchanged.

69 Unlike pharmaceuticals containing chemical entities, it is not possible to have an identical version of a biopharmaceutical (or biologic). Hence, the generic versions of biopharmaceuticals are either called follow-on biologics or biosimilars. Under the US law, a biosimilar is a pharmaceutical, which is "highly similar" to a biopharmaceutical and which does not have

both *data* and *market* exclusivities: providing for four years of data exclusivity and an overlapping 12 years of market exclusivity. Moreover, under BPCIA there is no requirement for the biological entity to be new. Theoretically at least, a biosimilar may also be filed as a biologic (though in this case it will have to provide a complete test data dossier) and receive test data exclusivity protection. This option is especially attractive as the cost difference between the two is not significant. The BPCIA also does not provide for exclusivity for subsequent modifications in the biologic.

Most of the countries that concluded FTAs with the US, EU and EFTA also enacted domestic laws to give effect to the test data exclusivity provisions of the FTAs.

The developments in the last few years show that test data exclusivity protection has spread both in scope and in breadth. The length of protection has been extended under more recent FTAs and national laws; test data relating to biologics have also been included in the fold of protection; an increasing number of countries have introduced test data exclusivity in their national laws and exceptions to the exclusivity are neither well understood nor well implemented. The existing test data exclusivity provisions are highly complex and vary between FTAs and national laws. The IDEAS framework discussed in the next section attempts to bring order to this confusing and chaotic area.

Index of Data Exclusivity and Access (IDEAS)

The Index of Data Exclusivity and Access (IDEAS) has been developed based on relevant provisions in 35 FTAs and 23 national laws. The use of indexes in the field of intellectual property law and policy is hardly new.[70] IDEAS, nonetheless, is an innovation over existing indexes in two important ways. It is, to my knowledge, the only index that compares FTAs and implementing laws. Moreover, other indexes assess strength of IP protection, whereas IDEAS measures the strength of an FTA and the national law provision in improving access to medicine in the presence of test data exclusivity (i.e., how much flexibility it includes for promoting access to both originator and generics medicine).[71]

"clinically meaningful differences in terms of safety, purity and potency" with the biopharmaceutical it is similar to.: 42 U.S.C. § 262(i)(2). For a brief introduction of biologics see United States Food and Drug Administration, *FDA 101: Biological Products*, www.fda.gov/downloads/ForConsumers/ConsumerUpdates/ucm048367.pdf, 2008, accessed 2 June 2014.

70 For a literature review of the existing IP indexes see GIPC, Global Intellectual Property Center, U.S. Chamber of Commerce, "Measuring Momentum: GIPC International IP Index" (2012) 10–2, www.theglobalipcenter.com/wp-content/uploads/2013/01/020119_GIPCIndex_final1.pdf, accessed 8 December 2015. With regard to the structure of IDEAS, the closest index is that developed by Ginarte and Park. See Juan C. Ginarte and Walter G. Park, "Determinants of Patent Rights: A Cross-national Study" (1997) 26 Research Policy, 283–301.

71 For the full analysis of test data exclusivity provisions in 35 FTAs and 23 national laws on IDEAS see Owais Shaikh, Access to Medicine versus Test Data Exclusivity: safeguarding flexibilities under international law, (Berlin: Springer, 2016) 129–208.

IDEAS determines the extent to which test data exclusivity provisions in an FTA and the implementing law enhance access to medicine. IDEAS provides an objective framework for comparison of such provisions across multiple FTAs, between an FTA and the implementing law, across different national laws and other combinations. For example, data exclusivity provisions of geographically proximate FTAs/national laws can be analysed on IDEAS. Similarly, provisions can be analysed according to hub and spoke relationships (for example US as hub and FTA parties as spokes), etc.

IDEAS ranks the FTA and national law provisions on test data exclusivity based on how much flexibility they provide for access to medicine. It quantifies aspects of test data exclusivity provisions by assigning them a value between 0 (least access) to 4 (most access). This is done by answering 25 questions about the provision itself. These questions are separated into four categories – namely:

1 Category A: Proximity to Article 39(3) TRIPS (six questions);
2 Category B: Strength of test data exclusivity protection (six questions);
3 Category C: Duration of test data exclusivity protection (seven questions);
4 Category D: Inclusion of exceptions/access enabling provisions (six questions).

The questions have binary answers – *yes* or *no* – except in the case of length of test data exclusivity. The latter is expressed as an inverse percentage of maximum ten years' protection using the protection duration under the EU law as the base. For example, test data exclusivity of six years will be expressed as 0.4 on IDEAS (1–6/10).

FTAs on IDEAS

Analysing the various aspects of test data exclusivity provisions in different FTAs on categories A to D provides a clear picture in terms of the winners and losers in respect of access to medicine. Table 4.1 ranks in descending order various test data exclusivity provisions in FTAs according to the responsiveness to access to medicine.

With a score of 3.17, the Peru–EFTA FTA is the most pro-access FTA analysed under this framework. Its score on categories A and B are 1 out of 1 showing that it includes all the respective flexibilities in these two categories. Moreover, it is also the only FTA that scores above 3 on IDEAS.

On the other end is the Australia–US FTA with a score of 1.17. As can be seen, its individual category scores are pretty dismal except for Category A. This shows that the Australia–US FTA is weak on flexibilities on the whole and not just on certain specific aspects. Hong Kong is half way on the scale with 2. It is strong on the first two categories but weak on the latter two.

The mean of all FTAs scores on IDEAS is 2.16 (the dotted circle in Figure 4.1), which is very close to midpoint of the scale (i.e., 2), despite the fact that 24 out of the 35 FTAs plotted on IDEAS are above the midpoint.

Figure 4.1 also provides a comparison of the US, the EU and the EFTA FTAs with each other and among themselves (7 out of 13 US FTAs, 11 out of 14 EFTA FTAs and 5 out of 8 EU).

Table 4.1 FTA ranking and scores on IDEAS

			Category Scores			
Rank	*Countries*[72]	*IDEAS Score*	*A*	*B*	*C*	*D*
1	PE (EFTA)	3.17	1.00	1.00	0.50	0.67
2	CO (EFTA)	3.00	0.83	1.00	0.50	0.67
2	PE & CO (EU)	2.83	0.67	1.00	0.50	0.67
4	NAFTA (US)	2.67	1.00	0.83	0.50	0.33
5	PE (US)	2.67	1.00	0.67	0.50	0.50
6	PA (US)	2.67	1.00	0.67	0.50	0.50
6	CO (US)	2.67	1.00	0.67	0.50	0.50
6	CL (US)	2.55	0.83	1.00	0.21	0.50
9	TN (EFTA)	2.52	1.00	0.83	0.36	0.33
9	KR (EFTA)	2.52	1.00	0.83	0.36	0.33
9	EG (EFTA)	2.52	1.00	1.00	0.36	0.17
12	CL (EFTA)	2.38	1.00	1.00	0.21	0.17
12	Cent. Am. (EU)	2.38	0.67	1.00	0.21	0.50
14	CA (EU)	2.37	1.00	0.83	0.20	0.33
15	CAFTA-DR (US)	2.36	0.67	0.67	0.36	0.67
16	JO (US)	2.31	1.00	0.83	0.31	0.17
17	SG (EU)	2.21	0.50	1.00	0.21	0.50
18	LB (EFTA)	2.20	1.00	0.83	0.20	0.17
19	RS (EFTA)	2.17	1.00	0.83	0.17	0.17
19	AL (EFTA)	2.17	1.00	0.83	0.17	0.17
21	UA (EFTA)	2.06	1.00	0.67	0.23	0.17
22	Cent. Am. (EFTA)	2.05	0.67	0.83	0.21	0.33
22	KR (EU)	2.05	0.67	0.83	0.21	0.33
24	HK (EFTA)	2.00	0.83	0.83	0.17	0.17
25	UA (EU)	1.71	0.33	0.83	0.21	0.33
26	GE (EU)	1.70	0.33	0.83	0.19	0.33
26	MD (EU)	1.70	0.50	0.67	0.20	0.33
28	MA (US)	1.67	0.50	0.50	0.17	0.50
29	ME (EFTA)	1.66	0.67	0.67	0.16	0.17
29	BA (EFTA)	1.66	0.67	0.67	0.16	0.17
31	OM (US)	1.50	0.50	0.33	0.17	0.50
31	BH (US)	1.50	0.50	0.33	0.17	0.50
31	KR (US)	1.50	0.67	0.33	0.17	0.33
34	SG (US)	1.38	0.33	0.67	0.21	0.17
35	AU (US)	1.17	0.67	0.17	0.17	0.17

72 For full country names, see the Annex at the end of this chapter.

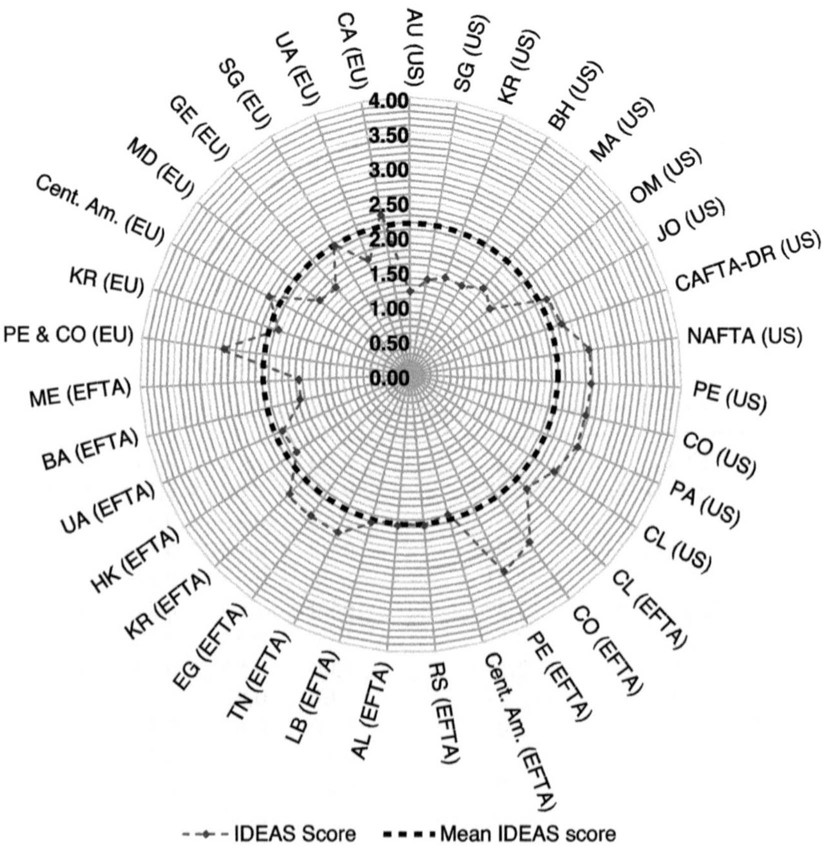

Figure 4.1 Comparison of FTAs on IDEAS

Twenty FTAs are above the mean FTA score. Moreover, when the scores are categorized geographically, the FTAs from the Americas, especially those of Peru, Colombia and Chile, consistently score higher as compared to the countries of other regions. Eight of the top ten FTAs are with the countries of the Americas.

National laws on IDEAS

The national provisions on test data exclusivity can also be assessed on IDEAS. In this analysis national laws of 23 countries have been included as they have at least one FTA containing test data exclusivity requirement. This allows a cross-comparison between the FTA obligation and its implementation in the national law.

Table 4.2 shows that Peru's national law provisions on test data exclusivity are most responsive to access to medicine among the laws analysed on IDEAS.

Table 4.2 National law ranking and scores on IDEAS

			Category Scores			
Rank	*Countries*	*IDEAS Score*	*A*	*B*	*C*	*D*
1	PE	2.50	0.83	0.50	0.50	0.67
2	CL	2.17	0.67	0.67	0.50	0.33
3	MX	2.02	1.00	0.50	0.36	0.17
4	EG	1.86	0.83	0.67	0.36	0.00
5	CR	1.71	0.67	0.67	0.21	0.17
6	DO	1.69	0.67	0.50	0.36	0.17
6	CO	1.69	0.67	0.50	0.36	0.17
8	JO	1.55	0.83	0.50	0.21	0.00
8	PA	1.55	0.50	0.50	0.21	0.33
10	SV	1.52	0.83	0.33	0.36	0.00
10	GT	1.52	0.67	0.50	0.36	0.00
12	UA	1.51	0.33	0.67	0.34	0.17
13	HN	1.36	0.50	0.50	0.36	0.00
14	NI	1.21	0.67	0.33	0.21	0.00
15	CA	1.18	0.50	0.33	0.34	0.00
16	BH	1.17	0.83	0.17	0.17	0.00
17	OM	0.84	0.67	0.00	0.17	0.00
18	ME	0.82	0.33	0.00	0.16	0.33
18	AU	0.71	0.33	0.17	0.21	0.00
20	SG	0.71	0.17	0.17	0.21	0.17
21	RS	0.66	0.33	0.00	0.16	0.17
22	KR	0.64	0.00	0.50	0.14	0.00
23	HK	0.50	0.33	0.00	0.17	0.00

However, with a score of 2.50 on the scale of 4, the Peruvian law scores far below that of its FTAs.[73] Hong Kong is last on this table with only 0.50, much below the score of 2.00 in its FTA with EFTA. This shows that the national provision on test data exclusivity in Hong Kong seriously lacks inclusion of various flexibilities that were part of the FTA itself.

Figure 4.2 maps national law scores and enables their comparison with each other as well as with their mean and the corresponding FTAs scores.

Figure 4.2 reveals stark difference between the FTAs scores and those of the national provisions on test data exclusivity. The gap between the national law and FTA scores reveal that countries do not implement all the flexibilities available under respective FTA provisions. This gap is especially wide in the case of Hong

73 For countries having more than one FTA, a "Final FTA" score has been calculated and the national law is compared with that score in Figure 4.2.

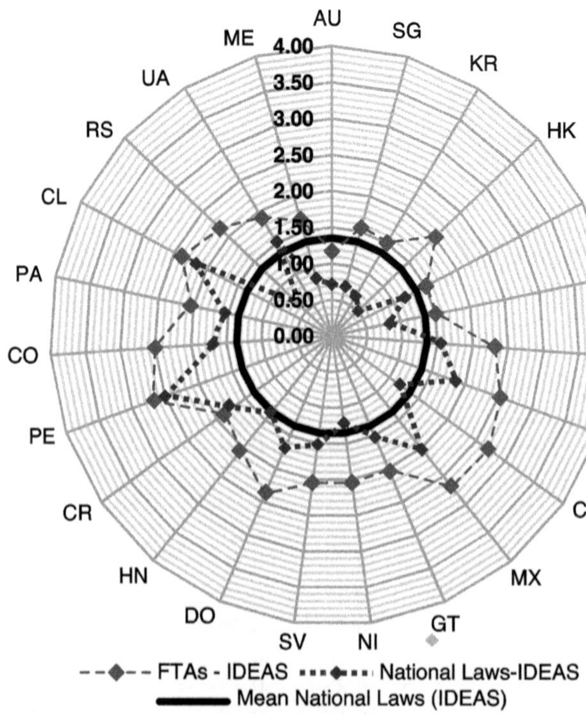

Figure 4.2 Comparison of national laws on IDEAS

Kong, Canada and Serbia. The mean of national law scores is a dismal 1.35, far below IDEAS midpoint. 10 out of 23 national laws are below the mean score. Moreover, 7 national laws score below 1 whereas the lowest FTA score was 1.17 – that of Australia–US FTA. Similarly, unlike the FTAs, none of the national laws has a score above 3.

IDEAS shows that the national provisions on test data exclusivity as compared to the corresponding FTA provisions are much less access oriented. And this is a major concern as measures for promotion access to medicine can only be undertaken if they are available under the national laws.

Implications and recommendations

As discussed above, in the last 13 years, the obligations in the US, the EFTA and the EU FTAs drove an increasing number of countries to introduced test data exclusivity in their domestic laws. This is despite the absence of convincing empirical evidence regarding fruition of promises attached with this exclusivity. In fact, the evidence is contrary as presented in the 'Introduction' above. There is, indeed, an immediate need for studying the impact of test data exclusivity in developing countries that have introduced it more than five years ago.

During the Uruguay Round, the collective opposition of the majority of the negotiating parties resulted in the removal of the reference to test data exclusivity from Article 39(3) TRIPS. Unfortunately, this unity did not carry through later, at least not outside the multilateral platform of the WTO. Most countries failing to realize the growing importance of intellectual property in international trade negotiations and ultimately under national laws, did not produce a sustainable human resource that could provide valuable input in the area of IP. The failure to understand the economic and social impact of IP in the medium- and long-run led many countries to bargain it in return for increased market access in the other party's market under FTAs. This is ironic as the quantitative barriers would any way come down sooner than later and the benefits of preferential trade would erode,[74] whereas compromises made with respect to IP without having any regard to local innovation, competition as well as access, are not time limited.

It is high time for countries to understand the loss in the bargain made by accepting test data exclusivity obligations in trade agreements. For their own sake, they have struck a deal with dubious impact on innovation and an assured negative impact on access to medicine. But more than that they may have shifted the interpretation of the TRIPS Agreement to their detriment! The success achieved by retaining the flexibility to interpret "protection against unfair commercial use" in line with their specific economic and social needs is gradually eroding. With more countries adopting rules on test data exclusivity, the danger that test data exclusivity would become the exclusive interpretation of "protection against unfair commercial use" is becoming real. IFPMA estimates that around 50 countries already have either national laws or international obligations in this area.[75] Countries eager to enter the EU Single Market have to provide test data exclusivity as part of their commitment to align their laws with that of the EU *acquis*.[76] The same is foreseen with countries that are part of the European Neighbourhood Policy[77] and probably the countries with whom the EU has signed interim trade agreements.[78] On the other hand, the US shift from bilateral to regional trade deals appears to expedite the spread of TRIPS-plus obligations including test data exclusivity.

74 Jan Wouters and Bart De Meester, *The World Trade Organization: A Legal and Institutional Analysis* (Antwerp: Intersentia, 2007) 34–44.

75 IFPMA (2000).

76 Countries applying for EU Membership have to adopt, implement and enforce current intellectual property rules of the EU. European Commission, *Enlargement: Conditions for Membership*, 2013, www.ec.europa.eu/enlargement/policy/conditions-membership/index_en.htm, accessed 8 December 2015.

77 European External Action Service, *European Neighbourhood Policy (ENP)*, www.eeas.europa.eu/enp/index_en.htm, accessed 8 December 2015.

78 These interim agreements do not contain substantive provisions on intellectual property. However, they contain *Rendezvous Clauses* regarding inclusion of IP in ultimate trade agreements with the EU. See, for example, Article 37 of the Framework Economic Partnership Agreement between the EU and the countries of the East African Community.

Amongst all this, the Most-Favoured Nation principle in the TRIPS Agreement (Article 4) exacerbates the problem by requiring that privileges, favours and advantages granted by one country to another would also be unconditionally granted to other WTO Members. Hence, test data exclusivity provisions may be part of a bilateral agreement, but their effect is plurilateral.

Nonetheless, it is still possible for those countries that have already introduced test data exclusivity as an FTA obligation to manage the damage. Similarly, countries that are in the negotiation stage of an FTA or those that are going to enter into one, can also prepare themselves before they haggle on test data exclusivity and market access options.

Managing the damage

Countries having commitments regarding test data exclusivity in FTAs should explore national laws of the countries having similar FTA provisions. This will provide new interpretive insights with regard to implementation of the provision. Countries that negotiated an FTA before the Doha Declaration should incorporate it in the main text ensuring that it is used in interpreting the FTA test data exclusivity provisions.

Countries should also analyse FTAs of their FTA partner(s) with other countries to assess what kind of concessions/flexibilities have been offered to others regarding test data exclusivity that may be absent from their FTAs. Once such concessions/flexibilities have been identified, FTAs may be renegotiated to incorporate them. At the same time, within their own FTAs and in others, the exceptions provided to patent protection, specially for protecting public health and promoting access to medicine, such as compulsory licensing (e.g., Article 17.9.7 Australia–US FTA and Article 16.7.6 Singapore–US FTA) may be made applicable *mutatis mutandis* to test data exclusivity. The most-favoured nation clause in the FTAs should be expanded to cover exceptions and limitations to test data exclusivity in other FTAs of the parties.[79] This will allow an automatic application of exceptions not included in the FTA.

Negotiating test data exclusivity provision

In addition to the above, countries should prepare beforehand for negotiating test data exclusivity in FTA. Only then a good deal can be had. As TRIPS does not require test data exclusivity, developing countries have ample room to construct a system incorporating maximum flexibilities if they have to include test data exclusivity in their FTA.

79 Max Planck Institute for Innovation and Competition (MPI), "Principles for Intellectual Property Provisions in Bilateral and Regional Agreements" (2013), para 25, www.ip.mpg.de/fileadmin/user_upload/Principles_for_IP_provisions_in_Bilateral_and_Regional_Agreements_final1.pdf, accessed 8 December 2015.

Countries must enter negotiations with a clear strategy and mandate regarding IP, generally, and test data exclusivity, especially.[80] Trading IP concessions against non-IP concessions lacks sustainability. With regard to test data exclusivity, it should only be on the negotiating table when there is gain in the same area, for example through assured investment in local production of originator pharmaceuticals. Assessing this gain would only be possible if prior impact assessment studies have been conducted.[81]

It is equally important that countries prepare their own negotiating text of test data exclusivity provisions and not simply accept the template by the other party. These templates fail to take into account specific economic and social conditions of individual countries and may not contain flexibilities incorporated in other FTAs.

Specifics of test data exclusivity provisions in FTAs

Test data exclusivity provisions in an FTA have different variables that can be adjusted to create a pro-access exclusivity regime.[82] For example, a reference to Article 39(3) TRIPS allows the conditions of that provision to be incorporated in the FTA, unless specifically contracted out. EFTA FTAs, except with Hong Kong, Costa Rica and Panama, Montenegro, and Bosnia and Herzegovina include such a provision. Similarly, specific reference can be made to Articles 7 (Objectives) and 8 (Principles) of the TRIPS Agreement (for example, Article 11.1 Singapore–EU FTA).

With regard to the duration, there is no requirement of having *at least five years* of exclusivity. This period has been adopted as a convention starting with the US Hatch-Waxman Act. Therefore, countries may negotiate for the shortest possible term of protection. Countries should also negotiate for *market* exclusivity rather than *data* exclusivity. The former paves the way to avoid a *de facto* exclusivity period and makes possible the use of "regulatory review exemption" for an applicable patent.[83] Similarly, the term of test data exclusivity must not be given

80 MPI (2013), paras 11–13.

81 See, for example, Paul Grootendorst and Aidan Hollis, "The Canada-European Union Comprehensive Economic & Trade Agreement: An Economic Impact Assessment of Proposed Pharmaceutical Intellectual Property Provisions" (2011), www.canadiangenerics.ca/en/news/docs/02.07.11CETAEconomicImpactAssessment-FinalEnglish.pdf, accessed 2 June 2014, for an assessment of the impact of the Canada–European Union Comprehensive Economic and Trade Agreement on pharmaceuticals.

82 In this regard also see Carlos M. Correa, "A Model Law for the Protection of Undisclosed Data" in Ricardo Meléndez-Ortiz and Pedro Roffe (eds), *Intellectual Property and Sustainable Development: Development Agendas in a Changing World* (Gloucestershire: Edward Elgar Publishing Limited, 2009) 370; and R. Weissman, "Data Protection: Options for Implementation" in Pedro Roffe, Geoff Tansy and David V. Eugui (eds), *Negotiating Health: Intellectual Property and Access To Medicines* (London: Earthscan, 2006) 151.

83 If the term of *data* exclusivity falls towards the end of the patent term, or exceeds it, regulatory review exemption may be rendered ineffective by prohibiting the regulatory authority from accepting the generics' application during the term of *data* exclusivity.

as a *minimum*. Rather, evidence shows that many FTAs provide the possibility to curtail the protection for less than the given period when needed (for example, Article 1711(6) NAFTA, Article 6.11.2 Colombia–EFTA FTA and Article 231(2) Peru–Colombia–EU FTA). Another provision present only in one FTA requires that the test data exclusivity period in one party must not exceed that in the originating country, the other party or in the exporting country (Article 4, Annex V Tunisia–EFTA FTA). This acts as an incentive for originator companies to apply for registration at the earliest for longer test data exclusivity protection.

FTAs also do not have to include protection against disclosure of test data where test data exclusivity is included. This is because Article 39(3) provides that WTO Members have an obligation to protect test data against disclosure except where protection against unfair commercial use of test data is provided.

Another provision to avoid in FTAs is the exclusivity for new use/indication, which has the potential to extend test data exclusivity perpetually, though with regard to specific uses and indications only. Historically, this exclusivity was not part of the EFTA FTA, but the recent ones with Ukraine, Montenegro and Bosnia and Herzegovina require this exclusivity. Same is true with the recent EU FTAs with Moldova and Georgia.

Most of the FTAs do not prohibit reliance on foreign marketing approval. Applicants of generic pharmaceuticals rely on foreign market approvals if the originator pharmaceutical product has not been approved in the country or has not been filed at all. In the latter case, a prohibition on reliance on a foreign market approval would result in total blackout of access to medication for specific ailments. Countries negotiating FTAs with the EU and EFTA should know that none of their current FTAs prohibit such reliance.

Apart from the above, many countries came up with creative solutions to restrict the exclusivity and its impact. For example, to assure that originator pharmaceuticals are launched in their markets, CAFTA-DR parties included in the FTA that test data exclusivity would only be available if the approval application is filed within five years of the first approval date (Article 15.10.1(b)). Article 4(d) of Decree 2085–2002 of Colombia and Article 91(d) Law 19039 of Chile require that after national approval the originator pharmaceutical product should be launched in the market within a specific period to enjoy continued test data exclusivity protection. The Canadian law provides that test data exclusivity is not applicable if originator products are not launched in the Canadian market (§ C.08.004.1 (5) Food and Drug Regulations).

Exceptions and limitations to test data exclusivity are conspicuously weak in the existing FTAs. As mentioned above, the Doha Declaration and reference to Articles 7 and 8 of the TRIPS Agreement should be included in the main FTA text. Unlike some FTAs, where these provisions are only applicable to patents (e.g., Article 10.34 Korea–EU FTA), countries can ensure that they are also applied in case of test data exclusivity. In the same manner, provisions on compulsory licensing should automatically apply to test data exclusivity. Language to this end must be included in the FTA to avoid any ambiguity. Another important mechanism absent from all FTAs is the opposition procedure with respect to the grant to test data exclusivity. It is only provided in the national law of Peru (Article 9 of Supreme Decree No. 002-2009-SA). Remedy against anti-competitive use of test data should also be part of the FTA, which is already provided in some FTAs of the US, the EU and the EFTA. FTAs may also require renewal of exclusivity throughout the term of protection, similar to patent renewals. An important alternative to test data exclusivity is reliance on test data against compensation (Article 4, Annex V Tunisia–EFTA FTA, Article 4, Annex V Lebanon–EFTA FTA and Article 3, Annex VIII Korea–EFTA FTA). Last but not the least, the preambles of the FTAs as well as general provisions on the chapter of IP should contain pro-access language. The preamble provides the overall framework of interpretation according to Article 31 of the Vienna Convention on the Law of Treaties.

Conclusion

The spread of test data exclusivity in national laws, especially of developing countries, at a rapid pace is a cause of concern. Countries have to realize that it is neither a standard in international IP law nor it is a bilateral issue. Their complicity in accepting test data exclusivity in their laws is gradually eroding the flexibility of Article 39 with regard to protection of test data against unfair commercial use. Countries becoming WTO Members now are required to provide for test data exclusivity. New WTO Members such as Russia and China accepted to introduce test data exclusivity for six years (one year more than required under the Hatch-Waxman Act in the US). Countries should collectively oppose or, if not possible then, create a more pro-access standard for test data exclusivity. Refusing to include test data exclusivity in FTAs is not unprecedented. Recently India opposed inclusion of a provision on the exclusivity in FTA negotiations with the EU that could jeopardize access to affordable generic pharmaceutical products for millions of people around the globe.

Countries should enter into FTA negotiations on test data exclusivity provisions after carefully considering their socio-economic and political imperatives. A careful analysis of FTAs of the other party should be undertaken. However, the exercise does not end here. Countries have creatively applied their FTA obligations related to test data exclusivity that can be studied for a better understanding and implementation. IDEAS provides an important framework for studying both the FTA and national law provisions. Its usefulness for policy-makers is especially in providing the information in a succinct and in depth manner.

Country codes in IDEAS

AU	Australia
BH	Bahrain
CA	Canada
CL	Chile
CO	Colombia
CR	Costa Rica
DO	Dominican Republic
EG	Egypt
SV	El Salvador
GT	Guatemala
HN	Honduras
HK	Hong Kong
JO	Jordan
KR	Korea
MX	Mexico
ME	Montenegro
NI	Nicaragua
OM	Oman
PA	Panama
PE	Peru
RS	Serbia
SG	Singapore
UA	Ukraine

5 Patent Linkage Regulations

The Importance of Context and of Balancing Competing Interests

Bryan Mercurio

Introduction

The pharmaceutical industry relies on innovation for its continued success and innovative companies spend billions of dollars annually on research and development (R&D) in order to develop the next generation of drugs. Humanity has without a doubt benefited, and continues to benefit, from industry development. Intellectual property rights (IPRs) play a key role in the pharmaceutical industry and in the advancement of R&D and innovation. While IPRs – and, more specifically, patents – are important for most industries and sectors, they are of particular importance to the pharmaceutical industry due to the high cost of product development, protracted product development timelines and the low rate of success with each new product line. For this reason, when a company develops a successful product it relies on the period of monopoly sales to recoup costs and provide incentive to reinvest profits into R&D in order to ensure it keeps producing innovative products. The granting of high-quality patents thus sustains the industry and benefits society.

Of course, the patent system balances the incentive to create with broader societal interests as governments seek to provide their populace with quality healthcare, including ample access to affordable and safe medicines, while at the same time restraining rising healthcare costs. In many jurisdictions, healthcare costs are rising both as a percentage of government spending and at a rate faster than gross domestic product (GDP),[1] necessitating cost-cutting measures such as

1 See, i.e., Amitabh Chandra, Jonathan Holmes and Jonathan Skinner, "Is This Time Different? The Slowdown in Healthcare Spending" (2013) Brookings Papers on Economic Activity 261, 264; European Commission Directorate-General for Economic and Financial Affairs European Economy, Economic Policy Committee, "The 2009 Ageing Report: Economic and Budgetary Projections for the EU-27 Member States (2008–2060) European Economy" (2009), Table 31, 127 (predicting total healthcare spending will rise from 6.7 per cent of the EU27's GDP in 2007 to 8.2 per cent in 2060); Masahiro Nozaki, Kenichiro Kashiwase and Ikuo Saito, "Health Spending in Japan: Macro-fiscal Implications and Reform Options" (August 2014) IMF Working Paper WP/14/142 38, 5, 13 (predicting healthcare spending will rise from 9.5 per cent of GDP in 2010 to between 13 and 15.5 per cent by 2030); William Hsiao and Winnie Yip, "China's Health Care Reform: A Tentative Assessment" (2009), 20, China Economic

the reduction of pharmaceutical expenditures through greater use of generic pharmaceuticals.[2]

This chapter focuses on patent linkage, which refers to the practice of national pharmaceutical registration authorities "linking" the granting of marketing approval – the right to market the drug – with the patent status of an originator drug,[3] thus preventing the relevant authority from granting marketing approval (i.e., registration of a generic drug for sale on the market) while the drug is under patent: without patent linkage, that is, the patent status of the pharmaceutical or any ingredient therein is simply irrelevant to the registration process. During recent years, as a result, patent linkage provisions have spread and led to many debates. Industry advocates argue that patent linkage protects IPRs, while others view it as simply adding to the rights of the patent holder and providing a "period of market exclusivity that is significantly extended beyond that for the originating patent (e.g., on the new active substance or new chemical entity)".[4] Regardless of one's position on the merits, with the industry seeking ways to extend monopoly selling periods, it is clear that pharmaceutical linkage "represent[s] a novel and evolving intellectual property paradigm for pharmaceutical products . . . [that is] rapidly evolving in a global context, and is poised to become an increasingly important determinant of the availability and cost of essential medications worldwide".[5]

Various factors must, however, be considered when evaluating the desirability and successes of patent linkage, including the policy intent behind implementation, public health and economic policy, clarity of the relevant laws and regulation as

Review 613, 614 (detailing the rise in healthcare spending of 16 per cent annually since the mid-1980s compared with an average growth rate of 7–8 per cent).

2 See, i.e., Hong Kong SAR 2012–13 Budget, Hong Kong Sar Finance Bureau 426 (2012), www.budget.gov.hk/2012/eng/pdf/e_budgetspeech2012-13.pdf; IMS Institute for Healthcare Informatics, "The Global Use of Medicines: Outlook through 2017", www.imshealth.com/en/thought-leadership/ims-institute/reports/global-use-of-medicines-outlook-through-2017 (November 2013) 2, 19 (predicting the share of generic pharmaceuticals in Japan to rise to 60 per cent by 2017 for a savings of between US$9–$11 billion dollars). See also Giuseppe Carone, Christoph Schwierz and Ana Xavier, "Cost-containment Policies in Public Pharmaceutical Spending in the EU" (2012), 2 European Economy, 461, Table 4, 13, 40–42 (a generic prescription rate of 80 per cent would reduce pharmaceutical spending by 33 per cent).

3 See Drug Price Competition and Patent Term Restoration Act, 1984, commonly known as the Hatch-Waxman Act. Drug Price Competition and Patent Term Restoration Act of 1984, 98 P.L. 417 (24 September 1984); 21 U.S.C.A. para 355(c)(3)(D) reprinted in 21 C.F.R. para 314.108 (1993). See also Bouchard et al (n. 5) 4.

4 Ron A. Bouchard, Richard W. Hawkins, Robert Clark, Reidar Hagtvedt and Jamil Sawani, "Empirical Analysis of Drug Approval-Drug Patenting Linkage for High Value Pharmaceuticals" (2010), 8, Northwestern Journal of Technology and Intellectual Property, 174, 176–177. See generally, Ron A. Bouchard, Jamil Sawani, Chris McLelland, Monika Sawicka and Richard W. Hawkins, "The Pas de Deux of Pharmaceutical Regulation and Innovation: Who's Leading Whom?" (2009), 24, Berkeley Technology Law Journal, 4, 1461.

5 Ron A. Bouchard et al, "Global Pharmaceutical Linkage Regulations: A Proposed Analytical Framework" (2011), 12, Minnesota Journal of Law, Science & Technology, 2, 1, 42.

well as the potential for judicial interpretation and other developments to influence or change the balance of competing health-related interests.[6]

This chapter therefore reviews the implementation of patent linkage in several jurisdictions before highlighting and evaluating critical factors which influence the economic and health-related effect of the regime. The second section briefly reviews the historical development and basics of patent linkage (from its beginnings in the US with the passage of the Hatch-Waxman Act) and surveys the implementation of patent linkage regulations in select jurisdictions. As such, it introduces the differences in each jurisdiction with a view to understanding the impact of patent linkage on the health and economics of a jurisdiction, the reasons for adopting patent linkage and the factors which should influence policy direction and choices regarding patent linkage. The third section offers critical commentary and analysis on key issues such as the policy justification for linking marketing approval to patent status, which patent or patents should be "linked", the use of injunctions to enforce patent linkage and the effect of patent linkage on competition. The fourth section concludes the chapter.

Development of patent linkage

Linking patent status to marketing approval

Patent linkage extends the monopoly selling period (or exclusivity) of an originator's pharmaceutical in the market by a period equal to the time it takes for a generic manufacturer to gain regulatory approval, usually between 6 and 24 months in developed markets. However, while the purpose of most patent linkage regulations is "to provide monopoly rights to private firms in exchange for new and innovative drugs while at the same time facilitating the timely entry of generic drugs",[7] public health advocates rather view such provisions as a means for extending monopoly pricing and delaying access to more affordable medicines.

The TRIPS Agreement does not mandate, or even mention, patent linkage. This is despite the existence of patent linkage in the US throughout the Uruguay Round negotiations which led to the creation of the TRIPS Agreement. Simply stated, the negotiating parties were aware of but chose not to include such protection in the international agreement. By not mentioning the subject, TRIPS neither requires nor prohibits patent linkage. Patent linkage is therefore a so-called "TRIPS-Plus" provision which lies beyond the mandate and scope of the World Trade Organization (WTO).[8] Nonetheless, since the US incorporated patent

6 See ibid 8.

7 Bouchard et al (n. 4), 181, FN 44 (citing numerous government Regulatory Impact Analysis Statements).

8 Patent linkage is therefore a so-called "TRIPS-Plus" provision which lies beyond the mandate and scope of the WTO. That being said, some countries, such as Cambodia, have agreed to include a strict form of patent linkage in its WTO accession package. See World Trade

linkage into its legislative framework, several other jurisdictions have followed the path. Most have agreed to introduce provisions as part of free trade agreements (FTAs) with the US, others have adopted such provisions without any external pressure. Patent linkage now exists in a diverse range of countries, including China, Japan, Mexico, South Korea, Singapore and Canada. In contrast, the European Union (EU) considers patent linkage to be unlawful.[9]

Most often patent linkage provisions include a notification requirement, and precludes the granting of marketing approval for a generic drug while the relevant patent remains in force (i.e., until it expires or is invalidated), or even prohibits health authorities from reviewing an application for marketing authorization while a patent remains in force. The recently negotiated US–Korea FTA (KORUS) provides an example of the patent linkage commitment:

> Where a Party permits, as a condition of approving the marketing of a pharmaceutical product, persons, other than the person originally submitting safety or efficacy information, to rely on that information or on evidence of safety or efficacy information of a product that was previously approved, such as evidence of prior marketing approval in the territory of the Party or in another territory, that Party shall:
>
> (a) provide that the patent owner shall be notified of the identity of any such other person that requests marketing approval to enter the market during the term of a patent notified to the approving authority as covering that product or its approved method of use; and
> (b) implement measures in its marketing approval process to prevent such other persons from marketing a product without the consent or acquiescence of the patent owner during the term of a patent notified to the approving authority as covering that product or its approved method of use.[10]

Organization, "Report of the Working Party on the Accession of Cambodia" (2003) 44, WT/ACC/KHM/21.

9 In contrast, the EU considers patent linkage to be unlawful; see art 81 of Regulation (EC) No. 726/2004 and art 10.6 and 126 of Directive (EC) No. 2001/83. See, further, the preliminary findings of the European Commission inquiry on the pharmaceutical industry: European Commission, "Pharmaceutical Sector Inquiry: Preliminary Report", DG Competition Staff Working Paper (28 November 2008), www.ec.europa.eu/competition/sectors/pharmaceuticals/inquiry/preliminary_report.pdf, 113, accessed 04/04/2016.

10 KORUS, art 18.9.5. For similar versions, see US–Oman FTA, art 15.9.4, Jan. 19, 2006; CAFTA-DR FTA, art 15.10.2, 5 August 2004; US–Australia FTA, art 17.10.4, 18 May 2004; US–Panama FTA, art 15.10.4(a) and (b). In other FTAs, less onerous variations have been used. For instance, art 4.23(b) of the US–Jordan FTA (2000) requires applicants to provide notification only. Note that US–Panama FTA, art 15.10.4(c) and (d), provides for "an expeditious administrative or judicial procedure in which the person requesting marketing approval can challenge the validity or applicability of the identified patent; and effective regards for a successful challenge of the validity or applicability of the patent".

As demonstrated below, implementation also differs and in some countries (including the US), patent linkage requires the drug registration authority to maintain a registrar of patents and to verify the patent status of any drug during the registration process. Whatever the form, patent linkage extends the traditional role of marketing authorities, which is to determine the safety and efficacy of the drug at issue. In this regard it is worth quoting the Canadian Supreme Court in noting the inherent tension between the two different regimes:

> The [patent linkage regulations] lie at the intersection of two regulatory systems with sometimes conflicting objectives. First, is the law governing approval of new drugs, which seeks to ensure the safety and efficacy of new medications before they can be put on the market . . . [This] process culminates (if successful) in the issuance of [marketing approval] to an applicant manufacturer by the Minister of Health on the advice of his officials in the Therapeutic Products Directorate. The [] objective is to encourage bringing safe and effective medicines to market to advance the nation's health. The achievement of this objective is tempered by a second and to some extent overlapping regulatory system created by the Patent Act . . . . Under that system, in exchange for disclosure to the public of an invention, including the invention of a medication, the innovator is given the exclusive right to its exploitation for a period of 20 years.[11]

Jurisdictional differences

We now turn to reviewing the law and operation of patent linkage in select jurisdictions.

United States

Patent linkage first appeared in the US as part of the Hatch-Waxman Act (1984). Until then, the Food and Drug Administration (FDA) treated data submitted by an originator as a trade secret;[12] competitors could not access the data when seeking to obtain marketing approval for generic versions of the patented

11 *AstraZeneca Canada Inc. vs Canada (Minister of Health)* 2 S.C.R. 560, [2006] SCC 49(Can.), para 12.

12 See 21 U.S.C. § 355(b)(1)(A). For background on reform attempts, see Ellen J. Flannery and Peter Barton Hutt, "Balancing Competition and Patent Protection in the Drug Industry: The Drug Price Competition and Patent Term Restoration Act of 1984" (1985), 40, Food Drug Cosmetic Law Journal, 269; Ronald L. Desrosiers, "The Drug Patent Term: Longtime Battleground in the Control of Health Care Costs" (1989), 24, New England Law Review, 115; Gerald J. Mossinghoff, "Overview of the Hatch-Waxman Act and Its Impacts on the Drug Development Process" (1999), 54, Food and Drug Law Journal, 187; Robin J. Strongin, "Hatch-Waxman, Generics, and Patents: Balancing Prescription Drug Innovation, Competition, and Affordability" (2002), NHPF Background Paper, www.nhpf.org/library/background-papers/BP_HatchWaxman_6-02.pdf, accessed 04/04/2016. For a modern

pharmaceutical. While this did not bar generic companies from conducting their own clinical trials, the complexity of conducting duplicative trials as well as the unlikelihood of recouping the R&D costs (not to mention the ethical concerns of repeating trials to achieve an already established result) meant that generic competitors could not apply for marketing approval during the term of patent protection, and even left the originator a period of time thereafter as generic competitors prepared and applied for marketing approval.

The Hatch-Waxman Act allowed generic companies to seek marketing approval from the FDA *before* the expiration of patent protection[13] (for exploitation after the term of patent protection) without having to conduct their own clinical trials. To file an Abbreviated New Drug Application (ANDA), generic companies merely have to prove the bioequivalence of their version with the originator pharmaceutical product.[14] Under the patent linkage system, the Act, however, "links" the patent status of a pharmaceutical (under the Patent Act) to marketing approval (under the Food, Drug and Cosmetic Act)[15] so the FDA is now prohibited from granting marketing approval to a generic product so long as the originator company filing a New Drug Application (NDA) "listed" or "registered" at least one patent contained in the approved drug in the "Approved Drug Products with Therapeutic Equivalence" (commonly referred to as the "Orange Book").[16] While the Act does not allow generic competition on the market during the term of patent protection, it does provide a financial sweetener to facilitate early entry of generics into the market by granting a generic company that successfully challenges the validity of a patent with its own six-month period of market exclusivity; meaning for the first six months following the invalidation of the patent, only the generic which successfully challenged the patent is allowed onto the market in competition with the originator company.[17] These measures were not implemented in isolation, however, but came as part of a "grand bargain" which, *inter alia*, provided the branded pharmaceutical/originator company with a limited (but secure) period

review of the Act, see Robert A. Armitage, "The Hatch-Waxman Act: A Path Forward for Making it More Modern" (2014), 40 William Mitchell Law Review, 1200.

13 35 U.S.C. para 271(e)(1) (2000 & Supp. 2005). The US Supreme Court has consistently expanded the boundaries of the exemption. See, e.g., *Eli Lilly and Co. vs Medtronic* [1990] 496 US 661; *Merck KgaA vs Integra Lifesciences I, Ltd.*, 545 U.S. 193 (2005); *Momenta Pharm. vs Amphastar Pharm* [2012] 686 F.3d 1348.

14 21 C.F.R. (2007), pt 211. Generic manufacturers also must demonstrate that the product is manufactured according to Good Manufacturing Practice. These measures come as part of a "grand bargain" which provided the originator with a secure period of exclusivity (between three and five years) and the opportunity for patent term extensions as a result of regulatory delay.

15 35 U.S.C. (2006) paras 1–376; Federal Food, Drug and Cosmetic Act, 21 U.S.C. (2006) paras 301–397.

16 21 U.S.C. (2006) para 355(j)(7)(A). For background, see Andrew A. Caffrey and Jonathan M. Rotter, "Consumer Protection, Patents and Procedure: Generic Drug Market Entry and the Need to Reform the Hatch-Waxman Act" (2004), 9 Virginia Journal of Law and Technology, 1, 4–7.

17 21 U.S.C. (2000 & Supp. V 2005) para 355(j)(5)(B)(iv).

of data protection/exclusivity (between three and five years) and the opportunity for patent term extensions as a result of regulatory delay.

Under the Hatch-Waxman Act, a generic producer can file an ANDA to facilitate entry of a generic equivalent but must certify that:

1 the drug has not been patented;
2 the patent has already expired;
3 the date on which the patent will expire, and that the generic drug will be placed on the market until that date passes; or
4 that the patent is not infringed or is invalid.

Referred to as paragraph I, II, III and IV certifications, the first three are relatively straightforward whereas a paragraph IV certification is more complicated to administer. In such an instance, the ANDA applicant must notify the innovator company of its filing and describe the reasons why the patent will not be infringed or is invalid or unenforceable.

Following receipt of the notice, the originator is given a 45-day period to file a lawsuit for infringement (submission of a paragraph IV certificate to the FDA triggers an infringement for purposes of the Federal Court). If the originator files a lawsuit for infringement, FDA approval is stayed for 30 months. Thus, the mere *claim* that a valid patent exists over the drug triggers an *automatic* 30-month injunction. When this period expires, the FDA can issue tentative marketing approval. While this allows an ANDA applicant to enter the market, most do not actually market the product until resolution of the litigation in order to avoid what could be significant liability for damages if the court ultimately finds infringement of a valid patent.

In the main, the Act facilitated the entry of generic pharmaceuticals into the US market, but it also provided an opportunity for anti-competitive behaviour, raised questions in regards to both the economic and health benefits of the "grand bargain", and transformed the FDA from a governmental agency solely concerned with the safety and efficacy of a pharmaceutical product into a quasi-"patent enforcement agency" which relies on the information provided by the originator in the NDA to restrain approval of generic equivalent drugs.[18]

The Hatch-Waxman Act undoubtedly facilitated the entry of generic pharmaceuticals into the US market. For instance, in updating the seminal work of Grabowski and Vernon, Berndt and Aitken found the rate of generics as a total

18 Brook Baker, "Ending Drug Registration Apartheid – Taming Data Exclusivity and Patent/Registration Linkage" (2008), 34 American Journal of Law and Medicine, 302, 307. For this reason, some question the value of such a register. See, e.g., Bouchard et al (2010) (n. 4), 174. See, contra, Commonwealth of Australia, "Pharmaceutical Patents Review Report 2013", 149–154 (recommending the addition of a "transparency" register in order to ease the burden on generic manufacturers in searching for relevant patents on pharmaceutical products).

percentage of prescriptions had risen from 18.6 per cent in 1984 to 74.5 per cent in 2009.[19] At the same time, however, the Act also provided an opportunity for gaming and anti-competitive behaviour and serious questions have been raised in regards to both the economic and health benefits of the "grand bargain". Foremost among the concerns are the delayed introduction of generic competition resulting from multiple patents over one drug and the resulting evergreening strategies of the branded industry as well as agreements whereby potential generic competitors agree not to compete with the branded drug in exchange for monetary remuneration.[20]

Canada

Prior to amendments introduced in 1987 and the introduction of patent linkage in 1993, Canada possibly operated the most pro-generic pharmaceutical regimes in the developed world. Compulsory licensing – that is, when a government allows someone to produce a patented product or process without the consent of the patent owner – was introduced in Canada in relation to the manufacturing of patented medicines (and food) in 1927,[21] and expanded to include the importation of medicines in 1969.[22] With little discretion to deny an

19 Ernst R. Berndt and Murray Aitken, "Brand Loyalty, Generic Entry and Price Competition in Pharmaceuticals in the Quarter Century after the Waxman-Hatch Legislation" (2010), NBER Working Paper No. 16431, www.nber.org/papers/w16431, accessed 04/04/2016, referring to Henry G. Grabowski and John M. Vernon, "Brand Loyalty, Entry, and Price Competition in Pharmaceuticals after the 1984 Drug Act" (1992), 35 Journal of Law and Economics, 331; Henry G. Grabowski and John M. Vernon, "Longer Patents for Increased Generic Competition in the US: The Waxman-Hatch Act after One Decade" (1996), 10 PharmacoEconomics 110.

20 See, e.g., Federal Trade Commission, "Generic Drug Entry Prior to Patent Expiration: An FTA Study" (July 2002); European Commission, "Pharmaceutical Sector Enquiry: Final Report" (8 July 2009), para 383; Matthew Avery, "Continuing Abuse of the Hatch-Waxman Act by Pharmaceutical Patent Holders and the Failure of the 2003 Amendments" (2008–2009) 60 Hastings Law Journal, 171; Caffrey and Rotter (n. 16); C. Scott Hemphill and Mark A. Lemley, "Earning Exclusivity: Generic Drug Incentives and the Hatch-Waxman Act" (2011), 77 Antitrust Law Journal, 947. The same is true of the Canadian system; see, e.g., Monika Sawicka and Ron A. Bouchard, "Empirical Analysis of Canadian Drug Approval Data 2001–2008: Are Pharmaceutical Players 'Doing More with Less'?" (2009), 3 McGill Journal of Law and Health, 87, 151; Bouchard et al (n. 4 (2010)); Edward Hore, "Patently Absurd: Evergreening of Pharmaceutical Patent Protection under the Patented Medicines (Notice of Compliance) Regulations of Canada's Patent Act" (2004), www.canadiangenerics.ca/en/news/docs/patently_absurd_04.pdf, accessed 04/04/2016.

21 *Patent Act*, S.C. 1923, c 23, s 17. The scheme limited the issuance of a compulsory licence to where the medicine's active ingredient was manufactured in Canada. For this reason, only a handful of licences were ever issued; see Margaret Smith, "Patent Protection for Pharmaceutical Products", Background paper (November 1993).

22 Throughout the 1960s, several commissions reviewed the compulsory licence scheme, with recommendations ranging from minor tweaks to the system to the abolishment of patents on pharmaceuticals. Smith (n. 21), citing Canada, Royal Commission on Patents, Copyright and Industrial Design, "Report on Patents of Invention" (1960) Queen's Printer, Ottawa, 1960,

application for a compulsory licence and royalty rates fixed at 4 per cent of the net selling price,[23] generic manufacturers flourished in Canada[24] and Canadians enjoyed some of the most affordable drug prices in developed countries.[25]

Canada's pharmaceutical patent regime, however, became unattractive by the 1980s[26] and despite substantial regulatory reforms,[27] became untenable with the proclamation of new rules prohibiting discrimination on the basis of field of technology or country of invention/manufacture under the Uruguay Round negotiations on IPRs (the TRIPS Agreement), a pathway furthermore confirmed in the soon to be concluded North American Free Trade Agreement (NAFTA). Changes came through Bill C-91 of 1992 which abolished the compulsory licence regime and introduced patent linkage laws – Patented Medicines (Notice of Compliance) Regulations SOR/1993-133 (Can) – modelled on the Hatch-Waxman Act.[28] Under the Regulations, drugs cannot be placed on the market without a Notice of Compliance (NOC) being issued by the Minister of Health based on the safety and efficacy of the drug at issue.[29] An originator submits a New Drug Submission (NDS) based on "test data" (i.e., clinical trials) and subsequently lists on a register patents for which they have received regulatory approval,[30] whereas generic companies submit an Abbreviated New Drug

92–97; Canada, Department of Justice, Restrictive Trade Practices Commission, "Report Concerning the Manufacture, Distribution and Sale of Drugs" (1963), Queen's Printer, Ottawa, 516–524; Canada, Royal Commission on Health Services, "Report of the Royal Commission on Health Services" (1964), Queen's Printer, Ottawa, 1701– 1709; Canada, House of Commons, Special Committee on Drug Costs and Prices "Second (Final) Report of the Special Committee of the House of Commons on Drug Costs and Prices" (1966/67), Ottawa, Queen's Printer, 42.

23 See Christopher Scott Harrison, "Protection of Pharmaceuticals as Foreign Policy: the Canada–U.S. Trade Agreement and Bill C-22 versus the North American Free Trade Agreement and Bill C-91" (2001), 26 North Carolina Journal of International Law & Commercial Regulation, 457, 507 (FN 282); Milan Chromecek, "The Amended Canadian Patent Act: General Amendments and Pharmaceutical Patents Compulsory Licensing Provisions" (1987), 11 Ford International Law Journal, 3, 504, 527–528.

24 Generic manufacturers also benefited from the establishment of provincial programmes to reimburse the cost of medicines for certain groups of individuals and legislation which required the purchase of generic-equivalent medicines where available. Smith (n. 21).

25 Harrison (n. 23) 547. See generally, Thomas K. Fulda and Paul F. Dickens, III, "Controlling the Cost of Drugs: the Canadian Experience" (1979), 1(2) Health Care Finance Review, 55.

26 See generally Smith (n. 21); Canada, Commission of Inquiry on the Pharmaceutical Industry, *The Report of the Commission of Inquiry on the Pharmaceutical Industry, Minister of Supply and Services*, Ottawa, 1985 (commonly referred to as the Eastman Commission).

27 Bill C-22 (1987) 35–36 Eliz. 2, ch 41 (1987), amending the Patent Act, R.S.C., ch P-4 (1970). See also Smith (n. 21). See, further, Chromecek (n. 23) 526–534; Brian W. Gray, "New Changes to the Patent System" (1988), 4 Food Drug Cosmetic Law Journal, 43, 641, 645–646.

28 Patented Medicines (Notice of Compliance) Regulations SOR/1993-133 (Can).

29 Food and Drug Regulations, C.R.C., ch 870 (1978).

30 Patented Medicines (Notice of Compliance) Regulations SOR/1993-133, §§ 3, 4 (Can). In 2008, after several inconsistent Federal Court decisions and consideration by the Supreme Court of Canada in *AstraZeneca Canada Inc. vs Canada*, [2006] 2 S.C.R. 560, 2006 SCC 49 (Can), the government issued revised guidance notes supporting the view that patents

Submission ("ANDS") demonstrating bioequivalence to the listed product.[31] The Canadian regulations directly link marketing approval with the patent status of the drug in that the minister is prohibited from issuing NOCs to generics until it has addressed each patent listed in the application; in practice, this means waiting until the expiry of all listed patents or challenging the validity of the patents via a Notice of Allegation (NOA).[32] If the generic issues an NOA, the originator company has a 45-day window to apply for judicial review requesting that the NOC not be issued to the generic applicant.[33] By taking such action, the originator delays the possibility of an NOC being issued for 24 months, or until the court has determined the issues or the patent expired, whichever is earliest.[34] Thus, by commencing proceedings the originator receives an *automatic* injunction without having to prove the validity of the patent or its claim. In the proceedings, the court is tasked with determining whether the generic manufacturer's allegations are "justified". If the court finds in the negative, it will issue an "order of prohibition" preventing the minister from issuing the NOC until the expiration of the patent expiry. Judicial review under the NOC Regulations is summary in nature and limited to a determination on the issuance of an NOC under the Food and Drug Regulation. Thus, the proceedings are not an action for infringement or a determination of the validity of the patent, but instead are of a more limited nature. The overlaps with infringement proceedings are obvious, and unsurprisingly there have been instances where the NOC proceedings have deemed patents invalid or non-infringed while a court in an infringement proceeding has subsequently found the patent to be valid or infringed. Such a system increases the cost of litigation and uncertainty. This aspect of the Canadian system is somewhat unique, and its usefulness and purpose can be questioned. For critics, relief may be coming as the completed but not yet in force Comprehensive Economic and Trade Agreement between Canada and Europe might streamline the "dual litigation" procedures into a single claim.[35]

The other main point of difference between the Canadian version of patent linkage and that of the US is that Canada does not grant any period of exclusivity to the first generic challenging the validity of the patent. This lack of incentive

listed on the register contain at least one specific claim to the medical ingredient, formulation, dosage form or use for which approval has been granted. For the latest version, see Guidance Document: Patented Medicines (Notice of Compliance) Regulations, www.hc-sc.gc.ca/dhp-mps/alt_formats/pdf/prodpharma/applic-demande/guide-ld/patmedbrev/pmreg3_mbreg3-eng.pdf, accessed 04/04/2016.

31 Food and Drug Regulations, C.R.C., para C.08.002.1.

32 Patented Medicines (Notice of Compliance) Regulations SOR/1993-133, (Can) paras 5(1)(a), 5(1)(b) and 5(3)(a).

33 Ibid para 6(1).

34 Ibid para 7.

35 Daphne Lainson, Nancy Pei and Sheldon Hamilton, "Text of CETA finalized – finally!", Smart & Biggar online post (6 August 2014) www.smart-biggar.ca/en/articles_detail.cfm?news_id=882&utm_source=iContact&utm_medium=email&utm_campaign=IP%20Update&utm_content=IP+Update+Aug6+CETA+finalized, accessed 04/014/2016.

fundamentally changes the "bargain" and shifts the benefits of patent linkage, and it is curious that a dearth of literature exists which explains Canada's decision not to provide an incentive to generics as per the US law.

Like in the US, studies have questioned the economic and health benefits of patent linkage in Canada and in one such study, Bouchard concludes that "rent-seeking behavior by brand-name pharmaceutical firms to leverage loopholes in the regime is passed on in the form of continued monopoly costs to the public".[36]

In this regard, the negative effects of patent linkage may actually be more acute than in any other jurisdiction given the nature of the previous system and apparent effect of the change on the local generic pharmaceutical manufacturing industry and price of medicines in Canada.

Australia

Australia's adoption of patent linkage flows from the Australia–United States Free Trade Agreement (AUSFTA) which prevents a marketing authority from approving a product where a patent is claimed and requires that a generic applicant notify the rights holder of its request for marketing approval.[37]

Australia thus added a new section 26B to the Therapeutic Goods Act 1989 (Cth), requiring applicants for marketing approval to certify that their product does not infringe a valid patent claim or that the patent holder has been notified of the application.

Following much debate, the government introduced what has been termed an "anti-evergreening" measure in the form of a new section 26C, which is designed to ensure that following generic certifications under s26B, patent holders desiring to institute infringement proceedings must certify that the proceedings are being commenced in good faith, have reasonable prospects of success and will be conducted without unreasonable delay.[38] If the certification is found to be false or misleading then the patent holder could face fines of up to AUD$10 million. Unlike the automatic injunctions in the US and Canadian regulations, Section 26D furthermore requires patent holders seeking interlocutory injunctions to prevent the marketing of generic pharmaceuticals to first notify the Australian attorney-general (who shall be deemed a party in the proceedings) and obtain leave from a court. Where the application for an interlocutory injunction is unsuccessful, the court has the authority to order compensation to the applicant as well as to the federal and/or state/territory government in order to recoup losses to the Pharmaceutical Benefits Scheme (the government system for purchasing and distributing subsidized prescription medicines to Australians).

36 Ron A. Bouchard, "I'm Still Your Baby: Canada's Continuing Support of U.S. Linkage Regulations for Pharmaceuticals" (2011), 15 Marquette Intellectual Property Law Review, 71, 114. See also Sawicka and Bouchard (n. 20); Bouchard et al (2010) (n. 4); Bouchard et al (2009) (n. 4).

37 AUSFTA , art 17.10.4.

38 On "reasonable prospects of success", see s26C(4).

The Australian regulations, despite creating implementation tensions with the US,[39] seem to offer an enhanced level of protection against abuse not explicitly evident in other systems.

Finally, it should be noted that Australia did not create an "Orange Book" equivalent patent register. Thus, while a generic must ascertain the existence (or non-existence) of a patent and certify to the Therapeutic Goods Administration (TGA) that they have done so, the *Therapeutic Goods Act* neither provides an "Orange Book" equivalent register nor verifies the accuracy of the certification. While this eases the burden on the TGA (the body responsible with granting marketing approval in Australia), it does make the verification process more difficult for the generic applicant.

More recently, the government published a comprehensive report (commissioned by the former government) recommending the creation of a "transparency register", which would include all patents owned by, or licensed to, the originator and relevant to the relevant drug.[40] Correspondingly, the report recommended that originators be limited to commencing infringement proceedings only in respect of a patent listed on the register. The report did not support several features common in other linkage regulations, including "the introduction of the features of the Orange Book that provide for an automatic stay on generic applications for regulatory approval should an originator commence court proceedings, nor those that prevent generic manufacturers from undertaking all the steps necessary to prepare to enter the market upon expiry of the relevant patent, which includes obtaining regulatory approval".[41] The intention behind the call for the creation of a register seems to be one of reducing costs and increasing transparency and certainty to generic companies seeking to apply for marketing approval, not as a way to increase evergreening and delay the introduction of generics onto the market. The report, however, is unlikely to be implemented by the current government.

Patent linkage in other jurisdictions

Other jurisdictions with patent linkage operate similar regimes, with the usual variations noted above. For instance, Singapore adopted a version of patent

39 See "Letter From Robert Zoellick, USTR, to Mark Vaile, Australian Minister for Trade" (17 November 2004), www.ustr.gov/assets/Trade_Agreements/Bilateral/Australia_FTA/Implementation/asset_upload_file393_6951.pdf, accessed 04/04/2016. The International Federation of Pharmaceutical Manufacturers Associations was particularly critical of the "bad faith" penalty, calling it both "excessive" and "unprecedented". Daniel Pruzin, Global Pharmaceutical Group Slams Amendments to U.S.–Australia FTA (2004), 21 Intl. Trade Rptr., 43, 1739, 1762. Other commentators believe the amendments are inconsistent with the TRIPS Agreement. See Christopher S. Rugaber, "Disputes Over Copyright, Pharmaceutical Issues Could Delay U.S.–Australia Pact" (2004), 21 Intl. Trade Rptr., 42, 1701, 1721.

40 *Australian Pharmaceutical Patents Review Report* (n. 18), 154.

41 Ibid 152–153.

linkage closely related to that of the US in compliance with obligations undertaken in the Singapore–US FTA (2004), with four categories of generic applications.[42] Under Section 12A of the Medicines Act applicants are required to provide a declaration to the Health Sciences Authority (HSA) stating whether there are any relevant patents in Singapore. Under what is referred to as Category B, the applicant can contest the validity of the patent by providing the patent holder with a notice of the application setting out the reasons why the applicant believes the application does not infringe the patent ("Notice to Proprietor of Patent"). The originator is given 45 days to commence an infringement claim against the generic, which triggers an *automatic* 30-month injunction against the granting of marketing approval. If the patent holder takes no action, the HSA may proceed to grant the marketing approval. This process is, of course, lifted from the paragraph 4 certification process in the US.

Unlike the US, Singapore does not maintain a patent register equivalent to the Orange Book nor does it provide an incentive to generics to challenge the validity of the patent with a period of exclusivity granted to the first successful generic challenger. Moreover, Singapore has undergone some implementation issues involving its patent linkage regime as a result of its choice to simply add Section 12A to the Medicines Act in lieu of introducing an amendment to the Singapore Patents Act to add a new cause of action – this is in contract to the US Patent Code, which statutorily provides the submission of an application for a patented drug is an infringement. In *AstraZeneca vs Sanofi-Aventis*, the court clarified the procedural ambiguity by holding that Section 12A of the Singapore Medicines Act, read together with the accompanying regulations, constitutes a cause of action separate and independent from a patent infringement action under the Patents Act.[43]

In the case, Sanofi-Aventis applied to the HSA under Section 12A of the Singapore Medicines Act for marketing/licensing approval to import a cholesterol-reducing drug into Singapore despite the fact that at least one patent on the drug was held by AstraZeneca. Sanofi-Aventis served a Notice to Proprietor of Patent on AstraZeneca stating the reasons why it did not believe its drug infringed AstraZeneca's patent. AstraZeneca duly commenced an action against Sanofi for a declaration of patent infringement if Sanofi were to import the products into Singapore. Sanofi-Aventis responded by seeking to strike out AstraZeneca's action for a declaration of infringement on the ground that the action was frivolous, vexatious or an abuse of process of the court, since AstraZeneca failed to allege any instance of a past act of infringement in its claim. The court agreed with AstraZeneca that the responsive action is not one for patent infringement made pursuant to the Patents Act, but upon Section 12A of the Medicines Act, which when read with other regulations forms a separate cause of action for which a

42 Medicines Act (1975) Section 12A.
43 *AstraZeneca AB (SE) v Sanofi-Aventis Singapore Pte Ltd* [2012] SGHC 16.

patent holder can seek a declaration of infringement.[44] Thus, the court did not agree with Sanofi-Aventis that Section 12A of the Medicines Act merely provides notification to inform the patent holder of an application for marketing/licensing approval relating to a patented product, but does not provide the patent holder with a right or cause of action to commence infringement proceedings.

Initiated in 1993, patent linkage in Mexico is a simpler version of the US system in that it requires the Mexican Institute of Industrial Property (IMPI) to maintain a patent register and for the Federal Commission for Protection against Sanitary Risks (COFEPRIS) to only grant marketing approval to patent holders (that is, to deny marketing approval to generics) but does not make use of certifications. The system does not provide for automatic injunctions nor does it grant exclusivity to the first generic challenging the validity of the patent. Upon creation, the IMPI stated that the regulations were limited to patents covering active ingredients – meaning that formulation patents were not listed in the registry or used by COFEPRIS for marketing authorization determinations. After more than 40 Mexican District Court decisions, the Mexican Supreme Court (in a 3:2 decision) agreed with all but two of the District Court decisions that the registry should include patents covering active ingredients and product patents including those covering pharmaceutical formulations and new use (but not to process patents);[45] in so doing, the Supreme Court expanded the scope of patent linkage in Mexico.

Korea introduced patent linkage in 2012 in order to comply with its obligations under the Korea–US FTA, and while the regime contains a number of features taken from the US the regime is substantially different in a number of ways which protect the integrity of the system and ability of generics to enter the marketplace. Becoming fully operational on 15 March 2015, the Korean regime makes use of a patent register called the "Green List" (the equivalent of the US "Orange Book") whereby patent holders can list patents pertaining to the substance, formulation, composition or medical use which are "directly relevant" to the approved medical product.[46] Importantly, patents must be listed on the Green List *before* the granting of regulatory approval; meaning a patent holder cannot

44 In so doing, the court rejected the arguments from Sanofi-Aventis that (1) Section 12A of the Medicines Act did not provide for a cause of action separate and independent from a patent infringement action under the Patents Act; and (2) correspondingly, that the Patents Act only deals with actual infringements and there is no separate mechanism provided for threatened infringements.

45 See Alejandro Luna, "Mexico: Supreme Court Upholds the Worth of Formulation Patents" (Mondaq, 11 October 2010), www.mondaq.com/x/111840/Patent/Supreme+Court+Upholds+The+Worth+Of+Formulation+Patents. See also "Formulation Patents Included in the Linkage Gazette for the First Time", Olivares News Brief (2012), www.olivares.com.mx/En/Knowledge/News/FormulationpatentsincludedintheLinkageGazetteforthefirsttime, accessed 04/04/2016.

46 Enforcement Regulations of Korea Pharmaceutical Affairs Act, Decree No. 162 (18 October 2012), art 30*ter*, para 3.

continue to add patents to the register in an attempt to forestall generic marketing approval or facilitate infringement claims.[47]

Another important difference with the US scheme is that the regulatory authority, the Korean Ministry of Food and Drug Safety (MFDS), does not simply list all patents claimed by the patentee but instead reviews the substance of the "Patent Listing Applications" to ensure the relationship between the patent claims and approved product are legitimate and has the authority to change, narrow, edit and delist patent claims for failing to meet the requisite standard.[48] Moreover, and again similarly to the US and others, generic applicants must notify the patent holder (with seven days) of its application for marketing approval, but the notification requirement does not apply when the generic applicant states that it will not begin selling the medicine until the expiration of the listed patents (or when there is consent of the patent holder).[49]

Like the US, the patent holder is given 45 days from notice to institute infringement proceedings against a generic applicant; but a major point of difference is that Korea does not provide for automatic injunctions. Instead, injunctions will only be granted where there is a "need to prevent significant damage" and are limited to a 12-month period from the date of notice (as opposed to a 30-month automatic injunction in the US).[50] Moreover, and importantly, the injunction applies to generic *sales*, not to the granting of marketing approval.

Korea operates a bifurcated system where generics can instigate validity and scope of claim proceedings before the IP Tribunal/Patents Court, while patent holders can claim for infringement in the High Court. Again similarly to the US, Korea provides for a period of exclusivity to the first generic company to successfully challenge the validity of a pharmaceutical patent. Unlike the US, which offers a six-month period of exclusivity to the first generic applicant, Korea offers a 12-month period to the first generic (covering the same type and amount of active ingredient, dosage form, usage, dosage and indication) which files a scope confirmation trial or action *before* filing for marketing approval.[51]

It is premature to comment on the effect of Korea's patent linkage system, but at first instance the system appears to have more effectively balanced the interests of the branded industry in protecting its rights with generic interests bringing cheaper drugs to market and consumer interests in promoting a competitive environment than other jurisdictions.

China's version of patent linkage is more limited than the versions reviewed above, merely requiring a statement of non-infringement from the applicant.

47 Ibid art 30*ter*.

48 Ibid at art 24, para 10; art 30*ter*, para 5. The Korean scheme also applies to biologic medicines, whereas in the US biologics are separately regulated.

49 Ibid at art 30*quarter*, para 1.

50 Korea Food and Drug Administration, Implementation Plan of Patent-Drug Approval Linkage (30 October 2007), www.mfds.go.kr/index.do?mid=50&seq=2705&cmd=v, accessed 04/04/2016.

51 Ibid.

China does not maintain a patent register; [52] however, its scheme does apply to all applications (as opposed to only those relying on data from the original applicant) and only allows generic applicants to apply for marketing approval within two years of the expiration of the patent.[53] In cases where a patent exists and remains valid, the regulatory authority's approval will only take effect from the date of the expiration of the patent – thereby eliminating the opportunity of the generic to challenge the validity of the patent by bringing the drug to market. The system does not provide for automatic injunctions when a patent holder claims a patent, issue certifications or offer inducements to generic companies to challenge the validity of patents.

Patent linkage may not feature in China's regime for much longer; in December 2013, the regulatory authority – the Chinese Food and Drug Administration (CFDA) – introduced a proposal to remove patent linkage from the regulations. Citing the burden on generic applicants to identify all relevant patents without the equivalent of an Orange Book, CFDA did not follow the rout of Australia by recommending the introduction of such a register but instead pointed out that it does not have any functional linkage or way to share information with the State Intellectual Property Office (SIPO) and thus recommended the abolishment of the system. The CFDA's recommendation is understandable given the system is not operating as anticipated due to a lack of available information and "generic versions of patent-protected drugs are frequently approved before patent expiry".[54] Given the low level of transparency (i.e., applications for marketing approval and drug dossiers are not made public) coupled with the difficulty to compel production of evidence and the more challenging task of obtaining an interim injunction to combat the alleged patent infringement, some believe the recommendation to abolish patent linkage could lead to an increase in patent infringement in the pharmaceutical sector.[55]

Patent linkage is not explicitly provided for in a number of prominent jurisdictions, and even prohibited in the EU.[56] However, and despite the European Commission stating that it will "act against patent linkage",[57] patent linkage has crept into the laws and regulations of several member states in what has been referred to as "ghost linkage".[58] Although the extent to which EU member states

52 Drug Registration Regulation art 11.

53 Ibid art 13.

54 Freshfields Bruckhaus Deringer, "Proposed Amendments to Drug Registration Rules", China Life Sciences (December 2013), http://www.freshfields.com/en/knowledge/China_life_sciences.

55 Ibid.

56 See above footnote 9.

57 European Commission, "Executive Summary of the Pharmaceutical Sector Inquiry Report" (8 July 2009), ec.europa.eu/competition/sectors/pharmaceuticals/inquiry/communication_en.pdf, 23.

58 European Commission Final Report (n. 20, 23). See also European Commission Preliminary Report (n. 9) 14, 113 and Table 22; European Generic Medicines Association, "Patent-related Barriers to Market Entry for Generic Medicines in the European Union: A Review of

have adopted patent linkage has been exaggerated,[59] several member states have in the recent past or still maintain some form of linkage. For instance, Hungary still requires an applicant to sign a declaration stating they do not intend to infringe the patent and the authority will not approve the application without the statement.[60] Moreover, until 2012, Italy only granted marketing approval to generic applicants within one year of expiry of the patent and even then the marketing approval only became valid upon expiry of the patent.[61] Likewise, prior to 2011, Slovakian regulatory authorities rejected applications for marketing approval if a patent existed over the active ingredient of the drug, with amendments in 2011 making marketing approval valid only upon the expiration of patent protection.[62] In this regard, generic manufacturers in Italy could not and manufacturers in Slovakia cannot challenge the validity of a patented pharmaceutical by bringing its version onto the market thereby insulating the patent holder from challenge. Furthermore, until 2012, Portugal allowed patent owners to bring infringement proceedings against the authorities responsible for marketing approval using a plethora of administrative law provisions aimed at preventing an infringement of industrial property rights by public bodies.[63]

Weaknesses in the Current European Patent System and their Impact on the Market Access of Generic Medicines", May 2008, pp23–24 (hereinafter "EU Generics"). The term "ghost linkage" is used in Bouchard et al (n. 5), 35.

59 Many of the assertions and even statistics cited in the *European Commission Preliminary Report* (n. 9) cannot be verified and appear to be incorrect.

60 Art 7(3) of Decree 52/2005 of the Ministry of Health.

61 Art 68(1*bis*) of the Code of Industrial Property (*Codice della proprietà industriale*) introduced with art 38(2) law no. D.Lgs. no. 131 of 13 August 2010, and repealed by art 83(1) of law no. D.L. no. 1 of 24 January 2012 as converted with amendments into law no. 27 of 24 March 2012.

62 See *Zákon o liekoch a zdravotníckych pomôckach a o zmene a doplnení niektorých zákonov*, Official Journal no. 362/2011 item 117, 3110. According to the World Health Organization (WHO)'s Pharmaceutical Sector Country Profile Questionnaire of 2013, the new law does not include provisions on patent linkage but there is no indication that the link has been abandoned. See point 4.01.12, 30, www.who.int/medicines/areas/coordination/Slovakia_country_profile.pdf?ua=1, accessed 04/04/2016.

63 See Associação Portuguesa da Indústria Farmacêutica, Comments on the Preliminary Report in the pharmaceutical sector inquiry, point 2.3 7–10, www.ec.europa.eu/competition/consultations/2009_pharma/apifarma.pdf, accessed 04/04/2016. The revised law (official journal of 12 December 2011 first series no. 236 5258) prevents the marketing authorization from being altered, suspended or revoked because of existing proprietary rights. See Letter from the IP Federation (London) to Manuela Romano de Castro / British Embassy in Portugal concerning the new law; www.google.com.hk/url?sa=t&rct=j&q=&esrc=s&source=web&cd=1&cad=rja&uact=8&ved=0CB0QFjAA&url=http%3A%2F%2Fwww.ipfederation.com%2Fdocument_download.php%3Fid%3D1164&ei=memsVISZC4bcmAWEr4KICg&usg=AFQjCNHlH9SflNmn6d14BLjj5AdZ_-jUlg&sig2=KJLy9mSH9jVZPhmXo80JXA, accessed 04/04/2016. This is in contrast to the situation under the old law, where cases were often filed against the regulatory authority for failing to adequately protect patent rights. See "EU Generics" (n. 58) 23 (reporting that over 70 cases were initiated against the regulatory authority in 2007); *European Commission Final Report* (n. 20) 315: 'Certain originator companies allege that by granting marketing authorisation, the authorities willingly

Commentary and analysis

Patent linkage is valuable to the branded pharmaceutical industry because it can delay market access to generic medicines. Such delays bring economic rents to the branded pharmaceutical industry, but at the expense of the government and consumer forced to pay higher prices for pharmaceuticals beyond the normal patent period. On the one hand, patent linkage delays the entry of generic competition by three to five years in some markets,[64] against a delay of seven months in the EU.[65] Importantly, the European Commission found the extended delay in generic competition occurs even when litigation determines the patent is invalid, which in many jurisdictions happens in the majority of instances.[66] There is, on the other hand, no evidence that patent linkage boosts innovation or benefits to public health. Taken together, the merits of patent linkage for most jurisdictions remain questionable – especially for countries without significant pharmaceutical industry.

From a legal perspective, the introduction of patent linkage has reversed the burden of proof: it is now for the generic applicant to prove that it does not infringe upon a patent, not for the owner of the private right to enforce its patent once infringed. This transformation of a private property right (normally depending on the owners' willingness and desire to enforce into a public right enforced by a governmental authority) is a significant departure from traditional IP norms but that IPRs are private rights, not rights which are enforced by government, is often lost by the branded pharmaceutical industry. For instance, AstraZeneca stated in the context of Canadian law that patent linkage – including presumably the need for an automatic injunction – was needed to "prevent infringement" from occurring and attempted to reiterate its point by stating that in Canada it was difficult to obtain an interlocutory injunction after the product has been placed on the market. These statements are an astonishing reversal of the traditional view of IP protection and enforcement and a brazen attempt at institutionalizing the burden shift to generic applicants and governmental authorities.

The "prevention of infringement" severely curtails the scope of activities of generic manufacturers and completely removes the right and opportunity for generic manufacturers to "willingly and knowingly" take the "calculated risk" of making and placing a product on the market without authorization from the patent owner in the belief either that the patent is invalid (and thus unenforceable) or because they have found a way to circumvent the claims made in the patent.

collude in the alleged infringement. These originator companies therefore argue that no marketing authorisation should be granted until the allegation of patent infringement has been settled. Occasionally, actions are accompanied by a threat to sue the marketing authorisation body for damages if marketing authorisation is granted."

64 Bouchard et al (n. 5) 30.

65 *European Commission Final Report* (n. 20) 8.

66 Ibid.

Such action is one cornerstone of the patent system, whereby a competitor can bring the product to market and, if sued for patent infringement, directly challenges the validity of the patent. Taking away this right of action, without a corresponding move making it easier to challenge a patent by administrative means, transforms the challengeable presumption of validity of the patent into a much more secure property right. While patent linkage may delay the introduction of generic competition onto the marketplace, some differences amongst regimes matter.

In the US, the policy intent is clear: to stimulate the development of innovative drugs while at the same time facilitate the timely entry of generic competition to the marketplace. This purpose has been confirmed in the jurisprudence,[67] but perhaps more importantly is encompassed in a statement of Senator Orrin Hatch when the Hatch-Waxman Act came into force: "The public receives the best of both worlds – cheaper drugs today and better drugs tomorrow."[68] In 1993, Canada relied on essentially the same justification for introducing patent linkage.[69] Likewise, throughout the AUFTA negotiations patent linkage was promoted to Australians as necessary in order to promote continued investment into pharmaceutical R&D.[70]

Using the same justification for every jurisdiction seems oddly misplaced. The formula used to encourage innovation and the development of drugs, or even to adequately secure an appropriate level of pharmaceutical patent enforcement or facilitate the entry of generic competition into the market, differs in every jurisdiction. Simply stated, what is missing from the sweeping justification for patent linkage is the appropriate comparator, or baseline legislation, from which each proposed measure should be judged. For instance, the pre-1984 law in the US treated test data as a trade secret and clearly hampered the entry of generic competition into the market by providing a de facto extension of monopoly sales.[71] The bargain reached to provide additional forms of protection in exchange for providing an easier pathway for generics to enter the market seemed appropriate to the US.

In Canada, however, generic competition has historically been encouraged and local production facilitated through compulsory licensing of pharmaceuticals. Far from facilitating the timely entry of generic competition of the market, patent linkage seems to have harmed the once-thriving domestic generic industry and led to an increase in the price of drugs.[72] Moreover, with Canada's limited domestic

67 See, e.g., *Mylan Pharmaceutical vs Bristol-Myers Squibb Co.* (2000), 268 F.3d 1323, 1326.

68 Congressional Record – Senate at 23764 (10 August 1984) as cited in Bouchard et al (n. 5) 10.

69 See, e.g., Canada Gazette, 140, 24 (17 June 2006). See also Bouchard et al (n. 5) 10–11 FN48.

70 See, e.g., Thomas A. Faunce and Joel Lexchin, "Linkage Pharmaceutical Evergreening in Australia and Canada" (2007), 4 Australia and New Zealand Health Policy, 1.

71 H.R. Rep. No. 98–857, pt. 1, 17 (1984), cited in Bouchard et al (n. 5) 11 (FN 50).

72 Brett Skinner, "Generic Drugopoly: Why Non-patented Prescription Drugs Cost More in Canada than in the United States and Europe" (23 August 2004), 82, Public Policy Sources,

market (with a population of slightly more than 30 million), it is unlikely that patent linkage has increased innovation or R&D in the pharmaceutical sector. While the specifics of legislation in Australia, Mexico, South Korea and elsewhere differ, the broader point is that the baseline in these jurisdictions was more similar to Canada than the US and therefore it is unlikely that patent linkage has stimulated R&D and innovation or even promoted quicker or easier entry of generic competition. Simply stated, the policy justification for patent linkage in the US is not relevant to jurisdictions with different baselines.

The differences between and among nations matter, and with the high cost of litigation it is questionable whether patent linkage is beneficial to most nations. More specifically, patent linkage (in addition to other laws and regulations which attempt to balance enhanced protections for the rights holder with encouraging generic entry into the market) may work in larger markets – and in particular the US, with approximately 40 per cent of the worldwide market – where the value of entry into the marketplace is high. In smaller jurisdictions, the benefits of entry into the market are more limited, and the costs of litigating a patent claim mean the benefits are marginal or negative, even with exclusivity on offer for the first generic entrant (as the US and Korea offers). In such jurisdictions, the net result of patent linkage is to delay generic entry into the market, with higher overall costs to the healthcare system.

Moving on to operational differences existing in current regimes, one divergence worthy of further exploration is the scope of linkage between the patent and marketing approval. Issues such as whether the first/“main” patent or multiple patents should be allowed to be linked (and placed on the register if a registration system is in place) and what type of patent should qualify for linkage, are fundamental to the scope of patent linkage. To date governments have responded in very different ways, seemingly without any empirical data or justification for their decisions.

The issue is important as it relates to both health and economics – the allowance of multiple patents for inventions beyond the chemical entity and follow-on patents could lead to patent holders gaming the system so as to delay the introduction of generic competition. Legislators in the US recognized the potential negative effects of multiple patents, but nevertheless allowed multiple patents to be registered in the belief that delay to generic entry would be limited.[73] This belief seems mistaken, as the Federal Trade Commission in 2002 found significant evidence of gaming to delay market entry of generic competition.[74] In hindsight, it is not difficult to see how this occurred. In the US (and Canada), courts have struggled to determine the appropriate threshold for what is a patent relevant

Fraser Institute, www.fraserinstitute.org/sites/default/files/Generic_Drugopoly.pdf; Joel Lexchin, “Intellectual Property Rights and the Canadian Pharmaceutical Marketplace: Where Do We Go from Here?” (2005), 35 International Journal of Health Services, 2, 237, 243; Bouchard et al (n. 5) 11.

73 See House Report No. 98–857(I); H.R. (I) 8–30, cited in Bouchard et al (n. 5) 12–13.

74 Federal Trade Commission (n. 20).

to the marketed drug, and therefore eligible for registration, and when forced to do so have taken a broad approach to the term relevance.[75] Meanwhile, marketing authorities (such as the FDA) are not experts in patent law and likewise take a broad approach to listing. The result is multiple patents registered for each drug.[76] More worrying is the trend of pharmaceutical companies producing large amounts of follow-on drugs each with their own register-able patents, which have the effect of delaying entry of generic competition.[77] For these reasons, allowing only the "main" patent(s) to be registered/linked is perhaps the single most important decision a jurisdiction can take to prevent the balance being tilted too far in favour of the originator and against entry of generic competition.[78]

Limiting linkage to the "main" patent(s) is also critical in determining the suitability of a patent register. With pharmaceutical patents being complex in nature, and with dozens of patents over high-value drugs, the health authorities' ability to determine the relevance of a patent to a generic application is questionable. With courts even having difficulty in distinguishing true innovation worthy of patent protection from non-patentable discoveries, it seems unrealistic to expect the health and marketing authorities to authenticate the claims of the patentee. For this reason, most jurisdictions maintaining a register simply list all patents asserted by the original applicant. But such a practice has been susceptible gaming by the branded industry, which constantly adds new patents and engages in "evergreening" so as to forestall competition. For this reason, some public health advocates heavily criticize the patent register. On the other hand, as mentioned above, a study commissioned by the Australian government recommended the addition of a patent register so as to provide certainty to the generic applicant (who can better identify which patents are registered) and limit infringement proceedings to a finite number of patents per product (i.e., those registered). In this regard, the use of a patent register would discourage excessive litigation, not only against generic applicants but also against the marketing authorities, so long as the patent owner was precluded from litigating over patents not listed in the register. The Korean approach adds an additional layer of protection in that its authorities vet applications instead of simply listing all patents identified by the originator. While this adds complexity to the system it also serves to improve the quality of the register and limit litigation expenses. In contrast, a register which simply lists all patents identified by the originator and also allows litigation

75 See, e.g., *Mylan Pharmaceuticals vs Bristol-Myers Squibb Co.* (2000) 268 F.3d 1323. In Canada, see *AstraZeneca vs Apotex, Minister of Health* 2004 FC 1277.

76 Bouchard et al (n. 5) 18; Bouchard et al (n. 4 (2010)); Hemphill and Lemley (n. 20).

77 This point has been analysed at length in the literature. See, e.g., Bouchard et al (n. 5) 18; Bouchard (2010).

78 See Hore (n. 20); Avery (n. 20). Alternatively, the Korean approach which does not simply list all claimed patents but instead reviews the substance of the "Patent Listing Applications" to ensure the relationship between the patent claims and approved product are legitimate prior to listing could be a model to follow in an effort to stem the flow of listings and litigation.

involving patents not listed in the register casts doubt upon the usefulness of the register and begs the question of its purpose.

Another issue is the availability to rights holders of automatic injunctions upon the initiation of infringement litigation, which features in US, Canadian and Singaporean patent linkage regulations. Unsurprisingly, evidence compiled over the last decade and a half indicates that automatic injunctions increase both the number of patents per high-value product and litigation.[79] In other words, patent linkage results in evergreening – this is especially the case where the regulations provide for automatic injunctions – with evidence from the US suggesting that pharmaceutical companies abuse the registration process by listing a substantial number of patents not entirely related to the drug in the Orange Book, or even list additional patents subsequent to an ANDA application from a generic company.[80] Furthermore, not only does the evidence point to increased litigation following the introduction of patent linkage, but also to an increase in the time it takes a generic to come to market. To some, the main problem lies with the plaintiff receiving an automatic injunction without even having to demonstrate the validity of the patent.[81] To this end, the *EC Pharmaceutical Sector Final Report* found the mere threat of automatic injunctions sends a strong chilling effect to generic competitors, with data "illustrat[ing] the strength of the link between patent-related exchanges and patent litigation".[82]

Of course, while the US provides for an automatic injunction it balances out this benefit to originators by granting the first generic to successfully challenge the validity of a patent a 180-day period of exclusivity. Such a measure serves to induce generics to challenge patents and in the process stimulate generic competition and a reduction in overall healthcare costs.[83] Unlike the US, most adherents to patent linkage do not balance the automatic injunction with any market-based incentives to generics. As mentioned above, with litigation costs being high and the returns on offer limited (in most countries) for generics the potential rewards do not justify the expense. Thus, the branded industry receives the benefit of automatic injunctions without any the corresponding benefit to the

79 See footnote 20.

80 Bouchard et al (n. 4 (2010)).

81 In this regard, the Federal Court of Canada stated: NOC Regulations, "by merely commencing the proceeding, the applicant obtains what is tantamount to an interlocutory injunction for up to 30 months without having satisfied any of the criteria a court would require before enjoining issuance of an NOC". *AstraZeneca vs Apotex, Minister of Health* 2004 FC 1277. At least in the US, patent issues can be resolved in one step and without the threat of severe damages. This is not the case in Canada, where the two-step process involves the summary proceedings under the linkage regulations often followed by infringement litigation. But automatic injunctions are not solely to blame for the increased delays. Perhaps more damaging to consumers are settlements between branded and generic firms which serve to delay the introduction of generics into the market.

82 *European Commission Final Report* (n. 20) para 458.

83 There is, however, some evidence to suggest that the exclusivity period is not working as designed. See Federal Trade Commission (n. 20).

generic industry. In this regard, Australia's regulations could serve as a useful model to others. Australia does not provide for automatic injunctions but instead requires the originator to seek an injunction through a court order, with penalties for failing to act in good faith.[84]

Another, more systemic, issue is how patent linkage fits with experimental use provisions, particularly where a "Bolar" or regulatory review exception is written into legislation which expressly allows a generic to "use" the patented pharmaceutical for the purpose of preparing an application for marketing approval. The WTO panel in *Canada–Pharmaceutical Patents* held that such practice fit within the perimeters of the exception clause (Article 30) of the TRIPS Agreement.[85] To some commentators, linkage acts as a barrier to countries wishing to resort to the regulatory exception to Article 30. This may be an overstatement, as even with patent linkage a regulatory review exception allows a generic to prepare and submit an application for marketing approval during the patent term; even if such application cannot be approved until the expiration of the patent, it can be approved immediately upon the expiration of the patent and thus generic drugs would come to market several months before they would if no regulatory review exception was in place.

That being the case, many jurisdictions suffer from having vaguely worded and opaque regulatory review exceptions. For instance, Section 75(b) of the Hong Kong Patent Ordinance reads: "The rights conferred by a patent shall not extend to acts done for experimental purposes relating to the subject-matter of the relevant patented invention." The lack of clarity and precision in the language could be interpreted narrowly or broadly and in this sense it is unclear whether, for instance, the term "experimental purposes" covers conducting tests using a patented subject matter as part of an application for the pharmaceutical regulatory approval. Thus, and despite the fact that a regulatory review exception is entirely consistent with the TRIPS Agreement, it remains unclear whether such conduct is consistent with Hong Kong patent law.[86] The vagueness and undetermined nature of legislation such as this illuminates the need for patent linkage to be introduced in conjunction with a clearer and more tailored research exemption which specifically includes patent use to facilitate an application for regulatory review in order to minimize delays to the introduction of generic competition upon expiration of the patent.

84 See also, the approach taken by Korea, detailed at text of footnotes 47–51.

85 *Canada–Patent Protection of Pharmaceutical Products*, WT/DS114/R, para 7.84 (17 March 2000).

86 This is a common problem, as the incorporation of "bolar" provisions vary widely. See Christoph de Coster, Julia Bödeker and Paul England, "Not All Bolar Exemptions Are the Same", TaylorWessing Synapse (September 2013), www.taylorwessing.com/synapse/september13.html; Darren Smyth, "More on Amendments to Bolar Provisions – This Time in Ireland" (IPKat Blog, 11 August 2014), www.ipkitten.blogspot.hk/2014/08/more-on-amendments-to-bolar-provisions.html.

Even though the EU does not maintain a patent linkage regime, its "bolar" exception can serve as a model in providing generic manufacturers with the comfort that: "[c]onducting the necessary studies and trials with a view to the application [for marketing approval] and the consequential practical requirements shall not be regarded as contrary to patent rights or to supplementary protection certificates for medicinal products".[87] Such a statement would explicitly allow generic manufacturers to "use" the patent in conducting the necessary studies, tests and trials before making an application for marketing approval and, in certain jurisdictions, challenging the validity of the patent via certification (i.e., paragraph 4 certification of the US).

As importantly, care must be taken to ensure that patent linkage does not conflict with or impede compulsory licensing provisions and the right of countries to take measures to protect public health. This would seem to necessitate legislation which suspends patent linkage in the event that the government issues a compulsory licence (for either domestic use or export under the waiver of Article 31 of the TRIPS Agreement).[88] Failing to legislate in such a manner could result in a situation where an importer or local manufacturer cannot obtain marketing approval to sell the drug subject to the compulsory licence in the jurisdiction. Somewhat surprisingly, such legislative protections are virtually unknown to this author in any jurisdiction.

Patent linkage may well have a place in domestic legislation and form part of the balance between innovators and users. That being said, countries should be aware of the potential consequences of each aspect of patent linkage and respond accordingly. In every case, countries would be well advised to take these general principles and 'best practices' guidelines into consideration:

- Patent linkage should not forestall the development of generic competition or unduly delay an application for marketing approval.
- Patent linkage should not completely forestall a generic manufacturer from challenging the validity of a pharmaceutical patent. Likewise, the grant of marketing approval should not be a defence to any action for infringement. Where patent linkage does delay the registration of a generic product, marketing approval should take effect on the day the patent expires or is invalidated.
- Patent linkage should apply only to patents involving the primary active ingredient(s) and not to compositions, dosage, new use and process patents.

87 See, e.g., European Directive 2004/27/EC (amending Directive 2001/83/EC) on the EU code relating to medicinal products for human use. The scope of the clause, however, remains unclear. See European Generic Medicines Association (n. 58) 23–24. See also Belgian alendronate litigation (2007) ibid 24–25. In this regard, see also the European Commission Pharmaceutical Sector Preliminary Report (n. 9) 260.

88 WTO General Council, "Implementation of Paragraph 6 of the Doha Declaration on the TRIPS Agreement and Public Health", Decision of the General Council of 30 August 2003, WT/L/540 and Corr.1 (1 September 2003).

- When a country uses a patent register, patent claims attempting to halt generic marketing approval should be limited to patents listed on the register at the time of the application for marketing approval.
- Regulations should not allow for automatic injunctions following a claim for patent infringement, but rather should only be granted after the plaintiff has made a prima facie case that the patent in question is valid. In any event, requiring a mandatory notice provision whereby a generic applicant must inform the patent holder of its application should provide enough time to allow the latter to determine whether it should initiate an infringement proceeding (as opposed to presuming the validity of the patent).
- Where automatic injunctions are granted, an exclusivity prize should exist for the first generic to successfully challenge the validity of the patent.
- As a matter of expediency, efficiency and legal harmonization, all claims involving marketing authorization and patent infringement should be heard in a single forum, so far as possible.
- Attempts to prevent or delay generic competition through payments and other inducements from the innovator company should be illegal, whether through competition law or otherwise.

Conclusion

This chapter highlights a point often lost on commentators: while patent linkage provisions are growing in number, every system operates in a slightly different manner and therefore can have a different effect on the availability of medicines. Some jurisdictions prohibit the granting of marketing approval while a patent remains valid, others simply require notification to the originator and still others allow marketing approval to be granted only within a set period of time prior to the expiration of the patents. In addition, all patent linkage laws and regulations have one, some or all of the following four features: patent register, certification process, temporary injunction and period of exclusivity for the first generic to successfully challenge the validity of a patent.

What is rather worrying is that while all patent linkage regimes have presumably been designed to suit the particulars of the differing jurisdictions, there is little evidence that any of the systems reduce costs, increase access to medicines or promote innovation. Perhaps the most worrying part of patent linkage is that despite almost all the empirical evidence suggesting it has negative health and economic effects on a country, only one country is considering its removal and more countries are adopting it as law. As more countries adopt patent linkage, empirical evidence on the effect of the various forms of patent linkage should also grow. If used wisely, such evidence can form the basis of a tardy but informed debate on the benefits and detriments of patent linkage.

To this end, governments must think carefully before adopting a regime of patent linkage, and ensure its introduction follows a systemic review which takes into account policy priorities and objectives and fully accounts for all potential costs.[89] This is, of course, what occurred when the US introduced patent linkage in 1984 as part of a broad law aimed at balancing promotion of innovation and safeguarding public interests, including through the early introduction of generic competition in the marketplace.

Any review of patent linkage would necessitate not only an evaluation of the economic benefits/costs and of potential models and choices (i.e., a patent registry, automatic injunctions, exclusive marketing periods for the first generic to challenge, penalties for frivolous claims, etc.) but also of the basic framework, including how patent linkage intersects with other patent and relevant regulatory laws. Foremost among such issues is the relationship between patent linkage and the regulatory review exception. In a number of jurisdictions, the regulatory review exception is vaguely worded and ill-defined. Introduction of patent linkage without a more precisely worded research exemption could create disharmony within the law, as would provisions which conflict with or impede compulsory licensing.

The recently instituted patent linkage regimes in Australia and South Korea can perhaps serve as a model to others. Both regimes agreed to patent linkage as part of FTAs with the US, but tailored the regime to their own needs. With no signs of the trend towards patent linkage abating, the hope is that more countries take such a considered approach. Important lessons can be learned from the experiences of others, and better and more precise drafting could go a long way in negating some of the most undesirable aspects of patent linkage.

89 In this regard, Taiwan announced it will implement patent linkage but only following a review of the experience from several US FTA partner countries. Yu-Tzu Chiu, "Taiwan to Create Patent Linkage System For Drugs in Quest for TPP Membership" (15 August 2014), BNA International Trade Daily.

Part II

Balancing Patent Protection with Available Flexibilities

6 The Bolar Exception

Legislative Models and Drafting Options

Carlos Correa

Introduction

The basic principle of patent law is that once the term of a patent has expired, the protected subject matter becomes a part of the public domain. Hence, it can be freely used, including for commercial purposes, without the interference by the former patent owner. This allows competitors to enter the market immediately after such expiry, eventually leading to lower prices for consumers and welfare gains.

Pharmaceutical products, however, cannot be marketed[1] without prior authorization of the competent regulatory agency. Such authorization is conditional upon the submission and approval of an application that normally has to be accompanied with certain pieces of information. Regulatory requirements differ among countries. Despite some efforts towards harmonization,[2] there is considerable diversity in respect of what evidence is required, the applicable procedures, and how long it can take to obtain the approval.

In general, national regulations on marketing approval differentiate between pharmaceutical products that include new chemical entities or biological molecules – for which pre-clinical and clinical studies demonstrating efficacy and safety are needed – and "generic" or "similar" versions of drugs (hereinafter "generic products"), for which information regarding efficacy and safety has already been submitted and evaluated by the same or other regulatory authorities. In this latter case, as discussed below, although the requirements imposed to the applicants vary amongst countries, generally abbreviated, simplified procedures are applied.

1 The same applies to other regulated products, such as agro-chemicals. This chapter focuses on pharmaceuticals.
2 Notably by the International Council for Harmonization of Technical Requirements for Pharmaceuticals for Human Use (ICH). ICH, however, is a non-governmental organization where the "majority of the WHO member countries have no voting rights and which is dominated by pharmaceutical industry groups" (Rema Nagarajan, "Conflict of interest in setting norms for pharmaceuticals in WHO", The Times of India, 17 May 2014, http://timesofindia.indiatimes.com/city/delhi/Conflict-of-interest-in-setting-norms-for-pharmaceuticals-in-WHO/articleshow/35261958.cms).

These abbreviated procedures are significantly shorter than those required for the approval of pharmaceuticals incorporating new molecules. However, the authorization of a generic drug does take some time: it has been estimated that procedures for marketing approval of generics may delay their commercialization by two to three years[3] or more in countries with generic pharmaceutical manufacturing capability. This, in turn, delays such entry in other countries importing generic products.[4]

The interface between the regulations for marketing approval of medicines and patent law explains the need for what has been termed as the "early working" or "Bolar exception" (hereinafter "Bolar exception"). If a producer of a generic or similar version is bound to wait until the last day of the term of patent(s) covering a pharmaceutical product, the owner of expired patent(s) will enjoy a *de facto* additional period of monopoly power, as long as a generic version of the product obtains market permission from the regulatory authority. During this period there can be no competition and, hence, the owner of the expired patent may continue to charge a monopolistic price.

Since governments and consumers would benefit from lower prices as the result of generic competition, the Bolar exception may play an important role in reducing the burden on health budgets and increase access to more affordable pharmaceuticals. Studies for the US show, for instance, that drugs experiencing first generic entry in 1999–2000 maintained a share of 44 per cent of units at one year following first generic entry; in the period 2011–2012 the gain of market share by generics was much faster: originator products retained an average of only 16 per cent of units at one year (11 per cent in the case of products with sales greater than $250 million (in 2008 dollars) prior to first generic entry).[5]

The Bolar exception, first introduced by the US "Drug Price Competition and Patent Term Restoration Act" of 1984 (and more commonly known as the "Hatch-Waxman Act"),[6] intended to strike a compromise between the so-called "innovator" and generic pharmaceutical producers. Generic producers were allowed to use the patented subject matter for the purpose of regulatory procedures before the expiry of relevant patent(s), while innovator companies were given the

3 This delay may be longer for biosimilars, to the extent that additional testing is required.

4 Jashree Watal, "Bolar Exception to Patent Rights: Some Economic Implications" (SCP Seminar on Exceptions and Limitations to Patent Rights, 3 November 2014), www.wipo.int/edocs/mdocs/scp/en/scp_21/scp_21_ref_watal.pdf. In Europe, the registration of a generic medicine usually takes one to two years, but can sometimes take longer (see British Generic Manufacturers Association, "Generic FAQs", www.britishgenerics.co.uk/about-generics/generics-faqs).

5 Henry Grabowski, Genia Long and Richard Mortimer, "Recent Trends in Brand-Name and Generic Drug Competition", 2013, Journal of Medical Economics, http://fds.duke.edu/db/attachment/2575.

6 35 USC § 271(e)(1): " . . . it shall not be an act of infringement to make, use, offer to sell, or sell within the United States or import into the United States a patented invention . . . solely for uses reasonably related to the development and submission of information under a Federal law which regulates the manufacture, use, or sale of drugs or veterinary biological products."

right to request, under certain circumstances and within some limits, an extension of the patent term to compensate for the delay in the FDA's approval process. The analysis of welfare implications of this Act indicated that

> . . . from the perspective of economic welfare, the Act is the source of large potential positive gains of two types. First, it eliminated costly scientific testing which served no valid purpose. Second, the Act lowered prices to consumers with some elimination of deadweight losses and large transfers from producers to consumers.[7]

The name of the exception derives its origin from the earlier decision by the US Federal Circuit in *Roche Products, Inc. vs Bolar Pharmaceutical Co., Inc.* (733 F.2d 858, 1984). The court held in this case that the experimental use exemption to patent infringement narrowly provided under US law (35 U.S.C. § 271(a)) did not allow for testing undertaken by Bolar Pharmaceutical to obtain marketing approval of a generic product. The "Hatch-Waxman Act" overturned this decision only a few months after its issuance.

This chapter briefly addresses, first, the regulatory requirements applicable to marketing approval of pharmaceutical products. Second, it examines the Bolar exception in the light of the Agreement on Trade-Related Aspects of Intellectual Property Rights ("the TRIPS Agreement"), particularly on the basis of the findings of a World Trade Organization (WTO) panel that examined the consistency of such exception with Article 30 of the said agreement. Third, it analyses how the Bolar exception has been introduced in different countries without any intention, however, of presenting the full panorama. Finally, the chapter discusses several aspects that need to be considered in drafting and interpreting a Bolar-type provision.

Marketing approval of pharmaceuticals

The marketing approval of a pharmaceutical product incorporating a new molecule generally requires tests in animals to assess its pharmacodynamic, phamacokinetic and toxicological profile, before tests in human beings are carried out. The latter are conducted in different phases, under protocols that vary in accordance with therapeutic classes and even among drugs within one therapeutic class. In "phase I" (focused on toxicity and bioavailability) a small group of healthy volunteers receive the candidate product for a short period; "phase II" has as a primary objective to assess the new substance's effectiveness. In "phase III" trials are conducted on a number of patients (often involving several hundred volunteers) for substantial periods (depending on the therapeutic class and the purpose of

7 W. Viscusi, J. Vernon and J. Harrington, *Economics of Regulation and Antitrust* (2nd edn, MIT Press, 1997), 857.

the study[8]) to determine efficacy and safety including side effects, drug interactions and specific dosage for different indications.[9]

In addition to these test data, national authorities normally require information on the quantitative and qualitative composition and other attributes of the product, as well as on manufacturing methods. Marketing approval is granted for a specific drug used as a specific therapy.

While these requirements apply to *new* pharmaceuticals, the marketing approval of a generic product is subject to simplified procedures. For instance, the US Food and Drug Administration (FDA), as well as other regulatory authorities, do not require the repetition of pre-clinical and clinical studies to establish safety and effectiveness. Instead, the submission of data is required showing that the generic product is bioequivalent (i.e., that it performs in the same manner as the "innovator" drug, including the time it takes the drug to reach the bloodstream (bioavailability), tested in 24 to 36 healthy volunteers).[10]

Other regulatory authorities, however, do not require demonstration of bioquivalence in all cases; it is sufficient to show chemical equivalence with the "originator" product. Under some regulations, for instance, chemical equivalence and evidence that the product has been approved by the regulatory authority of a country that applies high standards for assessing efficacy and safety are sufficient to register a generic product. The time needed to market a generic product after the expiry of a patent will be generally shorter in countries that provide for such kind of approval by reference.

In the case of biologicals (therapeutic substances consisting of or derived from biological sources, such as vaccines, proteins, hormones), which account for a growing share of the pharmaceutical market,[11] special requirements apply. There has been considerable debate regarding the approval of "biosimilars" once the respective patents have expired. In many cases, biologicals – such as those for anti-cancer therapies – are highly priced[12] and the early introduction of biosimilars may have a major impact in terms of access to treatment.

8 For instance, the approval of the second indication of a known medicine may require clinical studies involving a small number of volunteers for a short term. For example, a US company obtained FDA approval for a colchicine product ("Colcrys") to treat acute gout pain on the basis of clinical studies involving 185 patients for one week (see Aaron S. Kesselheim and Daniel H. Solomon, "Incentives for Drug Development – The Curious Case of Colchicine" (NEJM, 14 April 2010), www.nejm.org/doi/full/10.1056/NEJMp1003126.

9 Long-term animal toxicity studies are also undertaken to determine the effects of the prolonged exposure and on subsequent generations.

10 See FDA, "Abbreviated New Drug Application (ANDA): Generics", www.fda.gov/Drugs/DevelopmentApprovalProcess/HowDrugsareDevelopedandApproved/ApprovalApplications/AbbreviatedNewDrugApplicationANDAGenerics/.

11 It is estimated that biologicals account for 20 per cent of the global pharmaceutical market. See, e.g., Ralf Otto, Alberto Santagostino and Ulf Schrader, "Rapid Growth in Biopharma: Challenges and Opportunities" (December 2014), www.mckinsey.com/insights/health_systems_and_services/rapid_growth_in_biopharma.

12 John Gapper, "The Unhealthily High Price of Cancer Drugs" (3 June 2015), www.ft.com/cms/s/0/9033f5fc-09d6-11e5-b6bd-00144feabdc0.html.

While the "innovator" companies have argued that it is not possible to show equivalence (or "biosimilarity") for biologicals as in the case of chemical entities,[13] several countries have adopted regulations to make it possible to obtain an abbreviated or simplified marketing approval of biosimilars.[14] Applicants need to submit a series of data (such as product characterization, *in vitro* and/or *in vivo* studies, toxicity studies, some clinical studies, etc. to allow comparability with the "innovator" product), which differ among jurisdictions. Biosimilars have been available in Europe since 2006. Specific guidelines concerning the scientific data needed to establish similarity between the referenced and the similar biologic products have been developed, so as to fulfil the requirements of Annex I of Directive 2001/83/EC.[15] The biosimilarity is established on the basis of analytical models, manufacturing process as well as clinical models. In the USA, the "Biologics Price Competition and Innovation Act" (BPCIA) of 2009 established an abbreviated pathway for biologicals[16] which are shown to be biosimilar to an FDA licensed reference product.[17] Many developing countries, such as Argentina,[18] India[19] and Colombia,[20] have also adopted guidelines on the subject to speed up the registration of biosimilars.

13 Thus, it has been argued that clinical studies should be repeated for each bisosimilar, which would significantly raise the cost of entry of competitive products. It has also been suggested that biosimilars should not be allowed to use the same non-proprietary name as the "innovator" product, in order to distinguish them from the "innovator" products. The US Federal Trade Commission has opposed a proposal by the US FDA to distinguish biological products through the use of a randomly assigned unique four letter suffix following the product's non-proprietary name, on the ground that "price competition is more intense when the products are seen as close substitutes for one another". See, e.g., Michael Mezher, "Industry, Patient Groups Weigh in on FDA's Biosimilar Naming Guidance" (29 October 2015), www.raps.org/Regulatory-Focus/News/2015/10/29/23487/Industry-Patient-Groups-Weigh-in-on-FDAs-Biosimilar-Naming-Guidance/#sthash.vauDaJJN.dpuf.

14 See Chapter 3 in this volume.

15 See http://ec.europa.eu/health/files/eudralex/vol1/dir_2001_83_consol_2012/dir_2001_83_cons_2012_en.pdf.

16 See FDA, "Scientific Considerations in Demonstrating Biosimilarity to a Reference Product Guidance for Industry" (April 2015), www.fda.gov/downloads/DrugsGuidanceCompliance RegulatoryInformation/Guidances/UCM291128.pdf.

17 The approval of the first biosimilar accepted in the US – Novartis's drug "Zarxio", which contains the same active ingredient as Amgen's "Neupogen" – was the subject of litigation based on the interpretation of some aspects of the BCPIA. In March 2015 a US District Court judge dismissed Amgen's claim. See, e.g., Reuters, "Judge Rejects Bid by Amgen to Block Biosimilar Drug by Novartis" (19 March 2015, The New York Times), www.nytimes.com/2015/03/20/business/judge-rejects-bid-by-amgen-to-block-biosimilar-drug-by-novartis.html?_r=0.

18 ANMAT Disposición 7729/11 and Disposición 7075/11.

19 Government of India, "Guidelines on Similar Biologics: Regulatory Requirements for Market Authorization in India" (2012), http://dbtbiosafety.nic.in/Files%5CCDSCO-DBTSimilar Biologicsfinal.pdf.

20 Germán Velásquez, "La Sana Victoria de los Biotecnológicos" (Semana, 20 September 2014), www.semana.com/nacion/articulo/la-sana-victoria-de-los-medicamentos-biotecnologicos/403469-3.

Although generic products and biosimilars[21] are normally subject to conditions for marketing approval much less complex and time- and investment-consuming than those for new molecules, the time needed to obtain such approval may considerably delay the commercialization of competitive products after the expiry of the relevant patents, if the procedures for approval are not initiated before that date. As mentioned, this time-lag would allow the owner of the expired patent(s) to prolong the monopolistic position. On the contrary, allowing for generic products and biosimilars to enter the market immediately after patent expiry may make available cheaper alternatives to the "innovator" product. While the latter will inevitably lose its market share, it can still be sold at a high price as a result of marketing strategies and brand loyalty.[22]

The Bolar exception serves the interest of the public as well as governments and social security systems that bear the cost of medicines. There is ample evidence indicating that, after the first generic is introduced following patent expiration, price is reduced, albeit it may not be initially significant. In the US, for instance, the introduction of the second generic, on average, has been reported to reduce the price by half, and that when a larger number of generic manufacturers enter the market, the average price may fall to 20 per cent or less of that of the brand-name product.[23]

Consistency of the Bolar exception with the TRIPS Agreement[24]

In accordance with the TRIPS Agreement, patents confer exclusive rights to the holder of making, using, offering for sale, selling, or importing (except to the extent that parallel imports are allowed)[25] for those purposes a protected

21 In the remainder of this chapter, references to "generics" or "generic products" are intended to encompass biosimilars as well.

22 Richard E. Caves, Michael D. Whinston and Mark A. Hurwitz, "Patent Expiration, Entry, and Competition in the U.S. Pharmaceutical Industry: An Exploratory Analysis" (1991), 7 Brookings Papers on Economic Activity 1; Richard G. Frank and Davis S. Salkever, "Pricing, Patent Loss and the Market for Pharmaceuticals" (1992) 59(2), Southern Economic Journal 165; Henry G. Grabowski and John M. Vernon, "Brand Loyalty, Entry, and Price Competition in Pharmaceuticals after the 1984 Drug Act" (1992), 35(2) Journal of Law and Economics 331; Milt Freudenheim, "Cleaning Out the Medicine Cabinet" (The New York Times, 11 September 1997), www.nytimes.com/1997/09/11/business/cleaning-out-the-medicine-cabinet-prescription-drug-makers-reconsider-generics.html?pagewanted=all; Jorge Gonzalez Rodriguez et al, "Can Branded Drugs Benefit from Generic Entry?: The Role of Detailing and Price in Switching to Non-Bioequivalent Molecules" (2008) 25(4), International Journal of Research in Marketing 247, www.sciencedirect.com/science/article/pii/S0167811608000578.

23 See www.express-scripts.com/art/pdf/kap17Medications.pdf.

24 This section is partially based on Carlos M. Correa, *Trade Related Aspects of Intellectual Property Rights*, vol. 6 (Commentaries on the GATT/WTO Agreements, Oxford University Press, 2007).

25 See Article 6 of the TRIPS Agreement.

product.[26] These rights, however, are subject to exceptions under the general requirements contained in Article 30 of the agreement.[27]

The consistency of the "Bolar exception" with Article 30 of the TRIPS Agreement was tested in a case initiated in November 1998 by the European Communities and their member States (EC) against Canada, which had introduced a Bolar exception in 1991. The challenged provision explicitly allowed a third party to use the patented invention to submit the information required for marketing approval (in Canada or abroad) as well as to stockpile the product (for up to six months) for release immediately after the expiry of the patent.[28]

In March 2000, the WTO panel concluded that Canada was not in violation of the TRIPS Agreement in terms of its practice of allowing the development and submission of information required to obtain marketing approval for pharmaceutical products carried out without the consent of the patent holder. However, Canada was found to be acting inconsistently with the agreement in terms of its practice of manufacturing and stockpiling pharmaceutical products during the six months immediately prior to the expiry of the 20-year patent term.[29]

The admissibility of exceptions to patent rights is subject, under Article 30 of the TRIPS Agreement, to three conditions which, in the view of the panel, are:

> . . . cumulative, each being a separate and independent requirement that must be satisfied. Failure to comply with any one of the three conditions results in the Article 30 exception being disallowed.[30]

The panel added that:

> The three conditions must, of course, be interpreted in relation to each other. Each of the three must be presumed to mean something different

26 Article 28.1(a) of the TRIPS Agreement.

27 Article 30: "Members may provide limited exceptions to the exclusive rights conferred by a patent, provided that such exceptions do not unreasonably conflict with a normal exploitation of the patent and do not unreasonably prejudice the legitimate interests of the patent owner, taking account of the legitimate interests of third parties."

28 Patent Act, Section 55.2(1): "It is not an infringement of a patent for any person to make, construct, use or sell the patented invention solely for uses reasonably related to the development and submission of information required under any law of Canada, a province or a country other than Canada that regulates the manufacture, construction, use or sale of any product." Patent Act, Section 55.2(2). "It is not an infringement of a patent for any person who makes, constructs, uses or sells a patented invention in accordance with subsection (1) to make, construct or use the invention, during the applicable period provided for by the regulations, for the manufacture and storage of articles intended for sale after the date on which the term of the patent expires". In accordance with the Manufacturing and Storage of Patented Medicines Regulations, "the applicable period referred to in subsection 55.2(2) of the Patent Act is the six month period immediately preceding the date on which the term of the patent expires".

29 WT/DS114/R.

30 Ibid, para. 7.20.

> from the other two, or else there would be redundancy. Normally, the order of listing can be read to suggest that an exception that complies with the first condition can nevertheless violate the second or third, and that one which complies with the first and second can still violate the third. The syntax of Article 30 supports the conclusion that an exception may be "limited" and yet fail to satisfy one or both of the other two conditions. The ordering further suggests that an exception that does not "unreasonably conflict with normal exploitation" could nonetheless "unreasonably prejudice the legitimate interests of the patent owner".[31]

The consideration of the three conditions established by Article 30 as "cumulative" does not find support in the text of the provision nor is it justified under an interpretation in accordance with the Vienna Convention on the Law of the Treaties. As noted in the "Declaration on Patent Protection. Regulatory Sovereignty under TRIPS" elaborated under the auspices of the Max Planck Institute for Innovation and Competition (MPG):·

> Contrary to what a panel of the WTO's Dispute Settlement Body seemed to assume (cf. WT/DS114/R of 17 March 2000), the three conditions are not cumulative. The three-step test may be understood to require a comprehensive overall assessment rather than a separate and independent assessment of each criterion. Failure to comply with one of the three conditions need not result in the exception being disallowed.[32] The first condition to be met under the referred to Article 30 of the TRIPS Agreement is that the exception must be "limited". In accordance with the WTO panel:
>
> > The word "exception" by itself connotes a limited derogation, one that does not undercut the body of rules from which it is made. When a treaty uses the term "limited exception", the word "limited" must be given a meaning separate from the limitation implicit in the word "exception" itself. The term "limited exception" must therefore be read to connote a narrow exception – one which makes only a small diminution of the rights in question.[33]

In the absence of other indications, the panel concluded that it would be justified in reading the text literally, to focus on the extent to which legal rights have been curtailed, rather than the size or extent of the economic impact. In support of this conclusion, the panel noted that the following two conditions of Article 30 ask more particularly about the economic impact of the exception, and provide two sets of standards by which such impact may be judged. The term "limited

31 Ibid, para. 7.21.

32 MPG, "Declaration on Patent Protection: Regulatory Sovereignty under TRIPS", www.mpg.de/8132986/Patent-Declaration.pdf, 8.

33 WT/DS114/R, para. 7.30.

exceptions" is the only one of the three conditions in Article 30 under which the extent of the curtailment of rights as such is dealt with.[34]

By adopting a narrow concept of "limited", the panel focused on the extent of the curtailment of rights and not on the economic implications thereof. Hence, an exception with little economic effects might be disallowed under this doctrine even if the patent owner is not negatively affected in practice. The panel's view that the economic impact of the exception must be evaluated under the other conditions of Article 30 unduly narrows down the scope of admissible exceptions.

The language of the second condition established by Article 30 (the exception should not "unreasonably conflict with the normal exploitation" of the patent) was substantially borrowed from Article 9(2) of the Berne Convention. Canada argued that "exploitation" of the patent involved the extraction of commercial value from the patent by "working" the patent, either by selling the product in a market from which competitors are excluded, or by licensing others to do so, or by selling the patent rights outright. The EC defined "exploitation" by referring to the same three ways of "working" a patent, but differed on the interpretation of the term "normal".[35] In the panel's view, "normal" is "regular, usual, typical, ordinary, conventional".[36] The panel did not take a position with regard to the empirical or normative connotation of the concept. It held that:

> . . . the term can be understood to refer either to an empirical conclusion about what is common within a relevant community, or to a normative standard of entitlement. The Panel concluded that the word "normal" was being used in Article 30 in a sense that combined the two meanings (para. 7.54).

The normal practice of exploitation by patent owners, as with owners of any other intellectual property right, is to exclude all forms of competition that could detract significantly from the economic returns anticipated from a patent's grant of market exclusivity. The specific forms of patent exploitation are not static, of course, for to be effective exploitation must adapt to changing forms of competition due to technological development and the evolution of marketing practices. Protection of all normal exploitation practices is a key element of the policy reflected in all patent laws.[37]

The panel's reasoning is questionable since the right to exclude the use of the patented subject matter by third parties is not a form of exploitation of the patent, but a legal power established by law that may be exercised or not. However, the panel analysis led to the conclusion that in the case of the Canadian provision there was not conflict with the "normal" exploitation of a patent. As a result,

34 Ibid, para. 7.31.
35 Ibid, para. 7.51.
36 The New Shorter Oxford English Dictionary, p1940.
37 WT/DS114/R, para. 7.55

it was not necessary to elucidate whether the Canadian exception was reasonable or not.

The third condition of Article 30 requires that the exception does "not unreasonably prejudice the legitimate interests of the patent owner". While the EC argued that that "legitimate interests" were essentially "legal" interests, in rejecting this interpretation the panel considered that:

> To make sense of the term "legitimate interests" in this context, that term must be defined in the way that it is often used in legal discourse – as a normative claim calling for protection of interests that are "justifiable" in the sense that they are supported by relevant public policies or other social norms. This is the sense of the word that often appears in statements such as "X has no legitimate interest in being able to do Y".[38] The panel added that "a definition equating 'legitimate interests' with legal interests makes no sense at all when applied to the final phrase of Article 30 referring to the 'legitimate interests' of third parties" (para. 7.68).

In relation to the last part of Article 30 "taking account of the legitimate interests of third parties" – which is absent in Article 9(2) of the Berne Convention and in Article 13 of the TRIPS Agreement – the panel noted that:

> Absent further explanation in the records of the TRIPS negotiations, however, the Panel was not able to attach a substantive meaning to this change other than what is already obvious in the text itself, namely that the reference to the "legitimate interests of third parties" makes sense only if the term "legitimate interests" is construed as a concept broader than legal interests.[39]

Based on this reasoning and other convergent arguments, [40] the panel concluded, as noted, that the Canadian Bolar exception was consistent with the TRIPS Agreement. The panel ruling dismissed the argument suggesting that the owner of an expired patent had a right to a *de facto* extension of its monopoly resulting from the delay in the approval of generic products. However, as the panel found that the stockpiling provision was inconsistent with Article 30 of the TRIPS Agreement, and Canada subsequently amended its legislation in this regard.[41]

38 Ibid, para. 7.69.

39 Ibid, para. 7.71.

40 Thus, it rejected the argument that the Canadian exception was discriminatory (and hence incompatible with Article 27.1 of the TRIPS Agreement). It is worth noting that the challenged Section 55.2(1) applied to any regulated products, and not only to pharmaceuticals, that it allowed for submission of information in other countries and that it was not linked to an extension of the patent term.

41 Patent Act SC 1993, C.2, Section 5 5.2(1): "It is not an infringement of a patent for any person to make, construct, use or sell the patented invention solely for uses reasonably related to the development and submission of information required under any law of Canada, a

The Bolar exception in national laws

Since this panel decision, the Bolar exception has been incorporated in many national laws.[42] It is clearly one of the "flexibilities" allowed by the TRIPS Agreement widely recommended to mitigate the negative impact that patents may have on access to medicines, particularly in developing countries.[43] There are differences, however, regarding the scope of acts shielded from infringement claims.

In the US, a number of court cases have clarified some aspects of the Bolar exception under the Hatch-Waxman Act.[44] In *Eli Lilly and Co. vs Medtronic*, the Supreme Court affirmed that the exception not only applied to drugs but also to medical devices.[45] In *Merck KGaA vs Integra Lifesciences I, Ltd*,[46] the same court reversed the decision by the Federal Circuit and held that pre-clinical studies, if undertaken with the intent of making a submission to the FDA, even if the product was not finally made,[47] were exempted under 35 U.S.C. § 271(e)(1). The court stated that "[t]here is simply no room in the statute for excluding certain information from the exemption on the basis of the phase of research in which it is developed or the particular submission in which it could be included",[48] and that the application of the exception was not limited to situations in which a pharmaceutical candidate had already been identified and was being tested in order to obtain the FDA approval. The Supreme Court thus confirmed that the Bolar exception applied to pre-clinical and clinical studies related to safety and efficacy of a drug, including studies on the mechanism of action, pharmacology and pharmacokinetics. It held that a reasonable basis for believing that the experiments will produce the types of information that are relevant to a new drug application was sufficient for the Bolar exception to apply. In a later decision, the Federal Circuit considered that the exception also covered post-approval testing,

province or a country other than Canada that regulates the manufacture, construction, use or sale of any product . . . (6) For greater certainty, subsection (1) does not affect any exception to the exclusive property or privilege granted by a patent that exists at law in respect of acts done privately and on a non-commercial scale or for a non-commercial purpose or in respect of any use, manufacture, construction or sale of the patented invention solely for the purpose of experiments that relate to the subject-matter of the patent."

42 World Intellectual Property Organization (WIPO), "Exceptions and Limitations to Patent Rights: Experimental Use and/or Scientific Research" (report prepared by the Secretariat of WIPO for the SCLP, Twentieth Session Geneva 27 to 31 January 2014 (SCP/20/4)).

43 Germán Velásquez, Carlos Correa and Xavier Seuba, "IPR, R&D, Human Rights and Access to Medicines – An Annotated and Selected Bibliography" (South Centre, Geneva, 2012).

44 Anthony Tridico, Jeffrey Jacobstein and Leythem Wall, "Facilitating Generic Drug Manufacturing: Bolar Exemptions Worldwide" (WIPO Magazine, June 2014, www.wipo.int/wipo_magazine/en/2014/03/article_0004.html).

45 496 US 661 (1990).

46 545 US 193 (2005).

47 Merck tested patented RGD peptides, in vitro and in vivo, covered by five Integra patents in an effort to develop integrin antagonists as angiogenesis inhibitors.

48 *Merck KGaA vs Integra Lifesciences I, Ltd* 545 US 193, 202 (2005).

"even if the information collected [was] never submitted to a regulatory agency, provided that the agency require[d] such testing or the retention of records for possible inspection".[49]

In European countries, the experimentation *on* an invention (as opposed to *with* an invention) has been generally allowed, without excluding acts done for commercial purposes. Case law on this exception relating to pharmaceutical or agrochemical products accepted, for instance, research undertaken to find out more information about a product, provided that it was not made just to convince licensing authorities or customers about the virtues of an alternative product, and to obtain further information about the uses of a product and its possible side-effects and other consequences of its use.[50] In a case decided in 1997 by the German Federal Supreme Court[51] concerning erythropoietin, the court held that "the intention that is associated with an activity begun and carried out for research purposes cannot render such an activity infringing merely because the results of the research will not solely serve research purposes but above all will serve commercial purposes", thereby suggesting that research done for submitting the results of trials to the drug regulatory authority might be admissible under certain circumstances.

The situation was clarified in the European Union in 2004 through Article 10(6) of the Directive 2001/83/EC (as amended) in accordance to which:

> Conducting the necessary studies and trials with a view to the application of paragraphs 1, 2, 3 and 4 and the consequential practical requirements shall not be regarded as contrary to patent rights or to supplementary protection certificates for medicinal products.

This directive – which entered into force in October 2005 – exempts the use of a patented invention that is made to comply with the requirements for the marketing approval for generic medicines.[52] Since it does not clarify the terms "studies and trials", it has not led to the full harmonization within the EU, where many differences in the implementation of the exception exist.[53] On the one hand, while some countries (such as the United Kingdom, Belgium, Cyprus, Ireland, the

49 Anthony Tridico, Jeffrey Jacobstein and Leythem Wall, op. cit.

50 W. Cornish "Experimental Use of Patented Inventions in European Community States", 29 IIC 7 (1998), 736; see also Carlos M. Correa, "International Dimension of the Research Exception" (SIPPI Project, AAAS), http://sippi.aaas.org/intlexemptionpaper.shtml.

51 Clinical Trials II [1998] RPC 423.

52 Article 27(d) of the Agreement on a Unified Patent Court reiterates the Directive's exception: "The rights conferred by a patent shall not extend to any of the following: . . . (d) the acts allowed pursuant to Article 13(6) of Directive 2001/82/EC 1 or Article 10(6) of Directive 2001/83/EC 2 in respect of any patent covering the product within the meaning of either of those Directives".

53 András Kupecz and others, "Safe Harbors in Europe: An Update on the Research and Bolar Exemptions to Patent Infringement" (2015), 33, Nature Biotechnology, www.nature.com/nbt/journal/v33/n7/full/nbt.3273.html, 710.

Netherlands and Sweden) only seem to apply the exception to activities relating to marketing approval of generic medicines and biosimilars, other countries (such as Austria, Bulgaria, the Czech Republic, Denmark, Estonia, Finland, France, Germany, Hungary, Italy, Latvia, Lithuania, Luxembourg, Malta, Poland, Portugal, Romania, Slovakia, Slovenia and Spain) exempt uses in trials related to the development of new products.[54] On the other, some countries (such as Austria, Germany, Denmark and Italy) seem to also allow trials undertaken to comply with regulatory requirements abroad.[55]

The question whether outsourcing of an active pharmaceutical ingredient to a generic producer is exempted was considered in 2013 by the Polish Supreme Court in *Astellas Pharma Inc. Polpharma SA Pharmaceutical Works* (CSK 92/13). With regard to the argument that the supplier was unable to ensure that the purchaser effectively used the acquired product for the purposes allowed under the Bolar exception, the court ruled that the sale of the patented active ingredient, irrespective of its purpose, was not covered by it and constituted a patent infringement.[56]

In a similar case, the Düsseldorf Court of Appeal disagreed with the first instance decision that the sale of an active ingredient would be covered by the exception only if the supplier was the co-organizer of the tests and studies for regulatory approval.[57] The Court of Appeal referred in 2014 to the Court of Justice of the European Union (CJEU) the question whether the Bolar provision covered outsourcing and whether the supplier was bound to take measures to ensure that the active ingredient would only be used for obtaining regulatory approval.[58]

The Bolar exception has been adopted in many Latin American countries, such as Argentina (Law No. 24.766 of 1996),[59] Dominican Republic (Law No. 20–00 on Industrial Property of April 2000), Brazil (Law No. 10.196/2001), Chile (Patent Law, Article 49), Andean Community (Decision 689)[60] and Uruguay

54 The same would apply in Norway and Switzerland; see Anthony Tridico, Jeffrey Jacobstein and Leythem Wall, op. cit.

55 Ibid.

56 The court also refused to refer to the Court of Justice of the European Union for a preliminary ruling regarding the interpretation of the Bolar exemption. See Marta Koremba and Aleksandra Karpińska, "Poland: Outsourcing of API manufacture is not Covered by the Bolar Exemption" (6 February 2014), www.twobirds.com/en/news/articles/2014/global/life-sciences/poland-outsourcing-of-api-manufacture-is-not-covered-by-the-bolar-exemption.

57 See "CJEU – Referral Düsseldorf Court of Appeal Re Third Party Supply for Bolar Exemption" (EPLAW Patent Blog, 15 January 2014), www.eplawpatentblog.com/eplaw/2014/01/cjeu-referral-d%C3%BCsseldorf-court-of-appeal-re-third-party-supply-for-bolar-exemption.html.

58 See C-661/13, http://curia.europa.eu/juris/liste.jsf?language=en&num=C-661/13. Since the case was later withdrawn, the CJEU did not issue an interpretation on the subject.

59 The exception was not contained in the patent law adopted in 1995, but later incorporated it in the law dealing with test data and confidential information.

60 The incorporation of the exception into national laws is, however, facultative.

(Law No. 17.164, Article 39). Interestingly, the exception was introduced in some countries as a result of the implementation of free trade agreements (FTAs) with the US, which typically contain such exception.[61] These FTAs, however, seem only to exempt the use of the protected product to file for the marketing approval of a generic drug. They also provide that "if the Party permits exportation, the product shall only be exported outside the territory of that Party for purposes of meeting marketing approval requirements of that Party", thereby limiting the possibility of invoking the exception to seek regulatory approval in a foreign country. In Mexico, the Bolar exception is not recognized under the Mexican Industrial Property Law, but under Article 167*bis* of the Reglamento de Insumos para la Salud (Regulations on Health-Related Consumable Goods), in accordance to which it shall be possible to undertake studies, tests, or experimental production of product, the substance or active ingredient of which is protected by a patent, to request registration of a generic version of the same, within a period of three years before the expiration of the patent.

Most countries in Asia provide for the Bolar exception, albeit with different scope. In some countries it is limited to marketing approval in its own territory (e.g., Pakistan, Singapore), while in others (e.g., India, Philippines, Israel) acts relating to submissions in other countries are also exempted in some cases.[62] In Japan, acts relating to the marketing approval of medicines were deemed by the Supreme Court as covered by the patents law's experimentation exception. In a unanimous decision, the court in *Ono Pharmaceuticals Co., Ltd vs Kyoto Pharmaceutical Industries, Ltd* confirmed that tests during the patent term to obtain data required for regulatory approval were not infringing under Section 69(1) of the Japanese patent law.[63] Bolar-type provisions are also available in other jurisdictions, such as New Zealand and Australia.[64]

While some African countries have introduced a Bolar exception, the number of the countries that have done so seems lower than in other regions.[65] The Bangui Agreement Relating to the Creation of an African Intellectual Property Organization (OAPI), with the membership of 27 countries, currently does not include a Bolar exception among those provided for patent rights (Article 8, Annex I). The 2007 review[66] of the national legislation in 39 out of the 47 sub-Saharan African countries found, although most of them, including least-developed

61 See, for instance, Article 15.9.5 of the DR-CAFTA, https://ustr.gov/sites/default/files/uploads/agreements/cafta/asset_upload_file934_3935.pdf. See also the FTAs US–Chile, US–Colombia, US–Peru.

62 Anthony Tridico, Jeffrey Jacobstein and Leythem Wall, op. cit.

63 Jennifer A. Johnson, "The Experimental Use Exception in Japan: A Model for U.S. Patent Law?" (2003), 12(2) Pacific Rim Law & Policy Journal, 516.

64 See below.

65 See WIPO, "WIPO Regional Seminar on the Effective Implementation and Use of Several Patent-Related Flexibilities" (Bangkok, 29–31 March 2011), www.wipo.int/edocs/mdocs/patent_policy/en/wipo_ip_bkk_11/wipo_ip_bkk_11_ref_topic3.pdf.

66 Sisule Musungu, "Access to ART and Other Essential Medicines in Sub-Saharan Africa: Intellectual Property and Relevant Legislations" (Report commissioned by the United

countries, provided patents for pharmaceutical products, the level of the incorporation of the flexibilities, including the Bolar exception, was very low. Only three countries (Kenya, Namibia and Zimbabwe) specifically provided for the Bolar exception. Since the review, however, some African countries have incorporated it. For instance, a new Section 69A was introduced in the South African Patents Act by the legislative amendment in 2002 providing for an exception applicable to any regulated products. The provision specifies that the making, use or importation of the patented product must be "on a non-commercial scale" to submit "information required under any law that regulates the manufacture, production, distribution, use or sale of any product". Bolar exceptions can also be found in the laws of North African countries. For instance, in Egypt patent law exempts from patent infringement acts if "a third party proceeds, during the protection period of a product, with its manufacturing, assembly, use or sale, with a view to obtain a marketing license, provided that the marketing starts after the expiry of such a protection period". In Morocco, a Bolar exception was introduced by the FTA with the US, with the limitation regarding submissions of information in other countries noted above.[67]

Designing a Bolar exception

The previous overview suggests that there are several aspects that should be taken into consideration in drafting a Bolar exception. They are briefly referred to below.

Covered products

As mentioned above, some Bolar exceptions apply to all products subject to regulatory approval (e.g., under the laws of New Zealand and Canada).

Under some formulations, however, the exception is limited to health products for human use, including pharmaceuticals and medical devices (such as in the US, in accordance with courts' interpretation), while in some cases only pharmaceuticals are covered (Australia's Bolar exception, for instance, expressly excludes medical or therapeutic devices). In the EU and the US, producers of veterinary products may benefit from the Bolar exception as well.

While public health concerns deserve particular attention, the most reasonable approach would seem to cover under the exception all regulated products, since there is no solid argument to differentiate between health-related and other products, the marketing of which is subject to prior regulatory approval. This does

Nations Development Programme (UNDP), http://apps.who.int/medicinedocs/documents/s18248en/s18248en.pdf, 13.

67 A similar provision is contained in the FTAs entered into by the USA with Bahrain. See S. Musungu and C. Oh, "The Use of Flexibilites in TRIPS by Developing Countries: Can They Promote Access to Medicines?" (Study 4C Commission on Intellectual Property Rights, Innovation and Public Health, 2005), www.who.int/intellectualproperty/studies/TRIPSFLEXI.pdf.

not mean, however, that exceptions limited to pharmaceuticals (or sub-categories thereof, such as medicines) would be inconsistent with the TRIPS Agreement since, as noted by the WTO panel in *Canada–Patent Protection of Pharmaceutical Products*, a special treatment based on public health considerations is justified under Article 27.1 of said agreement.[68]

Specific or general

It has also been mentioned above that a Bolar-type exception has been recognized through the interpretation of more general exceptions allowing for research and/or experimentation on a patented invention. This may be the outcome of courts' interpretation (like in the case of Japan) or be provided for by the statute. For instance, the patent law of Croatia (1999) exempts:

> . . . acts done for the purposes of the research and development of the subject matter of the protected invention, in particular: making, using, offering for sale, importation, or exportation of the protected product, where such acts are reasonably connected with the experiments and tests necessary for the registration of the human and veterinary medicines, medical and veterinary products or preparations for the protection of plants (Article 5.2).

Permitted acts

In order to undertake testing of a generic product for approval by a regulatory authority, the applicant normally needs to work with samples of the drug embodying a patented invention. The required materials may be obtained through importation or production by the applicant. These possibilities are specifically spelled out in some laws (e.g., South African Patent Act). It is desirable to follow this approach in order to give certainty to both patent owners and generic producers about the scope of their rights.

Of particular importance is also to clarify whether outsourcing of an active ingredient to conduct the necessary tests is covered by the exception. As noted above, this issue has been controversial in Europe. In order to achieve its purpose, a well-formulated Bolar provision should make it clear that outsourcing is not infringing. If it were not allowed, many generic producers (especially small and medium enterprises) could be *de facto* prevented from undertaking trials exempted under the exception, thereby limiting generic competition and its potential price-reduction effect.

Some differences in the scope of the exception may stem from the wording used to refer to the relationship between the acts that are exempted and their purpose. Expressions like "acts for regulatory approval", "acts solely for uses reasonably

68 WT/DS114/R, para. 92.

related to regulatory approval" or "acts exclusively aiming at regulatory approval"[69] may lead to various determinations regarding what types of activities are effectively shielded from infringement claims.

Pre-clinical and/or clinical trials

Most Bolar exceptions do not clarify whether they apply to pre-clinical or clinical studies, or both. As noted above, in *Merck vs Integra*, the US Supreme Court ruled that pre-clinical studies involving patented compounds may be exempted from patent infringement under 35 U.S.C. § 271(e)(1), to the extent that there is a reasonable basis to believe that those studies will produce information relevant to an application to be filed with the FDA. This seems the right solution, as there is no reason to distinguish between early and late stages of research involving a patented product.

A pro-competitive Bolar exception may also cover post-approval testing required by a regulatory authority, even if the information is not actually submitted to it. The *Momenta Pharm. vs Amphastar Pharm.* (686 F.3d 1348, 2012) provides an example of a US precedent confirming the coverage under the Bolar exception of such testing.

Generic versions and/or new products

Another important dimension of the Bolar exception is whether it is only applicable to obtain the marketing approval of a *generic* product, or also to research that may lead to the development of a *new* product.

Some national laws do not distinguish whether the patented invention is used for the marketing approval of a generic or the development of a new pharmaceutical product. For example, Article 8 of Argentine law 24.766 of December 1996 states that:

> When a product or process is protected by a patent, any third party shall be able to use the invention before the expiration of the patent, with experimental aims and to gather the information required for the approval of a product or process by the competent authority, for its commercialization after the expiration of the patent.

The Thai Patent Act B.E 2522 (1979), as amended by B.E 2535 (1992), provides that the patentee's exclusive rights shall not apply to:

> . . . any act in respect of applications for drug registration, the applicant intending to produce, sell or import the patented pharmaceutical when the patent expires (Article 36.4).

The doctrine developed by US courts, as referred to above, is also relevant in this respect. The Canadian courts have likewise extended the Bolar exception to

69 See WIPO, Exceptions and Limitations to Patent Rights, op. cit., para. 132.

include material that is not submitted to a regulatory authority but is subject to potential inspection, including samples and data stored pursuant to regulatory requirements.[70]

A Bolar exception should apply to submissions relating to generic products as well as if the application for the approval of a generic product is not filed, for instance, because the tests did not produce outcomes of immediate use.

Term to file an application

Can testing and research be conducted under a Bolar exception at any time during the life of the relevant patent? Normally, generic producers will start such activities within a reasonable period before the expiry of the patent, once the commercial attractiveness of a product can be established with some certainty, and there is no need to wait for a long period before the investment made to obtain the required authorization can be recouped.

Most national laws do not address this issue; the decision when to start the procedures is left to the interested parties. In the case of the Mexican law, however, the defence under the Bolar-like exception, as noted, is available only when a patent on a chemical is within three years of expiration.

Submissions in foreign countries

Some laws contain Bolar-type exceptions that only permit acts relating to the submission of an application in the respective country, while others also allow, as mentioned above, to make submissions abroad.[71] There is no solid justification for a limitation regarding submissions in foreign countries. The legitimate interests protected under a patent granted in the country where trials take place are not affected by acts made in another jurisdiction. Patents are of territorial nature. Whether the submission of information in a foreign country, before the expiry of a patent granted there, is admissible or not is a matter solely subject to the law of that country.

Taking advantage of the precedent set by the Canadian Bolar exception, many countries allow acts the purpose of the registration of generic products in foreign countries. For instance, the patent law of Croatia, mentioned above, explicitly refers to exportation of the protected products. Brazilian Law 10.196 (2001) contains an exception for acts performed by non-authorized third parties, regarding patented inventions, which aim exclusively at the production of information, data and test results directed to procure commercial registration, in Brazil or any other country, to allow the exploitation and commercialization of the patented product, after the termination of the patent (Article 43 (VII)). Section

70 See Anthony Tridico, Jeffrey Jacobstein and Leythem Wall, op. cit.

71 In the case of Israel, this is limited to other countries where a Bolar exception is also recognized.

107(a) of the Indian Patents Act more broadly exempts acts relating to the development and submission of information required by law "in India or in a country other than India". A similar far-reaching exemption is also found in the Universally Accessible Cheaper and Quality Medicines Act of 2008 (Section 72(4)) of the Philippines.

Extension of the patent term

The introduction of the Bolar exception, as provided for in most countries, has not been linked to an extension of the term of the respective patent, as it is the case of the USA, given the particular circumstances under which that exception was introduced. There is nothing in the TRIPS Agreement or in other international instruments requiring an extension of the patent term as a condition for providing for a Bolar exception. Canadian law scrutinized and found WTO-consistent in *Canada–Pharmaceutical Patents* (except with regard to the stockpiling of products) likewise did not grant such an extension.

Conclusion

The Bolar exception has clear pro-competitive effects, which are of particular importance in the area of public health. Since the exclusive rights of the patent owner are not affected during the patent term, its incorporation into patent regimes (or other relevant legislation) is amply justified. The Bolar exception is one of the important flexibilities allowed by the TRIPS Agreement. In fact, its recognition long preceded the adoption of that agreement, and is today broadly accepted in developed and developing countries. Law-makers and courts should be aware of a diversity of aspects that determine, in practice, the scope of acts permissible under the exception. The broader the formulation of the exception in terms of covered products, sources of samples, type of trials allowed, time to undertake them, and geographical scope, the more competitive environment is ensured that will benefit consumers, health providers and other public agencies.

7 Compulsory Licensing

Threats, Use and Recent Trends

Chang-fa Lo

Introduction

There are many different perspectives from which one could look at compulsory licensing of pharmaceutical patents. From the intellectual property rights (IPRs) perspective, compulsory licensing is a limitation of exclusive rights which are enjoyed by a patent holder and, at the same time, an important component of the patent system. Under the Agreement on Trade-Related Aspects of Intellectual Property Rights (the TRIPS Agreement), a compulsory licence is a flexibility available for WTO Members which need the patented products or processes in order to cope with serious situations in their jurisdictions. From the public health perspective, compulsory licensing is an important scheme for countries, especially for developing and least developed countries, to acquire available and affordable drugs that are needed for public health purposes.

This chapter will discuss the threat, use and recent trends of compulsory licensing. The second section defines the meaning and functions of compulsory licensing. The third section reviews the requirements under the TRIPS Agreement. Section four provides recent examples. The fifth section proposes factors that should be considered when adopting compulsory licensing in order to maintain the balance between the accessible and affordable drugs for developing countries, on the one hand, and the legitimate interest of pharmaceutical patent holders, on the other.

Meaning and functions of compulsory licensing

Exclusive rights of patent holders and compulsory licensing as a limitation

Under Article 28.1 of the TRIPS Agreement, a patent holder shall have exclusive rights to prevent third parties from unauthorized making, using, offering for sale, selling, or importing a patented product (where the subject matter of a patent is a product) or the product obtained directly by a patented process (where the subject matter of a patent is a process). According to Article 28.2, patent owners shall also have the right to assign the patent and to conclude licensing contracts.

The purpose of exclusive rights is to prevent others from activities that could undermine the value of patents to patent holders. Although the exclusive rights are supposed to be protected by Members of the World Trade Organization (WTO), there are certain exceptions and limitations. The TRIPS Agreement provides some flexibilities (but with detailed requirements) for countries, mainly developing and least developed countries, to alleviate difficulties in implementing the obligations under the TRIPS Agreement. Compulsory licensing is one of such flexibilities. It allows third parties to use a patent without the patent holder's authorization. Hence compulsory licensing is a limitation to exclusive rights conferred to patent holders under TRIPS Article 28.

Compulsory licensing as an important flexibility for developing countries

Developing countries generally consider that compulsory licensing is "one of the key instruments that may limit the exclusive rights of the patent owner when needed to fulfill certain objectives of public policy, particularly in order to ensure the availability of alternative sources for the supply of medicines at lower prices".[1]

At the Fourth Ministerial Conference of the WTO in Doha in 2001, ministers adopted two declarations, one of which – the Doha Ministerial Declaration – stresses the importance attached to implementation and interpretation of the TRIPS Agreement "in a manner supportive of public health, by promoting both access to existing medicines and research and development into new medicines".[2] Based on the decision, the ministers also adopted a "separate declaration" – that is, the "Doha Declaration on the TRIPS Agreement and Public Health" (hereinafter "Doha Public Health Declaration")[3] to support public health and to promote access to medicines and research and development (R&D) for new drugs. It includes the following main points.

First, the Doha Public Health Declaration recognizes the importance of intellectual property protection for the development of new medicines, on the one hand, and "the concerns about its effects on prices", on the other. Ministers also agreed that "the TRIPS Agreement does not and should not prevent members from taking measures to protect public health" and affirmed that the TRIPS Agreement "can and should be interpreted and implemented in a manner supportive of WTO members' right to protect public health and, in particular, to promote access to medicines for all".[4]

1 Carlos M. Correa, "Implications of Doha Declaration on the TRIPS Agreement and Public Health" (2002), 15, http://apps.who.int/medicinedocs/pdf/s2301e/s2301e.pdf, accessed 15 January 2016.

2 Doha Ministerial Conference, Ministerial declaration, WT/MIN(01)/DEC/1, adopted on 20 November 2001, para. 17.

3 Doha Ministerial Conference, Declaration on the TRIPS Agreement and public health, WT/MIN(01)/DEC/2, adopted on 14 November 2001.

4 Ibid, paras 3, 4.

Second, ministers further reaffirmed "the right of WTO members to use, to the full, the provisions in the TRIPS Agreement, which provide flexibility for this purpose".[5] The flexibilities include: applying the customary rules of interpretation of public international law so as to have each provision of the TRIPS Agreement to be read in the light of the object and purpose of the Agreement as expressed in Articles 7 and 8 of the TRIPS Agreement. They also affirmed "each member's right to grant compulsory licences and its freedom to determine the grounds upon which such licences are granted" and "each member's right to determine what constitutes a national emergency or other circumstances of extreme urgency, it being understood that public health crises, including those relating to HIV/AIDS, tuberculosis, malaria and other epidemics, can represent a national emergency or other circumstances of extreme urgency".[6]

Third, ministers recognized that WTO members with insufficient or no manufacturing capacities in the pharmaceutical sector could face difficulties in making effective use of compulsory licensing under the TRIPS Agreement and thus they instructed the Council for TRIPS to find an expeditious solution to this problem and to report to the General Council before the end of 2002.[7]

Fourth, ministers reaffirmed the commitment of developed country members to provide incentives to their enterprises and institutions to promote and encourage technology transfer to least developed country members pursuant to Article 66.2 and agreed that the least developed country members will not be obliged, with respect to pharmaceutical products, to implement or apply Sections 5 and 7 of Part II of the TRIPS Agreement or to enforce rights provided for under these sections until 1 January 2016, without prejudice to the right of least developed country members to seek other extensions of the transition periods as provided for in Article 66.1 of the TRIPS Agreement. They further instructed the Council for TRIPS to take the necessary action to give effect to this pursuant to Article 66.1 of the TRIPS Agreement.[8]

Later on, a number of WTO Decisions were adopted to further implement the Doha Public Health Declaration, including the following:

1 *Decision on the Extension of the Transition Period under Article 66.1 of the TRIPS Agreement for Least Developed Country Members for Certain Obligations with Respect to Pharmaceutical Products*, adopted by the TRIPS Council on 27 June 2002 to implement the second and third sentences of paragraph 7 of the Doha Public Health Declaration. Under the decision, least developed countries are not required to protect pharmaceutical patents and test data until 1 January 2016.

5 Ibid, para 4.
6 Ibid, para 5.
7 Ibid, para 6.
8 Ibid, para 7.

2 *Decision on Least Developed Country Members – Obligations under Article 70.9 of the TRIPS Agreement with Respect to Pharmaceutical Products*, adopted by the General Council on 8 July 2002 in order to achieve the objectives of paragraph 7 of the Doha Public Health Declaration. Under this decision, least developed countries are not required to grant exclusive marketing rights to pharmaceutical products that are subject of a patent application until 1 January 2016.
3 *Decision on the Implementation of Paragraph 6 of the Doha Declaration on the TRIPS Agreement and Public Health*, adopted by the General Council on 30 August 2003 concerning "waivers" granted for countries that cannot manufacture the pharmaceuticals themselves concerning the limitations on exports under compulsory licence. This will be explained below.
4 *Decision on the Amendment of the TRIPS Agreement*, adopted by the General Council on 6 December 2005. The decision adopts a protocol of amendment to amend the requirement regarding the limitation on exports of generic products under a compulsory licence. The amendment will come into force after two thirds of members have accepted it, and will replace the August 2003 decision.

Functions of compulsory licensing in the pharmaceutical sector

Compulsory licensing allows third parties to use patented subject matter without the authorization of the patent holder. Rules governing compulsory licensing can apply to inventions in all fields of technology. For instance, TRIPS Article 31(c) mentions semi-conductor technology being potentially subject to compulsory licensing, but under stricter restrictions.

Among fields of technology and industrial sectors where compulsory licensing can be applied, the most controversial and frequently applied is the pharmaceutical sector. This is also the most difficult area because compulsory licensing does not only involve legal requirements, but also raises industrial policy issues (including the brand name drug industry and the generic industry) and the issues of the right to health.

As will be discussed below, compulsory licensing is more commonly used by developing countries. But this does not mean that developed countries do not use the mechanism for certain public interest purposes. For instance, in the United States, there are compulsory licensing provisions applicable to patents for the pollution control devices under the Clean Air Act and patents involving nuclear materials.[9] However, for pharmaceutical patents, the frequent users of compulsory licensing are developing countries, especially those with strong generic industries.

There are a number of functions provided by the compulsory licensing to assist making medicines more affordable and available for patients. First, it can bring

9 Cole M. Fauver, "Compulsory Patent Licensing in the United States: An Idea Whose Time Has Come" (1988) 8 Northwestern J. Int'l L. & Bus., 670.

generic products to the market. The availability and affordability of drugs can be critical in the countries where healthcare resources are limited and the average standard of living is low. For instance, it is reported that in 2003, Malaysia issued "government use" compulsory licences on three patented AIDS medicines. It imported generic versions of the drugs from India. As a result, the average cost of treating an HIV/AIDS patient in Malaysia was reduced by 81 per cent (dropping from US$315 to $58 per month) and the number of HIV/AIDS patients treated in government hospitals and clinics increased from 1500 to 4000.[10] In this case, the effect on drugs availability and affordability is apparent. However, whether or not, and to what extent, compulsory licensing will enhance the availability and affordability of medicines depends on the different factors.

Second, compulsory licensing can be imposed to counteract anti-competitive use of patent protection. This is explicitly mentioned in TRIPS Article 31(k), which says that the WTO Members are not obliged to apply the conditions set forth in subparagraphs (b) (the prior negotiation requirement) and (f) (the requirement of being authorized predominantly for the supply of the domestic market) where such use is permitted to remedy a practice determined after judicial or administrative process to be anti-competitive. Also, the need to correct anti-competitive practices may be taken into account in determining the amount of remuneration in such cases. Such function is also useful for making drugs more available and affordable in those markets where the anti-competitive use of pharmaceutical patents occurred.

Third, compulsory licensing basically requires parties to negotiate a voluntary licence at the first stage, before resorting to compulsory licensing. Such possibility can encourage or push patent holders to grant a voluntary licence. And, of course, voluntary licensing provides similar functions of enhancing availability and affordability of medicines in the market, but perhaps to a lesser extent because the licence fee involved in the voluntary licensing arising even from the threat of compulsory licensing could still be higher than the fee involved in the compulsory licensing.

Fourth, compulsory licensing can help developing countries access and utilize new technologies. This is because when a generic company is permitted to use a patented process or product, it would be able to unveil, to conduct detailed research on and to practise the invention or technology. This definitely helps the enhancement of technologies in the industry and could also help the economy of the country which grants compulsory licensing. This, in turn, will also help this country improve its capability of making drugs more available and affordable.

10 Chee Yoke Ling, "Malaysia's Experience in Increasing Access to Antiretroviral Drugs: Exercising the 'Government Use' Option" (2006) Intellectual Property Rights Series 9, Third World Network 14, http://www.twnside.org.sg/title2/IPR/pdf/ipr09.pdf, accessed 15 January 2016.

Requirements under TRIPS Agreement

Compulsory licensing is not created by the TRIPS Agreement. As a matter of fact, it was already provided by the Paris Convention for the Protection of Industrial Property of 1883. Article 5 A(2) of the convention states: "Each country of the Union shall have the right to take legislative measures providing for the grant of compulsory licences to prevent the abuses which might result from the exercise of the exclusive rights conferred by the patent, for example, failure to work." The purpose of the compulsory licensing is to counteract the abusive use of exclusive rights granted to the patent holder. The TRIPS Agreement has broader purposes for applying compulsory licensing but subject to specific requirements.

TRIPS Article 31 (entitled "Other Use without Authorization of the Right Holders") is a detailed provision on the requirements of compulsory licensing:

> Where the law of a Member allows for other use[11] of the subject matter of a patent without the authorization of the right holder, including use by the government or third parties authorized by the government, the following provisions shall be respected:
>
> (a) authorization of such use shall be considered on its individual merits;
> (b) such use may only be permitted if, prior to such use, the proposed user has made efforts to obtain authorization from the right holder on reasonable commercial terms and conditions and that such efforts have not been successful within a reasonable period of time. This requirement may be waived by a Member in the case of a national emergency or other circumstances of extreme urgency or in cases of public non-commercial use. In situations of national emergency or other circumstances of extreme urgency, the right holder shall, nevertheless, be notified as soon as reasonably practicable. In the case of public non-commercial use, where the government or contractor, without making a patent search, knows or has demonstrable grounds to know that a valid patent is or will be used by or for the government, the right holder shall be informed promptly;
> (c) the scope and duration of such use shall be limited to the purpose for which it was authorized, and in the case of semi-conductor technology shall only be for public non-commercial use or to remedy a practice determined after judicial or administrative process to be anti-competitive;
> (d) such use shall be non-exclusive;
> (e) such use shall be non-assignable, except with that part of the enterprise or goodwill which enjoys such use;

11 "Other use" refers to use other than that allowed under Article 30.

(f) any such use shall be authorized predominantly for the supply of the domestic market of the Member authorizing such use;
(g) authorization for such use shall be liable, subject to adequate protection of the legitimate interests of the persons so authorized, to be terminated if and when the circumstances which led to it cease to exist and are unlikely to recur. The competent authority shall have the authority to review, upon motivated request, the continued existence of these circumstances;
(h) the right holder shall be paid adequate remuneration in the circumstances of each case, taking into account the economic value of the authorization;
(i) the legal validity of any decision relating to the authorization of such use shall be subject to judicial review or other independent review by a distinct higher authority in that Member;
(j) any decision relating to the remuneration provided in respect of such use shall be subject to judicial review or other independent review by a distinct higher authority in that Member;
(k) Members are not obliged to apply the conditions set forth in subparagraphs (b) and (f) where such use is permitted to remedy a practice determined after judicial or administrative process to be anti-competitive. The need to correct anti-competitive practices may be taken into account in determining the amount of remuneration in such cases. Competent authorities shall have the authority to refuse termination of authorization if and when the conditions which led to such authorization are likely to recur;
(l) where such use is authorized to permit the exploitation of a patent ("the second patent") which cannot be exploited without infringing another patent ("the first patent"), the following additional conditions shall apply:

    (i) the invention claimed in the second patent shall involve an important technical advance of considerable economic significance in relation to the invention claimed in the first patent;
    (ii) the owner of the first patent shall be entitled to a cross-licence on reasonable terms to use the invention claimed in the second patent; and
    (iii) the use authorized in respect of the first patent shall be non-assignable except with the assignment of the second patent.

1. The utilizing parties: it is provided in the preamble of Article 31 of the TRIPS Agreement that the authorization can be granted for the use of the government or for the use of third parties authorized by the government. There are cases where the authorization was issued for the governmental use of the patented drugs and cases where the authorization was issued to generic companies.

2. The domestic legislation: there must be domestic law allowing such involuntary authorization that sets forth the legal requirements and procedures for the government and companies to be followed when deciding the issuance of a compulsory licence.

3. Individual merits: compulsory licensing should not be granted on the general basis. It should be issued on the basis of the case-by-case assessment. Thus, a country would not be able to authorize all domestic generic companies to produce any patented HIV/AIDS drug.

4. Reasonable efforts/prior negotiation: the authorization can be granted only when, prior to the application for compulsory licence, the perspective licensee has made efforts to obtain authorization from the right holder on reasonable commercial terms and conditions and when such efforts have not been successful within a reasonable period of time.

The threshold for the requirement of making efforts needs to be decided together with the requirements of "reasonable commercial terms and conditions" and "reasonable period of time". The notion of "reasonableness" should be interpreted in connection with Articles 7 and 8 of the TRIPS Agreement. The developing status of a country should be taken into account to define reasonable commercial terms. The public health situation as well as the specific disease that the patented drug can treat should also be considered to decide the requirement of "reasonable period of time" for negotiating the authorization.

Such requirement can be waived in three situations – namely, national emergency, extreme urgency including public health crises and anti-competitive practices. Paragraph 5(c) of the Doha Public Health Declaration provides that "Each member has the right to determine what constitutes a national emergency or other circumstances of extreme urgency, it being understood that public health crises, including those relating to HIV/AIDS, tuberculosis, malaria and other epidemics, can represent a national emergency or other circumstances of extreme urgency."

5. National emergency and extreme urgency and the public non-commercial use: there are exceptions to the above requirement of making efforts or prior negotiation. In the cases of a national emergency or other circumstances of extreme urgency or in cases of public non-commercial use, the requirement of making effort or prior negotiation can be waived. In the situations of national emergency or other circumstances of extreme urgency, the right holder shall, nevertheless, be notified as soon as reasonably practicable. In the case of public non-commercial use, where the government or the contractor, without making a patent search, knows or has demonstrable grounds to know that a valid patent is or will be used by or for the government, the right holder shall be informed promptly.[12]

The factors of "national emergency" and "other circumstances of extreme urgency" are not defined. Article 31(b) of the TRIPS Agreement does not provide

12 Article 31(b) of the TRIPS Agreement.

clear guidance on the scope of or the decision for the two situations. The question what constitutes such emergency or extreme urgency situations was "vehemently debated".[13] There were concerns about the uncertainty especially from the perspective of developing countries for their application of the exceptions. According to the Doha Public Health Declaration, the TRIPS Agreement is to be read in light of the object and purpose of the agreement – that is, Articles 7 and 8. Ministers also affirmed in the Declaration "each member's right to grant compulsory licences and its freedom to determine the grounds upon which such licences are granted" and "each member's right to determine what constitutes a national emergency or other circumstances of extreme urgency, it being understood that public health crises, including those relating to HIV/AIDS, tuberculosis, malaria and other epidemics, can represent a national emergency or other circumstances of extreme urgency".[14] Accordingly, the scope of application is not restricted. HIV/AIDS, tuberculosis, and malaria are merely the illustrative ones. Most importantly, countries can decide for themselves the criteria of defining what constitutes national emergency and circumstances of extreme urgency; thus, the requirements can be eased.

6. Scope and duration: the scope and duration of such use shall be limited to the purpose for which it was authorized; and in the case of semi-conductor technology it shall only be for public non-commercial use or to remedy a practice determined after judicial or administrative process to be anti-competitive.[15] For instance, if a compulsory licence is issued for manufacturing Tamiflu, if there is an outbreak of bird flu, the duration of the compulsory licence should be limited to such incidence. However, it cannot be predicted when the outbreak will cease. Thus, there should be certain flexibility in determining the scope and duration of a licence.

7. Non-exclusive authorization: under Article 31(d) of the TRIPS Agreement a compulsory licence shall be non-exclusive. In other words, the government is not allowed to issue an exclusive authorization to a generic company, to prevent the patent owner from producing or selling the patented product, or to prevent the patent owner from authorizing other companies to produce a generic drug. This is to ensure that compulsory licensing is not used to grant monopoly to the licensee, that the patent holder still owns its right to utilize the patent, and that there will be competition in the market among brand name and generic drugs so as to make medicines more available and affordable.

8. Non-assignability: under paragraph (e) of Article 31 of the TRIPS Agreement, the licensed use shall be non-assignable, except with that part of the enterprise or

13 Mor Bakhoum, "TRIPS, Patent Rights and Right to Health: 'Price' or 'Prize' for Better Access to Medicine?" (2009) Max Planck Institute for Intellectual Property, Competition & Tax Law Research Paper No. 10–07.

14 The Doha Public Health Declaration, para 5.

15 Article 31(c) of the TRIPS Agreement.

goodwill which enjoys such use. The authorization does not allocate a property right to generic companies. The permission obtained from the government is merely to produce generic products to meet the demand in the country. Although generic companies can also make profits from selling products, the main purpose of such authorization is for public health (i.e., for making drugs more available and affordable for the patients).

9. The requirement of domestic supply: according to Article 31(f) of the TRIPS Agreement, the licensed use shall be predominantly for the supply of the domestic market of the Member authorizing such use. Although the requirement does not strictly prevent the possibility of supplying foreign markets, such supply should be kept to a minimal level. The phrase "authorized predominantly for the supply" indicates that not only the purpose of such authorization should be made for the purpose of supplying the domestic market, but also that the generic products are mainly sold in the domestic market. The term "predominant" indicates that products manufactured under a compulsory market can be sold in foreign markets only in rare and incidental cases.

The requirement of supplying the domestic market might not cause any problem for those countries having the necessary capacity to produce generic versions of patented drugs. However, for countries which do not have such manufacturing capacity, the requirement becomes a hurdle. While such countries are not able to produce generic drugs, other countries that have such capacity can be prevented from exporting generic drugs under this requirement.

Prior to the Doha Public Health Declaration, there were discussions about whether drugs produced under compulsory licensing can be imported into another country without the patent holder's consent.[16] This issue has been addressed in the declaration: paragraph 6 of the declaration recognizes such a problem by stating that "WTO members with insufficient or no manufacturing capacities in the pharmaceutical sector could face difficulties in making effective use of compulsory licensing under the TRIPS Agreement". Ministers thus instructed the Council for TRIPS to find an expeditious solution to this problem and to report to the General Council before the end of 2002.[17]

Based on this instruction, the WTO General Council adopted the above-mentioned "Decision on the Implementation of Paragraph 6 of the Doha Declaration on the TRIPS Agreement and Public Health" in 2003 to grant "waivers" under certain strictly defined terms. Paragraphs 2 to 4 of the decision contain three waivers. Paragraph 2 waives exporting countries' obligations under Article 31(f) – that is, the requirement of predominant domestic supply – to enable export of generic pharmaceutical products produced under compulsory licences. Paragraph 3 partially waives importing countries' obligations regarding the

16 Frederick M. Abbott, "The Doha Declaration on the TRIPS Agreement and Public Health: Lighting a Dark Corner at the WTO" (2002) 5 J. Int'l Econ. L. 469, 495–6.

17 The Doha Public Health Declaration, para 6.

payment of the adequate remuneration to the patent holder under compulsory licensing to avoid double payment. It only requires the exporting country to pay remuneration. Paragraph 4 waives export constraints for developing and least developed countries so that these countries can export within a regional trade agreement, when at least half of the members were categorized as least developed countries at the time of the decision.[18]

Later in 2005, the General Council of the WTO adopted the Decision on the Amendment of the TRIPS Agreement, which amended the requirement regarding the limitation on exports of generic products under a compulsory licence. The decision includes the "Protocol Amending the TRIPS Agreement" and "Annex to the Protocol Amending the TRIPS Agreement" proposing to add Article 31 *bis* the TRIPS Agreement. If the new Article 31*bis* becomes effective, it would make the waivers mentioned above permanent. Since there have not been enough support from WTO Members, the period for accepting the protocol was extended five times, with the latest extension being made in 2015 and the period being extended to 31 December 2017.[19]

There were no notifications of using the waivers after the decision was adopted in 2003 until in 2007 Rwanda notified the WTO of its importation of 260,000 packs of Apo-Triavir, a generic version of a patented HIV/AIDS drug manufactured by a Canadian pharmaceutical company Apotex Inc.[20]

It was not only developing countries lacking manufacturing capacity which started to utilize the waivers to import generic drugs; developed and some developing countries with the capacity of exporting generic drugs also began to make use of the waivers. For instance, Canada adopted the Canadian Access to Medicine Regime (CAMR) in 2005 to give effect to the waivers of the WTO. In 2007 the Canadian Intellectual Property Office granted the generic manufacturer Apotex a compulsory licence to produce and export to Rwanda 260,000 packs of Apo-Triavir and notified the WTO of its decision.[21]

10. Termination: under paragraph (g) of Article 31 of the TRIPS Agreement, the authorization for the licensed use shall be liable, subject to adequate protection of the legitimate interests of the persons so authorized, to be terminated if and when the circumstances which led to it cease to exist and are unlikely to recur; and the competent authority shall have the authority to review, upon motivated request, the continued existence of these circumstances. Again, this

18 See, further, Frederick M. Abbott and Rudolf V. Van Puymbroeck, "Compulsory Licensing for Public Health: A Guide and Model Documents for Implementation of the Doha Declaration Paragraph 6 Decision" (2005) World Bank Working Paper No. 61.

19 World Trade Organization, Amendment of the TRIPS Agreement – Fifth extension of the period for the acceptance by members of the Protocol amending the TRIPS Agreement, decision of 30 November 2015, WT/L/965.

20 International Centre for Trade and Sustainable Development, "Rwanda Tests Public Health Waiver" (1 October 2007) Bridges News 11(6), http://ictsd.org/i/news/bridges/4095/, accessed 15 January 2016.

21 Ibid.

is to ensure that the authorization is properly used only for the strictly defined situation.

11. Adequate remuneration: under paragraph (h) of Article 31 of the TRIPS Agreement, the right holder shall be paid adequate remuneration in the circumstances of each case, taking into account the economic value of the authorization. The decision of adequacy of the remuneration is difficult. If the remuneration is too low, it might not be fair to the patent owner and might be benefiting the generic companies too much. On the other hand, if the remuneration is too high, the generic companies might not be willing to produce the drugs or they might have to charge more for the generic drugs so as to cover their costs. Neither of these situations is desirable. Under the provision, the circumstances of each case are also to be considered. Economic development and general standards of living are among circumstances that should be taken into account for the purpose of deciding the level of remuneration.

12. Judicial review: under paragraphs (i) and (j) of Article 31 of the TRIPS Agreement, the legal validity of any decision relating to the authorization of such use shall be subject to judicial review or other independent review by a distinct higher authority in that Member, and any decision relating to the remuneration provided in respect of such use shall be subject to judicial review or other independent review by a distinct higher authority in that Member. This is particularly important to the patent holder. The scope of judicial review is broad. Any decision relating to the authorization is subject to such review. It is possible for the patent holder to request a judicial body or an independent body to review whether requirements of such authorization are met and whether the remuneration is adequate in light of the circumstances of the case.

13. Anti-competitive exceptions: under Article 31(k) of the TRIPS Agreement, WTO Members are not obliged to apply the conditions set forth in subparagraphs (b) and (f) where the licensed use is permitted to remedy a practice determined after judicial or administrative process to be anti-competitive; the need to correct anti-competitive practices may be taken into account in determining the amount of remuneration in such cases; competent authorities shall have the authority to refuse termination of authorization if and when the conditions which led to such authorization are likely to recur. The patent holder is granted a legal monopoly to exclude others from using a patent to manufacture and sell patented products. It is possible for the patent holder to exploit its legal monopoly position to prevent others from entering the market and engaging in competition. Such anti-competitive practice has an adverse effect on the functions of the market. The exceptions in this paragraph are designed to deter or counteract possible anti-competitive practices by the patent holder so as to make competition possible.

14. The cross-licensing and other requirements when two patents are involved: under paragraph (l) of Article 31 of the TRIPS Agreement, where the use is authorized to permit the exploitation of a patent ("the second patent") which cannot be exploited without infringing another patent ("the first patent"), the following additional conditions shall apply:

(i) the invention claimed in the second patent shall involve an important technical advance of considerable economic significance in relation to the invention claimed in the first patent;

(ii) the owner of the first patent shall be entitled to a cross-licence on reasonable terms to use the invention claimed in the second patent; and

(iii) the use authorized in respect of the first patent shall be non-assignable except with the assignment of the second patent.

This provision intends to ensure that when there are two related patents involved, the other related patent should be taken into account when granting a compulsory licence for a patent.

Uses and threats of compulsory licensing for pharmaceutical patents in some jurisdictions and the general trend

Uses and threats

A number of countries have already granted compulsory licensing for the production of pharmaceutical products including the following, commonly cited examples.

1. Thailand: the HIV/AIDS prevalence in Thailand was high in the 1990s and 2000s. The Thai government implemented its National Plan for Prevention and Alleviation of HIV/AIDS, but its budget declined by 14 per cent in the late 1990s. In addition to other transmission channels, it was estimated by a Thai Working Group that in 2000 around 12,500 of adult HIV infections were spread between spouses. Between 2004 and 2005, Thailand's Department of Disease Control requested patent holders to reduce prices for anti-retrovirals, but without a satisfactory outcome. In November 2006, the Thai Department of Disease Control and the Ministry of Public Health announced that it would issue a compulsory licence for Merck's Stocrin (Efavirenz) to the Government Pharmaceutical Organization of Thailand.[22] The Thai government decided to issue the first set of compulsory licences in 2007 on three patented drugs, including Merck's anti-retroviral efavirenz (Stocrin), Abbott Laboratories' anti-retroviral lopinavir/ritonavir (Kaletra) and Sanofi-Aventis' heart disease drug clopidogrel (Plavix).[23] The compulsory licences were for government use and the royalty rate was set at 0.5 per cent of the selling price. Abbott responded to the compulsory licence by announcing it would no longer register in Thailand new drugs, which could be important in Thailand due to its tropical climate. Allegation of violation

22 Timeline for Thailand's Compulsory Licenses, (2008) Program on Information Justice and Intellectual Property, https://www.wcl.american.edu/pijip/documents/timeline.pdf, accessed 15 January 2016.

23 Sirapapha Rungpry and Edward J. Kelly, "Compulsory Licensing Developments in Thailand" (2008) Aisa law IP Review 16http://www.tilleke.com/sites/default/files/compulsory_licensing_developments_TH.pdf, accessed 15 January 2016.

of Thailand's competition law was also initiated against Abbott for withdrawing its products from Thailand.[24]

2. Brazil: due to a serious HIV/AIDS problem, Brazil publicly announced its consideration of issuing compulsory licences for Nelfinavir and Efavirenz in 2001. The United States filed a complaint in the WTO and requested the establishment of a WTO Dispute Settlement panel concerning the "local working requirement" under Brazilian patent law later in 2001. The complaint was later withdrawn by the United States facing a highly negative public campaign. However, Brazil agreed to provide the United States with advance notification of compulsory licences and to discuss disputes with the United States through a newly formed Consultative Mechanism. A series of discounts was agreed upon by pharmaceutical companies. For instance, in 2003, the Government of Brazil reached a deal with Bristol-Myers Squibb to buy Atazanavir at a 76 per cent discount. During the same year, Brazil reached an agreement with Merck to buy Efavirenz at a discount of 25 per cent. In 2004, Brazil and pharmaceutical companies (Hoffman-La Roche, Gilead and Abbott) agreed to discount the five most expensive anti-retrovirals by 10 and 76 per cent.[25]

3. Indonesia: in 2012, the Indonesian government renewed a previous compulsory licence issued against HIV anti-retroviral (ARV) Sustiva (efavirenz) in 2007, as well as six more newly approved drugs, including abacavir (Ziagen), didanosine (Videx), combination lopinavir, ritonavir (Kaletra), tenofovir (Viread), the combination of tenofovir and emtricitabine (Truvada) and the combination of tenofovir, emtricitabine and efavirenz (Atripla). These therapies could be licensed by the government to local pharmaceutical companies to use the patents with 0.5 per cent royalty paid to the patent holder.[26]

4. South Africa: in South Africa, Article 15(C) of the Medicines and Related Substances Act 101 of 1997 allowed the South African Minister of Health to provide less expensive generic versions of essential medicines, including anti-HIV therapies, through compulsory licensing.[27] In addition to compulsory licensing, South Africa conducted an investigation against anti-competitive practices in order to push pharmaceutical companies to grant voluntary licences. For instance, in 2002 and 2003, the South African Competition Commission conducted an investigation against GlaxoSmithKline (GSK) and Boehringer Ingelheim (GI) concerning excessive pricing practices in respect of ritonavir, lamivudine,

24 Sean Flynn, "Appeal of Thailand Commission Order on Abbott's Refusal to Sell AIDS Medications in Thailand" (2008), http://www.wcl.american.edu/pijip/thai_comp_licenses.cfm, accessed 15 January 2016.

25 Timeline on Brazil's Compulsory Licensing, file:(2008) Program on Information Justice and Intellectual Property, https://www.wcl.american.edu/pijip/, accessed 15 January 2016.

26 IHS Markit, Indonesia issues compulsory licences against seven HIV, hepatitis drugs (10 December 2012) https://www.ihs.com/country-industry-forecasting.html?ID=1065972339, accessed 15 January 2016.

27 E.L. Saslow, "Compulsory licensing and the AIDS epidemic in South Africa" (1999) AIDS Patient Care STDS, 577.

ritonavir+lamivudine and nevirapine. Later in 2003, the South African Competition Commission reached a settlement with GSK whereby the latter extended a voluntary licence to Aspen Pharmacare in October 2001 and to grant up to three more voluntary licences on terms no less favourable than those granted to Aspen Pharmacare, among other agreed terms.[28]

General trend of uses

Many compulsory licences were issued in the 2000s (mostly, between 2003 and 2005). This coincides with the adoption of the two Doha Declarations in 2001. The users were developing countries which have domestic abilities to produce generic drugs. Least developed countries do not have such capacity and, thus, are not able to utilize the flexibility of compulsory licensing. The most frequently practised fields of drugs are related to HIV/AIDS, but there have also been other dealings with communicable or non-communicable diseases. During recent years, there have been fewer cases of compulsory licensing.[29] This is possibly due to the fact that the most important HIV/AIDS drugs had been subject to compulsory licensing and no other drugs are of such critical nature in the developing countries.

Looking into the future: Factors to be considered when issuing a compulsory licence

Compulsory licensing under Article 31 of the TRIPS Agreement can help to make generic drugs available in countries with a generic industry. It can also help to address the high price problem arising due to the exclusive rights granted to patent holders. However, this mechanism does not help less developed countries that do not have generic industries. The waivers largely solve the legal difficulty encountered by many less developed countries and enhance the access to affordable medicines in their jurisdictions.

As indicated above, there were only a modest number of pharmaceutical compulsory licences issued that mostly related to drugs for HIV/AIDS and occurred between 2003 and 2005.[30] This could mean that compulsory licensing is not critically important for developing countries in other fields of technology and other areas of pharmaceutical products; or that the needed compulsory licences had already been issued; or that the mechanism itself has already become a threat to the patent holder preventing from fixing excessively high prices for patented drugs.

28 James Packard Love, "Recent examples of the use of compulsory licenses on patents" (2007) KEI Research Note 2007:2.

29 Reed Beall and Randall Kuhn, "Trends in Compulsory Licensing of Pharmaceuticals since the Doha Declaration: A Database Analysis" (2012) 9(1) PLOS Medicine 1.

30 Ibid.

Compulsory licensing alone cannot be a panacea for all problems encountered by developing countries. At the same time, the improved features of the compulsory licensing under the waivers certainly help to improve the situation and allow nationals of developing countries to have better access to affordable medicines.

The TRIPS Agreement and the Doha Public Health Declaration has been already a balanced package concerning the available flexibility for developing countries. It is up to developing countries to decide whether to use such flexibilities. When deciding whether or not to use the flexibilities, especially compulsory licensing, protection of public health should be the first priority for policy-makers. In the opinion of the author, the factors to be considered by policy-makers should include the following, in addition to whether the requirements under TRIPS Article 31 are met:

1 Whether the public health resources are critically insufficient: the flexibilities are available for developing WTO Members. For other Members whose resources are more sufficient (including developed and high income developing countries), it might not be appropriate to rely on such a "last resort" because compulsory licensing can adversely impact right holders and is against the basic idea of granting exclusive rights.
2 Whether compulsory licensing can be used to force or urge pharmaceutical companies to reduce their prices or grant voluntary licences: voluntary price reduction and voluntary licensing are based on patent holders' decisions. To the maximum possible extent, countries should respect patent holders and should prioritize the possibility of urging pharmaceutical companies to grant voluntary licences, even though it would appear that most voluntary licences are issued as a result of a government's investigation against anti-competitive practices allegedly engaged in by the investigated pharmaceutical company.
3 Whether compulsory licensing is exclusively used to enhance the availability and affordability of essential medicines: although granting compulsory licences to domestic pharmaceutical companies could have a collateral effect of enhancing their technological capacity, this should not be the primary purpose behind the practice. The genuine purpose should be to enhance the availability and affordability of the essential medicines, which are essential components of human rights, especially the right to health.

Concluding remarks: A proper balance between affordable medicine and patent holder's legitimate interests

Compulsory licensing is an important flexibility under the TRIPS Agreement. One of its essential functions is to support public health by enhancing the availability of affordable pharmaceutical products. It has played a significant role in helping certain developing countries to get access to more affordable HIV/AIDS drugs. Looking at the recent cases of compulsory licensing, the reliance on such mechanisms has been decreasing. The TRIPS Agreement aims to achieve a proper balance between flexibilities and the interests of the right holders. This chapter suggests that certain additional factors need to be considered in order to make the flexibility more genuine in nature and in use. These factors should take into account the public health resources of the potentially licensing country, the possibility of not relying on the last resort option of using the compulsory licensing mechanism to induce pharmaceutical companies to reduce prices or to grant voluntary licences, and the avoidance of using the mechanism mainly to enhance domestic pharmaceutical industry. If such factors are also taken into account when deciding on the use of compulsory licensing, there could be an even better balance between affordable medicine and the legitimate interests of patent holders.

8 A Manufacturing for Export Exception

Xavier Seuba, Luis Mariano Genovesi and Pedro Roffe

Introduction

This chapter seeks to ascertain whether it is consistent with international intellectual property law to manufacture and export a product protected by a patent or a supplementary protection certificate to importing countries where the invention is off patent. We submit that a new exception to the rights of the patentee, or to the rights of the owner of a supplementary protection certificate, enabling the manufacture for exportation, would be necessary to conduct such an activity. Furthermore, we are of the view that the proposed exception is compatible with the Agreement on Trade-Related Aspects of Intellectual Property Rights (TRIPS).

In order to assess the new exception, the second section of this chapter discusses the features of patent exceptions, the diversity of exceptions in comparative patent law and the general rule relating to patent exceptions under the three-step test embodied in Article 30 of the TRIPS Agreement. Section three considers normative precedents in comparative patent law supporting the introduction of such an exception for manufacturing for export, particularly with respect to supplementary protection certificates (SPCs) and patent extensions. Finally, section four analyses the new exception in light of the three-step test, and addresses the requirement of being a "limited" exception, whether manufacturing for export unreasonably conflicts with a normal exploitation of the patent, and whether it unreasonably prejudices the legitimate interests of the right holder, taking into consideration the legitimate interests of third parties.

The impossibility to compete in foreign markets with products that are not protected in these markets but are, in fact, protected in the domestic jurisdiction either by patents or by supplementary protection certificates has for some time been the object of concern of some governments, economic actors and regional organizations. Industries that would benefit from a change of the present situation assert that the benefits in terms of jobs, revenues and taxes could be significant. In the majority of cases, these companies have in mind the differences in terms of protection that arise from the diverse approaches to estimate patent extensions and supplementary protection certificates. We will argue that even if the exception for manufacture and export is easier to defend in the context of patent extensions and supplementary protection certificates, this exception is also defensible during the normal life of the patent.

Before focusing on the new exception, it is probably useful to recall why manufacturing for export is considered an infringing activity. In this regard, even if TRIPS and most national patent laws do not mention exportation, nor manufacturing for exportation, among the activities that the right holder can impede, they have become associated with acts that fall within the *ius excluendi* of the right holder. In effect, if manufacturing for export is segmented into the different activities that need to be undertaken to implement it, several forbidden acts become apparent: manufacture, offer for sale and sale. This is the reason why its infringing status is generally upheld. Certainly, this conclusion is reached without taking into consideration the final destiny of the product, or the principle of connectivity among the acts of exploitation of the patent. It does not consider either that the right holder power to exclude could eventually not impact activities that result in profits abroad. All these justifications have been discarded, and it has become commonplace to understand that manufacturing for export is prohibited and, hence, an exception should be recognized.

Exceptions in patent law

Concept and characteristics

All intellectual property legal regimes contemplate limitations to the rights of the patent owner. Such limitations fall generally under the concept of "exception", a term that also extends to "limitations", "defences", "authorized acts" or, among others, "restrictions".[1] Thanks to patent exceptions, acts that typically fall within the right holder power to exclude (*ius prohibendi*) are tolerated. These acts do not require prior authorization by an administrative or judicial authority, and those executing them are not liable for patent infringement.

Even if exceptions are a consubstantial element of the patent system, they have become more relevant in recent times, for a host of reasons. First, exceptions permit governments to respond to situations that were previously addressed in the context of patent exclusions, the latter being gradually conceptualized in more restrictive terms in international treaties.[2] Second, exceptions are also understood as a proper channel to respond to technological changes arising in various fields

1 "Exceptions" in the strict sense refer to the acts that fall within the scope of TRIPS Article 30. A broader notion of "exceptions" includes so-called "flexibilities", such as exhaustion of rights, compulsory licensing and government use, which are subject to different legal requirements and are regulated in other TRIPS articles.

2 L. Bently, "Introduction by Lionel Bently", in WIPO Standing Committee on the Law of Patents, *Exclusions from Patentability and Exceptions and Limitations to Patentees' Rights*, SCP/15/3 Annex I, (2010), 31. Of course, some situations can be addressed either in the context of exceptions or in the context of exclusions, so it is a matter of choice which option will be followed. In some cases, therefore, an invention deemed non-patentable in one country is treated as an exception in a different country.

of technology,[3] the existence of new patentable subject matter and the need to respond to new practices, problems and materials.[4] This explains the emergence of new exceptions in comparative law and the diversity of interpretations of the same exception in different countries. Certainly, the flexibility of international norms relating to exceptions facilitates their receptiveness to new needs and situations.[5]

Patent exceptions in international and comparative law

The original version of the Paris Convention (1883) did not refer to exceptions as such. It was only in The Hague Conference for the review of the Paris Convention, in 1925, when an exception relating to patented devices forming part of vessels, aircraft or land vehicles was introduced.[6] That being the case, at the time of the Paris Convention several national courts already recognized that exception[7] and national legal systems acknowledged other exceptions, i.e. those relating to previous or personal use.[8] Progressively, many other exceptions were conceived and became standard.[9]

Currently, the international agreement that enumerates the longer list of patent exceptions is the Agreement on the Establishment of a Unified Patent Court (UPC).[10] The UPC Agreement combines the exceptions set forth in the

3 Take, for instance, interoperability exceptions. See M. Chapin, "Sharing the Interoperability Ball on the Software Patent Playground" (2008), 14, Boston University Journal of Science and Technology Law, 245.

4 L. Bently, op. cit., p67.

5 Ibid, pp3, 5.

6 "This Article concerns patents only. It was introduced into the Convention by the Revision Conference of The Hague in 1925 and has not been changed since, except for some minor modifications as to form". G. H. C. Bodenhausen, "Guide to the Application of the Paris Convention for the Protection of Industrial Property" (BIRPI, 1968) 82.

7 S. P. Ladas, *Patents, Trademarks and Related Rights: National and International Protection*, vol. 1 (Harvard University Press, 1975) 416.

8 E. Pouillet, *Traité Théorique et pratique des Brevets D'Invention et de la Contrefaçon* (13th ed., Marchal et Billard, 1889) 821, 891.

9 C. Garrison, "Exception to Patent Rights in Developing Countries" (UNCTAD-ICTSD Issue Paper 17, 2006).

10 There is no European unified text governing the award, legal regime and enforcement of patents. This concerns not only the European Union but also the broader geographical scope of the European Patent Organization. Three legal texts need to be taken into account in this context: the Strasbourg Convention of the Council of Europe, the Munich Convention setting up the European Patent Organization and the Luxembourg Convention, developed in the framework of the European Economic Community. The 1963 Strasbourg Convention on the Unification of Certain Points of Substantive Law on Patents and the Munich Convention on the Grant of European Patents of 1972 addressed the issues relating to patentability, validity, legitimacy, the process for the granting of a patent, the role of claims in defining the scope of the patents and the method for interpreting patent claims. They did not touch upon, however, capital issues such as the rights conferred by a patent or limitations on these rights. This means, in effect, that exceptions were not regulated in these texts.

Luxembourg Convention on the Community Patent, which never came into force, with other exceptions developed over the years by the European Union, such as the regulatory exception and those relating to agro-biotechnological inventions. In total, UPC in Article 27 lists 12 exceptions[11] and refers separately (Article 28) to rights based on prior use of the invention.[12]

With the exclusion of the UPC Agreement, exceptions have not been extensively regulated at the international level. On the contrary, treaties merely lay down the general conditions that exceptions should meet, but do not establish a strict regime nor a *numerus clausus* list of exceptions. Notably, this is the standard of treatment in Article 30 of the TRIPS Agreement.

With such a backdrop, it is unsurprising that a comparative study of exceptions finds notable differences across countries, as regards to both the list of exceptions and their respective scope and specificity. As international intellectual property treaties tend to codify existing laws, it is also unsurprising that expansion of exceptions has not occurred via international treaties but through regulatory and jurisprudential developments occurring in national jurisdictions.[13] At present,

In the European Union strict legal domain, the European Court of Justice has noted that exceptions are still subject to national patent law. See, for instance, case C-316/95, *Generics BV contra Smith Kline & French Laboratories Ltd.*

11 The Agreement on the Unified Patent Court lists: (a) acts done privately and for non-commercial purposes; (b) acts done for experimental purposes relating to the subject matter of the patented invention; (c) the use of biological material for the purpose of breeding, or discovering and developing other plant varieties; (d) the acts allowed pursuant to Article 13(6) of Directive 2001/82/EC1 or Article 10(6) of Directive 2001/83/EC2 in respect of any patent covering the product within the meaning of either of those Directives; (e) the extemporaneous preparation by a pharmacy, for individual cases, of a medicine in accordance with a medical prescription or acts concerning the medicine so prepared; (f) the use of the patented invention on board; (g) the use of the patented invention in the construction or operation of aircraft or land vehicles or other means of transport; (h) the acts specified in Article 27 of the Convention on International Civil Aviation of 7 December 1941; (i) the use by a farmer of the product of his harvest for propagation or multiplication by him on his own holding, provided that the plant propagating material was sold or otherwise commercialized to the farmer by or with the consent of the patent proprietor for agricultural use; (j) the use by a farmer of protected livestock for an agricultural purpose, provided that the breeding stock or other animal reproductive material were sold or otherwise commercialized to the farmer by or with the consent of the patent proprietor; (k) the acts and the use of the obtained information as allowed under Articles 5 and 6 of Directive 2009/24/EC1, in particular, by its provisions on decompilation and interoperability; and (l) the acts allowed pursuant to Article 10 of Directive 98/44/EC2.

12 The prior user has the authority to continue using the invention even if a patent has been granted in respect of such invention. See Article 28 of the Agreement on the Unified Patent Court and Article 37, Agreement relating to Community patents, "Protocol on the Settlement of Litigation Concerning the Infringement and Validity of Community Patents" (Official Journal of the European Communities L 401 (89/695/CEE), 30 December1989) 1.

13 In the United States, for instance, some limitations are found in the patents code while others are jurisprudential creations, sometimes codified *a posteriori*. Among the exceptions of legal origin mention can be made to the Bolar exception, the first inventor defence and the temporary presence of the patented invention in vehicles, ships and aircraft. On the other

more than 20 different exceptions can be identified in comparative patent law.[14] Certainly, their recognition varies across countries, and while some exceptions are widely accepted (i.e., those for experimental, teaching, and transportation-related purposes), some exceptions are found only in a single jurisdiction.[15]

Although the diversity of exceptions makes it difficult to classify them, a systematic approach to exceptions has identified three broad categories depending on the grounds on which they are based.[16] As a matter of clarification and depending on different perspectives to the rationale behind the patent system, one particular exception would find its justification in more than one of these three broad categories; thus, the examples that follow might overlap in the three identified categories.

The first category of exceptions finds its foundation under the same grounds commonly invoked for the granting of patents, namely to encourage investment in research and the disclosure of knowledge.[17] This category would include exceptions such as the use for research or scientific purposes, non-commercial use, prior use, private use and *de minimis* use exception.

A second category relates to the conflicts sometimes prevailing between protection of intellectual property and a range of public or social goods and interests. A number of exceptions to the patent owners' rights have been developed to address these potential conflicts. This would be the case of limitations for teaching purposes, the farmer's privilege or the possibility to consider treatment

hand, among the exceptions of jurisprudential origin can be included the exception for experimental nonprofit use, the doctrine of implied licence and the right to repair a patented product.

14 Among the currently existing exceptions, mention must be made at least to use for experimental purposes; acts done for private and non-commercial use; preparation of medicines in a pharmacy for individual cases; prior use; non-commercial use of living material as an initial source of variation or propagation; use by farmers of harvested plant propagating material for multiplication or propagation on own farm; use by farmers of breeding stock or other animal reproductive material for own agricultural activity, but not sale for commercial reproduction; indirect uses of production processes to obtain other products; importation or entry of small quantities of non-commercial goods in personal effects of passengers or sent in small packages; regulatory or "Bolar" exception; *de minimis* uses; use for teaching purposes; use of certain methods of treatment; use of the patented invention on ships, airplanes, land vehicles or other means of transport; actions related to decompilation and interoperability.

15 Such as those relating to "objects to be launched into space from French national territory", and "use of biological material already existing in nature which is not necessary for the industrial application specified in the patent", found respectively in France and Norway. See WIPO, "Standing Committee on the Law of Patents" (SCP_12_3 Rev.2 I) 11 and 21.

16 Some exceptions are so broadly defined that it is just impossible to group them in any functional category. Indeed, some exceptions in comparative law have gone very far in terms of generality, and mention for instance "Any other acts by third parties, provided that they shall not unreasonably hamper the normal exploitation of the patent, and shall not be unreasonably prejudicial to the legitimate interests of the patent owner taking into consideration the legitimate interests of others". Art. 9(6) *Egyptian Law No. 82 of 2002 Pertaining to the Protection of Intellectual Property Rights.*

17 L. Bently, op. cit., p55.

methods an exception to the patentee. Under the same category we could also include exceptions intended to impede intellectual property from becoming a barrier to trade,[18] a subset that includes exceptions relating to the entry of personal effects of passengers or goods sent in small packages (*de minimis exception*, cited also under the first category), as well as the Bolar or regulatory exception.

Finally, some exceptions are upheld so as to allow for the effective maintenance and functioning of the patent system.[19] This would be for instance the case of the experimental use exception, which allows putting, under certain conditions, into practice the disclosed invention and testing its main features. Indeed, patent law obliges the public disclosure of the invention, so that third parties can experiment with the invention and test whether the invention actually works and the necessary information has been disclosed for that purpose.

The general rule on exceptions

The general rule relating to patent exceptions is found in the TRIPS Agreement, where patent exceptions are regulated by importing into patent law the three-step test developed in the Berne Convention for the Protection of Literary and Artistic Works.[20] According to TRIPS Article 30, patent exceptions must be limited, not unreasonably conflict with the normal exploitation of the patent, and not unreasonably prejudice the legitimate interests of the patent owner, taking into account the legitimate interests of third parties.

Article 30 reflects an international consensus on a number of facets. First, it reflects consensus on the fact that the list of patent exceptions is open ended. Indeed, Article 30 is a flexible as opposed to a rigid test, since it does not limit exceptions to a particular circumstance or range of situations. In this sense, it should be recalled that the effort to adopt a *numerus clausus* list during the negotiations of TRIPS garnered little support.[21] However, it has been also

18 In line with the TRIPS Preamble and TRIPS Article 41.1.

19 L. Bently, op. cit., p57.

20 UNCTAD-ICTSD, *Resource Book on TRIPS and Development* (UNCTAD-ICTSD, 2005) 431. This is also the case of TRIPS Articles 13 (exceptions for copyright), 17 (exceptions for trademarks) and 26(2) (exceptions for industrial designs).

21 The European Union was one of the proponents of a limited list of exceptions. See MTN. GNG/NG11/W/26, 7 July 1998. Among the relevant documents in that context, *Vid.* Statement by Thailand at the meeting of 12–14 September 1988 (21 September 1988), MTN.GNG/NG11/W/27, p2; Guidelines and Objectives Proposed by the European Community for the Negotiations on Trade-Related Aspects of Substantive Standards of Intellectual Property Rights (7 July 1988), MTN.GNG/NG11/W/26, pp6–7; Existence, Scope and Form of Generally Internationally Accepted and Applied Standards/Norms for the Protection of Intellectual Property – Note prepared by the International Bureau of WIPO – Revision (15 September 1988), MTN.GNG/NG11/W/24/Rev.1, pp7–8; Compilation of Written Submissions and Oral Statements – Prepared by the Secretariat – Revision, 5 February 1988, MTN.GNG/NG11/W/12/Rev.1, p17; Proposal by the Nordic Countries for the Negotiations on Standards and Principles for Trade-Related Aspects of Intellectual

underlined that Article 30 should not be seen as opening the door to reinterpret the agreement,[22] thereby introducing a note of caution in this context with respect to absolute flexibility.

Another common understanding with respect to Article 30 relates to the fact that the criteria set forth therein are to be interpreted in accordance with national law and national priorities. This explains the existence of a large number of exceptions in comparative law, and was, in fact, an objective already intended in the original three-step test of the Bern Convention. As noted by Senftleben, due to its openness, the latter "gains the capacity to encompass a wide range of national limitations".[23]It is also important to underline that exceptions can pursue economic objectives. Moreover, as explored further in this chapter, some conflict may exist between the exploitation of the patent and exceptions, particularly when taking into account the interests of third parties.

There is no consensus, however, with respect to whether the conditions set out in Article 30 are cumulative. Thus, whereas some understand that each and every condition has to be fulfilled in order to render acceptable the exception,[24] others advocate for "a comprehensive overall assessment" of the exception, particularly in light of the third criteria set forth in Article 30 in line with the principle of proportionality. In this regard, "failure to comply with one of the three conditions need not result in the exception being disallowed".[25]

TRIPS Article 30 was the subject of an important dispute in the WTO in the *Canada-Pharmaceutical Patents*, where two exceptions of relevance to the sector

Property Rights (10 July 1989), MTN.GNG/NG11/W/36, p2; Standards and Principles Concerning the Availability, Scope and Use of Trade-Related Intellectual Property Rights – Communication from India (10 July 1989), pp6, 7, 17; Trade-Related Aspects of Intellectual Property Rights – Submission from the European Communities (14 November 1989), p8; Standards for Trade-Related Intellectual Property Rights – Submission from Hong Kong (29 November 1989), p6; *Draft Agreement on Trade-Related Aspects of Intellectual Property Rights* (EC Delegation), 29 March 1990, MTN.GNG/NG11/W/68, pp10, 11; *Communication of Argentina, Brazil, Chile, China, Colombia, Cuba, Egypt, India, Nigeria, Peru, Tanzania and Uruguay*, 14 May 1990, MTN.GNG/NG11/W/71, p10; *Communication of Brazil*, 31 October 1988, MTN.GNG/NG11/W/30.

22 M. Senftleben, "Towards a Horizontal Standard for Limiting Intellectual Property Rights? – WTO Panel Reports Shed Light on the Three-Step Test in Copyright Law and Related Tests in Patent and Trademark Law" (IIC vol. 37(4), 2006) 413. The *Canada–Generics* panel report noted that "the negotiators of the Agreement did not intend Article 30 to bring about what would be equivalent to a renegotiation of the basic balance of the Agreement". *Canada–Patent Protection of Pharmaceutical Products* WT/DS114/R, 17 March 2000, § 7.26.

23 M. Senftleben, op. cit., p. 411.

24 M. Senftleben, op. cit., p. 412. In this same sense, the panel could not be clearer in *Canada Pharmaceutical Patents*: "The three conditions are cumulative, each being a separate and independent requirement that must be satisfied. Failure to comply with any one of the three conditions results in the Article 30 exception being disallowed", § 7.20.

25 "Declaration on Patent Protection – Regulatory Sovereignty under TRIPS", www.mpg.de/8132986/Patent-Declaration.pdf, para. 22.

– the regulatory review exception[26] and the stockpiling exception[27] – were the object of analysis. The views of the panel report in this case – not appealed – permit a better understanding of TRIPS Article 30 and of the proposed exception for manufacturing for export.

The interpretation provided in *Canada-Pharmaceutical Patents* is more flexible than that made with respect to copyright exceptions by another WTO panel, in the case of *US-Copyright.*

That being the case, some claim that the case still implies a restrictive interpretation of the agreement,[28] and that some aspects of that interpretation may in fact "operate to deprive member countries of the real potential offered by the use of exceptions".[29] Indeed, the international normative framework enables a more flexible reading of TRIPS Article 30 than that made in the *Canada-Pharmaceutical Patents* panel report. A more flexible interpretation has in fact been supported in studies presented in the WIPO Standing Committee on the Law of Patents, and in the 2014 Declaration on Patent Protection issued by the Max Planck Institute for Innovation and Competition and supported by a number of scholars and international experts.[30]

The WIPO Standing Committee on the Law of Patents has put special emphasis on patent exceptions in the last decade. One of the studies that the Committee has commissioned endorses the view that "the use of exceptions has not been fully explored".[31] The study goes on to recommend, "careful thought be given to

26 The "regulatory review exception" allowed generic competitors to advance the administrative formalities in order to, at the expiration of the patent, obtain a speedy approval and rapidly compete with the originator. The goal was that of avoiding a *de facto* extension of the exclusivity period in benefit of the former patent owner. Indeed, if the generic manufacturer had to wait until the end of the patent, he could only begin the preparation of the relevant regulatory information at a very late stage. In its turn, this would lead to marketing delays and detrimental effects on pharmaceutical competition and medicines' prices.

27 This exception allowed generic producers to manufacture and stockpile the medicines during the period of patent protection. Generic competitors could in this way manufacture the product well in advance of the expiration of the patent term, and commercialize the medicines just after the patent expired. Without this exception, these would be considered patent infringing activities. The Canadian exception allowed conducting these activities during the "period specified in the regulations" – more precisely, six months (Manufacturing and Storage of Patented Medicines Regulations, SOR/93-134).

28 See *Declaration on Patent Protection*, op. cit.

29 L. Bently, op. cit., p71.

30 *Declaration on Patent Protection*, op. cit.

31 Among the initiatives, the committee has commissioned a significant number of studies on patent exceptions: *WIPO Standing Committee on the Law of Patents, Exclusions from Patentable Subject Matter and Exceptions and Limitations to the Rights, Document prepared by the Secretariat*, 4 February 2009, SCP/13/3; Experts' Study on Exclusions from Patentable Subject Matter and Exceptions and Limitations to the Rights, SCP/15/3; Overview of the Responses to the Questionnaire on Exceptions and Limitations to Patent Rights, SCP/18/3; Exceptions and Limitations to Patent Rights: Private and/or Non Commercial Use, SCP/20/3; Exceptions and Limitations to Patent Rights: Experimental Use and/or Scientific Research, SCP/20/4; Exceptions and Limitations to Patent Rights:

broader use of exceptions, and counsels that efforts should be made so as to ensure international norms do not stifle this important avenue for calibrating national patent policy".[32] The suggested flexibility with respect to exceptions responds to the understanding that they can be "finely tuned to ensure that an appropriate compromise is made within the patent system".[33]

The 2014 Declaration on Patent Protection, in light of the socio-economic benefits and costs of patents, addresses the central aspects of patent law with the objective of tailoring the system to the innovation process and to the need to sustain a competitive environment.[34] Concerning exceptions, the declaration takes the view that, contrary to what might be inferred from the *Canada-Pharmaceutical Patents* panel report, the three conditions found in Article 30 are not, in fact, cumulative. It also explores the meaning of these conditions, and it does so in a more open and flexible manner than the panel report. As it will be noted below, the declaration fundamentally emphasized the relevance of the principle of proportionality and the interests of third parties.

Precedents of the manufacturing for export exception

References to exportation in the community code for medicinal products for human use

In 2002, with the objective to "ensure that the European generics industry can compete in the world market",[35] the European Parliament proposed an amendment to the Code for Medicinal Products for Human Use. Pursuant to the suggested amendment, patent and supplementary protection certificates would not impede the grant of an authorization to export a generic product. This proposal and subsequent texts in the same line were, however, later abandoned.[36] The Council

Extemporaneous Preparation of Medicines, SCP/20/5; Exceptions and Limitations to Patent Rights: Prior Use, SCP/20/6; Exceptions and Limitations to Patent Rights: Use of Articles on Foreign Vessels, Aircrafts and Land Vehicles, SCP/20/7.

32 L. Bently, op. cit., p5.

33 They would be like 'dimmer switches', that can be turned down (to reduce costs), without necessarily turning off the light". L. Bently, op. cit., p65.

34 *Declaration on Patent Protection*, op. cit, para.1, Preface, p1.

35 European Parliament legislative resolution on the proposal for a European Parliament and Council directive amending Directive 2001/83/EC on the Community code relating to medicinal products for human use (COM(2001) 404 - C5-0592/2001 - 2001/0253 (COD)), p27.

36 One year later, in the same process of amendment, the Parliament insisted on mentioning exportation among the acts that are not considered contrary to the rights of the patentee or SPC owner. The Rapporteur included in this context the following explanatory statement:

> Medicines are not like other products. They are not sold or consumed in the way ordinary, everyday products are sold and consumed. Their use is unique, and everyone expects their medicine to be safe and effective. It is possible to find an optimum balance between competitiveness, research, health system needs and the development of generic

considered that those exceptions relating to medicinal products intended for export were not within the scope of a directive that was meant to regulate the marketing of medicinal products in Member States.[37]

Exportation exception in the European Union and Canada Comprehensive Economic and Trade Agreement

The Comprehensive Economic and Trade Agreement between the European Union and Canada (CETA) includes a "*sui generis* protection for pharmaceuticals".[38] In a lengthy provision, CETA regulates virtually all aspects of supplementary protection certificates without, however, using this term. Relevant for the purposes of the exception for manufacture for exportation is the assertion made therein in the sense that "each Party may also limit the scope of the protection by providing exceptions for making, using, offering for sale, selling or importing of products *for the purpose of export during the period of protection*".[39] To our knowledge, this is probably the only case where preferential trade agreements make a particular reference to exceptions beyond those that reiterate provisions identical to Article 30, TRIPS, and recognize the legitimacy of the regulatory exception. In the case

> medicines. This, at any rate, is the main aim here. While the Council appears to have abided by this balance which Parliament sought to achieve at first reading, there remain major differences of opinion on key issues. The definition of the term medicinal product must not allow for any confusion with what are known as "borderline products". The rapporteur therefore wishes to clarify this definition and intends to put forward proposals regarding the definition of the terms generic medicinal product and biogeneric medicinal product. Research and development also help to lay the foundations for health protection. We all know that innovation comes at a price. It is thus our duty to prevent European industry from being relegated to the second division in the global league and from trailing behind the United States and Asia, as that would be a disaster for Europe. This is why the amendment on data protection adopted at first reading has been retabled. Other issues such as the "switch", the duration of testing or making public monies available for pharmacovigilance work are important matters on which Parliament has already given its opinion. Lastly, the issue of information must not be overlooked. The rapporteur, who did not endorse the Commission's initial proposal at first reading, would therefore like the matter to be discussed in greater detail in the future.

Recommendation for a second voting on the common position adopted by the Council with a view to adopting a European Parliament and Council directive amending Directive 2001/83/EC on the Community code relating to medicinal products for human use, (10950/03/2003 – C5-0464/2003 – 2001/0253(COD)) p14.

37 COMMON POSITION (EC) No 61/2003 adopted by the Council on 29 September 2003 with a view to the adoption of a Directive 2003/ . . . /EC of the European Parliament and of the Council of . . . amending Council Directive 2001/83/EC on the Community code relating to medicinal products for human use (2003/C 297 E/02).

38 Article 20.27 which is the chapter regulating intellectual property rights. Similar texts have been proposed to other trade partners in ongoing trade negotiations, this being for instance the case of the TTIP.

39 Article 20.27.9.

of the latter, it is interesting to note that in most preferential trade agreements sponsored by the United States, the regulatory exception includes language expanding its scope to "exportation of such product" when the respective party so permits and for the sole purpose of meeting marketing approval requirements.[40]

The exception for manufacturing for exportation in the context of the European supplementary protection certificates

In Europe, and in line with the provisions of CETA, private actors have proposed the adoption of an exception allowing the export of generic and biosimilar products even if supplementary protection certificates are in force, provided that exportation is made to countries where the same product is not protected by a patent.[41] This would be an important amendment to the SPC Regulation,[42] since today European biosimilar and generic producers compete on unequal terms with manufacturers from countries where supplementary protection certificates or patent extensions do not exist or happen to expire earlier.[43]

These proposals have been echoed in the European Parliament. In the *Report on Reindustrialising Europe to Promote Competitiveness and Sustainability*, the commission was asked to propose legislation enabling European companies to manufacture generic and biosimilar medicines in the EU during the supplementary protection certificate period, following the expiry of patent protection. The immediate objective of such a measure would be to be ready for immediate introduction of the product following expiration of the SPC or to export to countries where no patent or SPC is in force. The report sustained as well that "such provisions could help to avoid the outsourcing of production and to foster job creation in the EU, as well as to create a level playing field between European companies and their competitors in third countries".[44]

40 See examples in US trade agreements with Australia (Art. 17.9.6), Chile (Art. 17.9.4), Colombia and Peru (Art. 16.8.5), DR-CAFTA (Art. 16.9.5) and KORUS (Art. 18.8.5).

41 "Manufacturing in an EU member state during the term of a supplementary protection certificate for medicinal products to export to other EU member states or third countries where a) a relevant patent and/or patent or product exclusivity term extension right is not in place or has expired, lapsed or ceased to exist in any other way, and/or b) in response to a compulsory license, shall not be regarded as being contrary to supplementary protection certificates for medicinal products." EGA, "An EU Advanced Manufacturing Provision for Export of Generic and Biosimilar Medicines to Third Countries" (Brussels: EGA, September 2013) 3.

42 Council Regulation (EEC) No 1768/92 of 18 June 1992 concerning the creation of a supplementary protection certificate for medicinal products.

43 EGA, "EU–US Transatlantic Trade and Investment Partnership" (Brussels: EGA, 6 May 2013).

44 *Report on Reindustrialising Europe to Promote Competitiveness and Sustainability (2013/2006(INI))*, 18 December 2013, Ref. A7-00464/2013, Rapporteur Mr Reinhard Bütikofer, para. 66

Manufacture for export exception in Australia

While some claimed that manufacture for exportation was already permitted by the Australian Patent Law,[45] the exception for manufacture for exportation was examined by a committee set up in 2012 to review the Australian patent law as regards to pharmaceutical patents.[46] The committee welcomed the arguments favouring such an exception, in particular the arguments relating to industrial development, employment promotion and the absence of actual harm to the interests of the patent owner.[47] In the opinion of the committee, however, this exception may contradict international rules, mainly those enshrined in TRIPS and the Australia–United States Free Trade Agreement (AUFTA). As noted, in the committee report, preferential trade agreements, particularly those signed with the US, include complex procedures to be followed by a generic pharmaceutical manufacturer to enter the domestic market when the patent is still in force. These provisions would not apply, in our view, in the case of the exportation exception that is principally targeting markets off patents.

The review panel report took generally a cautious approach, concluding that it was preferable to avoid litigation and not incorporate such an exception immediately. Instead, the committee suggested the adoption of an explicit exception of this nature in the context of an international normative reform. Meanwhile, it proposed the conclusion of voluntary agreements under which patent holders would not denounce generic manufacturers that produced for export to countries with no patent protection.[48] It is also our view that the analysis made by the committee adopts a restrictive interpretation of the

45 It was affirmed that the Australian Patents Act "already allows manufacture for export during the extension period, by virtue of section 78(1)(a). A plausible interpretation of this section is that, due to the territorial limitations of patent rights to Australia, the only act of exploitation of a pharmaceutical substance that constitutes infringement during the extension period, is exploitation for the purpose of therapeutic use in Australia." See A. F. Christie, S. Elkman and M. J. Howlett, "Review of Pharmaceutical Patent Extension and Springboarding Provisions in Various Jurisdictions" (Intellectual Property Research Institute of Australia (IPRIA), 2002) 9.

46 The so-called Pharmaceutical Patents Review Panel; vid. "Review of pharmaceutical patents in Australia", www.ipaustralia.gov.au/about-us/ip-legislation-changes/review-pharmaceutical-patents/, accessed May 2015.

47 According to the committee "Perversely, if the applicable patent has not expired in Australia, it seems that Australian generic manufacturers must establish manufacturing facilities overseas to serve those markets to avoid infringing Australian patent rights. This result offers no obvious benefit to the original patentee, for the drugs will be produced for the export market, but it prevents Australian business and its workers from producing them." T. Harris, D. Nicol and N. Gruen, "Pharmaceutical Patents Review Report" (Canberra, 2013) vi.

48 In this context the report argued: "The AUSFTA and TRIPS also place restrictions on manufacturers of generic pharmaceuticals wishing to export pharmaceuticals. If an extension of term has been granted for the pharmaceutical in Australia, and that extension has not expired, it is an infringement to manufacture the pharmaceutical without the patent owner's consent for export to a country where patent protection for the pharmaceuticals has expired or never existed." Ibid, p52.

Canada-Pharmaceutical Patents panel report compared to the approach we take on the matter as we argue in the following sections.

The exception for manufacture for exportation in light of TRIPS Article 30 and authoritative interpretations

The convergence between TRIPS Article 30 and the exception for manufacture for exportation can be sustained in two different but complementary ways. First, it can be argued that the new exemption is compatible with the criteria set forth in TRIPS Article 30 as interpreted in the *Canada Pharmaceutical Products* panel report. Second, the exemption becomes even more justifiable if the more flexible criteria relating to the meaning of TRIPS Article 30, in line with the 2014 Declaration on Patent Protection and the reports presented in the WIPO Standing Committee on Patents, are adopted.

The requirement of being a "limited" exception

Implementation of the criteria invoked in Canada-Pharmaceutical Patents

The recognition of exceptions to the rights of patent owners, even if these exceptions must be "limited", implies that the system recognizes some degree of tolerance with respect to activities that otherwise would be prohibited.[49] Therefore, if the expression "limited exception" evokes something less than full enjoyment of the patent holder right to exclude, the relevant question is how to craft an exception that restricts the right to exclude but does so with an intensity that can be considered "limited".

The *Canada-Pharmaceutical Patents* panel report affirmed that the terms "limited exception" must be strictly interpreted. According to the panel, "limited" qualifies the word "exception", which already has a connotation of something that is restricted. Therefore, "limited exception" must be interpreted as meaning that it entails a strict or narrow exception, involving just a small reduction of the patent owner rights.[50] In this line of reasoning, when determining whether an exception is "limited" the relevance should not be put on the "economic impact" of the exception, but on its impact on the patent holder rights.[51]

Taking into consideration the restriction of the patent holder's legal rights, the panel held that the stockpiling exception implied a substantial impact on the right

49 The principle of effectiveness in treaty interpretation requires giving meaningful effect to the terms found in an international text. Hence, it must be given full effect to "limited". As the International Court of Justice states, it would be contrary to the customary rules of interpretation considering that a provision found in an international text is devoid of sense and effect. *Corfu Channel Case (UK v Albania)* (Merits)[1949] ICJ Rep 4.

50 *Canada Pharmaceutical Products*, § 7.30.

51 Ibid, § 7.31, 7.32, 7.49.

holder *ius excluendi* and could not be considered "limited". In reaching this conclusion, the panel invoked two considerations.[52] First, stockpiling would hinder the patentee's rights to impede "making" and "using" the patented product, closely connected to the right to prevent the sale of the protected product. According to the panel, the absence of any limitation with respect to the quantity that could be produced under the stockpiling exception implied that the right holder's rights to impede manufacture and use were entirely suppressed.[53] Second, the panel refuted the arguments made by Canada in the sense that the exception was "limited" since it preserved the rights of the right holders in the market where the protection had been granted, since no sales would be made in Canada. The panel concluded that the commercial advantage obtained by the patentee during the months following the expiration of the patent were benefits that could be expected from the acts of "manufacturing" and "use" before the expiration of the patent.[54]

The panel did not, however, hold that stockpiling was *per se* inconsistent with TRIPS. On the contrary, it stated that the limits put on the stockpiling exception[55] were insufficient to be considered that the exception was "limited". In effect, six months was considered a relevant period in commercial terms, in particular because there was no limitation as to the quantity that could be produced and the markets that would be served.[56] Therefore, following the panel's interpretation, had the Canadian exception incorporated limits relating, for example, to authorized quantities, or in relation to targeted markets, it would have complied with the standard set forth in TRIPS Article 30.

In line with these arguments, the limitation of the right to impede the manufacture for export would be consistent with the principles of Article 30 if it had, at least, limitations as to the volume of production and markets. The presence of other limitations, even if not listed by the Panel, would strengthen the exception. The exception for manufacture for export is construed alongside limitations that enables holding that in this particular case the exception is of a "limited" nature.

First, an exception for manufacture for export does not impact the right holder's *ius excluendi* in a general way, but only in relation to objects intended for export to markets where no patent protection exists and thus subject to competition. Hence, the exception for manufacture for export is, by definition, limited in terms of quantity, since it does not allow unlimited production of the patented product but only the production for markets off patent. Second, unlike the *Canada-Pharmaceutical Patents* case, the exception for manufacture for export does not impact on the right to exclude non-authorized parties from the domestic

52 Ibid, § 7.36.
53 Ibid, § 7.34.
54 Ibid, § 7.35.
55 Stockpiling was, in effect, a limited activity since (i) only those benefited by the Bolar exception could invoke as well the stockpiling exception; (ii) the exemption covered only a certain and limited number of products; and (iii) it only lasted six months.
56 Ibid, § 7.38.

protected market, a right which can be fully exercised during the duration of the patent or the supplementary certificate.

Contemporary and broader criteria with respect to "limited"

The 2014 Declaration on Patent Protection states that in order to be considered "limited", an exception does not necessarily have to have limited effect on the right holder's rights. On the contrary, an exception is "limited" if its scope is proportionate to its object and purpose. Therefore, the exception must pursue a legitimate aim, be adequate to achieve its objective and does not exceed what is necessary and sufficient to achieve this objective.[57]

The first paragraph of the TRIPS preamble emphasizes the need to harmonize intellectual property protection and "legitimate trade".[58] The reference to legitimate trade and the broader contextualization of TRIPS within a legal regime favouring trade liberalization, makes it relevant underlining the situation that the new exception intends to address. In effect, the proposed exception would permit to respond to a situation where a commercial demand from a country where no exclusive rights exist at all cannot be satisfied. The barrier to international trade that the new exception intends to address would seem to go beyond the "effective and adequate protection of intellectual property", also underlined in the preamble.

The reference to legitimate trade must be read in conjunction with the objectives of TRIPS. Article 7 makes it clear that intellectual property rights are not granted in a vacuum, and that a range of economic and social objectives need to be taken into account when regulating intellectual property. In an instrumental approach to the protection of intangible assets, Article 7 refers to the promotion of technological innovation, the transfer of technology and, among others, the promotion of social and economic welfare.

Exceptions to patent rights may be instrumental to achieve the objectives mentioned in the Preamble and Article 7 of TRIPS. The unrestricted application of the right holder rights could in effect be contrary to the objectives of the agreement. Article 30 allows, in fact, limiting the full application of patent rights in light of the specific circumstances and other purposes relating to social and economic welfare.[59] As noted above, the new exception would permit to respond

57 *Declaration on Patent Protection*, op. cit., p8.

58 Article 31 of the Vienna Convention on the Law of Treaties (VCLT) provides that "[a] treaty shall be interpreted in good faith in accordance with the ordinary meaning to be given to the terms of the treaty in their context and considering its object and purpose". The "context" includes, *inter alia*, the preamble of the treaty. TRIPS preamble underlines Members' desire "to reduce distortions and impediments to international trade" and "ensure that measures and procedures to enforce intellectual property rights do not themselves become barriers to legitimate trade".

59 *Declaration on Patent Protection*, op. cit., para. 23, p8.

to a range of objectives at both the national (economic development, job creation) and the international level (public health protection, competition).

Exceptions cannot unreasonably conflict with a normal exploitation of the patent

TRIPS Article 30 establishes that exceptions cannot unreasonably conflict with the normal exploitation of the patent. The requirement of reasonableness is not found in TRIPS Article 13 dealing with copyright, and adds nuances when compared to the latter provision.[60] We analyse next whether the interpretation of this requirement made in the *Canada-Pharmaceutical Patents* case, as well as a related WTO report on exceptions, provide more flexible interpretations, enabling us to support the argument that the manufacturing for exportation exception meets this apparent stringent condition.

The interpretation made in the Canada Pharmaceutical Products *panel report*

The requirement to not unreasonably conflict with a normal exploitation of the patent relates to the economic impact of the exception.[61] In this case, what is "normal" and what is "exploitation" are the central elements of the analysis.[62] Additionally, if it is determined that the exception interferes with the "normal exploitation", it must still be decided whether such a conflict is "reasonable" or not.

First, "exploitation" is interpreted as the "commercial activity by which patent owners employ their exclusive patent rights to extract economic value of their patent".[63] Both the European Communities and Canada agreed in the proceedings with the meaning of "exploitation", which involves the extraction of commercial value through three forms of "use" – namely, selling the product in a market where competitors are excluded, granting others a licence to do so, and more directly by transferring the rights conferred by the patent.[64]

Second, the panel interpreted that "normal" alludes to the type of activity that is protected with Article 30. It gave to this word the ordinary meaning given in dictionaries, consisting in something "regular, usual, typical, ordinary, conventional".[65] For the panel "normal" has both an empirical connotation and a normative one:[66] it relates "to an empirical conclusion about what is common

60 M. Senftleben, op. cit., p 412.
61 *Canada Pharmaceutical Products*, § 7.49.
62 Ibid, § 7.59.
63 Ibid, § 7.54.
64 Ibid, § 7.51.
65 Ibid.
66 M. Senftleben, op. cit., p428.

within a given community"[67] and also to a standard to decide what right holders are entitled to.

After defining the meaning of the words "exploitation" and "normal" separately, the panel interpreted the scope of these words when put together. According to the panel, "normal practice" refers to the exclusion of "all forms of competition that could detract significantly from the economic returns anticipated from a patent's grant of market exclusivity".[68] Under this view, the protection of all normal types of exploitation is a key element reflected in all patent laws. The policy goals sustaining this legal regime can not materialize unless patent holders can effectively take advantage of their exclusivity during the relevant period.[69]

The panel then considered whether the market exclusivity following the expiry of the patent term could be considered part of the "normal exploitation". According to the panel, some basic rights granted to all patentees may give place to a period of market exclusivity following the expiration of the patent. This is for instance the case of the prohibition to manufacture and stockpile before the end of the patent term.[70] By contrast, an additional *de facto* exclusivity period resulting from exercising patent rights to prevent the necessary submissions for regulatory approvals would be anomalous.[71] The pharmaceutical sector combines administrative hurdles and patent exclusivity, something unusual for products commercialized in other industries.[72] Hence, allowing competitors to file marketing authorization submission is a rational possibility.

The exception for manufacture for export to countries where the patent has expired does not impact on the "normal exploitation" of the patent because it does not detract from the expected economic benefits deriving from market exclusivity in countries where the patent is still in force. Indeed, the benefits arising from the exclusive rights conferred by a patent generally rely on the commercial exploitation of the invention. This usually involves either the use of the patent by the titleholder to manufacture and sell the product, or the licensing of the patent. The right holder's rights to sell the product in a market where competitors are excluded, grant others the licence to do so, and directly transfer the rights conferred by the patent are not diminished by the new exception.

67 *Canada Generics*, § 7.54.
68 Ibid, § 7.55.
69 Ibid.
70 Ibid, § 7.56.
71 Ibid, § 7.57.
72 Ibid.

Interpretation of TRIPS Article 30 in the context of a more flexible criterion than those invoked by the Canada-Pharmaceutical Patents *panel*

According to the Max Planck Declaration on Patent Protection, an exception unreasonably conflicts with the normal exploitation of the patent if it impairs the efficiency of the patent as a mechanism to regulate prices. This, according to the declaration, occurs when the purported exception diminishes in an unjustified manner the incentives for innovation provided by the market.[73]

The economic exploitation of products made under the new exception for manufacture for export takes place in foreign markets, where the invention is off patent. Patents do not entitle right holders to control foreign markets, particularly to use the patent as a regulatory price mechanism in those markets. Therefore, the patent holder does not obtain from foreign markets where the invention is not patented a significant incentive to innovate. Indeed, in these markets it is competition, and not patent exclusivity, that is the factor determining the price of the product.

It does not unreasonably prejudice the legitimate interests of the right holder, taking into consideration the legitimate interests of third parties

The third condition set forth in TRIPS Article 30 requires that exceptions do not unreasonably prejudice the legitimate interests of the patent owner, taking account of the legitimate interests of third parties. In order to facilitate the analysis of this requisite, the three concepts –"legitimate interests of the patent owner", "unreasonably prejudice", "legitimate interests of third parties" – are examined separately. It should be reiterated that the reference to the interests of third parties is absent in the Berne Convention Article 9(2) and corresponding TRIPS Article 13.

Legitimate interests

The analysis of the third step, relating to the "legitimate interests" of the patent holder and third parties, led the panel to consider what these "legitimate interests" were. In this context, the panel distinguished between "legitimate interests" and "legal interest", and noted that the former have their own meaning, that of "justifiable" in the sense that they are supported by relevant public policies or other social norms.[74] Hence, the argument of the European Communities that the exception was limited to the rights of the right holder enshrined in Article 28.1

73 *Declaration of Patent Protection*, op. cit., para. 24, at p8.
74 *Canada Pharmaceutical Products*, § 7.69, 7.74 and 7.75.

of TRIPS,[75] without reference to any more particular normative claims of interest, was considered unacceptable by the panel.[76] From this perspective, the question posed was whether the benefits that the patent owner obtained after the expiration of the patent term, thanks to delays resulting from the regulatory process, were "justifiable".

The panel considered that patent holders did not have a "legitimate interest" on benefits arising after the term of the patent, which resulted from the delay imposed by the hurdles necessary to obtain regulatory approval and not the result from any WTO norm.[77] That interest was, in fact, neither so compelling nor so widely recognized that it could be regarded as a "legitimate interest" within the meaning of Article 30. For the panel, "Article 30's 'legitimate interests' concept should not be used to decide, through adjudication, a normative policy issue that is still obviously a matter of unresolved political debate".[78]

Unreasonably prejudice

Given the absence of a "legitimate interest" on the part of patent holders, and in line with the panel conception of the cumulative nature of the three-step test, the *Canada-Pharmaceutical Patents* panel did not go further in the analysis of Article 30. Accordingly, the scope and meaning of Article 30 reference to "unreasonable prejudice" has not yet been the subject of interpretation in the WTO dispute settlement system.

Nevertheless, the interpretation provided by a parallel WTO panel of a TRIPS article also mandating to not "unreasonably prejudice the legitimate interests of the right holder" can be relevant to our enquiry. The *US-Copyright* panel report interpreted TRIPS Article 13, on copyright exceptions, as a sister provision to TRIPS Article 30.[79] According to that report, "prejudice" implies damage, harm or injury. On its turn, "not unreasonable" connotes a slightly stricter threshold than "reasonable", a term that refers to something "proportionate", that is, "within the limits of reason, not greatly less or more than might be thought likely or appropriate", or "of a fair, average or considerable amount or size".[80]

According to the copyright panel, the most relevant question is which degree or level of "prejudice" may be considered "unreasonable", given that, under the third condition, a certain amount of "prejudice" has to be presumed justified as

75 When interpreting the condition to not unreasonably prejudice the "legitimate interests" of patentees the European Communities affirmed that legitimate interests referred to "legal interests". From this perspective, reference was being made to the full enjoyment of the patent rights enumerated in TRIPS Article 28. *Canada Pharmaceutical Products*, § 7.62.

76 Ibid, § 7.73.

77 Ibid, § 7.77.

78 Ibid, § 7.82.

79 Both provisions implementing the three-step rule have a similar drafting and find their origin in Article 9(b) of the Bern Convention.

80 *US-Copyright*, § 6.225.

"not unreasonable". Following the panel's view, prejudice to the legitimate interests of right holders reaches an unreasonable level if an exception or limitation causes or has the potential to cause an unreasonable loss of income to the copyright owner.[81]

Taking into account the legitimate interests of third parties

The *Canada-Pharmaceutical Patents* panel did not analyse an eventual conflict between the legitimate interests of the patent holder and the interests of third parties. Given that the panel found that no legitimate interests were affected by the Bolar exception, it also understood that no further analysis of the third condition or step on Article 30 was required. Nevertheless, both the expressions "third parties" and "legitimate interests" were, in effect, subject of interpretation by the panel.

The panel found that, in the context of Article 30, "third parties" are parties not entitled to perform the activities enumerated in TRIPS Article 28.[82] Therefore, by "third parties" it should be understood those having interests different from the patent holder interests.[83] Third parties include those who have an interest in relation to the availability, consumption, cost or production of products subject to patent protection. "Third parties" has, therefore, a broad sense, including "follow-on inventors; competitors and other market actors who need to operate on the market under conditions of effective competition; scientific and academic researchers who require access to the findings of basic research; consumers enjoying the benefits of technological advancement; the public at large in improved social, cultural and economic well-being".[84]

The *Canada Pharmaceutical Products* panel interpreted the term "legitimate interests" as those that are "justifiable", in the sense that they are supported by public policies and other relevant social norms.[85] In the context of patent exceptions, it exemplified this concept alluding to the experimental use exception and the fact that a public policy purpose of patent laws is to facilitate the

81 Ibid, § 6.229.

82 The citation is as follows: "parties who have no legal right at all in being able to perform the tasks excluded by Article 28 patent rights". *Canada Pharmaceutical Products*, § 7.68.

83 The European Communities argued in the case that the expression "legitimate interests of third parties" alluded to the eventual rights of the competitors to make, use or sell the patented product the day after the expiry of the patent. Consequently, the Bolar exception would not meet the third condition of Article 30 because it affected the "legitimate interests" of patent holders to prevent the exercise of *ius excluendi* granted by Article 28.1 of the TRIPS and there was no "legitimate interest" of competitors, since their rights to make, use and sell were born after the expiry of the patent, and the exception was important enough to be described as "unjustified". Ibid, § 7.64.

84 *Declaration on Patent Protection*, op. cit., para. 25 at p8.

85 *Canada Pharmaceutical Products*, § 7.69.

dissemination and advancement of technical knowledge. Thus, in case patent owners might prevent experimental use, that purpose would be frustrated.[86]

It remains, therefore, to be determined how the balance between the legitimate interests of patentees and the legitimate interests of third parties should be calibrated. In this regard it has been proposed to invoke in this context the principle of proportionality. In this sense, the Declaration on Patent Protection upholds the view that exceptions do not unreasonably harm the legitimate interests of patent holders if they are proportionate and reasonable,[87] taking into consideration "all affected interests".[88]

The implementation of the principle of proportionality in the balance between the legitimate interests of patent holders and third parties would, thus, at least require that:

(i) the exception is an effective means of protecting the legitimate interests of third parties as part of the objectives underlying public policy goals;
(ii) the exception is appropriate to accomplish the fulfilment of these objectives; and
(iii) the harm caused to the right holder is not excessive or disproportionate when compared to the benefits that the exception has on third parties.

The payment of an equitable compensation

The payment of an equitable compensation could be eventually proposed to do a final readjustment of the implementation of the three-step test. In a cumulative reading of the conditions of Article 30, as done by the WTO panel, if an exception satisfies the first condition (the exception is limited) and also the second (it does not interfere with the normal exploitation of the patent), but fails to meet the third condition (because it unreasonably prejudices the legitimate interests of the patent owner, taking into account the interests of third parties), then the payment of an equitable remuneration can be instrumental to rebalance the situation. Thus, the unreasonable prejudice of the rights of the patentee resulting from the exception can be reduced to a reasonable level by paying an equitable remuneration.[89]

This approach to reduce or mitigate the "unreasonable prejudice" was deliberated in the context of the discussions relating to Article 9(2) of the Berne Convention in the 1967 Stockholm Conference. In effect, "the principle was established that the payment of equitable remuneration, as a countermove to the adoption or maintenance of a limitation, can be taken into account".[90] So, an exception could even "unreasonably prejudice the legitimate interests of the

86 Ibid, § 7.69.
87 *Declaration on Patent Protection*, op. cit., para. 25 at p8.
88 Ibid, para. 26 at p9. M. Senftleben, op. cit., p151.
89 Ibid.
90 M. Senftleben, op. cit., p435.

author", provided that an equitable remuneration is paid. This principle can be extended, *mutatis mutandis*, to TRIPS Article 30. If an exception meets the conditions of being limited and not interfering with the normal exploitation of the patent, but does not meet the third condition of not unreasonably prejudicing the legitimate interests of the patent owner, taking into account the legitimate interests of third parties, then the eventual payment of an equitable remuneration could mitigate the negative impact of unreasonable prejudice.

The fulfilment of the third condition

In our argumentation, the consistency of the exception for manufacture for export in light of the third condition set forth in TRIPS Article 30 – legitimate interests of third parties – must still be determined. It is not enough to argue that the right to exclude recognized in TRIPS Article 28 is affected in order to claim that the "legitimate interests" of the patentee are prejudiced.[91] In this regard, we cannot identify any legitimate interest of the right holder, widely recognized by WTO Members as a legitimate interest policy that is negatively affected by the exception for manufacture for export.

Even if it is understood that the "legitimate interests" of the right holder are affected because the *ius excluendi* stipulated in TRIPS Article 28.1 is restricted, no prejudice to such rights can be observed. To paraphrase the *Canada Pharmaceutical Products* panel,[92] the question that needs to be answered is whether patent holders can claim a "legitimate interest" in the economic benefits that could result using their *ius excluendi* in order to prevent the manufacture for export to countries where there is no patent protection. In this regard, the said exception does not negatively impact right holders' entitlements because they have no "legitimate interest" in markets off patents.

Certainly, in exchange of disclosing an invention to the public, the patent holder has a "legitimate interest" in the exclusive exploitation of the patent, and to obtain the related economic benefits. However, the manufacturing for export exception does not appear to affect any "legitimate interest" of the right holder with respect to countries where there is no patent protection. The right holder maintains, in fact, the right to file, at any time of the term of protection, infringement proceedings to prevent others from the commercial sale of the patented invention in the territories where (s)he has been granted protection.

According to the *US-Copyright* panel report the decisive aspect is the degree of "prejudice" that may be considered "unreasonable", given that, under the third condition, it could be considered that a certain level of "prejudice" is reasonable. The threshold is found on whether the exception or limitation causes an unreasonable loss of income. In the case of the exception for manufacture for export the cause of potential loss of income will not be the result of the exception as such, but the fact that the invention is already in the public domain and,

91 *Canada Pharmaceutical Products*, § 7.73.
92 Ibid, § 7.61.

therefore, subject to the rules of economic competition. The potential loss of income to the patentee could be caused either by marketing products made in the country of export as well as from imports from third countries.

Finally, even if the "legitimate interests" of right holders were affected by the proposed exception, it would still be necessary to balance those interests with the legitimate interests of third parties. The TRIPS structure serves the purpose of achieving a balance between competing interests and ensures that patent rights claims do not prevent the achievement of other social objectives. As stated in the first paragraph of the preamble and in the objectives set out in Article 7, TRIPS is not intended to promote patent rights at the expense of legitimate trade, social and economic welfare and third parties' rights. It is in this context that, in order to achieve the balance sought by the reference to "third parties" in Article 30, the interests of the latter are recognized.

The "legitimate interests" of third parties are also implicit in TRIPS Article 8, since it empowers Members, when implementing the obligations under the Agreement, to take the necessary measures to protect public health and nutrition of the population, or to promote public interest in sectors of vital importance to their socio-economic and technological development. Once identified third parties' "legitimate interests" endorsed by political standards recognized by WTO members, it should be resolved then, applying the principle of proportionality, whether the new exception unreasonably prejudices patents owners' interests taking into account the legitimate interests of third parties.

Applying the principles mentioned above, relating to proportionality, we submit that the proposed exception meets the third condition of Article 30 of TRIPS. First, the exception is an effective means of protecting the legitimate interests of economic, social and technological development, in the case of both other economic actors and the society as a whole. Second, the exception is appropriate to accomplish the fulfilment of these objectives, since it enables the development of relevant investments, scientific research, creation of jobs and export promotion. Third, the exception does not cause prejudice to the right holder since he has no exclusive rights according to international intellectual property law in the export market and, conversely, the benefits in economic terms and development that produces the exception in favour of competitors, ends by tilting the test of proportionality in favour of the exception.

Finally, if it is understood that a breach of the third condition – to not unreasonably prejudice the legitimate interest of the patent owner, taking account of the legitimate interests of third parties – persists, it is still possible to establish that the use of the exemption might be subject to payment of an equitable remuneration, to compensate the eventual prejudice suffered by the patent owner.

Conclusions

Patent law recognizes that in certain circumstances it is necessary to use exceptions to meet public policy objectives such as, *inter alia*, the promotion of innovation, industrial development and competition, and to protect superior legal interests, such as health, nutrition and education. There is in this context a great diversity of exceptions across national legal orders.

All exceptions discharge users from liability for patent infringement, even if the acts carried out fall within the right holder *ius prohibendi*. There is a forceful trend, identifiable in both multilateral fora and academia, in favour of expanding the use of exceptions to respond to new situations.

TRIPS Article 30 sets forth the conditions under which WTO Members may regulate exceptions to patent rights in national laws. To this end, it establishes that exceptions should be limited; must not unreasonably conflict with the normal exploitation of the patent; and may not unreasonably prejudice the legitimate interests of the patent owner, taking into account the interests of third parties.

TRIPS Article 30 reflects an international consensus with respect to a number of points. First, exceptions are open ended and are not subject to *numerus clausus*. Second, only the general conditions to be met by exceptions have been agreed. Third, the conditions laid down in TRIPS Article 30 are to be interpreted in accordance with national law. Fourth, exceptions may pursue economic purposes and a conflict between the exploitation of the patent and the exceptions could exist. There is no consensus, however, as to whether these conditions are cumulative, contrary to the view of the *Canada-Pharmaceutical Patents* panel.

Beyond the applicability of the export exception during the normal life of the patent, in the case of supplementary protection certificates and patent extensions in general, they need to be seen as TRIPS-plus or extra measures, in the sense that they are not explicitly regulated by TRIPS. In both cases, they expand the temporary protection beyond the TRIPS minimum standard of 20 years. States, therefore, keeping in mind their international obligations, have the freedom to implement, within their own legal system and practice, these measures in the way that they deem appropriate. The manufacture for export should be conceived in the above cases as an exception to the right holder rights in the context of a new type of protection and, in the case of supplementary protection certificates, in the context of a new category of intellectual property.

The new exception is "limited" because it does not absolutely restrict the patentee's *ius excluendi*, but only with respect to products made for export. Moreover, the exception is also limited because, by definition, it has a restriction on the volume of production. Thus, the exception also has an implicit limitation with respect to destination, as it can only supply foreign markets off patents. As explicit in the TRIPS Agreement, measures and procedures to enforce intellectual property rights should not by "themselves become barriers to legitimate trade".

The exception for manufacturing for exportation does not affect the "normal exploitation" of the patent because it does not detract from any of the expected economic benefits that result from market exclusivity where the patent is granted. The exception does not prevent the owner from retaining full and exclusive rights to prevent the economic exploitation of the patented invention in the territory where the protection has been granted, and thereby obtain economic benefits during the term of protection. Likewise, the exception does not harm the "normal exploitation" of the patent because it does not hinder the efficiency of the patent as price regulation mechanism.

The exception also meets the third condition set in TRIPS to not "unreasonably prejudice the legitimate interests of the patent owner, taking account of the legitimate interests of third parties". It has not been possible to yet identify any legitimate interest – different from those resulting from the rights conferred by TRIPS Article 28.1 – which constitutes a policy norm widely recognized by WTO Members and which is concerned by the exception.

If, hypothetically, it is assumed that the term legitimate interests refers to the power to fully exercise the *ius excluendi*, it is similarly difficult to identify any impairment of such rights. Indeed, patent holders cannot claim a "legitimate interest" with respect to their potential economic benefits that could relate to their *ius excluendi* in preventing the manufacture of patented products for export prominently because they are not entitled to any exclusivity in the importing market.

Similarly, even if there were "legitimate interests" of the patent owners affected by the exception, it cannot be the cause of an unreasonable loss of income. The patent holder cannot expect or understand as guaranteed any income, derived from his/her exclusive rights in the exporting territory, in a foreign market that is off patent. The damage caused by the loss of potential income from abroad will not be the result of the exception for manufacturing for export, but will be due to the fact that the invention is not protected in the country of export and, therefore, subject to legitimate trade and competition.

Even if the exception caused unreasonably prejudice the legitimate interests of patent holders, by virtue of the proportionality principle the balance tips in favour of the legitimate interests of third parties benefiting from the exception. These legitimate interests include not only the patent holder but also follow-on inventors, competitors and other market actors who need to operate under conditions of effective competition, consumers and broadly the public at large. This is in line with the balance enshrined in TRIPS (Articles 7 and 8) between rights and obligations, and socio-economic development objectives. For many countries, moreover, the exception would be a feasible instrument to reconcile TRIPS and the protection of public health.

Finally, it is also possible to interpret TRIPS Article 30 in a more liberal way, as demonstrated by the declaration sponsored by the Max Planck Institute holding that the three requirements are not cumulative. Thus, the analysis of the fulfilment of Article 30 requires a global approach to the exception, different from the analysis of each of the requirements performed in *Canada-Pharmaceutical Patents*. From this more liberal perspective, it can only be confirmed the conformity of the new exception with TRIPS Article 30 and with the broad interpretation of that provision as given in the cited panel report.

Part III

A Broader View on Incentives for Pharmaceutical Innovation

9 The Price of Exclusivity

The Economics of Patent Extensions and Data Protection

Aidan Hollis and Paul Grootendorst*

Introduction

In most countries, there is pressure from the pharmaceutical industry to increase protection for patented drugs. Often, the most contentious aspect of trade agreements, such as the Trans-Pacific Partnership, is the coordination of new, higher standards to extend the effective exclusivity period of innovative pharmaceuticals. In this chapter, we explore the likely costs of policies that would lengthen the exclusivity period for new pharmaceutical products, using Hong Kong as a case study. Our approach is empirical in nature, and transparent. We show that plausible changes in the intellectual property provisions relating to pharmaceuticals would have modest effects on total drug spending.

It is widely accepted that there would be low levels of investment into the discovery and commercialization of new drugs (i.e., new pharmaceuticals and biologics) without some form of government support. Most governments thus support drug research and development (R&D). This support takes four forms:[1]

1. grants for basic biomedical research conducted in academic and public sector labs;
2. tax subsidies for clinical trials and other R&D costs;
3. patents and other forms of intellectual property (IP) protection that provide innovators a period of exclusivity in the sale of newly developed drugs;[2] and
4. prescription drug subsidies, typically extended through publicly funded insurance programmes to those who would otherwise have limited ability to pay.

* Aidan Hollis acknowledges the generous support of the Canadian Institutes of Health Research for this work, through an Emerging Team Grant on "Developing Effective Policies for Managing Technologies for Rare Diseases" and the European Research Council under the European Union's Seventh Framework Programme (FP/2007-2013)/ERC Grant Agreement no. 339239.

1 Paul Grootendorst, Aidan Hollis, and Aled Edwards "Patents and Other Incentives for Pharmaceutical Innovation" in Anthony J. Culyer (ed), *Encyclopedia of Health Economics* (Elsevier, 2014), 434–442.

2 See particularly Chapter 10 in this volume.

As discussed above, the focus of this chapter is the system of pharmaceutical IP protection, and, in particular, the financial impact of possible changes to IP provisions, using Hong Kong as a case study to ground the analysis in a real-life situation. We begin by summarizing the uses and purposes of various types of IP and then we develop an empirically plausible method to estimate the cost of given changes to the provisions.

As noted above and demonstrated throughout this volume, the goal of the pharmaceutical IP system is to provide drug companies with a time-limited period of exclusivity in the sale of a new drug. This allows the innovator both to capture the entire market and to sell profitably at a price that is higher than if the firm faced competition from producers of interchangeable generic products. These supra-competitive sales revenues create an incentive to invest in drug development.

Once exclusivity ends, generic entrants can capture most of the market of the innovator's product. The reason is that insurers normally reduce reimbursement levels to the price of the generic product; consumers are required to pay extra should they wish to continue using the innovator (i.e., "brand") product. Governments further facilitate generic substitution by permitting pharmacists to dispense generic drugs, even if the prescription is written for the brand name product. In many cases, patients are not even aware of the substitution.[3] Governments also facilitate generic entry by reducing the testing requirements for generic products. Whereas brand drugs must demonstrate safety and efficacy, generic drugs need to demonstrate therapeutic equivalence to the reference brand drug, which is a much lower hurdle.

The effective period of market exclusivity depends on the interplay of four types of IP regulations specific to pharmaceuticals, namely, patents, patent term extension, data protection, and linkage. We discuss each of these in turn, starting with the most common form of IP, the patent.

Patents

A patent provides its owner with a 20-year period of exclusive use of the invention disclosed in the patent. Market exclusivity offered by pharmaceutical patents, however, is less than 20 years owing to the lengthy drug development process. This is illustrated in Figure 9.1, which displays the timelines of drug development and patenting activity. Market exclusivity follows market authorization and ends with generic entry. Market authorization, in turn, follows a lengthy period of drug discovery, animal testing and formulation (the pre-clinical stage), the generation of data on drug safety and efficacy in human volunteers (clinical testing, typically using the randomized controlled trial design), and government review of these

3 It should be noted, however, that in jurisdictions without automatic substitution, where prescribers can veto substitution, the process of erosion of patentee market share by generics is relatively slow.

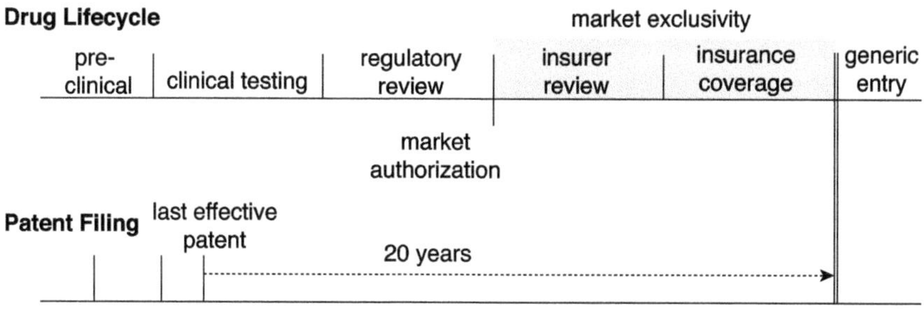

Figure 9.1 Drug lifecycle and patent filing activity

data (regulatory review). Prior to market authorization, the innovator will apply for a series of patents on the product; these normally cover, *inter alia*, the active ingredient, the biologic mechanism of action, therapeutic uses, and methods to synthesize the active ingredient. Not all of these patents will prevent generic entry; for instance, a generic firm might find a way to synthesize the active ingredient using a non-infringing process. Thus, the innovator receives 20 years of protection from the filing of the last patent that can prevent generic entry; this protection starts with the filing of the "last effective patent" in Figure 9.1. Normally, the last effective patent is filed prior to market authorization, so that by the time a drug actually gets to market, it may have only ten years remaining of the last effective patent.[4]

Patent term extension

As noted above, governments determine whether a new drug can be sold after reviewing the evidence regarding its safety and efficacy. Each month of review time reduces the period of market exclusivity by a month. Some governments compensate drug companies with additional patent life should the review time exceed some threshold (see Figure 9.2).

Patent term extension is operative in numerous countries, as summarized in Table 9.1. In the European Union (EU) and the United States (US), the five-year period may be extended by an additional six months subject to the completion of clinical studies of the drug on paediatric populations.

Data Protection

Data protection (DP) provides drug companies with a guaranteed minimum period of market exclusivity. The period of DP follows market authorization and

4 C. Scott. Hemphill and Bhaven Sampat, "Evergreening, Patent Challenges, and Effective Market Life in Pharmaceuticals" (2012), 31, Journal of Health Economics, 2, 327.

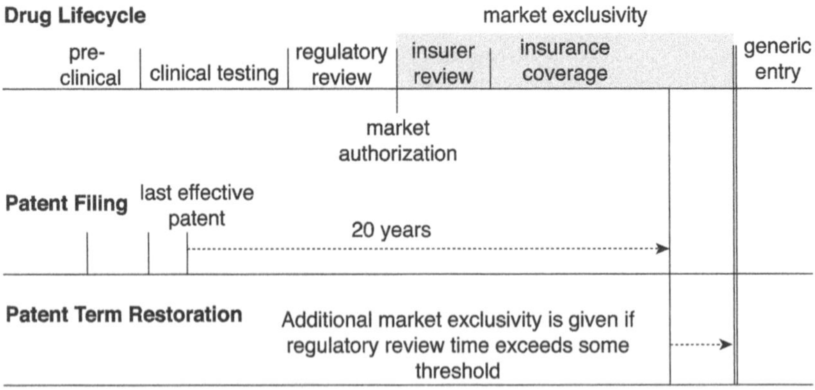

Figure 9.2 Patent term restoration

Table 9.1 Extension of protection term for pharmaceutical patents by country

Country	*Maximum term in years*
The US, EU, Australia, Japan, South Korea, Singapore, Russia	5
Canada[1]	2
Chile	Based on "unjustified administrative delay"[2]
China, India, Brazil, Saudi Arabia	0

Source: International Comparative Legal Guide to Patents 2016;[3] the European Patent Office[4]

1 The provision of the two-year patent term restoration in Canada, akin to the EU Supplementary Protection Certificate system, is an obligation under the Comprehensive Economic and Trade Agreement (CETA) between Canada and the European Union.
2 According to Article 53*bis* 2 of Chile's Law No. 19.039 on Industrial Property: "Supplementary protection will *only extend for the period proved as unjustified* administrative delay by the administrative organ called to decide said registration." See www.achipi.cl/wp-content/uploads/2010/09/Ley-N%C2%BA-19.039-sobre-Propiedad-Industrial-versi%C3%B3n-en-ingl%C3%A9s.pdf, accessed 11 March 2016.
3 International Comparative Legal Guides (2016) International Comparative Legal Guide to Patents, www.iclg.co.uk, accessed 11 March 2016.
4 European Patent Office, Asian Patent Information, www.epo.org/searching-for-patents/helpful-resources/asian.html, accessed 11 March 2016.

varies by country from five to ten years. Technically, during the DP period, generic firms attempting to obtain market authorization cannot rely on the evidence of drug safety and efficacy generated by the innovator firm. This deprives the generic firm the option of gaining approval by demonstrating therapeutic equivalence to the innovator brand. The only remaining option available to the generic firm is to demonstrate safety and efficacy *de novo* by repeating the clinical trials already

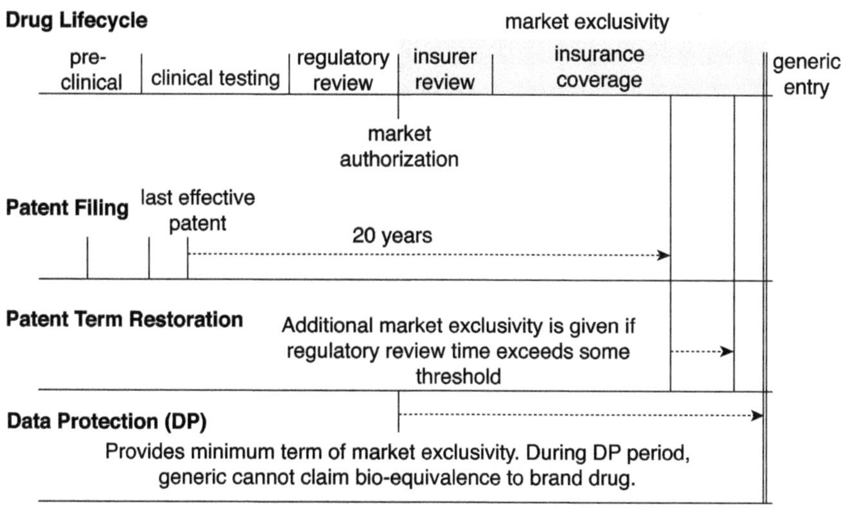

Figure 9.3 Data protection

conducted by the innovator. This option is virtually never pursued because of the high cost; indeed, testing costs account for about half of the total cost of drug development. Moreover, it is debatable whether ethics boards would allow human testing of a drug that was already shown to be safe and efficacious.[5]

DP extends market exclusivity only if the exclusivity provided by the other forms of IP, patents and patent term restoration are less than the minimum threshold. Otherwise, DP is not binding.

Sometimes, after the brand drug is on the market, the innovator will conduct a second set of clinical trials to obtain approval to market the drug for a new therapeutic indication. The DP rules need to accommodate this possibility. In particular, the regulator needs to determine if the second set of trial data is given data protection after the expiry of data protection on the primary trial data (i.e., the data that support the first therapeutic indication). If it were possible to allow generics to be substituted for the first indication, but not the second, then there would not be an issue. But neither the generic manufacturer nor the pharmacist know what indication a drug is dispensed for; it is not possible for them to prevent the generic being dispensed for the second indication. In effect, if data protection is not renewed, the second indication is not protected; but if data protection is designed to prevent sales of generics for the second indication, it would normally also block sales of the generic for the first indication. The solution in most jurisdictions has been for data protection to be granted only once for a given molecule.

5 Karin Timmermans, "Monopolizing Clinical Trial Data: Implications and Trends" (2007), 4, PLoS Medicine 2, 0206, 0207, www.journals.plos.org/plosmedicine/article?id=10.1371/journal.pmed.0040002, accessed 18 March 2016.

Table 9.2 Data protection term by country

Years	*Countries*
12	US (biologics only)
10	EU, EEA, Switzerland
8	Japan, Canada, Hong Kong
6	China, Korea, Turkey, Croatia
5	27 countries, US (small molecule drugs)

Source: IFPMA (2011);[1] Mercurio and Kim (2014)[2]

1 International Federation of Pharmaceutical Manufactures and Associations, "Data Exclusivity: Encouraging Development of New Medicines" (IFPMA, 2011).
2 Bryan C. Mercurio and Daria Kim, "Patently Lacking: A Call for Systemic Review of Pharmaceutical Law and Policy – A Case Study of Hong Kong" (2014), 9, Asian Journal of WTO & International Health Law and Policy, 1, 63.

Data protection has become quite common. Table 9.2 shows the set of countries with data protection. The most common duration is five years, though most Western European countries offer ten years of data protection. The general trend is an increase in data protection. Many countries have added or lengthened data protection as part of free trade agreements, especially with the US.

Linkage

A further form of IP protection for new drugs is so-called "linkage" regulation, under which the regulatory approval of generic drugs is linked to the brand drug's patent status. Such a system operates in the US, Canada, South Korea, Mexico, Australia and China. Linkage means that a generic firm must address outstanding patents on the brand drug before it can be granted marketing approval. In particular, a generic firm must demonstrate via litigation that the extant patents are either invalid or not infringed by its generic drug. The generic firm must await the expiry of patents that the court deems to be valid and infringed upon generic entry. If a generic firm elects not to engage in litigation, all patents are presumed to be valid and infringed upon generic entry.

A linkage system puts the onus on the would-be market entrant to demonstrate that it is not infringing. Normally, a potential infringer may simply enter the market and start selling, and the patentee has the burden of demonstrating infringement in order to obtain an injunction against the infringer. With linkage, the generic firm cannot enter until it has obtained a court decision that it is not infringing.

Evergreening

The innovative firm can use various strategies to extend market exclusivity. A common strategy in countries with particularly generous drug insurance is for the

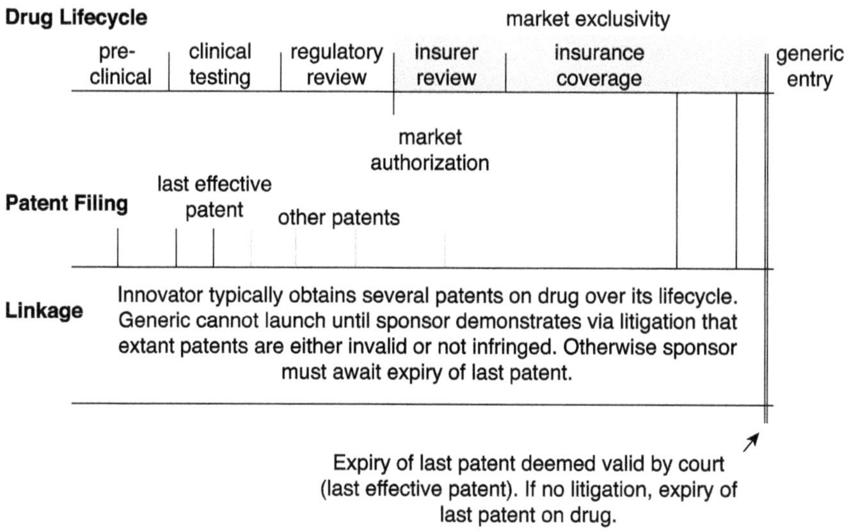

Figure 9.4 Linkage

patentee to launch a new, "improved" version of the drug as the exclusivity of the original drug draws to an end. This launch is normally accompanied by a promotional campaign that attempts to persuade physicians and patients to switch to the new drug. Examples include the launch of desvenlafaxine (Pristiq) to replace venlafaxine (Effexor), and the launch of esomeprazole (Nexium) to replace omeprazole (Losec). Whether this strategy is successful depends on the effectiveness of the promotion, the additional therapeutic benefits, if any, provided by the new drug, and most importantly, the willingness of the insurer to pay for the additional therapeutic benefits. Such strategies are commonly successful in the US market, even for new drugs which are only marginally better than the drugs they replace, owing to the generous drug reimbursement by many US insurers.[6]

Another way of extending exclusivity is for innovator firms to make settlements with generic rivals that have the effect of delaying generic entry. Since the branded product sells for much more than generic rivals, delaying entry and compensating the generic firm for its lost profits can be profitable for the brand. These kinds of settlements have attracted considerable attention from the Federal Trade Commission in the US and the European Commission in Europe.

While strategic behaviour by the patentee is not, in itself, a regulatory choice, it often depends on the nature of the IP policies, and how the courts interpret them. Thus, the actual period of exclusivity is determined by more than just the

6 David Whelan, "Little Pricey Pill" Forbes (25 March 2010), www.forbes.com/forbes/2010/0412/opinions-healthcare-nexium-hmo-prescriptions-heads-up.html, accessed 12 March 2016.

official patent term or data protection period. Instead, it depends on the number of forms of IP (patents, patent term restoration, data protection, and linkage), the precision of the language in each of these policies, and the ability of the policies to contemplate all possible contingencies. The greater the number of forms of IP and the less precise is the language, the greater the opportunity for patentees to engage in regulatory gamesmanship to protect their market. Each additional regulatory layer presents new opportunities for litigation, and new ways to use the rules in ways not anticipated by their designers.[7]

Exclusivity rules as part of the toolbox

It is important to appreciate that exclusivity restrictions are not the sole determinants of pharmaceutical expenditures – or the revenues of innovative pharmaceutical companies – in a jurisdiction. The length of exclusivity is only one component of spending on pharmaceuticals: volume, the rate of substitution to generics, and price also matter. As an example, Canada and the EU have recently negotiated a trade agreement in which the EU requested Canada to offer patent term extension and to extend data protection to match EU levels. There is some irony in this, since Canada already was spending more on pharmaceuticals per capita than virtually all EU countries.

Longer exclusivity is one way of increasing returns to pharmaceutical innovation, but if it is compensated by lower pricing, then there is no change in total expenditures or in the return to investment. Consider a simple numerical example. Suppose that the revenues from a product are $1 million per year over a 10-year exclusivity period, with revenues falling by US$100,000 each year after the exclusivity period. And suppose that the firm discounts future earnings at the rate of 10 per cent per year. This discount rate reflects the cost of capital for pharmaceutical firms. Now suppose that the exclusivity period is extended to 12 years (i.e., by 20 per cent); but prices fall by 6 per cent. The firm earns roughly the same revenues as before. In effect, while the period of exclusivity is an important component of total revenues, a small negative adjustment to price can wipe out the gains from longer exclusivity. The key is that longer exclusivity has an effect many years in the future, while any change in price has an immediate effect.

Similarly, the speed of substitution of generics for brands can have just as large an effect on brand revenues (and insurer expenditures) as changing the length of effective exclusivity. The decision as to what drugs are included in the formulary – or list of insured drugs – can also have a profound effect on the revenues of innovative drug companies and on the expenditures of insurers.

7 Canada provides a useful example. As of June 2014, Canada has 20-year patent terms, eight years of data protection, and linkage. These IP policies have been the subject of much litigation between brand and generic firms over the years. Indeed, even the Supreme Court has rendered many decisions in respect of pharmaceutical IP issues.

Therefore, to the extent that the government controls levers other than the length of exclusivity, there are various ways of achieving a given level of expenditure. In addition, it seems likely that the price and formulary are endogenous to the exclusivity rules: this is self-evident if the insurer has a fixed budget. Thus, the purpose of changing exclusivity rules should chiefly be to reallocate revenues between drugs, rather than to increase or decrease total spending. An increase in data protection might, in this thinking, simply transfer some of the revenues from drugs with long patent life to drugs with short patent life.

Hong Kong current exclusivity provisions

Currently, Hong Kong (HK) offers data protection of eight years, following the EFTA-HK trade agreement.[8] Neither patent term extension nor linkage are available in HK. We empirically explore in this section the effect of adding patent term extensions or longer data protection – we do not attempt to identify the likely effect of establishing formal linkage regulations, since any expenditure impacts are sensitive to the specific details of the regulations, which are not predictable.

As a starting point, we present data on the current average length of exclusivity in Hong Kong. Using the Hong Kong Drug Office database, we selected the 20 products that most recently attracted a first generic competitor. These products are shown in Table 9.3.

As Table 9.3 shows, the exclusivity enjoyed by brand drugs has recently averaged approximately 13 years. Two drugs, Zometa and Strattera, had exclusivity periods of less than the eight-year minimum guaranteed by the data exclusivity provisions in HK. Had the eight-year data exclusivity been applied to these two drugs, this would have increased the exclusivity period of Zometa by 2.2 years and Strattera by 4 months. Suppose that all drugs were guaranteed eight years' data exclusivity. What would be the average increase in exclusivity, across all 20 drugs, of increasing data exclusivity to ten years? The average exclusivity period would increase by 128 days, or roughly four months. At most 4 of the 20 drugs in this list would have seen any change as a result of data protection being ten years instead of eight.

In general, we observe that the average additional exclusivity time is not increased as much as the maximum possible increase. Patent term extension of up to five years does not extend the average period of exclusivity by five years, since some products qualify for less than the maximum extension, and some may not qualify at all. Moving from eight-year to ten-year data protection, to the extent that it is coincident with patent protection, may extend the average exclusivity by only a few months, though it may extend exclusivity by the full two years for certain products.

8 Mercurio and Kim (n. 11).

Table 9.3 Twenty most recently genericized drugs in Hong Kong

Proprietary name	*API*	*Originator company*	*MA of originator*	*Date of MA for first generic in HK*	*HK exclusivity (years)*	*Date of US generic approval*
Aciphex (Pariet)	Rabeprazole (sodium)	EISAI Inc.	8 June 1999	8 June 2009	10.0	8 November 2013
Aricept	Donepezil Hydrochloride	EISAI Inc.	12 March 1998	16 March 2011	13.0	26 November 2010
Arimidex	Anastrozole	Astrazeneca	22 August 1997	8 June 2009	11.8	28 June 2010
Aromasin	Exemestane	Pfizer	3 November 2000	7 August 2012	11.8	1 April 2011
Combivir	Lamivudine Zidovudine	GSK	5 September 1998	19 January 2012	13.4	25 May 2011
Cymevene for inj 500 mg (Cytovene)	Ganciclovir	Roche	8 December 1989	11 February 2014	24.2	21 June 2010
Lyrica	Pregabalin	Pfizer	12 February 2005	14 January 2014	8.9	3 July 2012
Micardis	Telmisartan	Boehringer Ingelheim	28 January 2000	18 October 2011	11.7	8 January 2014
Nimbex	Cisatracurium	GSK	22 August 1997	8 November 2013	16.2	3 February 2012
Pletal	Cilostazol	Otsuka	23 February 2001	21 June 2013	12.3	23 November 2004
Propecia	Finasteride	Merck	3 February 1999	28 October 2011	12.7	15 December 2006
Rilutek	Riluzole	Sanofi-Aventis	27 November 1997	6 January 2014	16.1	29 January 2003
Sirdalud (Zanaflex)	Tizanidine	Acorda	1 August 1995	21 August 2013	18.1	3 July 2002
Strattera	Atomoxetine	Eli Lilly	1 July 2005	20 March 2013	7.7	26 May 2017

Temodar	Temozolomide	Merck Sharp & Dohme	10 December 2005	7 January 2014	8.1	1 March 2010
Trusopt	Dorzolamide	Merck Sharp & Dohme	24 June 1996	5 October 2012	16.3	28 October 2008
Viramune	Nevirapine	Boehringer Ingelheim	28 December 1998	12 October 2012	13.8	22 May 2012
Xalatan	Latanoprost	Pfizer	23 June 1997	26 April 2013	15.9	22 March 2011
Zometa	Zoledronic acid	Novartis	28 January 2004	28 November 2009	5.8	4 March 2013
Zomig	Zolmitriptan	Astrazeneca	31 July 1998	30 September 2013	15.2	14 May 2013
				Average	**13.2**	

Source: Hong Kong Drug Office database, FDA Orange Book; drugs.com/availability/generic-strattera.html for forecasted Strattera US generic entry date

Estimating the cost impact of changed exclusivity provisions

The data above can help us estimate the cost of extending the average duration of exclusivity. To do so, first, we calculate the cost to insurers (and other payers) per year of exclusivity offered by the current IP system. We then determine the increase in years in exclusivity offered by the contemplated IP changes and multiply the two.

Cost to insurers per year of exclusivity offered by the current IP system

We assume that market exclusivity currently stands at 13.2 years, the average for the 20 selected drugs. Also, we use the BMI estimate of 2014 spending on patented drugs, HK$6.3 billion.[9] We assume that 85 per cent of the present value of sales of patented drugs occur before generic entry, and 15 per cent thereafter.[10] Discounted sales that occur after generic entry are small primarily because generics are assumed to capture most molecule level sales. But there are several other reasons. The innovator product price may decrease to compete with generics (although it can also increase); the total volume of sales of the molecule may decrease because of a reduction in promotional activities of the firm; and finally, the value of post-patent sales is discounted more heavily because it is further in the future.

Using the above figures, innovator firms collectively earn HK$6.3 billon x 85 per cent annually on pre-generic entry sales; this is equivalent to HK$6.3 billion x 85 per cent/13 = HK$406 million per year of exclusivity.[11] What is the cost to insurers per year of exclusivity? Without exclusivity, insurers are able to purchase the same drugs at generic prices; the cost to insurers of exclusivity is therefore the difference between expenditures without generics available and expenditures with. Expenditures with generics available depends on the generic price discount and the fraction of molecule level sales that would accrue to generics. A reasonable assumption is that within the first few years of generic entry, generics capture 70 per cent of sales of the molecule, and the innovator retains 30 per cent. Thus 70 per cent of the $406 million sales would be purchased at the generic price. Generic prices in HK are on average between 50 and 75 per cent of the interchangeable brand prices, so this implies that expenditures with generics available are 50 per cent x 70 per cent x $406 million and 75 per cent x 70 per cent

9 Business Monitor International, "Hong Kong Pharmaceuticals & Healthcare Report Q4 2013" (2013), 21.

10 This is calculated based on net present value of the revenue stream of a drug that is on the market for 30 years. Its sales increase linearly to the permanent volume over the first seven years. Upon generic entry at year 13, the brand drug's share of sales of the molecule falls to 30 per cent.

11 This calculation assumes steady state values of expenditure on patented drugs, and periods of market exclusivity.

x $406 million. Thus the additional cost to insurers per year of additional exclusivity would be in the range of HK$71 million to HK$142 million per year.

Increase in years in exclusivity offered by the contemplated IP changes

We first consider the effect on insurer drug costs of moving from eight to ten years' data exclusivity. Recall that this is forecast to increase the average duration of exclusivity by 128 days. The additional cost to payers from this change would be 128/365 times the additional cost per year of HK$71 million to HK$142 million. Thus, the effect of extending data protection from eight to ten years is predicted to be an increase in costs to insurers in the range of HK$25 million to HK$50 million per year. Spending in Hong Kong in 2014 on prescription pharmaceuticals is approximately HK$8.91 billion,[12] so the effect of extending data protection from eight to ten years would be approximately 0.3–0.6 per cent of the total.

Assessing the expenditure impact of patent term extension is more difficult, because of the difficulty of predicting which drugs would have been eligible for how much patent term extension. Fortunately, we can approach this by comparing to the outcomes of drugs in the US. Of the 20 most recently genericized drugs, 15 were genericized earlier in the US than in Hong Kong. Given that the US has a five-year patent term extension already in place, we use the US date of generic entry as a proxy for the earliest date of generic entry in Hong Kong given a counterfactual of a five-year patent term extension in Hong Kong.

Our approach to this calculation is as follows. For all the drugs for which the US had a later generic entry date, we use the US date; and for all the drugs for which Hong Kong had a later date, we assume that patent term extension would not have been relevant, and so we use the Hong Kong actual generic entry date. Using this mix of Hong Kong and US generic entry dates, the average period of exclusivity duration would have been 13.91 years, or 232 days longer than the model with zero patent term extension and eight-year data exclusivity. We can use the same methodology as above to calculate that the additional brand revenues would be approximately HK$150 million each year; while additional costs to the payers would be in the range of $37 million to $75 million.

Including both ten-year data exclusivity (as in Europe) and a five-year patent term extension would increase the average length of exclusivity even more, by approximately another 50 days.

Discussion

Increasing the number of different IP tools for pharmaceuticals would have a cost, as this article has shown. One of the most striking findings of the article is that for most drugs generic entry has occurred later in Hong Kong than in the US,

12 BMI (n. 9) 20.

despite the fact that in the US there is five years of patent term extension, five years of data exclusivity, further paediatric extensions, and linkage, while during the relevant time period Hong Kong had none of these. That is, Hong Kong already provides more generous exclusivity for most innovative pharmaceuticals than the US. This outcome has arisen most likely because Hong Kong is a small market with no prize attached to being the first generic. The US is a large market and it offers 180-day exclusivity as the sole generic to the first firm that is successful in litigation. This creates a very large prize, which encourages generics to enter as rapidly as possible.

Given that Hong Kong already offers, for most products, longer exclusivity than the US, and that it has recently added eight-year data exclusivity as part of its trade agreement with Europe, it is not obvious that there is a compelling case for Hong Kong to add yet more tools of exclusivity. If Hong Kong were to offer more generous pharmaceutical exclusivity provisions, it should take advantage of this to capture some available efficiencies from more active, rapid substitution to lower-cost generic drugs. Typically, there are substantial political obstacles to writing laws to increase the use of generic drugs, and so it makes sense to make revision of exclusivity laws a part of a larger reform that involves revisions to how generic drugs compete. Equally important, Hong Kong should be examining why generics enter in many molecules with such lengthy delays. It should also be reviewing generic drug pricing, which appears to be relatively high.

Hong Kong should also be looking ahead to the era of biologic drugs. Unlike small molecule drugs, biologics cannot generally be replicated perfectly, and this means that it may not be possible to create "bio-equivalent" generics. Hong Kong currently does not have a pathway to create biosimilars.[13] Since most of the blockbuster drugs of today are biologics, it is extremely important to design a biosimilar pathway as soon as possible.

While the discussion above is framed by the case of Hong Kong, there are implications to be drawn for other countries as well. The first observation is that when assessing potential exclusivity provisions, it is important to understand and carefully analyse the existing framework. For example, as we see in the case of Hong Kong, lengthening patent protection would have less impact than might be expected because generic entry is delayed by factors other than patent protection. Nominal exclusivity as defined by the rules is not necessarily the same as effective exclusivity. Second, there are often other changes that might accompany and soften the impact of extended exclusivity provisions; for example, facilitating generic entry or increasing post-patent generic penetration rates can have an important effect on total spending. Third, countries should be looking forward to and preparing for the ascendant role of biologics, which represent an increasing share of spending and operate under very different competitive rules.

13 Hong Kong Department of Health, Drug Office, "Guidance Notes for Registration of Biosimilar Products" (2016), www.drugoffice.gov.hk/eps/do/en/doc/guidelines_forms/Biosimilar_guidelines_revised_Final_ENG.pdf, accessed 12 March 2016.

10 Rationalizing Innovation Incentives under Drug Approval Regulation

National Policy Perspective

Daria Kim

Introduction

This chapter addresses issues related to the increasing role assigned to drug approval regulation in incentivizing pharmaceutical innovation. It focuses on the specific provisions under drug marketing approval regulation that intend to restrain the approval of a generic product in order to allow sponsors of innovative drugs to earn higher returns on research and development (R&D) investments. In doing so, these provisions essentially replicate the incentive model of patents. While previous research has provided a detailed account of drug regulatory incentives,[1] this chapter seeks to define a pertinent approach to their analysis from the national policy-making perspective.

Countries differ in terms of their policy priorities and technological capacities in the pharmaceutical sector. Historically, the development of the global pharmaceutical industry has been characterized by the asymmetric production and distribution of innovative medicines, with a handful of multinational companies concentrated in the high-income countries accounting for the major part of the new drug development.[2] More recently, growth in biopharmaceutical innovative activity has been observed in the middle-income countries.[3] While economic

1 See, e.g., V. N. Bhat, "Patent Term Extension Strategies in the Pharmaceutical Industry" (2005), 6 Pharmaceuticals Policy and Law, 109; Rebecca S. Eisenberg, "The Role of the FDA in Innovation Policy" (2007), 13 Mich Telecomm Tech L. Rev., 345; Margo Bagley, "Patent Term Restoration and Non-Patent Exclusivity in the United States" in *Pharmaceutical Innovation, Competition and Patent Law: A Trilateral Perspective* (Josef Drexl and Nari Lee, eds, 2011), 111; Yaniv Heled, "Patents vs. Statutory Exclusivities in Biological Pharmaceuticals – Do We Really Need Both?" (2012), 18 Mich. Telecomm. Tech. L. Rev., 423; John R. Thomas, "Toward a Theory of Regulatory Exclusivities" in *Patent Law in Global Perspective* (R. L. Okediji and Margo A. Bagley, eds, 2014), 345; Trevor Cook, "Data Protection and Market Exclusivities for Pharmaceuticals in the EU" (2014), 16 Pharmaceuticals Policy and Law, 19.

2 B. Achilladelis and N. Antonakis, "The Dynamics of Technological Innovation: The Case of the Pharmaceutical Industry" (2001), 30 Research Policy, 535, 537.

3 For recent trends in the localization of global pharmaceutical R&D, see Tim Wilsdon and Eva Fiz, "Encouraging Pharmaceutical Innovation in Middle-Income Countries" (2013), WIPO

analysis does not provide a conclusive answer as to what extent, and at what costs, intellectual property (IP) protection contributes to this trend, many countries have demonstrated willingness to enhance IP-type protection for pharmaceuticals under sector regulations. The global character of this trend can be attributed to the special obligations under bilateral and multilateral trade agreements.[4]

The concern is that, without solid policy and economic analysis, a sporadic implementation of exclusivity-based incentives might not benefit the functioning of the overall regulatory framework. Patent law and drug marketing approval regulation are two bodies of rules that pursue distinct policy objectives, are directed at different market failures, and enforced by separate authorities. Both play an important role as legal determinants of competition and innovation in the pharmaceutical sector. Similarities between patents and regulatory exclusivities, in terms of policy rationales and incentive mechanisms, have led some scholars to refer to the latter as "industry specific pseudo-patents", or instruments that award "patent-like protection" under the auspices of a drug authority.[5] Drug regulation can relate to the patent system in different ways (e.g., by strengthening patent protection for the originator drug, such as patent linkage), or providing an additional layer of protection (different types of marketing exclusivities awarded independently from the drug patent status). On the one hand, incentives under drug approval regulation have been viewed as an attempt to "fine-tune" sector regulation in order to respond to the industry's growing needs to support innovative activity.[6] On the other hand, they can entail considerable social costs by interfering with the availability of affordable drugs. By replicating the exclusionary mechanism of patent protection, regulatory exclusivities pose the same dilemma over the balance between static costs and dynamic benefits that has been the focus of policy and scholarly debate regarding patent rights. Namely, *to what extent can price competition be restrained to yield results in innovation in the most cost-benefit effective and efficient way?* The interaction between the patent system and marketing approval regulation raises the question of the *net* effect of regulatory interventions

Magazine, http://www.wipo.int/wipo_magazine/en/2013/02/article_0008.html, accessed 15 July 2015.

4 For the statistics on the special pharmaceutical provisions in regional trade agreements, see R. Valdés and Maegan McCann, "Intellectual Property Provisions in Regional Trade Agreements: Revision and Update" (2014), World Trade Organization, Economic Research and Statistics Division, http://www10.iadb.org/intal/intalcdi/PE/2014/14788.pdf (examining the sample of 245 regional trade agreements, notified to the WTO and in force by February 2014, and accounting for the increasing number of agreements that stipulate obligations to implement patent linkage and clinical data exclusivity).

5 Eisenberg (n. 1) at 364. See Thomas (n. 1) at 360 (arguing that the view of regulatory exclusivities "as a patent-like innovation promoter has both shortcomings and descriptive flaws").

6 Eisenberg (n. 1) at 364–365 (arguing that "[t]he patent system is a one-size-fits-all legal regime that applies essentially the same rules to inventions [across different industries] . . . . But the needs of these fields for patent protection differ greatly, making it difficult to fine-tune the patent laws to meet the needs of the pharmaceutical industry without upsetting the balance of protection and competition in other industries. . . . To the extent that the exclusivity needs of the pharmaceutical industry are different from those of other industries, it might be less problematic to fine tune the drug regulation rules than it is to fine tune the patent system").

on social welfare. At the core of the policy analysis lies the question: how should different regulatory instruments be integrated to achieve policy objectives in innovation in the most socially optimal way?

Reflecting on these issues, this chapter proceeds as follows. The second section provides a detailed perspective on how the patent system and drug regulation interact in innovation: at the level of policy objectives and individual provisions. It identifies exclusivity as the common denominator between the two systems and finds regulatory exclusivity to be of the superior quality compared to patents in several aspects. Section three reveals the complexities of the costs and benefits assessment of innovation incentives. In view of indeterminacy of their net impact, it proposes that decision-making regarding exclusivity incentives should integrate constructivist and ecological types of rationality. Section four concludes with policy recommendations.

The intersection between patent law and drug marketing approval regulation

The pharmaceutical regulatory framework encompasses a body of rules regulating the diverse processes, issues and legal relationships that constitute the contents of pharmaceutical policy.[7] Patent law and drug marketing approval regulation play a prominent role as legal determinants of competition in the drug market. Another area where the two systems intersect is innovation.

Patent law and drug regulations are government interventions directed at distinct types of market failures. Patent law addresses a market failure associated with the public good nature of certain goods, which production, distribution and consumption can be socially suboptimal. Patents are granted in return for the contribution to technical advancement and disclosure of an invention to the public, and under an assumption that profits raised under the limited legal monopoly will stimulate further innovation activity. Pharmaceutical patents can protect a product (a chemical compound) or a process (a method of producing drug ingredients, their composition and formulation). While patent law, in principle, applies to all areas of technology,[8] some provisions are of a particular relevance for pharmaceuticals (e.g., compulsory licensing for public health reasons; exceptions from patentability of diagnostic and therapeutic methods of treatment of humans; exemptions from infringement for uses of the patented subject matter for the purpose of drug regulatory approval).[9]

7 For the definition and contents of pharmaceutical policy, see, e.g., the World Health Organization, the World Intellectual Property Organization, the World Trade Organization, *Promoting Access to Medical Technologies and Innovation: Intersections Between Public Health, Intellectual Property and Trade* (2012), 33; the World Health Organization, *How to Develop and Implement Comprehensive National Drug Policy* (2001), 21–27; Andreas Seiter, *A Practical Approach to Pharmaceutical Policy* (2010), 117–120.

8 Art 27 of the TRIPS Agreement.

9 On compulsory licensing for public health reasons, see Chapter 7 in this collection; on the exceptions of patentability – Chapter 2; on the exemptions from infringement for uses related to drug regulatory approval – Chapter 6.

Regardless of the patent status, pharmaceutical products are, in most jurisdictions, subject to stringent testing and marketing approval requirements.[10] By enforcing standards for drug safety, efficacy and quality, the regulator addresses market failures of insufficient drug testing and asymmetric information about the claimed therapeutic effects.[11] The concern is that without the regulatory intervention, the drug market can turn into a "market for lemons"[12] or "snake oil".[13]

Although patent law and drug marketing approval regulation differ in terms of the rationales for regulatory intervention, they are inherently interrelated, being directed at drugs as the common subject matter of regulation. Notably, an increasing interaction between the two systems has been observed in the area of innovation and can be distinguished at the level of policy objectives and specific regulatory provisions.

The international IP system was intentionally designed to promote innovation.[14] Unlike patents, drug marketing approval regulation does not explicitly pursue innovation goals; however, it can have an appreciable "side-effect" on innovation that can go in two directions. On the one hand, the burden of compliance with marketing authorization requirements accounts for a substantial part of drug R&D costs and can discourage firms from undertaking innovative activity,[15] or a particular type of innovation that is more costly to develop.[16] On the other hand, drug standard regulation has been viewed as directing and promoting innovative activity.[17]

10 On the substantive and procedural requirements for drug marketing authorization, see, e.g., Enrique Fefer, "Pharmaceutical Legislation and Regulation" in *Managing Access to Medicines and Health Technologies* (World Health Organization, 2012).

11 For a discussion of market failure of information asymmetry and insufficient product testing in the pharmaceutical sector, see Evan R. Kwerel, "Economic Welfare and the Production of Information by a Monopolist: The Case of Drug Testing" (1980), 11(2) Bell J. Econ., 505–506 (noting that "the firm cannot appropriate the entire gain from testing [. . .] Hence, the firm will do less than the socially optimal amount.").

12 Ariel Katz, "Pharmaceutical Lemons: Innovation and Regulation in the Drug Industry" (2007), 14 Mich. Telecomm. Tech. L. Rev., 11.

13 Eisenberg (n. 1) at 371.

14 Art 7 of the TRIPS Agreement.

15 See Eisenberg (n. 1) at 346 (summarizing that "patents promote innovation by making it profitable, while drug regulation deters innovation, in furtherance of the competing goal of public health, by making it costly"); Henry G. Grabowski, John M. Vernon and Lacy Glenn Thomas, "Estimating the Effects of Regulation on Innovation: An International Comparative Analysis" (1978), 21(1) Journal of Law and Economics, 133; Sam Peltzman, *Regulation of Pharmaceutical Innovation: The 1962 Amendments* (American Enterprise Institute for Public Policy Research, 1974) (accounting for the reduction in innovative drugs as an effect of increased regulatory stringency).

16 See n. 71 and the accompanying text.

17 See Katz (n. 12) at 7 (arguing that "the regulatory framework is not solely a burden imposed on the industry, but also a valuable service of drug quality certification").

The interaction between the two systems in innovation at the provision level

Before the policy analysis of regulatory incentives can be addressed, this section briefly reviews the types of provisions emerging at the intersection between patent law and marketing approval regulation. These specific pharmaceutical provisions originated in the US and EU and have been subsequently replicated in other jurisdictions due to the obligations under bilateral and multilateral trade agreements.[18] The key element and common denominator of this type of incentives can be defined as *exclusivity* – the potential of legal protection to restrain generic competition. Two types of exclusivity can be distinguished: *patent-derived* (i.e., when protection under drug approval regulation builds on patent protection of a drug), and *patent-like* exclusivity (i.e., protection granted independently from patent law but essentially imitating its exclusionary model). Each is explained in turn.

Provisions extending or strengthening patent-derived exclusivity

Perhaps the most obvious example of the interaction between the patent system and drug regulation is *patent linkage* – a provision that requires the applicant to verify the non-infringing status of a drug as an additional criterion for marketing authorization.[19] In effect, patent linkage precludes a generic product from obtaining marketing authorization while the corresponding patent(s) is/are in force. Although patent linkage does not extend patent rights beyond the protection term, it fortifies a patent by strengthening its immunity to infringement (and eliminating the likelihood of invalidation as a result of the defence).

In the case of *patent term extension*, the two systems relate in such a way that term extension is justified as a "fair" compensation for the reduced effective patent life due to the lengthy marketing authorization procedures.[20] However, several

18 See the Bipartisan Trade Promotion Authority Act of 2002, Pub. L. No. 107–210, SEC. 2102 (b) (4) (mandating that "the provisions of any multilateral or bilateral trade agreement governing intellectual property rights that is entered into by the United States reflect a standard of protection similar to that found in United States law"). See Valdés and McCann (n. 4) at 8 (observing that multilateral agreements establishing the EEC, EFTA and the Andean Community originally did not stipulate specific pharmaceutical-related provisions as such "but rather established the legal frameworks within which such provisions were subsequently introduced"). See Michael Handler and Bryan Mercurio, "Intellectual Property" in *Bilateral and Regional Trade Agreements: Commentary and Analysis* (Simon Lester and Bryan Mercurio, eds, 2009), 308, 341 (concluding that "the US has in its [Preferential Trade Agreements] served to entrench amongst a growing number of developed and developing countries . . . ever-higher . . . standards of IP protection and the removal of certain flexibilities made available under multilateral instruments").

19 See Bryan Mercurio in this collection.

20 Effective patent life should be distinguished from the *effective market life* of pharmaceutical patents – i.e., the time from marketing approval for a branded product until the approval for a generic. See, generally, C. Scott Hemphill and Bhaven N. Sampat, "Evergreening, Patent

issues regarding the fairness argument can be raised. First, the patent holder is not prevented from exercising and enforcing exclusive rights before the marketing authorization is granted. During the period of clinical trials and regulatory review, the patent holder can still prohibit third parties from the unauthorized use of a patented invention. The patent holder can also dispose of patent rights by assigning or transferring them to an entity willing to undertake downstream product development. Second, the international minimum standard of a 20-year term of patent protection[21] is rather an arbitrary figure that cannot be expected to provide an adequate and optimal length of protection to fully recover R&D expenses across all technological fields and for all inventions.[22] The ability to appropriate R&D investment depends not only on the patent length but, to a greater extent, on the breadth of protection as defined by patent claims, as well as fact-specific determinants of actual market power.[23] The protection term that is "fair enough" to recoup R&D investment in one drug might not be enough for another.[24] Moreover, in other industries, the effective patent life can be shorter due to easier and faster competition by substitution, or a faster rate when technologies become obsolete.[25]

Regulatory exclusivities granted independently from patents

Clinical data protection (or data exclusivity) is a *sui generis* type of protection that prevents regulatory approval of a generic drug by referencing clinical data submitted by the originator company as a proof of drug quality, efficacy and safety. Clinical data is protected irrespective of the patent status of a drug. *De jure*, the two regimes function independently; *de facto*, data exclusivity protects test data

Challenges, and Effective Market Life in Pharmaceuticals" (2012), 31 J. Health Econ., 327, 328; Henry Grabowski and Margaret Kyle, "Generic Competition and Market Exclusivity Periods in Pharmaceuticals" (2007), 28 Managerial and Decision Econ., 491, 497.

21 Art 33 of the TRIPS Agreement.

22 Katz (n. 12) at 40 (arguing that under the patent term restoration "even if in an unregulated world, in which the effective patent life lasted the entire patent term, the flow of innovative drugs would have been lower compared to the present world, this would not tell us anything about how far from optimal the current patent system is. It is still possible that current patent terms are suboptimally short.").

23 Richard Gilbert and Carl Shapiro, "Optimal Patent Length and Breadth" (1990), 21(1) RAND Journal of Economics, 106, 107.

24 Suzan Scotchmer, "The Political Economy of Intellectual Property Treaties" (2004), 20(2), J. L. Econ. & Org., 415, 422 (speculating that "for some subject matter, protection in any one of the large markets, the United States, Europe, or Japan, is enough to compensate an inventor, regardless of where the inventor is domiciled").

25 Luigi Orsenigo and Valerio Sterzi, "Comparative Study of the Use of Patents in Different Industries" (2010), KITeS Knowledge, Internationalization and Technology Studies Working Paper 33/2010, 1, 8 (arguing that "[p]atents tend to be more important when R&D is highly capital intensive and highly uncertain (pharmaceuticals); conversely, when technical change is very fast and the effective life of an innovation is short, patents may not adequately reward innovators").

for the originator product that would be, in most cases, also covered by patent rights. Although, in many cases, the data exclusivity term expires before patent protection, it can play a role if patent rights could not be granted or cease before patent expiration. Theoretically, test data protection might not exclude generic competition if domestic law allows to approve an identical drug based on the submission of own clinical trial dossier. In practice, however, this is unlikely to happen since prices charged, on average, for generic products would not be sufficient to recoup the costs of conducting full-scale clinical trials.

Distinct from data exclusivity, *marketing exclusivity* protection precludes a drug authority from reviewing and approving an application for a drug analogue, even if the drug applicant provides its own clinical data.[26] Examples of this type of exclusivity are drugs with paediatric indications and orphan drugs.[27]

In some cases, patent protection can run concurrently with test data and marketing exclusivity.[28] One drug can be simultaneously or subsequently protected by different regimes. For instance, under the EU law, the formula "8+2+1" means that the originator's clinical data cannot be used for the purpose of a generic approval for eight years after the originator's drug approval (the data exclusivity term). During the subsequent two years, an application for a generic product can be reviewed and approved on the basis of the referenced data but cannot be launched on the market until the ten-year term, from the date of the reference product approval, expires (marketing exclusivity).[29] Thereafter, if the drug sponsor files for a new indication, an additional, non-cumulative year of protection can be granted. Another example is drugs with paediatric indications. Under the EU regulatory framework, for instance, such drugs can benefit from protection under the Supplementary Protection Certificate, marketing exclusivities and test data protection.[30]

The diversity of exclusivity provisions suggests that there is a room for legislative creativity in designing sector-specific incentives. Some peculiar types of exclusivities,

26 Marketing exclusivity provisions are jurisdiction specific; for a comparative overview of the US and the EU regulations, see Valerie Junod, "Drug Marketing Exclusivity Under the United States and European Union Law" (2008), 59(4), Food & Drug L. J., 479.

27 For an overview of orphan drug exclusivities in the US, EU, Australia and Japan, see Marilyn J. Field and Thomas F. Boat, *Rare Diseases and Orphan Products: Accelerating Research and Development* (2011), 29ff.

28 See Enrique Seoane-Vazquez et al, "Incentives for Orphan Drug Research and Development in the United States Orphan" (2008), 3(33), Orphanet Journal of Rare Diseases, doi:10.1186/1750-1172-3-33 (finding that orphan drug marketing exclusivity increased the average maximum effective patent by 0.8 years).

29 Art 10 of Directive 2001/83/EC (as amended) and Art 14 of Regulation 726/2004 (as amended).

30 For an overview of incentives for paediatric drug R&D under the EU framework, see the European Medicines Agency, "Report to the European Commission on companies and products that have benefited from any of the rewards and incentives in the Paediatric Regulation and on the companies that have failed to comply with any of the obligations in this Regulation" (2013) EMA/24516/2014 Corr.3.

such as exclusivities for terrorism countermeasures, personalized medicine, and race-based medicine, have been recently discussed in the US.[31] Although these provisions differ in terms of their modes of protection, they share certain features in common. First, they demonstrate a convergence in policy objectives between the patent system and drug approval regulation: drug marketing approval regulation, primarily directed at the mitigation of the risks related to drug safety and quality, aims to incentivize innovation, which is the main purpose of the patent system. The policy rationale behind regulatory exclusivities is very much in line with the incentive theory of patent rights.[32] Second, like patent rights, regulatory exclusivities have the potential to confer market power by excluding or restricting generic competition. In the case of patents, exclusivity emanates from the negative right to exclude third parties from using the patented subject matter. In the case of regulatory exclusivities, "immunity" to competition arises due to the administrative decision of a health authority not to accept, review or approve an application for a competing product.[33] In this sense, the patent office and drug authority act as market "gatekeepers". While a patent protects the "upstream gate" (i.e., excludes others from using a technology), regulatory exclusivities can block entry to the downstream product market.[34]

The major conceptual difference between patents and regulatory exclusivities is that patents are awarded in return for the contribution to technological advancement, public disclosure of an invention and the diffusion of knowledge.[35] The entitlement to exclusive rights and the scope of protection are conditioned on the contribution to the technological state of the art. In contrast, protection under regulatory exclusivities is not correlated with drug innovative characteristics. While the subject matter of patent protection is the outcome of upstream research, regulatory exclusivities intend to protect investment into downstream product development.

31 Thomas (n. 1) at 370–375 (discussing proposals for exclusivities for terrorism countermeasures, personalized medicine, and race-based medicine in the US).
32 On the incentive theory of patents in general, see Roberto Mazzoleni and Richard R. Nelson, "Economic Theories about the Benefits and Costs of Patents" (1998), (4), Journal of Economic Issues, 1031, 1034–1038. For the analysis of innovation rationale for clinical data protection, see Jerome H. Reichman, "Rethinking the Role of Clinical Trial Data in International Intellectual Property Law: The Case for a Public Goods Approach" (2009), 13(1) Marq. Intell. Prop. L. Rev., 1, 36–42; with regard to marketing exclusivities, see Valerie Junod (n. 26) at 483–485.
33 See Thomas (n. 1) at 349 (referring to data exclusivity and marketing exclusivities as "FDA-administered proprietary rights"); Eisenberg (n. 1) at 360–361 (referring to exclusivities under the Hatch-Waxman Act as "FDA-administered proprietary rights" and "valuable exclusionary rights").
34 Thomas (n. 1) at 355 (noting that regulatory exclusivities "offer the extraordinary advantage of pairing perfectly with product markets").
35 On the invention dissemination theory of patents, see Mazzoleni and Nelson (n. 32) at 1038–1040.

Furthermore, provisions differ in terms of the contestability of protection. Patent rights can be invalidated, revoked or reduced in scope. In contrast, the administrative decision of a health authority not to accept or review an application for a follow-on product cannot be disputed by third parties. In this sense, the exclusivity of patent rights appears to be probabilistic rather than actual.[36] In addition, the scope of patent rights is subject to limitations and exceptions, such as the exclusion of certain subject matter from patentability,[37] compulsory licensing,[38] and exemption from infringement for specific types of uses such as "Bolar" exemption.[39] Envisaged under the TRIPS Agreement, these provisions can be seen as "a broader institutional framework providing certain checks and balances to the exclusive rights of IPRs holders".[40] In contrast, regulatory exclusivities do not have a comparable system of public interest safeguards.[41] Unless a regulation provides for the presumptions addressing protection overlaps, there might be uncertainty as to which regime prevails (whether, for instance, a compulsory licence for a patent issued under patent or competition law can override patent linkage, data or marketing exclusivity).

On balance, exclusivity under drug regulation compared to patents appears of a superior quality due to its "virtual incontestability, self-enforcing nature, and scope of coverage".[42] This advantage can be offset by a more limited term of protection (bearing in mind that *de jure* patent term can elapse earlier if challenged by third parties; and the *de facto* market exclusivity of a patented drug can cease due to a generic entry prior to patent expiration).[43]

The implementation of additional incentives under drug regulation does not suggest "deficiency" of the patent system. On the contrary, the sector has generally been viewed as almost a unique example of the success of the patent system.[44] In this regard, regulatory exclusivities appear as a complementary, sector-specific type of protection responding to the industry's growing need for R&D investment.[45]

36 See Stuart O. Schweitzer, *Pharmaceutical Economics and Policy* (2007) 15 (stating that it might be "easy to overstate" the benefits of patent protection for research-based industry in terms of protection from competition). See generally Mark A. Lemley and Carl Shapiro, "Probabilistic Patents" (2005), 19 J. Econ. Persp., 75.
37 Art 27(3)(a) of the TRIPS Agreement. See Chapter 2 in this collection.
38 Art 31 of the TRIPS Agreement. See Chapter 7 in this volume.
39 See Chapter 6 in this collection.
40 Carsten Fink, "Promoting Checks and Balances" in *Intellectual Property and Sustainable Development: Development Agendas in a Changing World* (Ricardo Meléndez-Ortiz and Pedro Roffe, eds, 2009), 363, at 363.
41 In exceptional circumstances, marketing exclusivities can be overridden, e.g., if a competing drug candidate demonstrates clinical superiority.
42 Thomas (n. 1) at 357.
43 Grabowski and Kyle (n. 20) at 497.
44 See n. 55.
45 See Rebecca S. Eisenberg, "The Shifting Functional Balance of Patents and Drug Regulation" (2001), 20(5) Health Affairs, 119, 132 ("Although patents often take most of the credit for the profits of drug development, while drug regulation takes much of the blame for its costs, upon closer inspection these two legal regimes operate in tandem to limit competition in

Scholars have reflected on the increasing role of drug regulation in promoting innovation as a "shift in functional balance" and the changing role of the drug authority,[46] and a mark of "a new era" of incentivizing innovation through statutory exclusivities.[47] Others expressed concerns over the sporadic transplantation of new protection standards via bilateral and multilateral free trade agreements without adequate safeguards in the domestic legal and regulatory systems.[48] On the one hand, the superior quality of regulatory exclusivity, demonstrating a stronger resistance to generic competition, can potentially yield greater market power and higher returns on investment, securing further investment into drug R&D. On the other, it entails healthcare costs. These effects raise questions as to the cumulative effect of incentives on social welfare, as well as the integrity and balance within the overall regulatory framework.

lucrative markets for drugs"); Eisenberg (n. 1) at 365 (arguing that "[t]o the extent that the exclusivity needs of the pharmaceutical industry are different from those of other industries, it might be less problematic to fine tune the drug regulation rules than it is to fine tune the patent system"); Thomas (n. 1) at 358, 370 (arguing that "regulatory exclusivities are best seen as a means of promoting activities that the patent system, through its essential doctrinal framework, is unable to encourage"; and "regulatory exclusivities are best viewed as a means for encouraging socially beneficial acts that the patent system cannot protect under its own terms").

46 See generally Eisenberg (n. 45).

47 Heled (n. 1) at 424 (raising the question whether "the statutory exclusivity regime in biologics mark[s] the dawn of a new era in the protection and incentivizing of innovation and the beginning of a gradual replacement of the old patent system with modern schemes of statutory exclusivities; or is it just a peculiar case of a legal regime shaped by an unusually powerful industry").

48 See Max Planck Institute for Intellectual Property and Competition Law, "Principles for Intellectual Property Provisions in Bilateral and Regional Agreements" (2014), para 7 (stating that "IP provisions in bilateral and regional agreements have become increasingly detailed and prescriptive. They often transplant specific protection and enforcement standards from the domestic IP system of the IP-demanding country, while disregarding the exceptions, limitations and other checks and balances from that same system."); Pedro Roffe, Christoph Spennemann and Johanna von Braun, "Intellectual Property Rights in Free Trade Agreements: Moving Beyond TRIPS Minimum Standards" in *Research Handbook on the Protection of Intellectual Property under WTO Rules* (Carlos M. Correa, ed, 2010) 266, 312 (arguing that "there is an optimal level of IP protection, beyond which ever-increasing exclusive rights will prove counterproductive to society at large. . . . FTAs should be taken as an opportunity to modernize the domestic IP architecture by investing strongly in institutions and human resources in order to build systems of protection and enforcement around appropriate checks and balances that serve domestic policy objectives."); Pedro Roffe, "Intellectual Property Chapters in Free Trade Agreements: Their Significance and Systemic Implications" in *EU Bilateral Trade Agreements and Intellectual Property: For Better or Worse?* (Josef Drexl et al, eds, 2013) 17, 26 (noting with regard to IP enforcement provisions in FTAs that "the FTAs establish strict obligations that do transplant legal regimes, appropriate to their stage of development, but without at the same time providing for the checks and balances").

Considering regulatory exclusivities from the national policy perspective

Before addressing the question of how exclusivity-based incentives can be "organically" implemented under drug marketing approval regulation, policy-makers need some confidence in the working of this type of incentive as an innovation promoter.

Patent model of incentivizing innovation

Since drug exclusivities under marketing approval regulation tend to follow the model of the patent system, it is appropriate to recap its underlying economic logic. In theory, the patent system intends to stimulate the continuing innovation process by allowing innovators to appropriate R&D investments under temporarily restrained competition by imitation.[49] Economists, however, questioned whether the means are most suitable for the goals. In 1958, Fritz Machlup reporting to the US Congress famously concluded:

> If we did not have a patent system, it would be irresponsible, on the basis of our present knowledge of its economic consequences, to recommend instituting one. But since we have had a patent system for a long time, it would be irresponsible, on the basis of our present knowledge, to recommend abolishing it.[50]

Over half a century later, Richard A. Posner admits that:

> Unfortunately, economists do not know whether the existing system of intellectual property rights is, or for that matter whether any other system of intellectual property rights would be, a source of *net* social utility, given the costs of the system and the existence of alternative sources of incentives to create such property.[51]

Even more confusing is the acknowledgement that:

> . . . a belief that without legal protection the incentives to create [intellectual] property would be inadequate . . . cannot be defended on the basis of current knowledge.[52]

49 On the incentive theory of patent rights, see n. 32.

50 US Senate, *An Economic Review of the Patent System. Study of the Subcommittee on Patents, Trademarks, and Copyrights of the Committee on the Judiciary* (85th Congress, 2nd session, 1958), 80.

51 Richard A. Posner, "Intellectual Property: The Law and Economics Approach" (2005), 19(2) *Journal of Economic Perspectives*, 57, 59 (emphasis added).

52 William M. Landes and Richard A. Posner, *Economic Structure of Intellectual Property Law* (2003), 9.

As summarized by Daniel Cahoy, "the degree to which current patent systems promote innovative behavior remains surprisingly unclear".[53] Hardly providing a guidance for lawmakers,[54] these insights suggest a rather cautious approach to reinforcing the patent model through other regulatory instruments.

Yet, in the case of pharmaceuticals, patents have been viewed to play a prominent role in supporting innovation. Industry reliance on exclusive patent rights has been mainly attributed to the ease of imitating originator drugs, on the one hand, and significant R&D costs that without legal protection cannot be appropriated, on the other hand.[55] But is the objective of promoting investment in drug R&D compatible with the regulatory mandate of a drug authority?[56]

Drug authority as innovation promoter

While a patent application is assessed based on the contribution of a claimed invention to innovation, a candidate drug can be approved for marketing irrespective of its innovative characteristics. Insofar as innovative medicines provide an essential input for the healthcare system, encouraging innovation can be viewed as a complementary goal of drug regulation, in addition to consumer

53 Daniel R. Cahoy, "An Incrementalist Approach to Patent Reform Policy" (2006), Legislation and Public Policy, 101, 104.

54 See George L. Priest, "What Economists Can Tell Lawyers about Intellectual Property: Comment on Cheung" (1986), 8 Res. L. & Econ., 19, 21 (concluding that "economists have virtually nothing to say to lawyers"); Fritz Machlup, *The Production and Distribution of Knowledge in the United States* (1962), 176 (stating that "[t]he absence of any empirical evidence for either the claim or its denial that the patent system is an effective promoter of inventive research . . . is most frustrating"); World Intellectual Property Organization, "Report on the International Patent System, Standing Committee on the Law of Patents" (2008), SCP/12/3 Rev.2, 2 (concluding that "[i]nconclusive evidence on the role of the patent system in encouraging R&D and technology transfer makes it difficult to draw any clear-cut conclusions about the effectiveness of the patent system for economic development").

55 See, e.g., James Bessen and Michael J. Meurer, "Lessons for Patent Policy from Empirical Research on Patent Litigation" (2005), Boston Univ. School of Law Working Paper No. 05–22, 10, 27 (noting that "patent premium is greatest in the pharmaceutical industry", and while "the patent system has widely varying effects across different industries . . . [i]t provides critical incentives for research and development in a few industries including the pharmaceutical industry"); Richard C. Levin et al, "Appropriating the Returns from Industrial Research and Development" (1987), Brookings Papers on Economic Activity, 783, 796 (arguing that only in the drug industry "were product patents regarded by a majority of respondents as strictly more effective than other means of appropriation"); Edwin Mansfield, "Patents and Innovation: An Empirical Study" (1986), 32 Mgmt. Sci., 173, 175; Orsenigo and Sterzi (n. 25) at 7 (arguing that "the role of patents is likely to be higher . . . where imitation is easier, i.e. when the ratio between the costs of imitation to the costs of innovation is lower – e.g., chemicals, pharmaceuticals, machinery").

56 See Eisenberg (n. 1) at 372 (posing a similar question whether "it matter[s] whether one views FDA regulation as a means of protecting patients from unsafe or ineffective products or as a means of promoting investment in clinical trials of drugs"). The competence of a drug authority to enforce patents was, in particular, questioned with regard to patent linkage.

protection. What may raise concerns is not innovation objectives as such, but the means adopted for their achievement. One would assume that the affordability of drugs should be the priority of a drug authority; therefore, the implementation of provisions under drug regulation that eliminate the availability of generics contradicts its role as the healthcare provider. As a counterargument, one could speculate that, by maximizing exclusivities, the regulator secures a greater variety of innovative drugs in the future. In the context of IP rights, this dilemma is known as a trade-off between static and dynamic efficiency – that is, between more competitive prices in the short term, and potential benefits from increased innovative activity in the long term.[57] From the ethical perspective, the view that a drug authority should not enforce exclusionary rules that can impede the affordability to drugs appeals to the intuitive perception of "fairness". From the welfare perspective, exclusivities shall be justified if they prevent a situation, when "fairness can make everyone worse off"[58] in terms of innovative therapies.

Welfare considerations regarding exclusivity-based incentives

In general terms, welfare refers to "an overall condition [of] happiness and contentment . . . including one's standard of living in financial or material ways".[59] While it might be difficult to capture the effects on "happiness and contentment" in uniform values, methodologies have been developed in public policy planning that evaluate welfare implications of regulatory measures in terms of costs and benefits. Some methodologies account for the specifics of the pharmaceutical sector.[60] A regulatory measure is assessed in light of the policy objectives and in terms of the *effectiveness* and *efficiency* in reaching them. The former implies that benefits are greater than costs expressed in discounted terms;[61] the latter means that the benefit-cost ratio of a regulatory measure is higher compared to that of an alternative(s).[62] In order to perform a full-scale welfare analysis of drug exclusivities, one would need to identify, express in comparable values, and evaluate a full set of all possible costs and benefits entailed by regulatory

57 See William S. Comanor, "The Political Economy of the Pharmaceutical Industry" (1986), 24(3) Journal of Economic Literature, 1178, 1213. See, generally, David W. Barnes, "The Incentives/Access Tradeoff" (2010), 9(3) NW J. Tech. & Intel. Prop., 96.

58 Louis Kaplow and Steven Shavell, *Fairness versus Welfare* (2006), xviii.

59 Library Economics Liberty, "Wellbeing and Welfare", http://www.econlib.org/library/Topics/College/wellbeingandwelfare.html, last accessed 17 July 2016.

60 See, e.g., European Commission, *Competitiveness of the EU Market and Industry for Pharmaceuticals, Welfare Implications of Regulation* (2009).

61 The Organisation for Economic Co-operation and Development, *Policy Coherence: Vital for Global Development. Policy Brief* (2003), 97.

62 Ibid (emphasizing the importance of the benefit-cost ratio as it allows alternatives to be ranked according to their efficiency). See also Carl V. Patton and David S. Sawicki, *Basic Methods of Policy Analysis and Planning* (1986), 247 (noting that an "alternative [measure] with the highest benefit-cost ratio does not necessarily have the highest net present value").

intervention.[63] As much as such analysis is desirable, it is also unrealistic. As observed by Just et al:

> . . . [a]lthough a social welfare function is a convenient and powerful concept in theory, its practical usefulness has been illusory. Many attempts have been made to specify a social welfare function sufficiently to facilitate empirical usefulness but none have been widely accepted.[64]

Let us consider an example of how welfare considerations can be integrated into the analysis of a particular type of regulatory incentive – clinical trial data exclusivity. A study by Goldman et al[65] estimates the short- and long-term effects of a hypothetical increase of the term of protection for small-molecule drugs up to 12 years (from five years for new clinical data submission and three years of supplemental applications for new uses, as currently provided under the US law). The authors measure the effects of the extended exclusivity term on the revenues of pharmaceutical companies, new drug approvals and consumers' longevity. As acknowledged by the authors, the extension of data exclusivity protection would require a trade-off between current and future generations.[66] In summary, the study finds that the short-term effect of the term extension would be, on average, a 5 per cent increase in revenues, while the long-term effect would be 228 additional drug approvals in the US between 2020 and 2060. As a result, life expectancy would increase by 1.7 months, estimated to be worth $10,400 in net benefits.[67]

Taken as a given, how can the study results be interpreted? Do greater numbers unequivocally indicate a positive impact on innovation and welfare? Can the study's findings support the decisions of policy-makers regarding similar regulatory measures in other jurisdictions? The authors do not evaluate the social costs corresponding to the benefit of 228 additional drug approvals and a 1.7-month increase in life expectancy. A 5 per cent increase in revenues under restrained competition during the extended protection term represents the transfer from consumer to producer.[68] The value of such transfer is subject to demand elasticity that can depend on particular market factors as well as the country's public drug procurement and insurance system. The percentage of the increase in revenue does not tell us about the magnitude of deadweight loss. Theoretically, it is possible that the total dollar value of the increased longevity due to the introduction

63 See European Commission (n. 60) at 14–16.

64 Richard E. Just, Darrell L. Hueth and Andrew Schmitz, *The Welfare Economics of Public Policy: A Practical Approach to Project and Policy Evaluation* (2004), 41.

65 Dana P. Goldman et al, "The Benefits from Giving Makers of Conventional 'Small Molecule' Drugs Longer Exclusivity over Clinical Trial Data" (2011), 30 Health Affairs, 84.

66 Ibid, at 85.

67 Ibid, at 88.

68 Richard A. Posner, "The Social Costs of Monopoly and Regulation" (1975), 83(4) Journal of Political Economy, 807, at 807.

of a new drug ($10,400 multiplied by the hypothetical number of beneficiaries) is, in discounted terms, less than the dollar value of the corresponding consumer deadweight loss. If so, the term extension cannot be considered an *effective* measure to achieve such results in innovation.

Besides, the study does not assess alternative incentives. In theory, it is possible that other measures can work more efficiently, either by achieving the same level of innovation with lower costs, or a greater level of innovation via the same costs. It might also be so that the proposed term extension is not more efficient even if compared to the *current* term. Unless the costs corresponding to the claimed benefits are known, one cannot draw a clear conclusion regarding efficiency and effectiveness of extension of the protection term.

Additionally, it is important to define the assumptions, under which the forecast benefits can materialize. First, the extension of the term of clinical data exclusivity, or other exclusivity-based incentives, cannot be presumed to have an equal effect in different settings. Actual revenues would be subject to particular factors that determine competition in the market for the drug protected under data exclusivity, as well as the specificities of the national healthcare system (especially public drug procurement, insurance and reimbursement).[69] Second, the response of R&D productivity to investment cannot be readily predicted. Even if all profits earned under exclusivity protection are committed to further R&D, numerous factors can impact upon the rate, scope and value of R&D outcomes.[70]

Furthermore, the social value of R&D results would depend not only upon the investment but also the type and direction of R&D activity. Pharmaceutical patents have been criticized for motivating companies to allocate R&D resources to products that present minor improvements of the existing drugs rather than promoting fundamental research that might be more socially valuable, but less commercially attractive.[71]

69 As observed by Kaplow with regard to extending patent protection, "lengthening the patent life presumably increases the reward to the patentee by enhancing the opportunity for monopolistic exploitation. The amount that the reward will increase depends upon a number of factors, including the market value of the invention, the structure of the market involving the patented process or product, and the attributes of the patentee (such as marketing and production capacities) that determine its range of options within that market." Louis Kaplow, "The Patent-Antitrust Intersection: A Reappraisal" (1984), 97(8) Harv. L. Rev., 1813, 1823.

70 Ibid, at 1824 (noting that "[d]etermining the extent and types of increased [innovative] activity is a complex process whose outcome will vary substantially from case to case. Relevant factors include the potential return from further research and development, the risk involved in the undertaking, the nature of rivalry among firms"). See generally Fabio Pammolli, Laura Magazzini and Massimo Riccaboni, "The Productivity Crisis in Pharmaceutical R&D" (2011), 10 Nature Reviews Drug Discovery, 428.

71 Schweitzer (n. 36) at 15. See also Seiter (n. 7) at 14 (noting that while R&D costs are rising, "research productivity – that is, the relationship between investment in research and development (R&D) and output of successful new products – has been declining steadily in recent decades"); Ron A. Bouchard et al, "The *Pas De Deux* of Pharmaceutical Regulation and Innovation: Who is Leading Whom?" (2009), 24(4) Berkeley Tech. L. J., 1461, 1507

All this suggests that the study results cannot be taken at face value. Let us assume, nevertheless, that the benefit-cost ratio in discounted terms does show that the exclusivity term extension is an effective and efficient innovation incentive. Wouldn't then policy-makers wish to increase the protection term infinitely, in order to reach even greater benefits in innovation? The policy objective should not perhaps be viewed as to maximize legal protection for the sake of appropriability of returns on innovation, but to achieve innovation goals in an optimal way.

How can the optimal combination of incentives be defined?

Optimality can be distinguished at the level of policy objectives (i.e., as the "optimal" amount of innovation to cope with disease burden of a population) and at the level of policy implementation (i.e., as the integration of policy instruments to achieve the desired goals). Drug exclusivities, as they intended to incentivize drug R&D, concern the latter. By replicating the exclusionary model of patent protection, they pose the question of the optimal correlation of costs and benefits – the dilemma that has been in focus of economic analysis of patents well before the TRIPS Agreement set international legal standards, as well as thereafter.[72]

Ideally, the innovation incentive system "should strike a balance so that the economic rights of inventors are *sufficient* to encourage invention, innovation and the dissemination of useful technical information, but *not so excessive* as to unduly hinder competition, stifle follow-on invention, or harm the public".[73] It should furnish "the correct structure of rights [that] provides the optimal amount of

(arguing that "the multinational pharmaceutical industry is leaning away from breakthrough drug development towards less innovative products referred to variously as follow-on, incremental, supplemental, line extension, me too, and bioequivalent drugs"); David Dranove, Craig Garthwaite and Manuel Hermosilla, "Pharmaceutical Profits and the Social Value of Innovation" (2014), NBER Working Paper No. 20212, at 4 ("New products that are neither meaningful scientific advancements nor an expansion of treatment applications primarily represent business stealing with little welfare improvement").

72 See, e.g., William D. Nordhaus, *Invention, Growth and Welfare* (1969); Fredriek M. Scherer, "Nordhaus'" Theory of Optimal Patent Life: A Geometrical Reinterpretation" (1972), 62 Am. Econ. Rev., 422; Gilbert and Shapiro (n. 23); Kaplow (n. 69); Paul Klemperer, "How Broad Should the Scope of Patent Protection Be?" (1990), 21 RAND J. of Econ., 113; Nancy T. Gallini, "Patent Policy and Costly Imitation" (1992), 23 RAND J. Econ., 52; Vincenzo Denicolò, "Patent Races and Optimal Patent Breadth and Length" (1996), 44 Journal of Industrial Economics, 249; Ted O'Donoghue et al, "Patent Breadth, Patent Life, and the Pace of Technological Progress" (1998), 7 J. Econ. & Mgmt. Strategy, 1; Ian Ayers and Paul Klemperer, "Limiting Patentees'" Market Power Without Reducing Innovation Incentives: The Perverse Benefits of Uncertainty and Non-Injunctive Remedies" (1999), 97 Mich. L. Rev., 985; Landes and Posner (n. 52); John F. Duffy, "A Minimum Optimal Patent Term" (2005), UC Berkeley Recent Work; Daniel J. Gifford, "How Do the Social Benefits and Costs of the Patent System Stack up in Pharmaceuticals?" (2004), 12 J. Intell. Prop., 75.

73 Graham Dutfield, Lois Muraguri and Florian Leverve, "Exploring the Flexibilities of TRIPS to Promote Biotechnology in Developing Countries" in *Research Handbook On the Protection of Intellectual Property Under WTO Rules* (Carlos M. Correa, ed., 2010), 540, 541 (emphasis added).

incentives and results in the optimal output [and] optimal access".[74] Economic literature on *optimal* patent life is extensive and shows little consensus regarding the optimal measure of protection.[75] While many would agree that profits under protection should, at the minimum, cover expenditures incurred in innovative activities, views diverge with regard to the profit margin that would encourage further innovation (e.g., whether it should be "sufficient to cover development costs",[76] "include reasonable return on fixed-cost investment",[77] "just enough" to perform innovative activity,[78] or above "reasonable"[79]). There is also a lack of consensus as to what should count as social costs of patents.[80]

In the context of pharmaceutical patents, the balance is sought between the loss in static efficiency (i.e., temporary restraint on price competition) and gains in dynamic efficiency (i.e., the development of innovative medicines). As stated by Comanor:

> What is at issue here is the *appropriate* level of returns from pharmaceutical innovation. . . . The essential question is the extent to which competitive forces should be promoted or retarded so that the most desirable rate and pattern of innovation are induced. Some restrictions on competition may well promote innovation while others may not.[81]

The problem with the qualitative characteristics such as "just enough", "necessary", "sufficient", "appropriate", or "not excessive" is that, while they reflect certain

74 Barnes (n. 57) at 101.
75 Stanley M. Besen and Leo J. Raskind, "An Introduction to the Law and Economics of Intellectual Property" (1991), 5(1) Journal of Economic Perspectives, 3, 8.
76 Steven Shavell, *Foundations of Economic Analysis of Law* (2004), 145–146.
77 Mark A. Lemley, "Property, Intellectual Property, and Free Riding" (2005), 83 Tex. L. Rev., 1031, 1032.
78 S. Y. Wu, Michael A. Riddiough and Ronald Hansen, "Pharmaceutical Innovation, Product Imitation, and Public Policy" in *Drugs and Health: Economic Issues and Policy Objectives* (Robert B. Helms, ed., 1981), 272, 274 (arguing that protection should "provide just enough incentive for the innovator to perform his service and disseminate the fruits of innovation to the public at a maximum speed").
79 See F. M. Scherer, "Pricing, Profits, and Technological Progress in the Pharmaceutical Industry" (1993), 7(3) The Journal of Economic Perspectives, 97 (arguing that "[i]f profits were held to 'reasonable' levels on blockbuster drugs, aggregate profits would almost surely be insufficient to sustain a high rate of technological progress").
80 Social benefits of IP rights are usually defined in terms of induced inventive activity, and social costs in terms of deadweight loss resulting from prices above the competitive level. See Posner (n. 68) at 807. Gordon Tullock argued that social costs of monopoly should also include opportunity costs of the resources spent to obtain monopoly profits. See Gordon Tullock, "The Welfare Costs of Tariffs, Monopolies, and Theft" (1967), 5 Western Econ. J., 224. *Cf.* Gifford (n. 72). at 122–123 (arguing that "[t]o the extent that the exclusivity conferred on a patentee is necessary to generate an invention, the resulting deadweight loss is *not a social loss* at all", and only "to the extent that the exclusivity is unnecessary . . . it can become a social cost") (emphasis added).
81 Comanor (n. 57) at 1180 (emphasis added).

perceptions of the normative limitation of protection, it is hard to translate them into the legal rules that would ensure adequate return on innovative activity across all sectors, categories of innovative products and products within the same category. What these attributes suggest is that protection cannot be extended indefinitely and that rules need to balance competing interests. As aspired by the TRIPS Agreement:

> . . . protection and enforcement of intellectual property rights should *contribute* to the promotion of technological innovation and to the transfer and dissemination of technology, to the mutual advantage of producers and users of technological knowledge and in a manner conducive to social and economic welfare, and to a balance of rights and obligations.[82]

The ordinary meaning[83] of "to contribute" suggests that IP protection should not be viewed as bearing the *sole* responsibility for promoting innovative activity or providing the *full ex-post* compensation for the sunk R&D costs. On the one hand, the view of the contributory role of IP protection might alleviate the efforts to determine the elusive notion of "the optimal measure" of IP protection. On the other hand, it does not eliminate the problem of the policy decision-making regarding new drug exclusivities. As discussed above,[84] regulatory exclusivities can enhance the legal protection of innovative drugs against competition. According to the "net benefit principle" formulated by Barnes, "[a]n increase in exclusive rights to intellectual property is justified only when the value of increased creative activity resulting from increased incentives is greater than the value of the benefits lost from reduced access".[85] However, if we assume that, in a given context, costs and benefits *are* in optimal correlation, one cannot expect that a marginal increase in legal protection would yield a proportionate increase in innovation.[86] The relationship between legal protection and innovation is complex and subject to multiple factors.[87] As observed by Louis Kaplow, the "knowledge of the functional relationships between the separate links in the chain connecting patent life to social benefits remains quite limited".[88] If innovation incentives are *not* optimally correlated under the existing regime, the maximization of protection by provisions

82 Art 7 of the TRIPS Agreement (emphasis added).
83 Art 31 of the Vienna Convention on the Law of Treaties of 23 May 1969.
84 See earlier in chapter.
85 Barnes (n. 57) at 122.
86 See the United Nations Conference on Trade and Development, "Using Intellectual Property Rights to Stimulate Pharmaceutical Production in Developing Countries: Reference Guide" (2011), UNCTAD/DIAE/PCB/2009/19, 8–9 (concluding that "based on a number of recent studies, the conclusion has emerged that stronger patent protection does not necessarily lead to more innovation").
87 Richard Gilbert, "Looking for Mr. Schumpeter: Where Are We in the Competition-Innovation Debate?" in *Innovation Policy and the Economy* (Adam B. Jaffe, Josh Lerner and Scott Stern, eds, 2005), 159, 171ff.
88 Kaplow (n. 69) at 1824.

that underlie the same incentive logic can further aggravate the system misbalance. If there is no "ready-made" formula to identify and optimize *all* possible welfare effects of patents, how can additional, patent-like incentives be rationalized?

The rational approach to policy-making: Constructivist and ecological rationality

Quite naturally, one would expect that regulation in the area of pharmaceutical innovation should be based on rational decision-making. However, the unpredictable nature of drug R&D poses a considerable challenge for planning innovation policy. The rationality of policy-makers can be bounded by imperfect theoretical and empirical knowledge regarding determinants of R&D productivity. The preceding section suggests that the optimization of incentives necessitates balancing short- and long-term costs and benefits. The patent system has been argued to promote competition by substitution at the expense of restrained competition by imitation.[89] In the context of drug innovation, this means that the policy-maker needs to identify the measure of protection against generic competition that would yield maximum results in pharmaceutical innovation, beyond which incentives would be socially wasteful. To find such a golden mean can be viewed as an "impossible undertaking".[90] Should then any attempt to rationalize decisions regarding IP-type incentives be abandoned from the outset?

Socio-economic studies distinguish two types of rationality in decision-making: *constructivist* and *ecological*. Let us consider how these notions can assist policy decision-making regarding drug exclusivities. The *constructivist* type of rationality operates under an assumption that social order arises out of the "conscious deductive processes of human reason".[91] It "relies on the confidence in the human ability to understand the world around . . . and the complex causal structures of various phenomena".[92] In contrast, *ecological* – also known as evolutionary, "bottom up", or "home-grown" rationality – reflects an assumption that the identification of "maximizing strategies for a particular problem may not be

89 See Josef Drexl, "The Relationship between the Legal Exclusivity and Economic Market Power: Links and Limits" in *Intellectual Property, Market Power and the Public Interest* (Inge Govaere and Hanns Ullrich, eds, 2008), 13, 16.

90 US Senate, *Administered Prices in the Drug Industry. Hearings before the Subcommittee on Anti-Trust and Monopoly* (86th Congress, 2nd Session, Washington, DC, 1960), 114 (referring to an attempt "to determine the proportion of the higher price under patents that would be offset by new discoveries made possible by the awarding of patents" as an "impossible undertaking"). See also Katie Sykes, "Towards a Public Justification of Copyright" (2003), 61 U. Toronto Fac. L. Rev., 1, 5 ("No one can agree on, much less explain, what the correct balance should be between incentives to produce and public access to what is produced").

91 Vernon L. Smith, "Constructivist and Ecological Rationality in Economics" (2003), 93(3) American Economic Review, 465, 467.

92 K. Dholakia-Lehenbauer and E. W. Elliott, "Decisionmaking, Risk, and Uncertainty: An Analysis of Climate Change" (2012), 32(3), Cato Journal, 539, 545.

possible"; therefore decision-makers act according to "the rules of thumb or heuristics",[93] trying to match the strategy with the environment.[94] The main concern of ecological rationality is not about the optimization of the solution, but adaptation to the environment.[95] Known also as "domain-specific heuristics",[96] ecological rationality relies on the contextual, empirical understanding of the problem emerging from the collection and evaluation of the available evidence. Put simply, decisions should make sense in the given circumstances. In the context of IP law-making, this principle is in line with the idea of "tailoring" national IP legislation according to the socio-economic development and policy objectives of a particular country.[97] The guiding principle is that policy-makers should build the strategy, adopt decisions and develop the regulatory framework based upon the "cost-benefit balancing approach tailored to *local* circumstances".[98]

Efforts to base policy decisions on economic modelling are in line with the constructivist type of rationality. Ideally, to optimize the social costs and benefits of drug incentives, policy-makers would need to "have clearly defined objectives, carefully identified options for achieving them, accurate knowledge about how each option contributes to the objectives, and a full specification of the Social Welfare Function that identifies the optimal position on the tradeoff curve, and . . . they [would] then choose among the options so as to best achieve the objectives".[99] In view of the multiple dynamic effects on welfare that can be triggered by innovation incentives, the derivation of the "full specification of the social welfare function" appears unfeasible. Yet, welfare considerations can play an

93 Ibid, at 543 (stating that the approach based on ecological rationality "implies that determining global optima or maximizing strategies for a particular problem may not be possible").

94 Gerd Gigerenzer, "The Adaptive Toolbox" in *Bounded Rationality: The Adaptive Toolbox* (Reinhard Selden and Gerd Gigerenzer, eds, 2002), 37, 46.

95 Ibid, at 38.

96 Ibid.

97 On tailoring patent protection in the biopharmaceutical sector, see, e.g., Dan Burk and Mark A. Lemley, "Policy Levers in Patent Law" (2003), 89(7) Va. L. Rev., 1575, 1675–1686; Geertrui van Overwalle, "Policy Levers Tailoring Patent Law to Biotechnology: Comparing US and European Approaches" (2011), 1 UC Irvine Law Rev., 435–517; Benjamin N. Roin, "The Case for Tailoring Patent Awards Based on the Time-to-Market of Inventions" (2014), 61 UCLA L. Rev., 672; Dutfield et al (n. 73). For the clarification of the scope of national discretion under the TRIPS Agreement, see Max Planck Institute for Intellectual Property and Competition Law, "Declaration on Patent Protection: Regulatory Sovereignty under TRIPS" (2014).

98 Howard Latin, "Ideal versus Real Regulatory Efficiency: Implementation of Uniform Standards and 'Fine-Tuning' Regulatory Reforms" (1985) 37(5) Stan. L. Rev., 1267, 1276 (emphasis added). See the WHO et al (n. 7) at 20 (emphasizing the importance of empirical data in pharmaceutical policymaking and citing then WTO Director-General Pascal Lamy stating that those who "care deeply about health innovation and access to medicines would benefit . . . from the careful putting together of all the pieces of the empirical puzzle").

99 Robert Haveman, "The Big Tradeoff: Fundamental Law or Red Herring?" in *Handbook of Public Policy Evaluation* (2001), 7, 9.

important role, in particular, guiding the collection of the empirical data that can inform policy analysis of exclusivities.

On the costs side, policy-makers need to assess the impact of the additional protection for originator drugs on the generic entry and expenditures in the subsidized, out-of-pocket and private insurance segments of the drug market. Furthermore, from the national perspective, it appears important to consider whether producer surplus would support the innovative activity within the national pharmaceutical sector. In this regard, the extension of the data exclusivity term in Hong Kong SAR, discussed by Aidan Hollis and Paul Grootendorst earlier in this collection, can hardly be seen as a rational decision given the minuscule and stagnant R&D in the sector and heavy reliance on the import of branded drugs.[100]

Recent studies report that some countries, conventionally viewed as mainly importers of innovative medicines, are more actively pursuing innovation strategy in the pharmaceutical sector.[101] Oftentimes, such countries appear to have prioritized the biopharmaceutical sector as an area of deliberate policymaking and strategic development. An in-depth, multi-factor analysis of these examples can contribute to a more detailed understanding of the incentivizing role of the patent system behind these advancements.

Concluding remarks

This chapter intended to draw recommendations for decision-making regarding innovation incentives under drug regulation. Policy implications of the foregoing discussion can be summarized as follows:

100 B. C. Mercurio and D. Kim, "Patently Lacking: An Analysis and Call for Systemic Review of Pharmaceutical Law and Policy – A Case Study of Hong Kong" (2014), 9(1) Asian Journal of WTO and International Health Law and Policy, 63, 80–88. As argued by Pamela Samuelson, "[n]ations have incentives to adopt higher-protection rules when an already innovative domestic sector demonstrates a need for stronger rules to enable firms to recoup R&D investments, or when nations believe that doing so will spur investments and economic development in that field of innovation. Nations have incentives to adopt lower protection rules if they are predominantly users or net importers of products of that kind, if they aspire to incentivize investments in follow-on innovation, or if they believe that a lower-protection rule will induce more investments than a higher-protection." See Pamela Samuelson, "Intellectual Property Arbitrage: How Foreign Rules Can Affect Domestic Protections" (2004), 71(1) U. Chi. L Rev., 223, 224.

101 See, e.g., Rahim Rezaie et al, "Emergence of biopharmaceutical innovators in China, India, Brazil, and South Africa as global competitors and collaborators" (2012), Health Res. Policy Syst., 10; Chee-Ruey Hsieh and H. Löfgren, "Biopharmaceutical innovation and industrial developments in South Korea, Singapore and Taiwan" (2009), 33(2) Aust. Health Rev., 245; United Nations Educational, Scientific and Cultural Organization, "UNESCO Science Report: Towards 2030" (2015) (accounting on policy initiatives and the development trends in the biopharmaceutical sector in countries of Latin America, Africa, former CIS, South Asia).

- Innovation incentives under drug regulation tend to replicate or reinforce patent protection; decision-making regarding their implementation requires analysis of welfare implications.
- Policy objectives matter: the rationalization and assessment of drug incentives depend on how goals and priorities are defined and allocated within the pharmaceutical sector.
- There is no "ready-made" formula for how to optimize multiple welfare effects of different incentive instruments applicable to drugs. The question of whether to adopt regulatory exclusivities in addition to patent protection cannot be answered in abstract terms and necessitates a contextual, multi-factor assessment.
- Under uncertainty and imperfect knowledge about the functional relationship between legal protection and innovation, cost-benefit analysis should rely on empirical data and account for the dynamics of the domestic pharmaceutical industry and market, as well as the specifics of the national healthcare system.
- When considering the implementation of patent-like incentives under drug regulation, policy-makers need to reflect on how the patent system has been operating in the pharmaceutical sector, and its likely contribution to the benefits conventionally associated with patents such as technology transfer, FDI and the growth of national innovation capacity. Absent such evidence, alternative incentive models for drug innovation should be considered, especially those that target actual needs for medical treatment of the population and relate the reward with the therapeutic value of drugs.[102]

102 E.g., the Health Impact Fund project. See Aidan Hollis and Thomas Pogge, *The Health Impact Fund: Making New Medicines Accessible to All* (2008).

11 The Trans-Pacific Partnership Agreement and Its Implications for Access to Medicines

Jakkrit Kuanpoth

Introduction

Negotiated by 12 Pacific Rim countries – namely Australia, Brunei, Canada, Chile, Japan, Malaysia, Mexico, New Zealand, Peru, Singapore, the United States and Vietnam – parties to the Trans-Pacific Partnership Agreement (TPP) successfully reached agreement on all the outstanding issues in September 2015. As is the norm for comprehensive trade agreements, the TPP includes so-called "TRIPS-plus" provisions that increase standards of intellectual property (IP) protection to a level higher than required in the World Trade Organization (WTO) Agreement on Trade-Related Aspects of Intellectual Property Rights (TRIPS). As with all bilateral and regional international agreements on IP, the standards proposed in the TPP will bind and oblige participating countries to provide extensive IP protection.

This chapter argues that the TRIPS-plus provisions in the TPP will have a significant impact upon access to essential medicines by limiting countries' substantive ability to deal with public health problems and by restricting the measures the countries can take to pursue affordable drugs (e.g., restricting the right of governments to allow the production, marketing and import of generic medicines).

This chapter proceeds as follows. First, it commences with an overview of the TPP. The chapter will then examine the main provisions of the agreement relating to the legal protection of pharmaceutical inventions. It concludes by providing some analytical assessment as to whether or not the Trans-Pacific Partnership Agreement actually hinders access to medicines.

General background of the TPP

During the late 1980s, a number of countries, including Taiwan, South Korea, India, Thailand and Indonesia, were put under tremendous pressure by developed countries to improve their laws for the protection of IP. The United States (US), the world's largest trading nation, in particular, exerted bilateral pressure, by withdrawing or threatening to withdraw trade privileges they gave to developing countries under the Generalized System of Preferences (GSP). The developed countries also threatened to impose trade sanctions on the countries that failed to provide adequate and effective IP protection.[1] As a result of this pressure, the developing nations revised their IP laws to increase the protection level even before the adoption of the WTO TRIPS Agreement in 1994. In addition to the aggressive unilateralism and bilateralism, the industrialized countries' IP norm-setting activities continue to also take place on the plurilateral level. For example, when a country's government desires to apply for membership of the WTO, it must enter into specific bilateral negotiations with every interested WTO Member, which generally leads to the situation where the applicant is asked to make a large number of commitments not only to meet existing WTO obligations but also which go beyond existing WTO commitments.[2] Accession to the WTO therefore involves a complex technical process as well as bilateral negotiations with existing members.[3]

Yet, another complicating factor is that from the years from 2000 onwards there has been a proliferation of a large number of free trade agreements (FTAs). In recent times, major industrialized countries, particularly the US and the European Union (EU), have launched aggressive campaigns to negotiate bilateral and regional FTAs with a wide range of developed and developing countries.[4] Apart from these two, larger economies like China, Japan and Korea are also engaged in negotiating large numbers of FTAs with their trading partners. Several Latin counties, including Mexico and Chile, as well as regional groupings such as the Association of Southeast Asian Nations (ASEAN) and the European Free Trade Association (EFTA) are also active participants in the game. It therefore seems as if FTAs have become the new forum for trade negotiations.

There are several reasons for the expansion of the FTAs. First, the success of the North American Free Trade Agreement (NAFTA) and the moves toward a Free Trade Area of the Americas (FTAA) motivated other countries to adopt FTAs.[5] Secondly, the US and the EU aim to dominate rule-setting in the global trading system.[6] Those countries have realized the need for stepping up the pace of economic integration, and correspondingly the inability of negotiations at the WTO to provide for increased liberalization. FTAs therefore can help insure against the periodic difficulties of multilateral trade liberalization, and these two

1 For background information, see J. Kuanpoth, "Political Economy of the TRIPS Agreement" in Ricardo Meléndez-Ortiz and G Dutfield (eds), *Trading in Knowledge: Development Perspectives on TRIPS, Trade and Sustainability* (Routledge, 2003), pp45–56.

2 See J. Kuanpoth, "Patents and Access to Antiretroviral Medicines in Vietnam after WTO Accession" (2007), 10(3/4) Journal of World Intellectual Property, pp201–224.

3 R. J. Langhammer and M. Lucke, "WTO Accession Issues" (Kiel Working Paper No. 905, Kiel Institute of World Economics, February 1999).

4 For more information, see M. Schiff and L. A. Winters, *Regional Integration and Development* (OUP, 2003); Simon Lester, Bryan Mercurio and Lorand Bartles (eds), *Bilateral and Regional Trade Agreements: Commentary and Analysis* (2nd edn, Cambridge University Press, 2016).

5 Commission on Growth and Development, "The Growth Report: Strategies for Sustained Growth and Inclusive Development" (World Bank, 2008).

6 J. Morin, "Multilateralizing TRIPS-Plus Agreements: Is the US Strategy a Failure?" (2009), 12 Journal of World Intellectual Property, 191.

giant trading blocs and many others became weary of the slow progress in multilateral trade negotiations. Since trade liberalization was becoming more difficult under the WTO framework, trade negotiators have used bilateral and regional trade fora to achieve what they could not in the multilateral WTO forum, namely, *inter alia*, enforcing an inflexible, high level IP protection in developing countries. In such a forum, the developed countries can easily manage to set benchmarks with respect to all their trade objectives that will be difficult to achieve at the WTO.

The TPP Agreement is expected to be the world's highest standard agreement and perhaps will become the most important trade agreement in the 21st century. In this regard, the agreement will tie together the Pacific's largest economies and set standards of trade measures that cover a broad range of traditional and non-traditional trade and investment issues, such as local-content requirements in government contracts, higher standards of IP protection, the roles of state enterprises, liberalization of telecommunications, labour and environment standards and e-commerce.[7] Due to its rule that allows for membership expansion, the agreement could possibly expand to include countries such as South Korea, Philippines, Taiwan, Thailand and perhaps even China.

From the perspective of the negotiating countries, regional and bilateral FTAs will increase the volume of international trade and investment. The signing of non-multilateral trade agreements is the crucial economic factor for creating growth, efficiency and stability in their economy. A unified and borderless economic entity will present greater business challenges and opportunities for enterprises and investors of the signatory countries. It will also give exporters and investors from those countries greater access to lucrative integrated markets. However, it has been argued that the benefits derived from the trade agreements seem unbalanced, due to the fact that such agreements are negotiated by parties of unequal bargaining power. The power asymmetry is likely to influence the bargaining outcomes and will lead to unequal distribution of benefits causing unfairness and inequity in trading relations. Bilateral and regional FTAs will bring about several negative consequences for the smaller economies, particularly when they restrict those countries' ability to use the relevant policy space to implement their national development policies. The prospective costs of the bilateral trade treaties include various problems relating to monopoly, public health, education, food security, environment, labour rights, technology transfer, biodiversity management, etc.[8]

7 M. Lewis, "The Trans-Pacific Partnership: New Paradigm or Wolf in Sheep's Clothing?" (2011), 34 Boston College International and Comparative Law Review, 27.

8 C. M. Correa, "Implications of Bilateral Free Trade Agreements on Access to Medicines" (2006), 84 Bulletin of the World Health Organization, 401; P. Roffe and C. Spennemann, "The Impact of FTAs on Public Health Policies and TRIPs Flexibilities" (2006), 1 International Journal of Intellectual Property Management, pp75–93; T. A. Faunce and R. Townsend, "The Trans-Pacific Partnership Agreement: Challenges for Australian Health and Medicine Policies" (2011), 194(2) Medical Journal of Australia, pp83–86.

Before discussing implications of IP provisions under the TPP, let us briefly examine some other issues contained in the agreement. Commitments under the TPP are not limited to trade in goods and services but rather like many comprehensive FTAs are extended to cover several non-trade issues – principally investment, competition policy and government procurement. In many countries, there is widespread public concern over the adoption of those rules. For example, the TPP investment chapter offers features on investment such as: the right of establishment (permitting 100 per cent foreign ownership of companies in certain sectors); fair and equitable treatment; no restrictions on the free flow of capital into and out of the country; no performance requirements; investor-state-dispute mechanisms, etc.[9] For a developing country, incorporating such investment rules into national legislation may have severe consequences, including loss of the right to regulate the entry of foreign investors. The government would also no longer be able to give preferences or protection to local firms and small and medium-sized enterprises in sectors where commitments have been made without reservation. Local producers could be affected, as will be the government's right to subsidize, protect and prioritize certain sectors. Finally, any attempt by the government to regulate investment activities, such as imposing high environmental standards, could end up with the government paying millions of dollars in compensation to foreign investors under the investor-state dispute settlement mechanism.[10]

With the competition policy proposed in the TPP, parties are obliged to establish domestic competition policies and laws of a certain type which would restrict the sovereign right of each state to adopt laws preventing companies from resorting to practices which are prejudicial to the interests of the host country. Regarding government procurement, the TPP introduces a process whereby foreign bidders and contractors would be entitled to obtain a large share of the lucrative business of state projects in the host country. Under the WTO, Members do not undertake any obligations unless they willingly access to its plurilateral agreement on government procurement. Winning government contracts is undoubtedly lucrative in view of the fact that up to a significant proportion of countries' gross national product (GNP) goes to state projects.[11] If that is the case, the liberalization of government procurement raises the question of why this domestic spending should be treated as a trade issue.

9 United Nations Conference on Trade and Development (UNCTAD), "Investor–State Disputes: Prevention and Alternatives to Arbitration" (UNCTAD Series on International Investment Policies for Development, 2010).

10 L. Nottage, "The Rise and Possible Fall of Investor-State Arbitration in Asia: A Skeptic's View of Australia's Gillard Government Trade Policy Statement" (Legal Studies Research Paper No. 11/32, Sydney Law School, Social Science Research Network, June 2011); G. V. Harten and M. Loughlin, "Investment Treaty Arbitration as a Species of Global Administrative Law" (2006), 17 European Journal of International Law, 121.

11 See L. Davies and K. N. Schefer, "Government Procurement" in Simon Lester, Bryan Mercurio and Lorand Bartles (eds), *Bilateral and Regional Trade Agreements: Commentary and Analysis* (2nd edn, Cambridge University Press, 2016) pp299–323.

It is interesting to note that the TPP negotiations, like those of many other FTAs, were generally being conducted in a non-transparent manner. The FTA negotiating process of the US has been subject to particular criticism for lacking openness and transparency. The United States trade negotiators of the economic superpower are mandated to negotiate trade deals in secret and usually demand for closed and negotiations from their negotiating partners. Public access to draft agreement texts and other documents is restricted throughout the negotiation process, with only a trade advisory committee, largely dominated by industries, able to gain access to information. For example, the members of the Trade Advisory Committee on Intellectual Property Rights are mostly the representatives of US major research-based pharmaceutical companies and entertainment industry. They are the only interested private parties that are allowed to access and contribute comments on US proposals on IP matters.[12] The information that has been made publicly available is generally one-sided information, coming mainly from the government and those private groups. Public demands for a system of transparency, collaboration and participation of broader interest groups have been rejected. Overall, the closed-door policy not only prevented the vast majority of the public from fully comprehending the content of the negotiations, but also denied trade negotiators the opportunity to listen and exchange views with the public members.[13]

The secret nature of the bilateral and regional negotiations is contrary to the more open and transparent practice adopted by the WTO in its multilateral negotiations. The WTO generally makes all country proposals available to the public as a formal part of the negotiation process. They from time to time publish updates on the status of negotiations that generate public debates regarding various aspects of the negotiated issues. Likely as a result of dissatisfaction with the transparency, and numerous aspects of the norm-making process of the multilateral organizations, major developed countries have shifted their policy towards pursuing bilateral and regional trade agreements.

The secrecy in FTA negotiations allows the developed countries to establish acceptable higher trade standards. It also helps them to escape social movement attention and to avoid growing public opposition against international norm-making at the multilateral level.[14] As pointed out by Flynn et al, "[T]he strategy appeared tailored to avoid an open debate over the standards being proposed in

12 US Department of Commerce and the Office of the United States Trade Representative (USTR), "Charter of the United States Trade Advisory Committee on Intellectual Property Rights" (2010), www.trade.gov/itac/committees/Charters/Intellectual_Property_Rights_ITAC.pdf , accessed 4 September 2014.

13 S. Flynn, "Law Professors Call for Trans-Pacific Partnership (TPP) Transparency" (Infojustic, 9 May 2012), http://infojustice.org/archives/21137, accessed 4 September 2014.

14 J. Morin, "Multilaterlising TRIPs-Plus Agreements: Is the U.S. Strategy a Failure?" (2009), 12 Journal of World Intellectual Property, 175; D. Gervais, "Of Clusters and Assumptions: Innovation as Part of a Full TRIPS Implementation" (2009), 77 Fordham Law Review, 2353.

the agreement."[15] The US and EU are in particular pushing for poor countries to accept trade issues that will have public interest implications, such as threatening access to affordable generic medicines or generating environmental and resource depletion effects. This is probably the main reason why US and EU trade negotiators are reluctant to reveal their negotiating position to the public.[16]

So far the trade liberalization policies of most governments have deepened inequalities between different interest groups within a country. Most key decisions are worked out by a group of bureaucrats and business people. The vast majority of the population has very little real say in trade agenda. Governments of the negotiating countries never allow the public to participate in the many formal and informal meetings to which business people and trade councils are invited. As a result, the issues put up for negotiation, and the decisions made by the government, tend to be biased against grass-roots interests. By excluding the very people who have so far failed to benefit from trade liberalization, corporate-driven bilateral and regional trade deals like the TPP effectively undermine the sustainable development all governments say they are aiming for.

TPP provisions affecting access to medicines

The development of international IP law has become the subject of a growing concern among citizen groups, environmentalists, academics and the general public around the world, all of whom believe that the increased level of patent protection and enforcement of IP rights will increase the public burden. The WTO TRIPS Agreement set minimum standards of intellectual property protection, which all members of the WTO have to implement. Despite international concerns about the impact of the TRIPS Agreement upon development, IP standards continue to increase.[17] These strict TRIPS-plus IP standards are often used in bilateral and regional trade agreements and in treaties developed by the World Intellectual Property Organization (WIPO). We now turn to an overview of TRIPS-plus IP rules under the TPP.

Patent protection for living organisms

It may be noted that the patentability of biotechnological inventions has become the subject of growing controversies in many parts of the world. While the biotechnology industry is demanding a high degree of protection, citizen groups, environmentalists, scientists, farmers' organizations and religious leaders

15 S. Flynn et al, "U.S. Proposal for an Intellectual Property Chapter in the Trans-Pacific Partnership Agreement" (2012), 28, American University International Law Review, pp105–205, 110.

16 International Centre for Trade and Sustainable Development, "Bridges Weekly Trade News Digest" (ICTSD, 18 February 2011).

17 J. Kuanpoth, "TRIPS-Plus Intellectual Property Rules: Impact on Thailand's Public Health" (2006), 9(5) Journal of World Intellectual Property, pp573–591.

are running a worldwide campaign against the patenting of life forms. To those people, animals, plants, humans, microorganisms and their parts such as genes and cells, even if they are genetically modified, are not inventions because these life forms are the creation of God and Nature.[18]

On the issue of patentable subject matter, Article 18.37.1 of the TPP states that "each Party shall make patents available for any invention, whether a product or a process, in all fields of technology, provided that the invention is new, involves an inventive step and is capable of industrial application". Similar to what the TRIPS Agreement provides, the TPP permits the signatories to exclude from patentability plants, animals, essentially biological processes for the production of plants or animals, and methods of medical treatment. However, the TPP mandates Parties to protect "inventions that are derived from plants" (Article 18.37.4). In contrast, the TRIPS does not mandate the patentability of genetic information, in the form of either genes, parts of genes, DNA molecules, gene sequences, cell-lines, etc., although a country may choose to extend such protection under its domestic law. This can be seen from several countries' stance on the patentability of biotechnological inventions, which does not treat biomedical inventions as a separate category of potentially patentable inventions.[19]

In June 2013, it was decided in a US Supreme Court decision in *Association for Molecular Pathology vs US PTO*,[20] which received enormous publicity, that under 35 U.S.C. § 101 there would be no patent in isolated DNA in BRCA1 and BRCA2 genes. The decision extensively restricted the scope of the patenting of biotechnology of genes in general, and will have significant impacts upon patentability of genes in the US and other jurisdictions. It is interesting to see how Article 18.37.4 of the TPP will influence judicial decisions and will have an impact upon national patent systems, particularly regarding the patentability of genes, parts of genes, DNA molecules, etc., which are extracted or derived from plants.

As to plant breeding, many countries have adopted *sui generis* protection for plant varieties. The International Union for the Protection of New Varieties of Plants (UPOV) provides for one, but not the only *sui generis* system. The ambiguity of the term "effective *sui generis* system" under the TRIPS Agreement allows developing countries to avoid granting IP protection for plant varieties. Some developing countries, such as the Organization of African Unity (OAU),

18 J. H. Barton, "The International Breeders'" Rights System and Crop Plant Innovation" (1982) 216(4) Science; S. Sterckx, "Some Ethically Problematic Aspects of the Proposal for a Directive on the Legal Protection of Biotechnological Inventions" (1998), European Intellectual Property Review, 123–128; R. P. Merges, "Intellectual Property in Higher Life Forms: The Patent System and Controversial Technologies" (1988), 47 Maryland Law Review, 1051.

19 S. Hubicki and B. Sherman, "We Have Never Been Modern: The High Court's Decision in National Research Development Corporation vs Commissioner of Patents" in A. Kenyon, M. Richardson and S. Ricketson (eds), *Landmarks in Australian Intellectual Property Law* (Cambridge University Press, 2009), pp73–96; M. Rimmer, *Intellectual Property and Biotechnology* (Edward Elgar, 2008).

20 *Ass'n for Molecular Pathology vs Myriad Genetics, Inc.*, 133 S Ct 2107, 2118–19 (2013).

Malaysia, Thailand, India, etc., have flexibly implemented the TRIPS provision by incorporating the Farmers' Rights[21] and the access and benefit sharing (ABS) system under the Convention on Biological Diversity into their national legislation. Article 18.7.2 of the TPP limits this flexibility by requiring participating countries to join the UPOV 1991 Act. According to the UPOV 1991 Act, protection must cover vegetative or reproductive propagating material and extends to essentially derived varieties and harvested materials. The rights of farmers to save, use, exchange, or sell farm-saved seeds are constrained. TPP Parties will be prevented from taking the necessary steps to assure sufficient supply of seed and food for their populations. Since ensuring farmers' and breeders' access to seeds is crucial for countries with agriculture-based economies, such full-scale monopoly right will adversely affect food and agricultural sectors, and cause adverse effects on the interest of poor farmers, in particular when they are deprived of the right to save seeds.[22]

Second or further medical use of known pharmaceutical products

Non-medical uses claims are generally patentable in most countries, provided that the use of the known compound has not been known to the public (e.g., a new use of the known cosmetics). By contrast, national law and practices vary with regard to the patentability of second and further medical uses of known substances. Under patent laws of European countries, for example, methods of diagnosis, treatment and therapy applied on human or animal bodies are excluded from patentability. However, second and further uses of an existing medical product can be patented, provided that such uses meet the requirements of patentability and can be claimed as:

> Product X for use in the treatment of [disease].

Article 18.37.2 of TPP requires Parties to provide patent protection for new second or further medical uses of known pharmaceutical products:

> Subject to paragraphs 3 and 4 and consistent with paragraph 1, each Party confirms that patents are available for inventions claimed as at least one of the following: new uses of a known product, new methods of using a known product, or new processes of using a known product. A Party may limit those new processes to those that do not claim the use of the product as such.

21 The concept of Farmers' Rights adopted by the Food and Agriculture Organization (FAO) has the aim of compensating farmers who have been conserving plant genetic resources for the past centuries and thereby have contributed to the development of plant varieties. See Quaker United Nations Office (QUNO), "Developing Country Sui Generis Options for Plant Variety Protection" (January 2014), http://www.quno.org/resource/2014/1/developing-country-sui-generis-options-plant-variety-protection, accessed 04/03/2016.

22 G. Tansey, "Food Security, Biotechnology and Intellectual Property" (QUNO, 2002), pp3–6.

When a substance is already known to the public, the inventor cannot make patent claims to the substance as such. Alternative solutions for the research-based pharmaceutical company are: (i) to claim a new pharmaceutical composition; or (ii) to claim a new use of the product that is already known. First, it is common for a research-based pharmaceutical company to broadly claim pharmaceutical compositions containing the active ingredient (i.e., a formulated product containing a known active ingredient and appropriate additives). Yet, an invention used in one area may have applications in other areas. For example, an agrochemical substance may be used as a pharmaceutical product, or a well-known drug can have a new therapeutic application. Such second use may then be claimed either by the company that holds the patent over the substance as such, or by another company that has discovered such second use. Such a claim is advantageous for a pharmaceutical company as it is not limited to any specific pharmaceutical indication. The commercial use of the claimed compound for any use would constitute patent infringement.

The TRIPS Agreement does not require WTO Members to patent second use inventions. Some developed countries (e.g., US, EU and Japan) permit patenting new use inventions.[23] By mandating patentability of the second use of known drugs, the TPP will limit the freedom of countries to implement flexibility provided under the TRIPS Agreement. Medicines that are no longer patented as products could be patented as a second use, a new dosage of existing drugs, or a new combination of existing medicines. Patents for the subsequent uses of a known drug would thereby unnecessarily prolong the monopoly and deprive consumers of essential medicines.[24]

The TPP confirms the exclusion of patentability of medical practices, such as diagnosis, therapy, and surgery on the human or animal body (Article 18.37.3 (a)). The exclusion of methods of treatment is based on the grounds of ethical and social policy in order to protect medical practitioners from infringement claims.[25] However, it is rather unfortunate from the consumers' point of view that the TPP provision does not extend the exclusion to claims relating to second or further medical use of known pharmaceutical products.

23 In Europe, the issue was widely discussed in the first decisions of the European Patent Office's Enlarged Board of Appeal, G1/83, G5/83 and G6/83. The board affirmed the patentability of a second medical use, yet it is relatively clear that this is based not strictly on a legal interpretation of the relevant provisions, but on the assumption that such protection is useful in order to advance technological progress in the field of pharmaceuticals, and not contrary to the provisions in the European Patent Convention. Refusing protection for second medical uses is absolutely compatible with the obligation to grant absolute protection to pharmaceutical products and not contrary to TRIPS. The decision is rather one of economic policy, and the answer may well differ between developed and developing countries.

24 R. A. Castellano, "Patent Law for New Medical Uses of Known Chemical Compounds and Pfizer's Viagra Patent" (2006), 46(2) The Intellectual Property Law Review.

25 For a discussion of related ethical and practical issues, see D. Thomas, "Patentability Problems in Medical Technology" (2003), 34 IIC, 847.

Treaties related to intellectual property

The TPP demands that each party accedes to a number of IP treaties including the UPOV Agreement 1991, the Madrid Protocol, the Patent Cooperation Treaty, the Budapest Treaty and the Singapore Treaty on the Law of Trademarks. IP rights such as patents and trademarks are based on registration that involves prior search and examination as to whether or not certain subject matter meets protection requirements. As for patents, due to the sophisticated nature of inventions, full search and examination of an application become more and more difficult and can overload national patent offices. The treaties that TPP Parties are required to ratify or accede to provide for the system of international filing of applications for patents or trademarks in different countries. Applicants who seek to secure protection in several countries can obtain it through a single examination procedure which reduces application costs and time. Some treaties also provide for standardized procedures for obtaining and maintaining a patent or trademark. Some treaties, such as the Singapore Treaty on the Law of Trademarks, establish safeguards against a loss of rights due to procedural errors.

No doubt the requirement of accession to those treaties is an attempt to facilitate the international system for the administration of IP rights.[26] IP owners can benefit from using the existing mechanisms available under those procedural treaties as they provide for a means of securing protection in several countries that is faster and more effective than going through the national route.

Exclusivity protection for test or other regulatory data

Laws of most nations require pharmaceutical and agrochemical products to be registered with the competent authority before they can be put on the market. The company that seeks registration must submit data relating products' quality, safety and efficacy, the so-called test data. Although Article 39.3 of the TRIPS Agreement stipulates that all member states must protect the undisclosed data submitted for marketing approval, the requirement is limited to new chemical entities. Protection must be available against "unfair commercial use" and "disclosure" of data. The TRIPS Agreement does not require to provide exclusivity protection to the first person who submits the marketing approval data, generally the company that developed a new product.[27] This has left the Parties with considerable room to determine rules for the protection of undisclosed test data. For example, a country's legislation may not prevent third parties from using the test data, if that use does not constitute "unfair commercial use" or does not breach the "non-disclosure" obligation in the framework of unfair competition law. In addition, the regulatory authorities may rely on the data submitted by the

26 P. Drahos, "Expanding Intellectual Property's Empire: The Role of FTAs" (November 2003), www.grain.org, accessed 04/03/2016.

27 C. Correa, "Protection of Data Submitted for the Registration of Pharmaceuticals: Implementing the Standards of the TRIPS Agreement" (South Centre, Geneva, 2002).

originator company or on the evidence of a registration made in a foreign country to grant marketing approval for subsequent applications on a generic product.

Some developed countries, including the US and the EU Member states, grant TRIPS-plus protection in the form of data exclusivity in order to maintain technological and economic superiority of their manufacturers of medicines and agricultural chemicals.[28] The TPP follows this approach by requiring the Parties to grant exclusivity protection for at least:

1 ten years for data required for marketing approval of agricultural chemical products;
2 five years for data for a new pharmaceutical product;
3 three years for data for approving a new indication, new formulation or new method of administration of an existing medicines; and
4 eight years for data relating to a new pharmaceutical product that is or contains a biologic.

The requirement for data exclusivity seems absolute because the TPP does not contain any exceptions to the data exclusivity obligation.

According to the TPP, the exclusivity over test data must be granted to prohibit anyone from obtaining marketing authorization for the same or a similar product during the specified period on the basis of the originator's data without her consent from the originator of test data. The country must also prohibit anyone not having the consent of the originator company from submitting evidence on the basis of foreign marketing approval for that period from the date of marketing approval in the contracting country or the date of approval in the other country, whichever is later. This comprehensive data protection regime requires exclusivity to all kinds of pharmaceutical data submitted for marketing approval including pharmaceutical data with respect to drugs representing variations in formulations, dosage forms, new uses, or second indications. This commitment will limit the country's ability to flexibly implement Article 39.3 of TRIPS. In addition, if the data exclusivity is provided, it is unclear whether data exclusivity can be overridden if a compulsory licensing is issued for patent(s) covering the corresponding drug.

By implementing the TPP obligation to grant exclusivity over test data, a country will confer extra monopolistic protection to the pharmaceutical and agrochemical companies and create entry barriers for generic products. This TRIPS-plus obligation could generate negative effects in several ways:

1 By reducing competition in the private sector and thus limiting access to essential products, as the generic manufacturers, small companies in

28 US laws adopt an absolute exclusivity regime for pharmaceuticals and a limited-exclusivity regime for pesticides. See ibid at p8; M. Campolini, "Data Protection and Related Measures Under the New European Pharmaceutical Legislation" (2004), 162 Patent World, pp25–29.

developing countries such as India, will have to enter into a long and costly testing process before the marketing approval of a generic drug can be obtained.

2 By restraining the effectiveness of the compulsory licence system, as the relevant and essential data are not available due to the exclusivity protection. The person to whom a compulsory licence is granted will not be able to use the licensed invention efficiently and independently without the co-operation of the data originator.

3 By prohibiting the regulatory authorities of the contracting party from relying on marketing approvals in other countries, despite the fact that most developing countries currently do not have the expertise to assess and review clinical data for purposes of granting marketing approval.

Patent terms and extension

The period of patent from filing to the approval date remains unpredictable. It could take longer than ten years in some countries. The delay can be caused by a lack of human resources – particularly chemical and pharmaceutical patent examiners – at the national patent office. The problem of patent backlog for developing countries has become even more acute due to the weak institutional capacity in patent administration. The backlog of patent applications is the concern of patent holders, as it will increase the possibility of infringement from domestic companies during the pending periods. The patent term restoration or adjustment is envisaged to remedy the patent holders for the patent office delays. TPP Article 18.46.3 provides that "[i]f there are unreasonable delays in a Party's issuance of patents, that Party shall provide the means to, and at the request of the patent owner shall, adjust the term of the patent to compensate for such delays".

The 20-year patent term under the TRIPS Agreement is supposed to reward innovative efforts. The TPP provides for the so-called "patent term adjustment for patent office delays": Article 18.46.4 demands the Parties to adjust patent term in case of the delays for more than five years from the filing date or three years from the date the applicant has requested for examination of the application, whichever expires later. This compensation is not available under multilateral agreements of TRIPS or the Paris Convention. No doubt, this obligation will place additional burden on the developing countries participating in the TPP, especially when term extension affects patents on pharmaceuticals that are essential for the well-being of their population.[29]

Compulsory licences and access to medicines

The issue of access to medicines is a major problem in many developing countries – particularly Southeast Asian countries such as Thailand, Malaysia, Vietnam and

29 R. Lopert and D. Gleeson, "The High Price of 'Free' Trade: U.S. Trade Agreements and Access to Medicines" (2013), 41(1) The Journal of Law, Medicine & Ethics, pp199–223.

Indonesia. These countries experienced pressure from developed countries (the United States in particular) when considering implementing policies or measures that were not in line with the priorities of the developed countries. It is very important for countries to have sound legislation in order to be able to counter that pressure. The use of the judicial and administrative processes such as anti-trust laws and compulsory licensing seem to be the most effective and legitimate ways to encourage negotiations regarding prices of the needed medicines with the patent owners.[30]

An example of an attempt of the US to constrain the use of domestic regulation can be found in the bilateral free trade agreement between the US and Australia, which required substantial change in one of the world's most efficient drug procurement systems – the Pharmaceutical Benefit Scheme (PBS) used by Australia.[31] This was done purely for the benefit of multinational pharmaceutical companies and to inhibit other countries from adopting the Australian model. Under this scheme, acceptable prices for medication are calculated according to the health and economic benefits of the new drugs compared to existing treatments.

Health benefits are measured in terms of gains in life expectancy and quality of life, and economic benefits in terms of the reduction of treatment costs. These criteria are used for setting the maximum price for medicines that are to be financed by the public health system. Multinational companies always oppose the use of this measure. They contend that the use of patents against the will of the right holder in the form of compulsory licensing allows for the free-riding of their legitimate rights against the spirit of free trade.[32]

From the consumers' point of view, it is rather fortunate that the restraints on the use of the compulsory licensing and price control mechanisms do not appear in the TPP text. Article 18.6 confirms the Parties' commitment to the Declaration on TRIPS and Public Health and the "TRIPS/health solution", which refers to the WTO 2003 Decision[33] and the WTO 2005 Decision.[34] The same provision reiterates that the obligations of the TPP IP chapter "do not and should not prevent a Party from taking measures to protect public health". Further, Article 18.41 confirms that "[t]he Parties understand that nothing in this Chapter limits

30 G. P. Krikorian and D. M. Szymkowiak, "Intellectual Property Rights in the Making: The Evolution of Intellectual Property Provisions in US Free Trade Agreements and Access to Medicine" (2007), 10(5) Journal of World Intellectual Property, pp388–418.

31 S. K. Sell, "TRIPS-Plus Free Trade Agreements and Access to Medicines" (2007), 28(1), Liverpool Law Review, pp41–75; see also P. Drahos, "Intellectual Property and Pharmaceutical Markets: A Nodal Governance Approach" (2004), 77(2) Temple Law Review, pp401–424.

32 S. Ford, "Compulsory Licensing Provisions under the TRIPS Agreement: Balancing Pills and Patents" (2000), 15 American University International Law Review, 941.

33 The Decision of the General Council of 30 August 2003 on the Implementation of Paragraph Six of the Doha Declaration on the TRIPS Agreement and Public Health, WT/L/540.

34 The Decision of the WTO General Council of 6 December 2005 on the Amendment of the TRIPS Agreement, WT/L/641.

a Party's rights and obligations under Article 31 of the TRIPS Agreement, any waiver or any amendment to that Article that the Parties accept".

Under Article 31 of the TRIPS Agreement, WTO Members are permitted to use a compulsory licence of patents under certain conditions. A compulsory licence refers to a non-voluntary licence issued by the State to a third party without the consent of the patent holder, on the condition that the licensee pays reasonable remuneration to the patent holder in return. The grant of licence by State authorizes the licensee to perform acts covered by the patent exclusive rights (e.g., manufacturing, selling or importing the patented product). The system can help restrain market power of pharmaceutical patents holders and keep the prices of essential products at a reasonable level, as has been successfully used in some countries.

However, the rigid system of data protection under the TPP mentioned earlier may impede the effectiveness of compulsory licensing by preventing the registration of generic medicines, and thus negatively affect access to affordable life-saving medicines. It is, therefore, recommended that countries considering joining the TPP weigh socio-economic costs associated with policy constraints against potential benefits.

International cooperation and technical assistance

The TPP comprises both developed and developing economies. It calls for international cooperation activities among participating countries, with Article 18.13 stating: "[t]he Parties shall endeavour to cooperate on the subject matter covered by this Chapter, such as through appropriate coordination, training and exchange of information between the respective intellectual property offices of the Parties, or other institutions, as determined by each Party".

While the TPP emphasizes the importance of international cooperation on IP, it does not elaborate in detail how this obligation can be implemented. It might require technical assistance and capacity-building programmes relating to IP carried out by international organizations such as the World Intellectual Property Organization. The contention of developing countries is that capacity-building programmes should be tailored to cater for their developmental needs rather than as a means for promotion of IP enforcement in those countries. Related to this issue is the use of "model laws" intended to assist nations in the formulation and implementation of IP legal frameworks. It is important to note that many of these "model laws" incorporate TRIPS-plus provisions, which in general tie those countries to higher IP obligations than necessary had they adhered just to the basic TRIPS Agreement.

Technical assistance training should be multi-sectoral and include into their curricula sessions taught by professionals from diverse institutions, not only the WIPO.[35] It may be suggested, for example, that representatives from the medical

35 D. Vivas-Eugui and C. Bellman, "Towards Development Oriented Technical Assistance in Intellectual Property Policy-making" (ICTSD, Geneva, 2004); T. Pengelly, "Technical

care sector and NGOs should also be able to offer their insights regarding the impact of IP law on healthcare policies. Countries-recipients of technical assistance should send diverse groups of representatives to receive training including patent examiners, judges, police and prosecutors, etc. It is in the interest of the governments and public to take a more integrated approach to IP that, besides business-related issues, would also cover areas of healthcare, education and agriculture. In general, technical assistance should be tailored to individual needs of a country and aid in prioritizing IP in national development agenda.

Concluding analysis: Will the Trans-Pacific Partnership hinder access to medicines?

The debate on IP protection consistently touches upon the problems that are being faced by developing countries and the impact that IP implementation has on those countries. In particular, the impact upon and ability of local industries to use and produce new products are particularly felt in emerging economies as their growth is being slowed down because of the lack of access and use of advanced technology. It is universally accepted that access to good quality essential medicines could make a vital contribution to improving health and reducing mortality and morbidity. Those essential medicines would save lives and improve health only if they were available and affordable. However, many people in the developing world have not yet had regular access to the medicines they need. This has had a major impact on health, since most common illnesses in developing countries could be treated or alleviated with simple and inexpensive medicines. Trade globalization and the controversial TRIPS-plus provisions under various FTAs, including the TPP, have made the issue of access to medicines, and especially to patented medicines such as antiretroviral agents, more acute than ever. Therefore, it is necessary for a country to understand implications of TRIPS-plus obligations before it signs a treaty such as the TPP.

Below is the summary of the TPP IP issues that may hinder the accessibility of essential drugs:

- Patent applications for new uses, new methods of use, and new processes for using known substances will "flood" national patent offices and may prolong the monopoly periods of patents on medicines that should have potentially entered into the public domain.
- Requirements on data exclusivity will create entry barriers for generic medicines, as a drug authority cannot approve a generic product based on the originator's clinical and test data. Generic firms will be likely to wait until patent(s) expire rather than engaging in a long and costly testing process. It may also restrain the effectiveness of the compulsory licensing system unless the licensee is also exempted from submitting his/her own clinical data.

Assistance for the Formulation and Implementation of Intellectual Property Policy in Developing Countries and Transition Economies" (ICTSD, Issue Paper No. 11, 2005).

- Patent term extension, as required under the TPP, will give compensation for delays in issuing patents for pharmaceuticals. However, the term extension will allow the manufacturers of medicines to prolong their monopolistic control of the market longer than the conventional patent term, despite the fact that those companies are generally compensated by *de facto* deterrent effects of pending patents on generic producers such as by the advantage for being the first in the market or by using drug promotion campaigns to build up brand loyalty among consumers and medical practitioners. The original companies can also use various marketing techniques, such as brand name advertisement and trade mark protection, to secure their monopoly position even after the expiration of the patent term. Extending patent term will delay the potential introduction of affordable generic medicines and defer the day when consumers can benefit from generic competition.
- The TPP mandates patent linkage, whereby the national drug regulator is under the obligation to inform the holder of patents relating to medicines sought registration by a generic company. The authority is also required to withhold marketing approvals of the said medicine while the patent holder exercises his/her patent rights through judicial or administrative procedures. The linkage of drug registration with the patent status will impose an unnecessary burden on the drug authority and restrain the entry of generic medicines. The practice of linking patent status to registration obviously strengthens protection for IP rights.
- The previously mentioned TPP provisions, together with other provisions contained in the TPP including provisions on enforcement of IP rights and investor-state dispute settlement can deter governments from implementing TRIPS flexibilities, for example compulsory licensing, thus inhibiting the ability of nationals to access affordable life-saving medicines.

The TPP IP chapter will have serious effects on a developing country's substantive ability to deal with public health problems by limiting access to essential medicines for their poor population. The TRIPS-plus rule will limit flexibilities that the country currently has under the TRIPS Agreement. Developing countries considering joining the TPP therefore face a crucial dilemma – between greater access to export markets and greater access to needed medicines. As long as the problem of finding an adequate and equitable mechanism to stimulate health R&D in developing countries cannot be found, those countries may have to take extreme caution in signing bilateral and regional international agreements that oblige them to provide extensive IP protection that go beyond mandatory limits within the TRIPS Agreement.

Index

For Product Safety Concerns and Information please contact our EU
representative GPSR@taylorandfrancis.com
Taylor & Francis Verlag GmbH, Kaufingerstraße 24, 80331 München, Germany

www.ingramcontent.com/pod-product-compliance
Ingram Content Group UK Ltd.
Pitfield, Milton Keynes, MK11 3LW, UK
UKHW021722240926
475702UK00029BA/1809
9780367193386